Y0-BQT-149

CONTRIBUTORS

EDITOR

Veronica Wayner

CONTRIBUTING EDITORS

Timothy R.W. Kubik, Ph.D.
Lucia Rodriguez, Ed.D.
Gilbert Sewall
Roger W. Smith, *Copy Editor*
Diana Ayton-Shenker, *Copy Editor*

DESIGN

Margaret M. Wagner, *Text*
Douglas Tait, *Cover*

WRITERS

**SECTION I PREPARING FOR A MODEL U.N.
CONFERENCE**

Timothy R.W. Kubik, Ph.D.
Veronica Wayner, *UNA-USA*

CONTRIBUTING WRITERS

United Nations vs. Model United Nations
Brian Endless, *American Model United Nations
International*
Jean Gazarian, Ph.D., *United Nations Institute for
Training and Research (UNITAR)*
Effective Public Speaking
Michael Nwanze, Ph.D., *Howard University*
Preparing for a Crisis Committee
William Schlickenmaier, *Columbia University
Model United Nations*
International Criminal Court
Andrew Kim, *Duke University*
Model U.N. and the International Criminal Court
William Lim, *Independent Student Coalition for the
International Criminal Court*
India/Pakistan Crisis Simulation
Tomas Lopez, *Duke University*

**SECTION II REGIONAL PERSPECTIVES:
HOW NATIONS INTERACT**

Africa
Michael Nwanze, Ph.D., *Howard University*
The Americas
Amanda Marvin, *Baylor University*
Barbara Yu, *Yale University*
Asia
Manav Sachdeva, *Columbia University School of
International and Public Affairs*
The Commonwealth of Independent States
Eugene Oleynikov, *Seton Hall University*
Europe
John D. Giorgis, *Lake Erie International
Model United Nations*
The Middle East
Nicholas Howie, *Hobart and William Smith Colleges*
Matthew Kalloor, *Aberdeen University*

SECTION III REFERENCE

Michael Henry, *Dickinson College*
Nicholas Howie, *Hobart and William Smith Colleges*
Veronica Wayner, *UNA-USA*
Barbara Yu, *Yale University*

SPECIAL THANKS TO

The Annenberg Foundation, Better World Fund,
Deutsche Bank Americas Foundation,
The Goldman Sachs Foundation,
The New York Community Trust,
The New York Times Company Foundation, Inc.,
and The Ross Institute, for their generous support.

All previous writers of the 1998 and 1999-2000 editions
of *A Guide to Delegate Preparation*. Their work served as
a catalyst for the new edition.

Robert Wayner for his assistance, support, and advice in
the editing process.

A Guide to Delegate Preparation

Model U.N.

UNITED NATIONS ASSOCIATION OF THE UNITED STATES OF AMERICA

MODEL U.N. AND EDUCATION DEPARTMENT, UNA-USA

In the field of Model United Nations and U.N.-related educational activities and programs, UNA-USA offers materials and services for every level of participation. *Model U.N.: A Guide to Delegate Preparation* is one of many publications that UNA-USA is proud to produce in its effort to increase the number of students active in Model United Nations. Please feel free to contact your local UNA-USA Chapter or the National Headquarters (www.unausa.org) for further information.

TITLE PAGE. *Students from Georgetown University and McGill University, serving as staff members at the 2002 UNA-USA High School Model United Nations Conference, during an unmoderated caucus of the Security Council. (Photo: UNA-USA)*

CONTENTS

LIST OF BOXES

The Model United Nations (MUN), begun more than 50 years ago, is an authentic simulation of the debates and deliberations of U.N. bodies such as the General Assembly, the Security Council, and other multilateral organs, in which students step into the shoes of ambassadors of U.N. member states. Model United Nations is a unique, interactive educational experience that engages more than 250,000 students in the United States and other countries each year.

Through a combination of Model U.N. programs and the publication of high quality learning resources for primary, secondary and post-secondary school students, the United Nations Association of the USA (UNA-USA) is seeking to impart the skills, knowledge and attitudes necessary for the development of successful global citizens and leaders of the twenty-first century. We are convinced that the most important role that UNA-USA can perform over the long run is to greatly expand the reach of Model U.N. programs and publications in the U.S. and abroad and; subsequently, knowledge on global issues and the role of the United Nations in managing this new interdependent world.

Not surprisingly, the appeal of Model U.N. has been much greater following September 11. The appetite of American students of all ages and grade levels for information about cultures beyond America's borders has become almost insatiable. Most interestingly, according to some classroom teachers and other educators, it is not fear or security concerns that have driven the demand for better information, rather it is the recognition by students that they have been left out of the loop in a world that increasingly turns on an axis of global communication. We have discovered that young people want to be part of the bigger world, serving as citizens of global society. Model U.N. is an activity that is designed to help them do just that.

As Model U.N. prepares young people for life, this *Guide to Delegate Preparation* helps to make their Model U.N. experience a better one. The revised *Guide* includes new tips for Model U.N. participants as well as a Model U.N. scenario that can be used for a class or club simulation. The regional perspective and resource sections have also been updated and expanded.

We hope that the new edition of the *Guide* is helpful and informative. Let us know your thoughts or ideas on how we can make it better.

Have a great Model U.N. experience!

—*Lucia Rodriguez*
UNA-USA
Director, Education & Model U.N.
New York, New York

INTRODUCTION

Model United Nations (Model U.N., or MUN) is a simulation of the world's largest international organization, engaging hundreds of thousands of students around the world. Although Model U.N. conferences vary in size, type, and location, they all share a common goal: to engage individuals in the work of the United Nations. Through research, delegates (Model U.N. students) learn the function, scope, and issues of a U.N. committee. In simulations, delegates role-play as they prepare for their roles as mock ambassadors at a Model U.N. conference. During months of preparation for the conference, students:

- Gain knowledge of U.N. issues and learn how the United Nations operates;
- Become expert researchers, as they investigate multilateral issues from a national perspective;
- Acquire negotiation skills, as they role-play the representative of a particular country or non-governmental organization (NGO);
- Develop public speaking and debating skills, as they articulate "their" country's position on different issues; and
- Engage in consensus-building, while taking into account the views and opinions of other member states.

This preparation leads to a culminating event: the Model U.N. conference. Here, a delegate will have the opportunity to utilize the skills s/he has gained in preparation.

The intent of *A Guide to Delegate Preparation* is to help students prepare for a Model U.N. conference, while allowing them to examine the significance of the United Nations to the world. This *Guide* will introduce students to the main components of conference preparation, from crafting speeches to analyzing research, and advise readers on how to get the most out of their Model U.N. experience.

The *Guide* is divided into three sections: *Preparing for a Model U.N. Conference* (Chapters 1–4), *Regional Perspectives: How Nations Interact* (Chapters 5–10), and the *Reference.* Section one deals with the concepts and skills integral to Model U.N. **Chapter 1: Forming a Model U.N. Team** explores some of the basics of Model U.N., such as forming a team, choosing a conference, and raising funds to cover conference expenses. **Chapter 2: Modeling the U.N.** examines the U.N. system and how Model U.N. conferences simulate the United Nations. In **Chapter 3: Research and Interpretation**, delegates learn how to create a portfolio of the research they will need in preparation for a conference. **Chapter 4: Building Your Model U.N. Skills** explores the remaining areas in which Model U.N. delegates should be well-versed for a simulation, namely public speaking, rules and procedure, and resolution-writing.

The second section of the book, *Regional Perspectives: How Nations Interact,* deals with the current issues of the six regions of the world. **Chapters 5** through **10** discuss the political, social, and economic issues facing **Africa, the Americas, Asia and the Pacific, the Commonwealth of Independent States, Europe,** and **the Middle East.** Each regional perspective explores not only the issues that the country faces (such as civil war, human rights abuses, and the economy), but also how it works with the United Nations on these and related issues (such as peacekeeping, disarmament, human rights promotion and protection, and development).

The last section, the *Reference,* is an appendix of resources that will aid delegates in their research. These resources include a list of commonly used acronyms, a glossary of terms, Internet resources, important U.N. documents, and an annotated bibliography.

PREPARING FOR A
MODEL U.N. CONFERENCE

*A delegate studying a resolution during an
unmoderated caucus at the 2002 UNA-USA
High School Model U.N. Conference.
(Photo: Lauren Popkoff)*

PREVIOUS PAGE. *Delegates in discussion
during an unmoderated caucus.
(Photo: UNA-USA)*

Each year, hundreds of thousands of students participate in Model United Nations (Model U.N., or MUN) around the world. During the last 50 years or so, Model U.N. teams have been formed by different people at various points in time. There is no standard way to create a new Model U.N. team. However, there is helpful information that can be offered to assist you in the process.

In Model U.N., a student becomes a **delegate,** a representative of a U.N. member state, observer state, or nongovernmental organization (NGO). Each delegate is part of a larger group, called a **delegation.** Delegations are made up of individuals who are all representing the same country (See **Box 1.1**) at a **Model U.N. conference,** which is a simulation of the United Nations where students role-play ambassadors. (The minimum number of delegates needed to form a delegation varies with the conference you attend and the member state you represent.) The delegation of a country is expected to speak with one voice in stating and explaining its government's policies and interests. To register for a Model U.N. conference, you will need to form a delegation. The best way to accomplish this is to form a Model U.N. team.

FINDING A FACULTY ADVISOR

Your first step in organizing a Model U.N. team should be to find a faculty advisor. Like an advisor for any other extracurricular organization, this individual will be the liaison between the group and the school's administration, while also providing support in various areas of team development. Faculty advisors help the team maintain organization (by overseeing the group's leadership), prepare for conferences (by running simulations or advising on research), and make arrangements (such as travel plans or conference registration). When searching for a faculty advisor, first visit your school's Social Studies or Political Science department's chairperson and ask if s/he can suggest any individuals you may approach.

CLASS VS. CLUB

Most Model U.N. teams meet as either an extracurricular organization or class. In order to start a class, your group will need a faculty advisor who is highly knowledgeable about the Model U.N. program. S/he will have to approach your school's administration to approve adding the course to the curriculum. Depending on your state's school requirements or your university's degree requirements, it may be difficult to implement a new program. Speak to the administration, as well as your teachers, to see what would be involved in creating a Model U.N. course. In addition, visit UNA-USA's Education and Model U.N. website (www.unausa.org) to download syllabi that are used in Model U.N. classes on the high school and collegiate levels. Having that information for the teachers you approach will demonstrate that you are well prepared and serious about starting a Model U.N. class.

If you decide to start a Model U.N. club, approach your school's campus activities or guidance office to find out what procedures you need to take. In order to be recognized as a school-affiliated organization, your school's administration will most likely need to approve the club's formation. Your administration may even require you to draft a club charter or constitution (see **Box 1.2 Sample Team Charter/ Constitution**). These small hurdles can be overcome fairly easily, especially if your team has strong leadership.

1.1
REPRESENTING AN NGO

Throughout Section I there will be various references to role-playing your "member state". Nearly all of the preparation tips in the *Guide* can be utilized by delegates portraying non-governmental organizations (NGOs), as well. In addition, a section on researching NGOs can be found in Chapter 3: Research and Interpretation.

Your team may be required by your school to have a team charter or constitution outlining how it will operate and where responsibility will lie among members of the executive. Even if such a charter is not explicitly required, it is a good idea to create one so that members of your team are clear on how it will operate. Please note that these bylaws do not include the role of a faculty adviser but can be changed to include one.

The document should outline the following important areas:

- Purposes and Principles: Why the Model U.N. Team is being formed;

- Membership: How members are accepted, and in extreme cases expelled;

- Organs and Officers: What the decision-making mechanisms are for the team and what executive positions exist;

- Amendments: How amendments to the Charter / Constitution are made.

Here is a sample team charter or constitution:

CHAPTER I: PURPOSES AND PRINCIPLES

Article 1

The Purposes of the Model U.N. Team are:

1. To participate in Model U.N. Conferences and, in doing so, to represent and promote the school;
2. To promote a better understanding of the global political environment in which we live to the students of our community; and
3. To foster a dialogue based on tolerance and mutual understanding about various political issues.

Article 2

The Team and its Members, in pursuit of the Purposes stated in Article 1, shall act in accordance with the principle of the fundamental equality of all Members.

CHAPTER II: MEMBERSHIP

Article 3

1. Membership in the Model U.N. Team shall be open to all students of the school; Members accept the principles and purposes of the Organization contained within the present Charter.
2. The admission of a new Member to the

Organization will be effected by a decision of the President in full consultation with the Membership of the Team.
3. A Member who has persistently violated the principles and purposes of the Organization may be expelled upon a decision of the Team General Assembly.

CHAPTER III: ORGANS AND OFFICERS

Article 4

1. There are established as the principal organs of the Organization the University of XXXX Model U.N. Team: the General Assembly and the Executive Council.
2. There are established as the principal officers of the Organization: the President, the Vice President, the Secretary, the Head Delegate [when needed], and the Treasurer.
3. No person shall hold the office of President for more than a total of two years.
4. The operational year of the Organization shall be from May 1 to April 30 of the following year.

CHAPTER IV: THE GENERAL ASSEMBLY

Article 5

The General Assembly shall be composed of all the Members of the Model U.N. Team.

Article 6

1. The General Assembly shall convene once a year in April at a date and location fixed by the President.
2. The President shall solicit from the Team Members items for the agenda of the General Assembly and shall accept such items until three weeks prior to the meeting.
3. The President shall present a written and oral report on the operations of the Model U.N. Team to the annual meeting of the General Assembly.
4. The President shall inform the Members of the contents of the agenda at least one week prior to the date of the General Assembly.

Article 7

1. The President shall inform the Members of the Team of the names of those who have been granted the status of Voting Member of the General Assembly.
2. A Voting Member of the General Assembly

shall be defined as a Team Member who has participated in at least one Model U.N. during the course of the operational year.
3. All Members not granted the status of Voting Member shall be designated Observers.
4. The President may invite guests to sit at the General Assembly and confer on them the status of Observer.
5. Any Member who is not granted the status Voting Member may appeal to the Executive Council up to one week prior to the General Assembly for Voting Member status.

Article 8

The General Assembly shall be responsible for the general welfare of the Team and may debate any facet of the Team's operation or matters arising from the present Charter. The General Assembly shall be the highest decision-making body of the Team and may overrule nonprocedural decisions of the President or Executive Council by a two-thirds majority of all Voting Members.

Article 9

It shall be the goal of the General Assembly to reach all decisions by consensus. However, unless otherwise specified or agreed to by a majority of the Voting Members, all decisions of the Team shall be made by majority vote.

Article 10

1. The General Assembly may, by a resolution, adopt rules of procedure to govern the conduct of its meetings.
2. The President or his or her designee shall act as the Presiding Officer at the General Assembly.

Article 11

1. The General Assembly shall be responsible for the election of Officers in accordance with its rules of procedure.
2. All Officers elected by the General Assembly must receive the majority support of all Voting Members present [specify a quorum].
3. The General Assembly may, by a two-thirds majority of all Voting Members, remove any Officer from his/her position.
4. In accordance with Article 4 of the present Charter, the General Assembly may expel

a Member upon a two-thirds vote of all Voting Members.

Article 12

The President, at the request of the Executive Council or a majority of Team Members, may call an emergency meeting of the General Assembly. Such a meeting must be advertised at least three days prior to the emergency session. The roster of Voting Members shall be the same as that of the most recent regular General Assembly.

CHAPTER V: THE EXECUTIVE COUNCIL

Article 13

1. The Executive Council shall be composed of the President, the Vice President, the Secretary, the Treasurer, and the Head Delegate(s).
2. The Executive Council shall be responsible for the conduct of Team business, the promotion of the Team, and the execution of policies and decisions reached by the General Assembly.
3. All decisions of the Executive Council, unless otherwise noted, shall be taken by majority vote. The President shall vote only to break a tie.
4. The Executive Council shall be responsible for the sanctioning of projects/trips as official projects/trips of the Model U.N. Team.
5. Only those projects/trips that are sanctioned by the Executive Council shall be eligible to:
   a. receive financial or logistical support from the Team, and
   b. use the official logo of the Team, and
   c. make official statements claiming to represent the Team.
6. The Executive Council may, by majority, adopt its own rules of procedure and operation.
7. The Executive Council shall meet as needed and shall meet at least once a month.
8. For the purpose of financial transactions, the signatures of the President and Finance Officer shall be required.

Article 14

1. The President shall be responsible for the day-to-day activities of the Team and for overseeing the work of the Executive Council.

2. The President shall preside at meetings of the Executive Council.
3. The President shall, at the regular meeting of the General Assembly, present an oral and written report to the General Assembly on the conduct of Team business during the course of the preceding operational year.
4. The President shall act, unless otherwise noted, as the sole official spokesperson of the Team.
5. The President shall appoint the Head Delegates and, in the case of Officer positions left vacant, shall appoint interim Team officers.

Article 15

1. The Vice President shall be responsible for the internal health of the Team, including internal communication and academic integrity.
2. The Vice President shall fulfill the duties of the President if the President so authorizes or if the President is unable to execute the requirements of the office.
3. The Vice President shall be responsible for expanding the membership of the Team.

Article 16

The Secretary shall be responsible for, upon request from the President, communicating the affairs, activities, and achievements of the Team to the media and the community at large. The Treasurer shall be responsible for the financial activities of the team and for submitting financial reports to the President.

Article 17

1. For every sanctioned trip taken by the Team, the President shall appoint a Head Delegate.
2. The President shall notify the Team of openings for a Head Delegate and shall solicit volunteers from the Membership.
3. Should no volunteers present themselves, the President may appoint herself to the position. Should any member of the Executive Council act as a Head Delegate, that person shall receive no additional votes in the Executive Council.
4. The Head Delegate shall, unless already serving as an Officer of the Executive Council, relinquish his seat on the Executive Council upon return from the trip for which

he was assigned to serve as Head Delegate.

Article 18

1. The Head Delegate shall be responsible for overseeing all aspects of the trip on which she has been appointed to serve as Head Delegate.
2. The Head Delegate shall be responsible for all communication with the Conference staff for the trip on which he has been appointed to be Head Delegate.
3. The Head Delegate for a trip shall be responsible for, in conjunction with the resources of the Executive Council, securing transportation and accommodation. Furthermore, the Head Delegate shall ensure that all dues and or registration fees are collected and dispatched in compliance with prescribed deadlines.
4. The Head Delegate shall, in consultation with those Members participating in the trip, establish the country preference(s) of the Team.
5. The Head Delegate shall, in consultation with the President, establish the Team roster for the given trip.
6. The Head Delegate working in concert with the Vice President shall ensure that all academic materials related to the given conference are completed with the highest standards of academic quality in mind and are submitted to the conference in accordance with prescribed deadlines.

CHAPTER VI: TRANSITIONAL PROVISIONS

Article 19

The present Charter shall come into effect upon receiving the affirmative vote of two-thirds of Voting Members present [or a quorum] at a meeting of the Team General Assembly.

Article 20

The President shall inform all Team Members when the present Charter comes into effect.

CHAPTER VII: AMENDMENTS

Amendments to the present Charter shall require the two-thirds support of Voting Members present [or a quorum] at a meeting of the regular or emergency General Assembly

ORGANIZATIONAL STRUCTURE

Like any other club, your Model U.N. team will need a few dedicated individuals to take leadership positions. In creating your team's configuration, keep in mind that there is no official structure in organizing a Model U.N. team. Many organizations create a core of officers (such as a president, vice president, etc.) that direct the collective tasks of the group. (See **Box 1.3 Sample Organizational Structure.**) These officers perform their duties with the aim of achieving the goals the team has set for itself. Although this format is not used at the United Nations, it is one of the most common ways to organize a Model U.N. team. Not every aspect of the United Nations can be replicated in Model U.N. The United Nations is a large organization that operates continuously throughout the year, while a Model U.N. team is much smaller and usually operates anywhere from three to nine months.

In setting up your team's structure, choose a model that will meet the needs of the members of your team. Regardless of your structure, your team's officers should exhibit strong leadership skills and a firm understanding of the challenges facing a new organization.

RECRUITING MEMBERS

One of the common difficulties a new Model U.N. team faces is attracting a group of members that will consistently participate and contribute to the growth of the group. While finding dedicated team members is not easy, when it does happen, your group will flourish. In contemplat-

---

1.3 SAMPLE ORGANIZATIONAL STRUCTURE

THE PRESIDENT

A Model U.N. team president directs registration for a conference; chooses the country the team will represent; assigns committees; and sees that all delegates are progressing toward the team's goals. In many of these tasks, leadership by example is as effective as reliance upon authority.

THE VICE PRESIDENT

The vice president takes on the role of leader when s/he is unable to attend the Model U.N. class or meeting, and delegates tasks in support of the president. The vice president may have other duties, including overseeing member recruitment, but working together with the president is chief among them.

THE TREASURER

The treasurer is the organizing force behind the team's fundraising projects, and s/he must remain in constant contact with the president and/or faculty advisor to keep them apprised of the team's financial status. S/he should prepare a budget in the form of a spreadsheet

and routinely present it to the president and the faculty advisor.

THE SECRETARY

The secretary is the public relations officer and record keeper of the team. S/he must design a contact sheet or phone chain to keep the team informed of its decisions and commitments, and is in charge of taking attendance and keeping a record of each session. The secretary may also design or maintain the team's website.

THE ROLE OF THE HEAD DELEGATE

The head delegate manages affairs related to attending a conference as described above for the president of a team. In addition, the head delegate works with other more experienced delegates in training the delegation and enforcing deadlines. Before the conference, the head delegate must ensure that all members of a delegation understand the foreign policy of the country being represented. S/he also keeps the delegates informed about the work of committees apart from their own. If there is to be a head delegate, it is wise to have one for each country, and the head del-

egates of multiple delegations would have to share overall responsibility for the team as a whole.

THE ROLE OF THE HEAD DELEGATE'S DEPUTY

The head delegate's deputy is usually an experienced member of a delegation who can serve as a substitute when the head delegate is not available. Often, s/he will also assume the duties of the treasurer and secretary, described above. As such, this is primarily a support role, but also a key training position for future leadership.

THE ROLE OF THE DELEGATE

Remaining team memberss are tasked primarily with independent research on the issues before the committee to which they are assigned in consultation with the head delegate or instructor. If committee delegations have more than one member, it is wise to designate one of them as chief of staff for that committee. This is another excellent opportunity to prepare strong delegates for leadership roles in the future.

ing how to find members for your team, consider the following: students can't join Model U.N. unless they know about it. Thus, your best strategy will be to publicize your new team. Here are some commonly used methods:

- Invite others to your meetings. Post flyers that announce when your team meets. These flyers should briefly explain what Model U.N. is, as some students may not know. A perfect forum for publicizing your team is at the meetings of other student organizations. Contact these organizations and ask if they would let you speak to their members at a meeting for a few minutes. Additionally, you can ask your teachers or professors to make a similar announcement to their classes.
- Set up a table or booth at your school's extracurricular activities fair. It may attract new students at your school who are interested in getting involved in a club.
- Contact your school newspaper and ask them to write a story about the club. Give them background on Model U.N., and let them in on your club's future plans.

- Create a team website that features information on Model U.N., conferences you will attend, photos of your team in action, and contact information. If no one on your team is technologically savvy, contact your school's computer laboratory or information systems office to ask for help. Finally, find out if your campus activities office is willing to provide a link on the school's student organization webpage.
- Invite potential members to a simulation put on by your club. Observing a Model U.N. simulation may stimulate their interest.
- Spread the word among your classmates. Even if your friends are not able to join the team, chances are that they know others who would be interested.
- Find out if neighboring schools have Model U.N. teams. Your team members may be able to form a joint delegation with students from another school's Model U.N. group.

If your attempts to stir up interest in your team do not meet your expectations, remember this: some of the most established Model U.N.

Delegates in an unmoderated caucus at the 2002 UNA-USA High School Model U.N. Conference. (Photo: Lauren Popkoff)

teams in the country started with only one or two delegates. In fact, small delegations sometimes perform better at conferences than their larger counterparts. In Model U.N., the quality of a delegation is more important that the quantity of its delegates.

CHOOSING A CONFERENCE TO ATTEND

Approximately 350 Model U.N. conferences are held each year in more than thirty countries around the world. Your team will have to decide what type of conference it would like to attend.

To find a conference in your area, check UNA-USA's Calendar of Model U.N. Conferences (www.unausa.org). UNA-USA's Calendar enables you to search for a conference using location, date, and grade level as search options. You can also sign up for Model U.N. E-News (http://groups.yahoo.com/group/mun-e-news/), a listserve created by UNA-USA that allows thousands of Model U.N. participants to share information on conferences, resources for research, as well as internship and job opportunities.

Most Model U.N. conferences are organized by college and university Model U.N. clubs, although some are run by high schools, community groups, or non-profit organizations. Some have been running conferences for 50 years, while others are relatively new to the field. The best way to find information on a conference is to visit its website. To find its website, simply visit the Calendar of Model U.N. Conferences or perform a general Internet search. The conference website will often provide names, phone numbers, and e-mails of the Secretariat (senior conference staff members). Feel free to call or e-mail members of a conference's Secretariat. You will most likely get in touch with an enthusiastic Model U.N.er who is eager to answer your questions!

In deciding which conference to attend, you must consider several factors:

- **Size.** A conference's size can range from 15 to 3,000 participants. If your team is relatively new, it may choose to attend a small conference aimed at first-time participants. Small conferences often facilitate greater participation among Model U.N. novices, as smaller committees enable first-time delegates to become actively involved in the proceedings.

- **Location.** If the conference your team chooses to attend is held in another city, state, or even country, many expenses will be incurred. Your team may have to travel via car, bus, train, or airplane. Thus, finding an attractive rate will be a central concern. Keep in mind that other expenses, such as meals, will vary with location.

- **Lodging.** If your team is attending a multi-day conference that is out of town, team members will have to find lodging at a hotel, dormitory, hostel, or YMCA. Again, investigate which options your team can afford. If you plan to stay in the official conference hotel, make your reservations early before the space fills up. The hotel may also offer a discounted rate to conference participants who reserve rooms early.

- **Registration Fees.** Nearly every conference charges fees to its participants in order to cover the expenses of the event. Depending on the conference you are attending, you may have to pay fees per delegate (or student participant), delegation (country represented), school, and/or faculty member. Conference organizers may also charge miscellaneous fees and/or a late registration fee.

FUNDRAISING

Your school's administration may be helpful in funding your Model U.N. team. Make an appointment with your school's principal or dean to discuss the options available. You may be able to receive funding from your school's Social Studies or Political Science departments, student government, or campus activities fund. Approaching community organizations, such as the Kiwanis or Rotary Club, may also be fruitful. However, before meeting with any potential sponsors, create a presentation that showcases what Model U.N. is, how your team operates, and what expenses you will incur at a conference. Your

potential sponsors will appreciate knowing what their funds will support.

In approaching your school administration or other organization, keep the following in mind:

- Persistence is necessary in fundraising. If your potential supporter does not return phone calls or letters, keep trying. Your determination may pay off.
- Be flexible. If your school initially balks at funding your team's conference expenses, ask if it would consider simply paying registration fees. Your team may be able to find other sources of funding to make up the difference.
- Courtesy is key. Remember to thank your potential sponsors, even if they decline your request for financial support. Although you may walk away empty-handed this time around, your potential supporter will remember your courtesy the next time your team approaches him/her.

WHAT TO EXPECT IN THE MAIL

Once your have registered for a Model U.N. conference, the Secretariat may send you the following items:

- **Country assignment.** When registering for the conference, your team's leadership must choose country preferences to role-play (e.g. France, Japan, Guatemala). The earlier you send your country preferences in to the Secretariat, the greater your chances of obtaining your top choice. However, failure to receive your first, or even third, preference does not reflect badly on your team. Conference organizers often receive multiple requests for highly industrialized member states, such as the United Kingdom or the United States. However, in order to properly simulate the United Nations, conference organizers must assign various smaller member states to teams. Keep in mind that the role of developing countries

A delegate raises his placard in order to be placed on the speakers' list. (Photo: UNA-USA)

in the United Nations is quite powerful, and must be acknowledged by a delegate in order to understand the Organization. Also, in Model U.N., the size or wealth of the member state you are portraying has little impact on the success of your performance at a conference.

- **Delegate handbook.** The handbook will provide your team with the conference's rules of procedure, position paper and resolution format, and general information on conference proceedings. You may also receive additional information regarding deadlines for position papers, transportation and hotel instructions, and other logistical details.

- **Background guides.** Conference staff members create a background guide for each of the conference's committees. This guide is an informational aid that discusses the committee's mandate, the topics on the agenda, and questions delegates should consider in their research.

- **Additional materials.** Some conferences will send additional materials, such as issue summaries (a general brief on the agenda topics) and updates to the background guides (additional reports on late-breaking events pertinent to the committee).

In order to be effective Model U.N. delegates, students must understand the U.N. system, including the history and institutional relationships of the committee on which they will serve. (See **Box 2.1 The United Nations System: Principal Organs.**) This chapter presents a basic overview of that system with an eye toward understanding the U.N. committees that are typically simulated at a Model U.N. conference. (Further research into the U.N. system will be necessary, however, if you are to come to appreciate what the United Nations can, and cannot do. See **Box 2.2 Learning About the United Nations** for additional research resources.) In addition, the role of intergovernmental organizations (IGOs) will also be highlighted, as they play an important part in the actual U.N, as well as Model U.N.

Originally founded on October 24, 1945, The United Nations was established by 51 member states to preserve peace through cooperation and collective security. Since then, the United Nations has grown to include 191 member states and a vast constellation of organizations, programs, and other entities that fall into three main categories:

- The United Nations proper, the core of the system, consisting of six principal organs (General Assembly, Security Council, Economic and Social Council, International Court of Justice, Secretariat, and Trusteeship Council) and a large number of subsidiary organs. All six organs were established by the U.N. Charter in 1945.
- A number of commissions, programs, and funds established by and directly related to one of the six principal organs. In some cases, funding comes from the U.N. budget, but in others, funding comes from voluntary contributions, which makes them financially independent. The majority of these institutions report to the Economic and Social Council.

Examples include the U.N. Children's Fund (UNICEF) and the U.N. Development Programme (UNDP).
- Fifteen specialized agencies, which are independent organizations with their own budgets and governing bodies, that focus on social, cultural, economic, health, educational, and other humanitarian fields. All these agencies, some of which are even older than the United Nations itself, are now linked to the United Nations by specific international agreements. Examples include the Food and Agricultural Organization (FAO) and the World Health Organization (WHO).

UNITED NATIONS ORGANS

GENERAL ASSEMBLY

The General Assembly (GA) is the main deliberative body of the United Nations, consisting of all 191 member states. Each member state has one vote. The General Assembly has the power to debate any issue brought before it, to set the U.N. budget, and to elect officers. Decisions on important questions, such as those on peace and security, admission of new members, and budgetary matters, require a two-thirds majority, while other questions require only a simple majority. Although resolutions passed by the General Assembly have no legally binding force, they carry the weight of world opinion on major international issues, as well as the moral authority of the world community.

Due to the large number of agenda topics the General Assembly must address, the Assembly's work is divided into six main committees:

- First Committee—Disarmament and International Security
- Second Committee—Economic and Financial

▸ GENERAL ASSEMBLY

Main and other sessional committees

Other sessional committees

Standing committees and ad hoc bodies

Other subsidary organs

Programs and Funds

UNCTAD
United Nations Conference on Trade and Development

  ITC
  International Trade Centre (UNCTAD/WTO)

UNDCP
United Nations Drug Control Programme

UNEP
United Nations Environment Programme

UNHSP
United Nations Human Settlements Programme (UN–Habitat)

UNDP
United Nations Development Programme

  UNIFEM
  United Nations Development Fund for Women

  UNV
  United Nations Volunteers

UNFPA
United Nations Population Fund

UNHCR
Office of the United Nations High Commissioner for Refugees

UNICEF
United Nations Children's Fund

WFP
World Food Programme

UNRWA**
United Nations Relief and Works Agency for Palestine Refugees In the Near East

Other U.N. Entities

OHCHR
Office of the United Nations High Commissioner for Human Rights

UNOPS
United Nations Office for Project Services

UNU
United Nations University

UNSSC
United Nations System Staff College

▸ ECONOMIC AND SOCIAL COUNCIL

Functional Commissions

Commission for Social Development

Commission on Human Rights

Commission on Narcotic Drugs

Commission on Crime Prevention and Criminal Justice

Commission on Science and Technology for Development

Commission on Sustainable Development

Commission on the Status of Women

Commission on Population and Development

Statistical Commission

Regional Commissions

Economic Commission for Africa (ECA)

Economic Commission for Europe (ECE)

Economic Commission for Latin America and the Caribbean (ECLAC)

Economic and Social Commission for Asia and the Pacific (ESCAP)

Economic and Social Commission for Western Asia (ESCWA)

United Nations Forum on Forests

Sessional and Standing Committees

Expert, ad hoc and related bodies

Research and Training Institutes

INSTRAW
International Research and Training Institute for the Advancement of Women

UNICRI
United Nations Interregional Crime and Justice Research Institute

UNITAR
United Nations Institute for Training and Research

UNRISD
United Nations Research Institute for Social Development

UNIDIR**
United Nations Institute for Disarmament Research

▸ INTERNATIONAL COURT OF JUSTICE
▸ TRUSTEESHIP COUNCIL

Specialized Agencies*

▪ **ILO**
International Labour Organization

▪ **FAO**
Food and Agriculture Organization of the United Nations

▪ **UNESCO**
United Nations Educational, Scientific and Cultural Organization

▪ **WHO**
World Health Organization

WORLD BANK GROUP

▪ **IBRD**
International Bank for Reconstruction and Development

▪ **IDA**
International Development Association

▪ **IFC**
International Finance Corporation

▪ **MIGA**
Multilateral Investment Guarantee Agency

▪ **ICSID**
International Centre for Settlement of Investment Disputes

▪ **IMF**
International Monetary Fund

▪ **ICAO**
International Civil Aviation Organization

▪ **IMO**
International Maritime Organization

▪ **ITU**
International Telecommunication Union

▪ **UPU**
Universal Postal Union

▪ **WMO**
World Meteorological Organization

▪ **WIPO**
World Intellectual Property Organization

▪ **IFAD**
International Fund for Agricultural Development

▪ **UNIDO**
United Nations Industrial Development Organization

▸ SECURITY COUNCIL

Military Staff Committee

Standing Committee and ad hoc bodies

International Criminal Tribunal for the Former Yugoslavia

International Criminal Tribunal for Rwanda

U.N. Monitoring, Verification, and Inspection Commission (Iraq)

United Nations Compensation Commission

Peacekeeping Operations and Missions

Related Organizations

▪ **IAEA**
International Atomic Energy Agency

▪ **WTO**
World Trade Organization

▪ **WToO**
World Tourism Organization

▪ **CTBTO Preparatory Commission****
Preparatory Commission for the Comprehensive Nuclear Test Ban Treaty

▪ **OPCW****
Organization for the Prohibition of Chemical Weapons

▸ SECRETARIAT

OSG
Office of the Secretary-General

OIOS
Office of Internal Oversight Services

OLA
Office of Legal Affairs

DPA
Department of Political Affairs

DDA
Department for Disarmament Affairs

DPKO
Department of Peacekeeping Operations

OCHA
Office for the Coordination of Humanitarian Affairs

DESA
Department of Economic and Social Affairs

DGAACS
Department of General Assembly Affairs and Conference Services

DPI
Department of Public Information

DM
Department of Management

OIP
Office of Iraq Programme

UNSECOORD
Office of the United Nations Security Coordinator

ODCCP
Office for Drug Control and Crime Prevention

UNOG
UN Office at Geneva

UNOV
UN Office at Vienna

UNON
UN Office at Nairobi

▸ PRINCIPAL ORGANS OF THE UNITED NATIONS

Report to both the General Assembly and the Economic and Social Council

Report to Economic and Social Council

Security Council

▪ Specialized agencies and other autonomous organizations within the system

* Autonomous organizations working with the United Nations and each other through the coordinating machinery of the Economic and Social Council.

** Report only to the General Assembly

▪ Report to the General Assembly and the Security Council

Data courtesy of the United Nations Department of Public Information, January 2002

2.2 LEARNING ABOUT THE UNITED NATIONS

To gain in-depth knowledge of the United Nations and its subsidiary programs, delegates can turn to the U.N. home page, to UNA-USA's homepage, or to various journals and other publications of the U.N. Department of Public Information (UNDPI), as well as independent scholarly research.

Good general sources on the United Nations are available in print as well, including *Basic Facts About the United Nations*, from the UNDPI, and the *United Nations Handbook*, from the New Zealand Ministry of Foreign Affairs and Trade. Both are available from the U.N. bookstore, through the U.N. website,

and at other bookstores that have good selections in international affairs. These texts are updated annually, and are excellent sources for learning about the U.N. system. Recommended books on the United Nations are located in the Annotated Bibliography (page 221).

2.3 PREPARATION TIPS FOR DELEGATES OF THE GENERAL ASSEMBLY

- **Double delegations have their advantages.** Conferences often allow teams to "double" their representation in General Assembly committees. This simply means that your team will assign two delegates, working as a team, to represent your member state in the committee. This system has several advantages. First, an inexperienced team member can be paired with an experienced Model U.N. participant so that the former can learn the ropes at his/her first conference. Double delegations also come in handy during the busy moments of a committee session. For instance, one delegate can always remain in the committee room to follow debates, while the other can

stay involved in the discussions and negotiations that often occur outside in hallways.

- **Consider the size of your committee.** General Assembly committees tend to be quite large. Thus, it is often difficult to be heard amongst a crowd of 300 delegates. Ideal General Assembly delegates are not afraid to assert themselves in order to be heard.

- **Recognize the limitations of your committee.** While the General Assembly can and does debate whatever its members adopt for an agenda, its resolutions do not have the force of law, and will likely only receive the funding they require if the General Assembly reaches a high consensus on

financial priorities. While the General Assembly has the right to set the U.N. budget, it must do so in consultation with the Fifth Committee of the General Assembly, and under the guidance of the Advisory Committee on Administrative and Budgetary Questions (ACABQ). The same is true with resolutions relating to questions of peacekeeping or sanctions. While the General Assembly can, and often has, passed resolutions voicing its opinion on these issues, without the support of the Security Council, they become mere admonitions or condemnations, and are unlikely to produce results.

- Third Committee—Social, Humanitarian, and Cultural
- Fourth Committee—Special Political and Decolonization
- Fifth Committee—Administrative and Budgetary
- Sixth Committee—Legal

All draft resolutions are voted on in plenary meetings of the General Assembly, usually towards the end of the regular session (early September - mid December), after the main committees have completed their consideration of them and submitted draft resolutions to the plenary Assembly. (See **Box 2.3 Preparation Tips for Delegates of the General Assembly,** above.)

ECONOMIC AND SOCIAL COUNCIL

The Economic and Social Council (ECOSOC) is comprised of 54 member states, each serving a three-year term. Where the General Assembly debates broad issues of importance to the United Nations, ECOSOC is the principal organ charged with coordinating economic, social, and related work of the United Nations and the specialized agencies and institutions—known as the U.N. family of organizations. ECOSOC committees focus specifically on issues of economic and social development, supervising various U.N. programs, funds, and commissions, and gathering and distributing data and information related to these issues. Decisions of the ECOSOC require a simple majority.

Increasingly, ECOSOC committees also work directly with non-governmental organizations

- **Consider the size of the committee.** Committees of the Economic and Social Council can hold up to 54 member states, as well as selected NGOs. In this small setting, delegates must stay on their toes, as they will often have the opportunity to speak and ask questions in formal debate.
- **Recognize the limitations of your committee.** Committees of the ECOSOC are limited to creating or initiating studies and reports, making recommendations, preparing and organizing international conferences, and coordinating the activities of specialized agencies. Keep this mandate in mind when formulating resolutions.

- **Appreciate the importance of NGOs to your committee.** At some Model U.N. conferences, delegates have the opportunity to represent NGOs. Although NGOs do not have a vote in the ECOSOC, NGO representatives play an active role in the proceedings, disseminating information to member states and challenging them to solve the economic and social problems on the agenda.
- **Recognize the importance of building consensus.** Part of the influence of NGOs in ECOSOC committees has been the increasing realization that while a majority vote on an issue might be enough to carry a resolution or decision through a committee according to ECOSOC's charter, a unanimous or consensus decision may truly be necessary if the issue is to be resolved. Whereas a General Assembly delegate might be satisfied with a resolution that passes by a slim majority, an ECOSOC delegate needs to strive for full consensus, not only among member states, but also among NGO representatives who will play a key role in defining the success or failure of an issue once a vote is taken. Through their role as advocates in the mass media, and through their dedicated work in the field, NGOs have considerable leverage on ECOSOC issues.

(NGOs). The United Nations now officially recognizes over 1600 organizations that are independent of governments, as groups whose work is related to that of the United Nations, and therefore deserving of a role in U.N. proceedings. (See **Box 2.4 Preparation Tips for Delegates of the Economic and Social Council.**)

SECURITY COUNCIL

The Security Council is the 15-member organ responsible for maintaining international peace and security. The Council is composed of five permanent members (France, the People's Republic of China, the Russian Federation, the United Kingdom, and the United States—the victors of World War II), and ten rotating members elected to two-year terms from various world regions. A representative of each Security Council member must be present at U.N. Headquarters, located in New York City, at all times, ensuring the Council can function continuously. The presidency of the Council rotates on a monthly basis, following the English alphabet system.

Decisions on substantive matters require affirmative votes from a minimum of nine members, including all permanent members. U.N. member states that do not have a seat on the Council can participate in discussion, without a vote, if the Council agrees that member state's interests are affected by the issue under consideration.

To carry out its mandate, Council members rely on a range of alternatives—from investigations and mediation to sanctions and military action. In accordance to the statute of the U.N. Charter, all member states must accept and carry out the decisions of the Council. (See **Box 2.5 Preparation Tips for Delegates of the Security Council** and **Box 2.6 Preparing for A Crisis Committee.**)

INTERNATIONAL COURT OF JUSTICE

Located in The Hague, The Netherlands, the International Court of Justice (ICJ) is the principal legal organ of the United Nations. The Court is charged with settling legal disputes between states and giving advisory opinions on legal questions to other U.N. bodies. Only states that are parties to its Statute (which now includes all U.N. member states) are allowed to appear before the Court. The ICJ is composed of 15 judges of different nationalities, elected to nine-year terms by the General Assembly and the Security Council. These judges are independent magistrates, rather

2.5 Preparation Tips for Delegates of the Security Council

- **Be prepared for a crisis.** Security Council simulations often include a crisis: a topic for discussion taken from current events, but for which the delegates won't likely have had much opportunity to prepare. A surprise incursion by India into Pakistan, or a deadly terrorist attack using bio-toxins could interrupt the established agenda, and solving the crisis may require you to work deep into the night.

- **Researching is integral to your success.** Preparation for a Security Council simulation requires constant monitoring of current events, and a deep appreciation of your country's prior positions on all of the world's hotspots. If you are representing one of the five permanent members of the Council, you will be able to sift through the records of the Council to track your country's role over the entire half-century of its history. Some of this history will be easy to defend, but at other times, you will be forced to take a tough stance on a very tenuous position from the past. If you are one of the other ten rotating members, your country's policy might be more difficult to discern. However, most Security Council members now make an effort to post important positions on their websites at the U.N.

- **Recognize the importance of building consensus.** In the Security Council, decisions on substantive matters require nine votes, including the concurring votes of all five permanent members (referred to as "veto" power). Thus, permanent members wield considerable power in the Council.

2.6 Preparing for a Crisis Committee

Crisis committees are a unique phenomenon in the Model U.N. experience. In general, they are cabinet or political simulations that spend the majority of the conference focusing on spontaneous events. Although they can be more difficult to prepare for, crises committes are often the most rewarding experiences for delegates in Model U.N.

The most common crisis committee is the simulation of the U.S. National Security Council, the senior advisors that counsel the president on national security and foreign policy matters. However, recent conferences have run bodies as disparate as the Armenian Cabinet, Indian Cabinet, and Israeli-Palestinian peace talks (held before the beginning of the new intifada). Sometimes, conferences run joint crises, in which a crisis occurs simultaneously in two different committees, requiring each committee to react to the actions of the other.

Preparing for a crisis simulation differs greatly from preparing for a standard U.N. simulation. First, you do not represent a particular nation's views, but rather you are a member of a government or a political team. Preparation has to be both more specialized and more general. Topics will be given for research by the conference, but crises rarely grow out of these assigned issues. Instead, a fluency with the current state of the body being run is necessary, the environment in which the said body operates. Also, you need to have a good grasp of your "portfolio." For example, if you are the Minister of Economic Development in the Colombian Cabinet, you need to know the various crises facing Colombia, but you are also expected to know the economic situation better than, say, the Minister of Health, and be able to deal with the economic ramifications of any crisis that may arise, as well as be able to contribute to the general debate.

Rules of procedure in cabinets and political simulations vary, and many conferences will prepare their own. In general, rules are far less strict than in other Model U.N. simulations. Resolutions are rarely, if ever, presented, although this varies on a conference-by-conference basis, and resolutions may take on the form of press releases or "action orders" to various ministries. The majority of the time is spent in debate—generally a form of moderated caucus—dealing with crises as they arise.

The most important thing to do in preparing for a crisis simulation is to follow current events. Conference crisis directors can be very wily in devising intricate crises from what they see in the news every day. So, if you want to stay active in the committee, you should keep abreast of the major happenings in the world today. In addition, almost all national governments maintain websites where information can be found on the various members of the cabinet you will be simulating. Many countries also have English-language newspapers online which can be consulted to get an idea of domestic politics and potential flashpoints for conflict.

Delegates role-playing rebel leaders in Indonesia 2007, a joint crisis committee simulated at the McGill Model United Nations Assembly, January 2002.

than diplomats representing the interests of their countries.

The Court only hears cases in which the states involved have submitted to its jurisdiction. Since 1946, the Court has delivered 74 judgments on cases involving issues such as the right of asylum, non-interference in the internal affairs of states, hostage-taking, and territorial sovereignty.

THE SECRETARIAT

Made up of 8,900 international civil servants, the Secretariat is responsible for performing the day-to-day functions necessary to keep the United Nations running. The staff's duties range from administering peacekeeping operations to translating official documents. It is important to note that all members of the Secretariat are international civil servants, which means they are answerable to the United Nations for their activities rather than their home governments. In accordance with the U.N. Charter, member states agree to refrain from improperly influencing members of Secretariat in order to uphold the international character of the institution and its mandate.

The Secretariat is headed by the Secretary-General, who is appointed by the General Assembly (on the recommendation of the Security Council) for a term of five years. The current Secretary-General, Kofi Annan, of Ghana, is serving his second term. He is the first Secretary-General from the ranks of the U.N. staff, where he served in numerous positions, including Under-Secretary-General for Peacekeeping Operations. During his time in office, Annan has focused on reforming the U.N. through administrative and organizational measures, mobilizing international support for Africa, improving peacekeeping operations, and calling on member states to commit themselves to the goals of the Millennium Summit (see www.un.org/milleniumgials/index.html).

THE TRUSTEESHIP COUNCIL

The Trusteeship Council was established upon the founding of the United Nations to supervise the administration of Trust Territories, ensuring the populations of these territories progressed economically, socially, and politically. Another goal of the Council was to guide the Territories towards self-government and independence. In that respect, the Trusteeship Council was successful. In 1994, Palau became the last Trust Territory to become independent. Since then, the Council has suspended operations.

INTERGOVERNMENTAL ORGANIZATIONS

Intergovernmental organizations (IGOs) are institutions made up of governments, which give them the authority to make collective decisions to manage particular problems on the global agenda. The United Nations is the biggest IGO in the world, consisting of 191 member states. Several U.N. specialized agencies, such as the International Labor Organization, are also classified as IGOs. IGOs can focus on specific areas such as health (WHO), or military coordination (NATO), or they can deal with multiple issues (EU).

Below are descriptions of IGOs commonly simulated in Model U.N. Additionally, descriptions of other IGOs, including regional organizations, can be found in Section II: Regional Perspectives: How Nations Interact.

INTERNATIONAL CRIMINAL COURT

In Rome, on July 17, 1998, after a number of initial sessions beginning in 1995 and five weeks of intricate negotiations in six official U.N. languages, the Rome Statute of the International Criminal Court (ICC) was adopted at a diplomatic conference (Rome Conference). Under the Rome Statute, the ICC has the power to try those responsible for the most serious crimes of concern to the international community, including war crimes, genocide, and crimes against humanity. The adoption of the Statute by a vote of 121 was a watershed moment in efforts to ensure international justice. The Rome conference also created the U.N. Preparatory Commission for the ICC,

Model U.N. conferences are always looking for different and innovative new simulations, and the International Criminal Court (ICC) is the latest trend. Several conferences around the world have been simulating the ICC since 2001. However, there are some important details to be aware of when simulating the ICC. These caveats apply both to delegates and to conference organizers. •

The most important distinction is that the ICC does not operate in the same way as the International Court of Justice (ICJ), an older U.N. body that arbitrates cases between states. Instead, the ICC operates more like the ad hoc war crimes tribunals for Yugoslavia and Rwanda. Unlike the ICJ, the ICC prosecutes individual suspects in their capacities as government or military leaders. Therefore, delegates who have done ICJ simulations need to reorient themselves with respect to the rules of the ICC. At most conferences, delegates play the role of judges acting in their individual expert capacity, and not representing the position of any country.

The second distinction of the ICC is that while it works closely with the United Nations, the ICC is not a U.N. body. The ICC draws funding independently from the United Nations and also has an independent procedure for electing judges. The ICC is governed by the Rome Statute, and other human rights treaties are not applicable unless they are provided for within the Rome Statute. The ICC Assembly of States Parties is the governing body of the Court. While the crime of aggression is not yet within the purview of the ICC, aggression is one of the key areas of intersection between the ICC and the United Nations, as the Security Council has powers to deal with aggression under Chapter VII of the U.N. Charter.

Delegates should study the Rome Statute and other governing documents such as the Rules of Procedure and Evidence, the Elements of Crimes, and the Draft Relationship Agreement Between the ICC and the United Nations. They can be found online at http://www.un.org/icc. In the United States, the Independent Student Coalition for the ICC (http://www.isc-icc.org), a nongovernmental organization, maintains a website specifically for students, which includes information on simulating the ICC.

---

charged with framing proposals and draft texts as bases for the operation of the Court. All text has to be adopted by the Court's governing body, the Assembly of States Parties. Nine Preparatory Commissions have had successful sessions drafting substantive and administrative provisions for the Court, with a final session scheduled for July 2002.

Less than four years after the historic Rome Conference adopted the Rome Statute, it came into effect on April 11, 2002. At a special ceremony held during the 9th Preparatory Commission at the United Nations, ten states deposited their instruments of ratification, joining 52 others, to achieve and surpass the 60 ratifications necessary to bring into force the Statute to establish the Court. As provided for by the Rome Statute, the Court will have the authority to investigate and try persons accused of crimes committed after July 1, 2002. The Court itself will begin at a meeting of the Assembly of States Parties in September 2002. (See **Box 2.7 Model U.N. and the International Criminal Court.**)

THE WORLD BANK

The World Bank is a multilateral lending agency that directs its efforts toward reducing poverty by promoting sustainable economic growth for nations in need of assistance. While it was founded in 1944 to help restore the post-World War II economies of European nations, the World Bank has since focused on less-developed countries with efforts to help reduce national debts, educate citizens, and stabilize often-fragile economies. The Bank is an independent specialized agency of the United Nations, although their membership is fairly similar. It is funded through the sale of debt securities, capital earned on interest, and contributions from member states. The Bank has observer status in a number of U.N. bodies, including the General Assembly and the Economic and Social Council.

INTERNATIONAL MONETARY FUND

Established in 1946, the International Monetary Fund (IMF) is an international financial institution in charge of promoting free trade and exchange and overseeing the global economy, with the goal of mitigating problems such as large trade and budget deficits. The IMF includes 183 member countries, and works towards the creation of a collective economic policy through temporary financing, administering loans, and monitoring currency exchange policies. Unlike the World Bank, the institution is completely financed by its member states. Every country pays a quota subscription, a sum determined on the basis of its' economic position in relation to other members.

A main function of the IMF is to lend capital to countries that are experiencing balance-of-pay- ment difficulties. Member countries can borrow funds by accepting the IMF economic policies and conditions that typically involve removing trade barriers, increasing exports to earn hard currency for debt service, and promoting foreign investment through privatization and deregulation of labor and environmental laws.

United Nations <www.un.org>

Kegley Jr., Charles W. and Eugene R. Wittkopf. *World Politics: From War to Peace*, New York: Wadsworth Publishing, 147-155, 2000.

2.8 WEB RESOURCES ON THE U.N. AND IGOs

For more information on these committees, please visit their websites.

U.N. Organs

General Assembly: http://www.un.org/ga/

ECOSOC: http://www.un.org/esa/coordination/ecosoc/

Security Council: http://www.un.org/Docs/scinfo.htm

International Court of Justice: http://www.icj-cij.org/

Secretariat: http://www.un.org/documents/st.htm

Trusteeship Council: http://www.un.org/documents/tc.htm

Intergovernmental Organizations

International Criminal Court: http://www.un.org/law/icc/index.html

The World Bank: http://www.worldbank.org/

International Monetary Fund: http://www.imf.org/

2.9 UNITED NATIONS VS. MODEL UNITED NATIONS

Although Model United Nations aims to simulate committees of the United Nations accurately, there are important differences between the institutions that delegates should be aware of in order to prevent common misconceptions. These differences often exist for one of these reasons: 1) Model U.N. conferences work on a much shorter time frame, 2) Model U.N. participants are students, not experienced diplomats, and 3) Model U.N. organizers rarely have access to in-depth information on "real" U.N. practices and resources.

	UNITED NATIONS	MODEL UNITED NATIONS
Period of Time	Sessions usually last several months.	Conferences last one to five days.
Conference Attendees	Attendees are primarily diplomats.	Attendees are primarily students from elementary school, middle school, high school, or college.
Seating Arrangements	Most U.N. sessions seat delegates in alphabetical (English) order.	Delegates either sit in alphabetical order, or wherever they choose, based on individual conference rules.
Resolutions	Delegates may prepare draft resolutions either individually or in groups, which are circulated and subsequently merged to form a consensus. A draft resolution typically does not go to the floor until it is ready to be adopted by consensus. It is considered desirable for a draft resolution to pass by consensus, with no nation voting "no." Accordingly, more than 70 percent of all U.N. resolutions now pass by consensus.	Depending on the conference, several resolutions may reach the floor for discussion. It is typically after discussion has taken place in formal debate, that delegates merge resolutions, if at all. (Due to the short time frame of a Model U.N. conference, it is often difficult for students to come to a consensus.
Caucusing	95 percent of the U.N.'s time is spent in "behind-the-scenes" caucusing—after official meetings, during lunch or in the hallways. It is very rare, however, for the U.N. to suspend formal meetings to caucus.	Delegates may move for suspension of the meeting to caucus. At this time, the official session breaks and the delegates meet informally in different blocs to discuss and draft resolutions. Additionally, many students meet after hours to discuss committee work.
Speakers' Lists	Formal U.N. meetings typically work on a speakers' list, with each country speaking once, possibly with an additional right of reply. Once every country speaks, the meeting breaks and behind-the-scene work begins. Bloc groups and smaller bodies like the Security Council practice "informal consultation," in which all delegates speak freely, bound by the norms of diplomatic currency.	Many Model U.N. conferences have speakers' lists, with delegations allowed to speak multiple times. Other conferences use a less formal means of debate, with delegates raising their placards for their chairperson to recognize them to speak. Some conferences also combine this with "informal consultation" for smaller bodies.
Rules of Procedure	There are brief, formal rules of procedure for U.N. bodies. Some common rules are unwritten, and chairs occasionally make rulings without precedent, which stand if uncontested.	Conferences base their rules both on written U.N. rules and outside sources. The rules are often changed to help streamline a one to five-day conference. Also, particular rules have different uses in Model U.N. than in the actual U.N., like "right of reply."
Bloc Spokespeople	Typically, regional and diplomatic blocs elect a spokesperson to represent their consensus before the committee.	Bloc spokespeople are rarely used, as there is seldom time to form cohesive blocs or select consensus leaders.

Secretary-General Kofi Annan addresses a committee of the 1999 National Model U.N. Conference, sponsored by the National Collegiate Conference Association. (Photo: Daoud Mikhail)

Delegates in voting procedure at the UNA-USA 2002 High School Model U.N. Conference. (Photo: UNA-USA)

In addition to possessing a deep understanding of the U.N. system, Model U.N. delegates must research their member state, as well as the function and responsibilities of their committee and the issues before it. Effective diplomats spend considerable time preparing for U.N. sessions, and when a diplomat's government decides to take the initiative or assume leadership regarding an issue, he or she is expected to know the details of contentious aspects of the matter. To formulate policy decisions, foreign ministries must be able to analyze and interpret research. As a delegate in Model U.N., you must meet the same task.

RESOURCES

Much of your research for a Model U.N. conference can now be found on the Internet. Obviously, the U.N. website (www.un.org) will be your best resource, containing everything from your committee's history to resolutions passed on an agenda issue. UBISnet (http://unbisnet.un.org/) catalogues U.N. documentation from 1979 to the present, and offers current voting records and an index of speeches. The U.N. website also offers various other methodsof finding documents, including UN-I-QUE (http://libunique.un.org/), a user-friendly database that provides access to tens of thousands of documents, dating back to 1946. In addition, the *Guide's* Internet Resources (page 193) lists more than 300 websites of U.N. bodies, NGOs, IGOs, media forums, and research institutions.

Books, journals, and periodicals will also prove to be invaluable tools in your preparation. This publication's annotated bibliography, containing books on a variety of U.N.-related subjects, can be found on page 221. **Box 3.1 Reading Suggestions** offers a list of periodicals and journals often used by Model U.N. participants.

ORGANIZING A RESEARCH PORTFOLIO

Regardless of your committee assignment, one of the most important components of your preparation is a research portfolio. Your portfolio should be organized to ensure quick access at the conference. A three-ring binder is strongly recommended to gather all of your papers, as this will allow you to divide information into sections, and to have quick and easy access during conference sessions. In addition to your research, your portfolio should contain:

- All position paper(s) prepared for your committee;
- Rules of procedure for the conference;
- Your **Nation Guide** (page 23);
- A copy of the U.N. Charter; and
- Any relevant documents concerning your country and its positions that you feel may be helpful.

Other sections that should be included are outlined below.

BACKGROUND GUIDE

Your portfolio should contain a copy of your committee's background guide. Background guides are informational aids that assist delegates in their pre-conference work. Each committee has its own guide, which is usually written by the committee's director or president. Background guides generally include: an overview of the history and function of your committee, a summary of the agenda topics, past U.N. actions on these issues, questions to consider when formulating a resolution (see Chapter 4: Building Your Model U.N. Skills), and resources for research. The guide will give you an idea of the director or president's vision of the committee, and what you

Newspapers
Diplomatic World
    Bulletin
Disarmament Times
Earth Times
Financial Times
ICC Monitor
Los Angeles Times
Miami Herald
The New York Times
The Times (London)
Washington Post
International Herald
    Tribune

Journals
Foreign Affairs
Foreign Policy
Human Rights Quarterly
International
    Organization
International Security
The National Interest
World Policy Journal
World Politics

Magazines
The Economist
Far Eastern Economic
    Review
The InterDependent
Newsweek
U.N. Chronicle
U.S. News & World
    Report
World Press Review

Annuals
A Global Agenda:
    Issues Before the
    General Assembly
    of the United
    Nations

need to research and consider in order to be an active participant.

Although background guides are invaluable tools in Model U.N., simply reading your committee's guide will not sufficiently prepare you for the conference. Reading the guide will give you an overview of what delegates will debate at the conference, but it will not provide you with the specific information needed to communicate the interests and policies of your member state. For this, additional research is needed. The prepared delegates in your committee will have spent time researching your committee's history, the history and policy of their countries, and U.N. action in addressing the agenda topics.

COMMITTEE HISTORY

In order to thoroughly familiarize yourself with its mandate and functions, include a section devoted solely to the history and work of your committee. In addition to general information on the committee, search for relevant conventions, plans of actions, or conferences that relate to the issues before your committee at the conference. Learning about past actions the committee has taken on these issues will prevent you from suggesting a plan that the U.N. has already tried.

COUNTRY RESEARCH

Your portfolio must include basic information you have gathered on your country. A printout of at least one overview of your country from previously mentioned sources is recommended, but you should also have a good, detailed map, economic and demographic statistics on your country, and a brief history that you can trust to provide you with some context if something unexpected crops up during the course of the debate.

Basic information on your country is easily available in the CIA World Factbook (www. odci.gov/CIA/publications/factbook). However, it is best to begin with information from the websites or publications of that country itself. After all, if you are representing Thailand, it is more important to know what Thailand says about

itself, than it is to know how the CIA or other agencies view Thailand. Consider looking on the website of the permanent mission to the United Nations for the country you will represent. If that country does not have a website at the United Nations, check if they have an embassy website in your country, or contact them directly by email or a letter to ask for information. Identify yourself as a Model U.N. delegate desiring to represent the country as accurately as possible, and you may be surprised by what you get in response. With these resources, you should be able to complete the **Nation Guide** presented in this *Guide* (opposite), or develop a similar section in your binder with the same end in mind: knowledge of your country.

NGO RESEARCH

If your first Model U.N. assignment is to an NGO, you can use the same process of research described for countries. Like delegates representing a country, you need to be familiar with the principles and goals of your organization. Information about most NGOs is now often available from their websites, and those with adequate financial resources may also produce print materials such as pamphlets, studies or reports that you may obtain by request. Do not hesitate to contact the NGO you represent, as the organization will more than likely be very willing to assist you in promoting its perspectives on issues before the United Nations. Such information will be crucial in convincing the other delegations at the conference of the importance of your issues.

ISSUE BACKGROUND

Your portfolio should contain a general overview of the issue or issues on the agenda, focusing on the most significant and controversial aspects. The review should include references to previous U.N. actions and activity, especially citations of previous U.N. resolutions. It is not necessary to quote all of them at length; just note their basic thrust and the official U.N. resolution numbers. (However, you may elect to keep a copy of

3.2 NATION GUIDE: GETTING TO KNOW THE BASICS

Official country name:_____

Governmental system:_____

Head of state:_____

Official language(s): _____

Allies/blocs:_____

Major religions:_____

Major cities:_____

Climate:_____

Ports/waterways:_____

Infrastructure status:_____

Population:_____

U.N. dues payment status:_____

Environmental stance; e.g., problems, innovations:_____

Standard of living (UNDP Annual Report):_____

Development status:_____

U.N. peacekeeping role (Blue Helmets):_____

Has the U.N. ever had to intervene in any conflict involving this

nation? If so, where and what were the circumstances?_____

_____

_____

Has the United Nations ever cited this country for human rights

violations? If so, what were the circumstances? _____

_____

What are four problems/threats that currently seem to affect this

nation?_____

_____

_____

Ethnic/cultural issues:_____

Refugees problems:_____

_____

Trade blocs/associations:_____

_____

_____

Balance of payments/trade: _____

Military organization:_____

_____

Military expenditures (percent spent on defense):_____

Major weapons, arsenal, nuclear capability, etc: _____

_____

Percent of GNP spent on ODA (Overseas Development Aid): _____

Economic system: _____

Major exports/imports:_____

_____

_____

Major trade partners: _____

_____

_____

IMF, WB, GATT positions (debtor nation? donor nation?):_____

_____

_____

Agricultural products: _____

_____

_____

Industries:_____

_____

_____

Natural resources:_____

_____

Energy sources (both the type of energy and its origin):_____

_____

_____

Major conflicts both past and present: _____

_____

Date admitted to United Nations: _____

Based on your research, what do you feel is at the heart of this

nation's identity?: _____

_____

Try to find at least one recent article that is about or makes reference

to this nation (preferably from the past two weeks):_____

_____

important resolutions in your portfolio, so that you can refer to them during the course of debates.)

ISSUE POSITION

You should have material establishing **your country's position** on the relevant issues being discussed in your committee. If you are fortunate, you will have copies of specific statements made by a diplomat from your country or a spokesperson for your NGO. The information collected in this part of your portfolio should offer the reasons behind your position, and why you feel it is the correct one for all other nations to adopt. For your own information, note how important the issue is to your country, as this will guide you through negotiations. You should also speak with your teammates regarding the position your country takes on other issues. A prepared delegate should be able to discuss his or her country's views on a wide range of issues.

BLOC POSITION

Alternatively, you might find that your country does not have a position on one of your topics. That is not unusual and does not necessarily mean that you are failing at your research. What you should do in this case is establish your stance by ascertaining what the various bloc positions would be on this topic. A bloc is a cohesive alliance made up of a group of states with similar social, economic, and/or political interests. Blocs play an important role in coordinating and shaping the policies of many nations. This is especially true of smaller countries whose delegates find that combining their resources and votes is an effective way of advancing their positions against more influential nations. You should be aware of the **positions of major blocs** on the issues before your committee. First, address the position of your own bloc, paying particular attention to bloc members who might oppose your position. Next, identify and learn to discuss the positions of other key blocs. Become familiar with the major arguments used to support positions of other key blocs, as well as other positions that may be con-

trary to that of your bloc. Prepare yourself with material to show the weaknesses of these opposing views.

WRITING A POSITION PAPER

Before the Model U.N. conference begins, each delegate should prepare a position paper for his or her committee that defines each topic on the agenda, as well as that topic's relationship to the country's national interests. If you are working with a partner, you may each work individually on a single issue, but you must be sure that your positions do not contradict each other in principle.

Because of their importance in framing issues, conference organizers usually require that delegations submit completed position papers to their committees before the conference begins. A position paper is typically between 500 (high school) and 1,000 (college) words long and contains a brief introduction that frames each topic before the committee as your country sees it, as well as a comprehensive breakdown of your country's position on the topics. Alternatively, some conferences ask delegates to write a position paper on each topic on the committee's agenda. (See **Box 3.3 Sample Position Paper.**)

Regardless of its format, an excellent position paper must contain: (1) a clear statement of your country's position on each topic and an indication of why your country takes this position in the context of what it has already done in relation to the topic; (2) past U.N. actions regarding the topic; and (3) suggestions for a plan of action in addressing the issue. Keep in mind that you are not only attempting to demonstrate knowledge of the topic itself, but also of your country's relationship to it in the context of both historical and contemporary U.N. debates. To do this, you must:

* Frame your country's view of the topic by considering alternatives that have been proposed or pointing out specific regional blocs or countries that share your position;

- Examine previous resolutions or actions taken on this topic so as to propose or advance your opinion on what action should be taken, while attempting to alleviate the concerns of those who may oppose your position; and

- Intimate whether there is room for negotiation, while defending the position and propositions advanced above.

The position papers of your Model U.N. team are the collective building blocks of an overall, national position for the conference. Taking an overall, delegation-wide, national position will give your team its strategic focus during negotiation and debate at the Model U.N. conference. However, simply determining your country's position will not be enough. You should have a sound understanding of prior resolutions, conventions, charters, covenants, declarations, and documents that deal with the topic(s) that you have been assigned. Delegates who have thought through all sides of an issue, and can see the various possibilities for compromise will surprise a delegate who knows the issues from only one point of view. In addition, the more you know about all sides of the issue, the easier it will be to craft speeches, create resolutions, and negotiate.

3.3 SAMPLE POSITION PAPER

Committee: Commission on Human Rights
Topic: Violence Against Women
Country: The Kingdom of Denmark
Delegate: Simon Smith, Edgewater University

The Universal Declaration of Human Rights states, "no one shall be subjected to torture or to cruel, inhuman or degrading treatment or punishment." Although this doctrine was adopted in 1948, the world has fallen quite short of this goal. Violence against women pervades the borders of all states. Despite cooperative efforts at combating these gross human rights abuses, such as the adoption of the Declaration on the Elimination of Violence against Women, the United Nations has not been able to alleviate the injustice women worldwide experience daily.

The Danish Centre for Human Rights in Copenhagen, Denmark's foremost national human rights institution, serves to promote and protect human rights. The research it performs contributes to the passage of legislation concerning human rights in Denmark, as well as an increase in awareness. The Danish Centre addresses this committee annually regarding developments in human rights issues in Denmark, as well as the state of human rights internationally. Denmark has no record of committing major human rights violations, most importantly any targeted at women. In its 2000 Annual Report, Amnesty International also found no human rights violations against Danish women. Women are invaluable to Denmark's society and have achieved significant economic and social gains in the twentieth century. Currently, 75% of medical students in Denmark are women.

Denmark is confident that this body can help bring about an end to violence against women without compromising the sovereignty of a member state. There are several ways that this Committee can attack this problem while still following the principles of self-determination set forth by the U.N. Charter. Education, by far, is the most useful tool that this body can utilize to protect victims of this gender-based violence. Governments, U.N. agencies, and non-governmental organizations (NGOs) can plan a coordinated campaign that educates the population on the various ways women are violently targeted daily. Traditional views of women need to be changed in order to prevent atrocious practices, such as honor killings and female genital mutilation. Children of both sexes need to be taught at an early age to value the rights of women in order to prevent such violence in their generation.

Another way to stop this heinous violence would be to reproach member states that consistently violate treaties such as the Convention on Political Rights of Women (1952), the Convention on the Elimination of All Forms of Discrimination against Women (1979), and the Declaration on the Elimination of Violence against Women (1993). Although this Committee does not have the jurisdiction of imposing sanctions, it can pass resolutions that verbally condemn states that commit human rights violations and publicize such disapprobation. The U.N. High Commissioner for Human Rights can also meet with representatives of said governments to discuss possible solutions.

*A delegate looking over his
research during committee
session. (Photo: UNA-USA)*

In addition to improving your aptitude for research, your preparation for a Model U.N. conference will help you in developing or strengthening the following skills: role-playing, speech-making, negotiation, writing, and mastering rules of procedure. Many of these skills will help you not only at the conference, but also in instances of your every-day life, whether it be negotiating a raise at your after-school job or writing a paper for a class.

ROLE-PLAYING

In your role as a representative of a U.N. member state, your goal is to understand the country as if you were one of its citizens. The more you can identify with and behave as a person from that country, the better you will be at role-playing that country's diplomat. (This is referred to as "being in character".)

As a Model U.N. delegate, it is important to set aside all personal beliefs. You no longer represent the country of which you are actually a citizen, but, instead, the nation to which you are assigned at the conference. Other delegates at the conference will no longer refer to you by such names as Lucy, John, or Mike, but rather, as France, Haiti, the delegate from Iceland, or whatever member state you represent. In Model U.N., delegates must stay in the proper mindset: that of a representative, not a student. In committee, you are no longer stating your own opinions, but rather speaking as an ambassador representing the interests of your country.

Holding in-class simulations during your Model U.N. meetings or classes is an excellent way to practice role-playing, as well as build your other Model U.N. skills. **Box 4.6 India/Pakistan Crisis** features a scenario that your club or class can use as a pre-conference simulation.

SPEECH MAKING

Prior to arriving at the conference, you should prepare at least one opening speech presenting your overall position on the issues before your committee.

The components of your position paper may serve as a foundational statement, however it will not serve you to simply read your position paper. In order to keep your audience engaged, you must speak to them rather than at them. Learning to craft interesting speeches, as well as developing strong public speaking skills, is therefore, an important part of your Model U.N. preparation. **Box 4.1 Effective Public Speaking** offers suggestions for improving this skill.

When preparing your opening speech, remember that you are presenting your speech to students who are also role-playing in a mock U.N. debate. While your idea of a thoroughly professional speech may win a nod for your qualifications, posturing is easy to spot. A speech that does not consider its audience, both as individuals and according to the common sense of the committee, is likely to fall flat. Perhaps even more important, however, is the fact that your audience will be hearing, rather than reading your speech. Aural reception, the ability to listen, relies on clear, simple sentences, and not long-winded lists of information and facts. Often, a poetic or euphonic turn of phrase, or simple commonplace language, will stick in the minds of your audience throughout the entire length of the conference. Remembering these two foundations—audience and aurality—will help to give you a golden tongue when speaking before a large committee.

When creating your opening speech, begin by reading your position paper out loud, preferably to a friend or fellow delegate. Delete sentences that don't allow you to breathe effectively, or that cause your tongue to trip. If these sentences are critical to your position, rewrite them in a way that not only makes them easier to speak, but that will resonate with your audience and stick with them throughout the conference. As you begin to refine your text, change the font size to something large enough to read if you have to, and include stage directions such as bold text for emphasis, or ellipses . . . for dramatic pauses. While a memorized speech may impress some delegates, a forgotten line in your speech may cause you to lose focus and stumble on your words. Instead, have the text of your speech, or note cards, in hand when you get up to speak. You may not need to use them, but they may prevent you from making a serious mistake. As your experience grows, this will be less and less of a problem and, eventually, you will come to master the art of speaking on a topic with little or no assistance.

A finished speech should be a polished, easily presentable and clear articulation of your national policy on a specific issue. Since rules of procedure may leave you with only one or two minutes for each speech, you should make sure that you can deliver your message comfortably within that time frame. A successful speech will establish that you are a confident delegate, in command of the facts, and at home with your audience. If you are lucky, your speech will contain catchphrases that will become the defining terms of the debate on that topic. Indeed, a strong speech may even see some of its language adopted as the basis for a working paper, the first step on the way to a draft resolution by the committee. To assure this is the case, practice the delivery of your speeches before the conference, and revise them whenever necessary.

NEGOTIATION SKILLS

In Model U.N., delegates take part in negotiation, the act of coming to a consensus through discussion and compromise. Consensus building involves intense bargaining so that the interests of all member states are at least minimally met in agreements. To assist in this challenge, you can follow these basic principles of negotiations:

- Be personal. Before the committee is in session, learn the names of as many of the participants as possible, and use them frequently rather than calling someone by his/her country.
- Be calm and reasonable throughout. Maintaining your cool at all times gives you an unquestionable advantage.

4.1 EFFECTIVE PUBLIC SPEAKING

In Model U.N., a delegate becomes the member state that s/he is representing, assuming a new identity. For the assumption of this new identity to appear realistic, it is necessary for a delegate to portray his or her ideas effectively.

Below are some tips on effective public speaking.

- When speaking before the committee, you must appear informed. The more knowledgeable a delegate becomes on a topic, the better they will be to communicate ideas clearly to others.

- When trying to persuade the committee, you must stimulate the audience. One strategy is to stress and reinforce common beliefs or values of the audience (such as the dire need to address the issue of child trafficking) and attempt to intensify them. Another strategy is to incite people to take action. It is not enough to just talk about solutions; action must be taken to change the status quo.

- Have an effective delivery. When possible, speak extemporaneously, maintaining constant eye contact with delegates. Use note cards, if necessary. Avoid memorizing your speech. Once a mistake is made on one line, the following lines may be incorrectly delivered as well.

- Don't appear overconfident. A speech that is delivered with arrogance will fail to stimulate the audience. Instead, be diplomatic in your tone, showing courtesy to your fellow delegates.

- Remember that non-verbal communication accounts for much of your delivery. Avoid stiff body movement; move around if it makes you more comfortable. Movements you may perform absent-mindedly, such as touching your hair or tugging at your suit, will be noticed by your fellow delegates. Keep your hand movements to a minimum. Although some movements can be used to effectively illustrate a point, excessive waving will distract the audience.

- Sell. Successful negotiations are primarily the result of "selling" yourself and your objectives to others. Push the principles that will become the basis for consensus.
- Trade. Negotiations usually involve a series of compromises. If necessary, adopt an initial position from which you can compromise, but make sure this does not force you to betray the principles behind your position.
- Speak with as many delegates as possible. A deal with a few key delegates may not be enough to achieve the consensus of the committee.
- Don't overlook students who may not seem to be fully participating. It could be they are new delegates with a lot to say, but lack a clear understanding of how best to proceed. Reach out to them, and include them in your negotiations.
- Never lose focus. Three hours of careful negotiations can be forfeited in a few minutes of inattention.
- Always end on a positive note. Don't let setbacks shake your self-confidence.

All of your hard work and preparation will help you to keep these points in mind as you participate in a conference. After a few conferences, various approaches to these fundamentals will become part of the "conference personality" you develop. In the long run, the key to your success is a combination of substance and style that helps you to achieve the objectives you set on a regular basis.

Strategies and Tactics

From these fundamentals, most delegates develop certain tactics and strategies to respond to the specific challenges of a Model U.N. conference. In negotiating these challenges, some of these tactics have proven reliable and can be used frequently. Roughly, they can be divided into two main strategies related to the process of negotiation: initiation and mediation.

INITIATION

If done with modesty and respect, being the first one on your committee to speak, raise an issue, or offer a compromise will help you to win the recognition of other delegates. Some ways to accomplish this include:

- Sitting at the front of meetings. Be sure that your ideas or plan of action are the centerpiece.
- Providing leadership at each meeting. Be the first to get down to business.
- Having an overall plan for how the conference will go. Without one, most negotiations fail.
- Being the first to bring up major terms for agreement or compromise.
- Making an early concession. Early in the negotiations, try to satisfy the other party on a point that is very important to him or her.

MEDIATION

The ability to move negotiations beyond the initial phase of a discussion will distinguish you as a delegate who can keep the conversation going. If your country's policies or your personal style make it hard for you to be an initiator, than perhaps you can play a role as a mediator, someone who helps the committee along when the conversation gets stuck on difficult issues. Some ways to accomplish this include:

- Caucusing often. Leave the room to consult with other delegates whenever you think it is useful.
- Being courteous. Always try to be the delegate who makes sure everyone has a chance to speak in a caucus.
- Letting others finish their thoughts. Interruptions annoy people.
- Working to make all terms of agreement specific rather than permitting a broad range of interpretations. Unspecific language often ends up achieving only the lesser interpretations.
- Deferring discussion of sensitive points to those with something at stake.
- Breaking the tension—use humor, but do so judiciously. A joke in poor taste could prove costly.

- Renegotiating previous agreements if necessary. Remember, each day is a new ball game.
- Knowing the needs of the other side.
- Working toward agreement on next steps if an overall solution seems unachievable.

Related to this, you should also be mindful of the bloc policies you support. Survey the room at the beginning of a conference to determine which bloc will best support your position. Try to avoid making any specific commitments until you have determined the bloc you will support. Once you ally with a particular group, however, flitting back and forth to others to extract marginal advantages may risk the support of the group most closely aligned with your policies. In this sense, your disciplined ability to be a "team player" is important. Moving back and forth to convey information from one bloc to another so as to achieve a common goal is the essence of diplomacy. Playing two blocs against one another so as to achieve your national position will ultimately create suspicions and may undermine your own goals.

Always remember to think about how your actions will be perceived by others. As you negotiate, you will undoubtedly be impressed by those who are confident and well spoken enough that they can take their time to develop a position, and make compromises only when necessary. Often this is the result of effective organization, other times sheer charisma on the part of that individual, but the same things you admire in others can become the basis for establishing your own reputation. If you learn something from someone, thank that person. If someone else assists you in advancing your position on an issue, be ready to offer to do the same on an issue that is important to their country. Throughout your negotiations, remember that while you are representing another country in a simulation, you are also representing yourself.

WRITING AT THE CONFERENCE

Since most of the work in a Model U.N. conference is conducted through resolutions, the ability to write them well is necessary to stay active in the committee. A written document, such as a working paper or resolution, is both a tool for discussion, and the ultimate desired outcome of a Model U.N. committee. Members of every committee will work over the course of the conference to produce a document that will resolve the issues before it in the full spirit of multilateral diplomacy. To do so, these documents must capture the common sense of the committee, taking note of important exceptions where necessary, and striving for consensus where possible. While adoption of a resolution by a slim majority may allow you to claim a political success for your country in committee, in reality, most issues before the U.N. will not be solved unless the committee reaches a super-majority, or even unanimity on an issue. Seasoned Model U.N. delegates come to respect those delegates who are capable of producing consensus documents for their negotiating skills, patience, and commitment to the values of the U.N. such efforts require.

DRAFTING A RESOLUTION

Resolutions are either general statements or directives to specific organizations, U.N. bodies, or states. They are written in almost all committees at a Model U.N. conference, although some committees, such as the Commission on Sustainable Development and ad hoc committees, have other ways to conduct business. In practice, a resolution will be prepared by an individual nation or by a group of nations working together in caucus sessions to achieve common language. Resolutions are the final results of the writing, discussion, and negotiation that go on in your committee over the course of the conference.

Prior to formulating a draft resolution, delegates often create a **working paper,** a document that is informally distributed to the committee to form the basis for debate on specifics. Working papers can be written in point form, in prose, or in the actual format and wording of a U.N. resolution. They may be authored by one country or several countries. However, for a working paper to be formally introduced for debate and eventual voting, it must appear in the format of a **draft**

resolution and have been signed by a specified number of delegates (usually 20 percent of the committee). Once these prerequisites are met, the document is assigned a number by the chair and can be referred to in speeches as a "draft resolution". When formatting your working paper to become a draft resolution, the title of the topic should appear, as should the name of your committee. Each draft resolution is a very long sentence, with the sections separated by semicolons and commas. The subject of the sentence is the organ making the statement, such as the General Assembly, Economic and Social Council, or Security Council. The remainder of the draft resolution is divided into two parts: preambulatory and operative clauses.

PREAMBULATORY CLAUSES

The preamble of a draft resolution does everything but propose action or make any substantive statement on the topic at hand. The **preambulatory clauses** are often historic justifications for actions, or a set of terms framing the issue at hand that are agreeable to all parties. Each clause begins with a participle (see examples from the chart), and then cites past resolutions, precedents, and statements about the particular purposes of the action to be taken. Preambulatory clauses can include:

- Reference to the U.N. Charter;
- Citation of past U.N. resolutions or treaties that have been ratified on the topic under discussion;
- Mention of statements made by the Secretary-General or a relevant U.N. body or agency;
- Recognition of the efforts of regional or non-governmental organizations in dealing with the issue; and
- General statements on the topic, its significance, and its impacts.

OPERATIVE CLAUSES

Operative clauses are the position portion of the draft resolution, and are ideally set out to achieve your country's main policy goals on the topic. Each operative clause begins with a verb (see examples in **Box 4.2 Phrases for Introducing**

Resolutions) and ends with a semicolon. Operative clauses should be organized in a logical progression, and each clause should contain a single idea or proposal. Operative clauses that contain more than one idea or proposal can cause confusion, particularly if your committee proposes amendments to the draft resolution.

SPONSORS AND SIGNATORIES

Sponsors of a draft resolution are those countries that have been the principal authors of the document and agree with its substance. Although there can be a single sponsor of a resolution, such a scenario would not likely occur at the U.N., as other countries would want to be involved in the drafting process. Sponsors, in effect, control a draft resolution, and only sponsors can approve immediate changes. Thus, it is important that they are able to cooperate with one another through agreement on basic principles. Some delegates will seek to have their country's name placed as a sponsor on every draft resolution on the floor, regardless of its content. That does little to move debate forward, and may undermine your country's position because no one will be sure where you really stand.

At most conferences, 20 percent of the committee concerned must be sponsors or signatories to a resolution. **Signatories** are countries that may or may not agree with the substance of the draft resolution as it stands but still wish to see it debated so that they can propose amendments. If you are asked to be a signatory to a working paper and you agree, it simply means that you would like to see the working paper on the floor as a draft resolution. It does not necessarily mean that you support the document. Indeed, the document you do support will ultimately be the product of the work of your entire committee, not just the work of a select group.

AMENDMENTS

An **amendment** is a written statement that adds, deletes or revises an operative clause in a draft resolution. The amendment process is used to strengthen consensus on a resolution by allowing delegates to change certain sections. There are two types of amendments:

PREAMBULATORY PHRASES

Affirming
Alarmed by
Approving
Aware of
Bearing in mind
Believing
Confident
Contemplating
Convinced
Declaring
Deeply concerned
Deeply conscious
Deeply convinced
Deeply disturbed
Deeply regretting
Desiring
Emphasizing
Expecting
Expressing its appreciation
Expressing its satisfaction
Fulfilling
Fully alarmed
Fully aware

Fully believing
Further deploring
Further recalling
Guided by
Having adopted
Having considered
Having considered further
Having devoted attention
Having examined
Having heard
Having received
Having studied
Keeping in mind
Noting with deep concern
Noting with regret
Noting with satisfaction
Noting further
Noting with approval
Observing
Reaffirming
Realizing
Recalling
Recognizing
Referring

Seeking
Taking into account
Taking into consideration
Taking note
Viewing with appreciation
Welcoming

OPERATIVE PHRASES

Accepts
Affirms
Approves
Authorizes
Calls
Calls upon
Condemns
Confirms
Congratulates
Considers
Declares accordingly
Deplores
Designates
Draws the attention
Emphasizes
Encourages

Endorses
Expresses its appreciation
Expresses its hope
Further invites
Further proclaims
Further reminds
Further recommends
Further requests
Further resolves
Has resolved
Notes
Proclaims
Reaffirms
Recommends
Regrets
Reminds
Requests
Solemnly affirms
Strongly condemns
Supports
Takes note of
Transmits
Trusts
Urges

- A **friendly amendment** is a change to the draft resolution that all sponsors agree with. After the amendment is signed by all of the draft resolution's sponsors and approved by the director or president, it will be automatically incorporated into the resolution.
- An **unfriendly amendment** is a change that some or all of the draft resolution's sponsors do not support and must be voted upon by the committee. The author(s) of the amendment will need to obtain a required number of signatories in order to introduce it (usually 20 percent of the committee). Prior to voting on the draft resolution, the committee votes on all unfriendly amendments.

To sum up, the various stages of writing and signing committee documents follow a four-step pattern:

- Working in small caucus groups with common interests to produce **draft language** that will be agreeable for inclusion in a working paper;
- Shopping the **working paper** in the committee to gain the sponsors and signatories necessary for it to be formally introduced as a draft resolution by the chairperson of the committee;
- **Amending** the **draft resolution** by sponsors or other members of the committee; and
- Voting on draft resolutions. Any draft resolution that passes by a vote becomes a **resolution**. Once a resolution is passed, it is the official policy of that body.

Writing a draft resolution is much easier than it might initially seem. The language is technical, but the concepts are quite simple. It is worth practicing the format and style of resolution writing before you attend a conference. This can be done on your own, using **Box 4.3 U.N. Resolution** and **Box 4.4 Model U.N. Resolution**, as a reference. Please note, however, most conferences

4.3 U.N. RESOLUTION

Economic and Social Council
Resolution 1996/33 50th plenary meeting
25 July 1996

1996/33 Strengthening of the coordination of emergency humanitarian assistance of the United Nations

The Economic and Social Council,

Reaffirming the guiding principles and coordinating mechanisms for providing emergency humanitarian assistance as outlined in the annex to General Assembly resolution 46/182 of 19 December 1991,

Recalling other relevant Assembly resolutions, in particular its resolutions 47/168 of 22 December 1992, 48/57 of 14 December 1993, 49/139 A of 20 December 1994 and 50/57 of 12 December 1995, and Economic and Social Council resolution 1995/56 of 28 July 1995,

Taking note of the report of the Secretary-General,

1. *Requests* the Secretary-General, in close cooperation with relevant organizations of the United Nations system, to submit to the Council, at its substantive session of 1997, a comprehensive analytical report, including options, proposals and recommendations for a review and strengthening of all aspects of the capacity of the United Nations system for humanitarian assistance;

2. *Calls upon* the InterAgency Standing Committee to adopt clear work plans and timetables for the working groups established in the follow-up to Council resolution 1995/56 in order that the Secretary-General may have sufficient time to consider their recommendations;

3. *Urges* all relevant organizations of the United Nations system to actively participate in the follow-up process established in Council resolution 1995/56;

4. *Also urges* the governing bodies of the relevant agencies to complete their consideration of the follow-up to Council resolution 1995/56 in good time, no later than their first regular sessions of 1997, in order that the Secretary-General may have sufficient time to consider their recommendations;

5. *Calls upon* the Department of Humanitarian Affairs of the United Nations Secretariat to provide a conference room paper on the status of the discussions of the working groups of the InterAgency Standing Committee prior to each meeting of the governing bodies of the agencies, funds and programmes at which the follow-up to Council resolution 1995/56 is to be discussed so that governing body discussions can build on each other and on the work of the InterAgency Standing Committee;

6. *Encourages* Governments to ensure coherence in the direction given to the governing bodies of relevant agencies, organizations, funds and programmes of the United Nations system with the aim of improving the coordination and effectiveness of humanitarian assistance by the United Nations system;

7. *Calls upon* the Department of Humanitarian Affairs, in this context, to continue to convene regular, informal and open ended information meetings with Member States, observer States and relevant intergovernmental and other organizations on the review of the above mentioned issues so as to ensure that they are coherently addressed and appropriately reflected in the report of the Secretary-General.

4.4 MODEL U.N. RESOLUTION

General Assembly Third Committee
[*committee name*]
Sponsors: United States, Austria, Italy
Signatories: Greece, Tajikistan, Japan, Canada, Mali, the Netherlands, and Gabon
GA/3rd/l.1 [*draft resolution number*]

Strengthening U.N. coordination of humanitarian assistance in complex emergencies
[*topic title*]

The General Assembly,

Reminding [*underline or italicize first word or phrase*] all nations of the celebration of the 50th Anniversary of the Universal Declaration of Human Rights, which recognizes the inherent dignity, equality, and inalienable rights of all global citizens, [*use comma in preambulatory clauses*]

Reaffirming its resolution 33/1996 of 25 July 1996, which encourages Governments to work with established U.N. bodies aimed at improving the coordination and effectiveness of humanitarian assistance,

Noting with satisfaction the past efforts of various relevant U.N. bodies and nongovernmental organizations,

Stressing the fact that the United Nations is in a financial crisis and in dire need of reform, especially in the humanitarian realm,

1. *Encourages* all relevant agencies of the United Nations to collaborate more closely with countries at the grassroots level to enhance the carrying out of relief efforts; [**use semicolon in operative clauses**]

2. *Urges* Member States to comply with the goals of the U.N. Department of Humanitarian Affairs to streamline efforts of humanitarian aid;

3. *Requests* that all nations develop rapid deployment forces to better enhance the coordination of relief efforts of humanitarian assistance in complex emergencies;

4. *Calls* for the development of a United Nations Trust Fund that encourages voluntary donations from the private transnational sector to aid in funding the implementation of rapid deployment forces;

5. *Stresses* the continuing need for impartial and objective information on the political, economic and social situations and events of all countries;

6. *Calls upon* States to respond quickly and generously to consolidated appeals for humanitarian assistance; and

7. *Requests* the expansion of preventive actions and assurance of post-conflict assistance through reconstruction and development. [*end resolution with a period*]

prohibit delegates from bringing prepared working papers or draft resolutions to a conference out of a sense that it violates the multilateral spirit of the U.N. In keeping with that spirit, working papers should be written during the course of a conference, as it is then that they become draft resolutions.

RULES OF PROCEDURE

With representatives from up to 191 countries present and 2-3 topics to discuss, it is obvious that there is a need for some rules to regulate who speaks, on what, and when. The dais of your committee, led by a chairperson (or director at some conferences), will facilitate the committee, using a set of rules. The rules, known as parliamentary procedures, govern speech in a parliamentary body or assembly, and are an important part of diplomatic gatherings. (See **4.5 Shortsheet: Sample Model U.N. Procedural Rules**.) In general, these rules help to assure that the committee maintains order, but in practice, they can be used creatively to get your point across. In general, procedures divide conferences into "formal" and "informal" sessions, the specifics of which are outlined below.

FORMAL DEBATE

The formal sessions of a Model U.N. conference are important opportunities to demonstrate your confidence as a model delegate. Parliamentary procedures specified by the host organization will govern these portions of the Model U.N. conference, thus it is necessary to quickly appreciate how these specific procedures may differ from conferences you have attended before. Most conferences provide their procedures well in advance, and some even offer preparatory sessions so that you can get familiar with their unique procedures. Take advantage of these opportunities, and you will not only master the specifics for that conference, but broaden your appreciation of procedures in general.

During formal sessions, you should exhibit proper decorum at all times, including attention to the dress standards of the conference. Speaking will be limited to those who volunteer to be on a "speakers' list," a list of delegations that have submitted a specific request to speak, initially when called upon by the chair, or thereafter by note. Countries are added to the speakers' list in the order in which their requests are received, so waiting a moment to request your space on the speakers' list may mean waiting even longer to get a chance to speak. Once you are acknowledged to speak, your time will usually be further limited to a specific amount per speaker, perhaps anywhere from one to three minutes. During such speeches, remain focused on the speakers unless an urgent matter draws you out of the room. Show proper respect for other delegates. If you wish to speak, submit your name in writing to be added to the speakers' list, or use formal motions to be recognized (points of order, right of reply). Keep to the point. If you wish to respond to statements with which you disagree, use diplomatic language and save your harshest criticisms for informal rather than formal debates. This basic diplomatic courtesy will go a long way in winning the trust of others, and establishing your reputation as an experienced delegate.

Formal debate is also an opportunity to read the overall tenor of the conference. If the proceedings during formal debate tend toward the informal, if delegates quickly loosen up to get down to business, or if the chair seems willing to tolerate a more relaxed atmosphere, this should also be a cue to you to adopt the spirit of this committee. This is not to suggest that you should lower the high standards you set for yourself as a model diplomat, but an acknowledgement of one of diplomacy's oldest axioms: when in Rome, do as Romans do. Careful attention to the tenor of a conference will help you to alter your plans and strategies in a way that will ultimately allow you to continue to achieve the high standards of success you hold for yourself, and your assigned country.

INFORMAL DEBATE: CAUCUSING

While formal debate is an important tool for getting things started, most Model U.N. conferences

4.5 SHORTSHEET: SAMPLE MODEL U.N. PROCEDURAL RULES

MOTION	DESCRIPTION	VOTE REQUIRED TO PASS
Motion to set speakers' time	This procedural motion sets or changes the speakers' time. Two (2) delegates must speak for the amount of time proposed in the motion and two (2) delegates must speak against.	Simple majority
Motion to open and close the speakers' list	At some Model U.N. conferences, once the speakers' list is closed, it is closed for the remainder of the session or topic. However, at most Model U.N. conferences the speakers list can be opened and closed multiple times. Once the speakers list is exhausted, it means no one else wishes to speak, debate is over, and the committee moves into voting procedure. This motion requires an immediate vote.	Simple majority
Motion to suspend meeting	This motion is made to allow for a regular caucus or a moderated caucus, but its use also depends on the rules of the conference you attend. When moving to suspend the meeting, the delegate should specify the purpose and length of time of the suspension. This motion requires an immediate vote.	Simple majority
Motion to adjourn meeting	This motion ends the committee session until the next session, which may be held the following year. The motion is most commonly made to end a committee session for the purpose of lunch or dinner. It requires an immediate vote.	Simple majority
Motion to adjourn debate	This motion must not be confused with the motion to adjourn the meeting. A motion to adjourn debate is a tactic to put on hold and table all the work that the committee has completed on the topic under discussion. At some Model U.N. conferences you can table the topic by adjourning debate, move on to another topic, and return to the first topic at a later time. However, at most Model U.N. conferences, once you adjourn debate on a topic, the topic is considered tabled and cannot be discussed further. Two (2) delegates must speak for the adjournment of debate and two (2) delegates must speak against it.	Two-thirds majority
Motion to close debate	This motion is made to allow the committee to move into voting procedure. Once a delegate feels that the country's position has made clear, that there are enough draft resolutions on the floor, and that everyone is ready, she or he can move for the closure of debate. Two delegates must speak against the closure of debate, but none need speak for it.	Two-thirds majority
Point of order	During the discussion of any matter, a representative may rise to a point of order, and the chairperson in accordance with the rules of procedure immediately decides the point of order. A delegate may appeal the ruling of the chairperson, as noted below. The appeal is put to a vote, and the chairperson's ruling stands unless overruled by a two-thirds majority of the members present and voting. A delegate rising to a point of order may not speak on the substance of the matter under discussion.	
Point of Inquiry (also known as Point of Parliamentary Procedure)	When the floor is open, a delegate may move for a point of inquiry, in order to ask the chairperson a question regarding the rules of procedure.	
Point of Personal Privilege	A delegate may raise a point of personal privilege in order to inform the chairperson of a physical discomfort s/he is experiencing, such as the inability to hear another delegate's speech.	
Point of Information	After a delegate has given a speech in formal debate, s/he may choose to yield his or her time to points of information, questions other delegates may raise concerning the speech.	
Appeal to the chair's decision	This motion is made when a delegate feels that the chairperson has made an incorrect decision. The delegate formally challenges the chairperson by moving to appeal the chairperson's decision. This motion may be made orally or in writing. The opposing delegate speaks and the chairperson defends him or herself before the vote.	Two-thirds majority

also move into more informal procedures, such as a "moderated caucus," or "unmoderated caucus" in order to get down to business. Much of the same etiquette needs to be followed as when in formal debate, but the overall atmosphere is more relaxed.

MODERATED CAUCUS

In a moderated caucus, a mixture of formal and informal debate, delegates are called on in turn by the committee chair. More delegates have an opportunity to speak, and debate moves along more quickly. These caucuses are usually set for a short period of time, such as 5-10 minutes, in order to allow discussion of a particular aspect of a topic. You may wish to call for a moderated caucus simply because you are far down on the speakers' list and wish to speak, or because you feel a focused discussion on a particular issue will benefit the committee. Regardless, be sure to specify your reasons for calling for a moderated caucus, and the length of time you feel will be necessary. This will help you to win the votes necessary to move out of formal debate.

UNMODERATED CAUCUS

In an *informal* or *unmoderated* caucus, the same general rules apply with regard to shifting the mode of debate. Your motion should offer a reason and propose a time limit. If approved by the body, however, you will then have the opportunity to speak personally with any delegate in the room, provided you can get their attention or join the group in which they are meeting. Unmoderated caucuses are fast-paced, and can be fun and challenging opportunities to proceed more casually, all of which should be seized to build trust and respect among your colleagues. Note that often, the contacts and networks you establish during an unmoderated caucus may last into lunches, dinners, or social events at the conference, much as informal negotiations in the halls and corridors of the United Nations form lasting social and political connections that go far beyond the institutions walls.

During informal proceedings, present your position soundly and concisely and avoid attempts to monopolize discussion among other delegates. A willingness to account for the interests and needs of others, and a desire for flexibility and compromise without jeopardizing your own position will help to establish you as a diplomat whose commitment to multilateralism places an overall interest in unity and consensus. That said, this should not prevent you from asserting your leadership position if it is consistent with your role.

A good leader will know how to cooperate with others and credit others when its due.

AWARDS

If you role-play your part well at the conference, you may find yourself recognized by the dais of your committee at closing ceremonies. Conference organizers often give awards to individual delegations in each committee, as well as schools for the overall representation of a delegation in all committees. Many delegates feel that awards go to those who pass the most resolutions, or who are on the speakers' list most often, but this is often not the case. Awards usually go to those who succeed in accomplishing the tasks of the committee, rather than the individual responsible for getting the largest number of resolutions passed. It is much more important that delegates work toward a principled simulation of the diplomatic interactions that occur at the U.N., even if it means no resolutions are passed at all! Rather than focusing on your accomplishments at a conference, think about the process to those accomplishments, and whether they reflect the principle of multilateralism and the fundamentals that follow from it. Did you represent your assigned country realistically? If so, did you do so in a diplomatic manner? Were you willing to negotiate through topics for the benefit of the committee, or did you hold out simply to see your country as a sponsor?

What matters most, however, is that you learn the principles and skills necessary to play your part while learning the U.N. system. For many MUNers this is the most rewarding part of their Model U.N. experience; it is why they keep coming back to Model U.N., and why they continue to support the U.N. as a source of hope in a world they have come to understand better from their time as a Model U.N. delegate.

A FINAL NOTE

All of this may seem like quite a lot to remember, let alone master in preparing for a Model U.N. conference, and indeed, it is. While there are rare delegates who take to the experience of their first conference with great ease, for most participants it is not really until the end of their first conference that the rationale behind their preparations becomes fully apparent. Once a conference ends it is not uncommon to hear a fist-time delegate exclaim: "Now I know what to do at my next conference!" Comparatively, experienced delegates often tend to enjoy Model U.N. more after each conference attended. Advanced delegates look forward to participating in crisis committees, the most challenging simulations Model U.N. offers.

Finally, as a Model U.N. delegate, you will join legions of others around the world as an active participant in a global discussion of the U.N. agenda. You will experience what its like to step into the shoes of an ambassador to the United Nations, often playing the role of a negotiator, mediator, consensus-builder, or leader. If you are able to utilize the skills you have learned during preparation, as well as grasp the role the U.N. plays in the world today, then you are well on your way to mastering Model U.N.

ABOVE. *Delegates of the Legal Committee caucus outside their committee room at Old Dominion University's 2002 Model United Nations High School Conference. (Photo: UNA-USA)*

LEFT. *A bloc debates its response to a resolution on the floor. (Photo: UNA-USA)*

Model U.N. is both more enjoyable and rewarding if students practice debate before going to a conference. Learning proper procedure, and effective caucusing and speaking, takes experience. If you can get past the initial challenges of how to debate in Model U.N., focusing on the issue at hand becomes much easier—and more fun. Being able to work quickly, work well with others, and express yourself, are important elements of what it takes to succeed at Model U.N. This scenario, a simulation of the Security Council, can be practiced by a group of students either in a class or a club meeting. One student (or teacher) should serve as the president of the Council, introducing the scenario placed before them under the "Recent Events" heading. Students may represent member countries by themselves or in pairs. Students can use background information and bloc positions as bases for topic research, but may also perform additional research. A "Press Release" is included as an additional resource for this simulation session. This is to be distributed as a new challenge for delegates to face during their debate. It may be inserted into the simulation at the instructor or head delegate's discretion.

BACKGROUND INFORMATION

India and Pakistan are neighboring countries located on the southern tip of Central Asia. The history of the conflict between the two states dates back more than fifty years to 1947, when the countries gained independence from British colonial rule. Under the terms of the settlement, the area previously known as "British India" was divided into three segments: a Hindu majority area, which retained the name "India;" and two separate, Muslim-dominated areas, one of which took on the name of "Pakistan."

Prior to 1947, the former British India consisted of hundreds of autonomous principalities known as states. After the British rule ended, each state was required to join one of the two newly-formed countries, depending on the wishes of its people. However, despite the wishes of its citizens, Kashmir's ruler, a Hindu, decided to join a confederation with India,

even though the majority of citizens of Kashmir were Muslim. A dispute over Kashmir led to two of the three wars between Pakistan and India. In 1949, fighting resulted in the division of Kashmir into two separate parts: "Indian Kashmir" in India, and "Azad Kashmir" in Pakistan.

Despite two U.N.-sponsored cease-fires, hostilities between the two countries rose significantly in 1974, when India tested its first nuclear device, thereby ushering in a nuclear arms race in South Asia.

RECENT EVENTS

*The following facts may or **may not be factual** but are to be considered factual for the purposes of the Security Council simulation.*

I. On May 11, 1998, India conducted three rounds of nuclear tests in an underground faculty near its border with Pakistan. The tests were immediately condemned by the international community. Two days later, despite warnings of censure, India held two more rounds of nuclear tests. The United States promptly placed India under sanctions, freezing more than U.S. $20 million of previously committed financial assistance. Japan and the European Union followed suit with their round of sanctions.

II. In response to India's actions, Pakistan conducted five nuclear tests on May 28, 1998, and a sixth on May 30, 1998. Pakistan's actions were likewise met with condemnation and sanctions from the international community. The economic sanctions have seriously impacted both countries, as they are heavily dependent on international aid for assistance.

III. On December 13, 2001, following a period of relative calm, five assailants from a Kashmir-based, separatist attacked the Indian Parliament in New Delhi, killing nine people in addition to themselves. India and Pakistan soon sent thousands of troops to the Line of Control, the border between India-controlled and Pakistan-controlled Kashmir. Both countries proclaimed themselves ready for war, and each vowed to use nuclear weapons if the

other did. Weeks of tension eventually subsided, following Pakistani promises to crack down on religious extremists.

IV. On May 14, 2002, suspected Islamic militants opened fire on an army camp in Indian Kashmir, killing at least 30 people and wounding 40. Over the next several days, attacks continued across Kashmir, while Indian and Pakistani troops exchanged gunfire across the Line of Control. At the end of the month, Pakistan conducted two missile tests in two days, demonstrating its capability to strike India. The threat of nuclear conflict remained very real during the standoff, until Pakistani vows to address Kashmiri militants led both sides to back off of a full war footing. Nonetheless, the situation in South Asia remains very volatile.

V. The U.N. Security Council has been called upon to take immediate action in this matter and to further push India and Pakistan from the brink of total war.

COUNTRY AND BLOC POSITIONS

China
The People's Republic of China is a neighbor of both India and Pakistan. It has direct interest in the present situation between the two countries. China and India have not traditionally enjoyed good diplomatic relations. In contrast, China and Pakistan have been close allies in the past. China continues to hold considerable sway with Pakistan, and wishes to avoid any conflict that would destabilize its borders.

Bulgaria, Cameroon, Colombia, Guinea, Mauritius, Mexico
These nations have little to do with India and Pakistan. They wish to a see a quick and decisive end to hostilities. Their decisions could be affected by the positions of other influential nations on the Council.

France, Ireland, Norway, the United Kingdom
Western Europe is invested in avoiding a nuclear exchange between India and Pakistan. The United Kingdom in particular retains close historical ties to the region.

Russian Federation

Russia has traditionally been a strong ally to India in the past. Russian influence in Asia is challenged by China, which borders the conflicting states, and the United States, which has become a visible presence in the region over the past year. Like every other nation, however, it wishes to avoid an all-out war that could destabilize the region and become nuclear.

Singapore

A prosperous Asian nation, Singapore is particularly interested in averting a conflict in its hemisphere.

Syrian Arab Republic

Syria has been increasing its ties with Pakistan, to the point that it backs Pakistan on the Kashmir issue. Syria has expressed its desire to see a "self-determined" Kashmir. Syria, a Muslim nation, is sympathetic with Kashmir's largely Muslim population, but has little else invested in the region.

United States

The United States has particular interest in preventing an all-out war between India and Pakistan. Pakistani troops are currently aiding the U.S. campaign against al-Qaeda, by patrolling their border with Afghanistan in search of fleeing militants. Tensions with India, however, have caused many of those troops to be moved to the Line of Control. A war would leave Pakistan's Afghani border unprotected, and the nation itself in a very unstable state. Additionally, the United States would be left with the responsibility for the clean-up in the event of a nuclear exchange.

SOURCE: Adapted from UNA-USA's *Global Classrooms: Peacekeeping Unit.*

Students participating in an in-class simulation. (Photo: UNA-USA)

Department of Public Information—News Coverage Service

RENEWED CONFRONTATION BETWEEN INDIAN AND PAKISTANI FORCES AT LINE OF CONTROL SPARKED BY NEW TERROR ATTACK

Pakistan yesterday shot down two Indian military jets that were conducting air strikes over the Pakistan controlled area of Azad Kashmir, high in the Himalayan mountains. The Indian air strikes were launched in response to a terror attack launched by suspected Kashmiri militants that killed 16 and injured seven in New Delhi, the Indian capital. The heightened conflict could not have come at a worse time, with tensions between the nuclear states only now beginning to ease after a standoff in the Spring.

Yesterday afternoon, four armed militants and two suicide bombers launched a killing spree near a prominent office building in downtown New Delhi. The gunmen opened fire on pedestrians, as the bombers detonated explosives on street corners, in an echo of the December 13, 2001 attack on Parliament. Indian Prime Minister Atal Behari Vajpayee was quoted as pinning the attacks on "Pakistani terrorists," which provoked launching of the air strikes. Both he and Pakistan President Pervez Musharraf denounced the other side's "unprovoked aggression" as cause for "battle."

Hundreds of thousands of troops are already gathered along the Line of Control in Kashmir, and they continue to exchange fire at this hour. Both sides have also threatened to launch conventional missile strikes, in what marks their third standoff in recent months.

In view of these developments, the Security Council has scheduled another emergency session to once again attempt to resolve the conflict.

11

HOW NATIONS INTERACT:
REGIONAL PERSPECTIVES

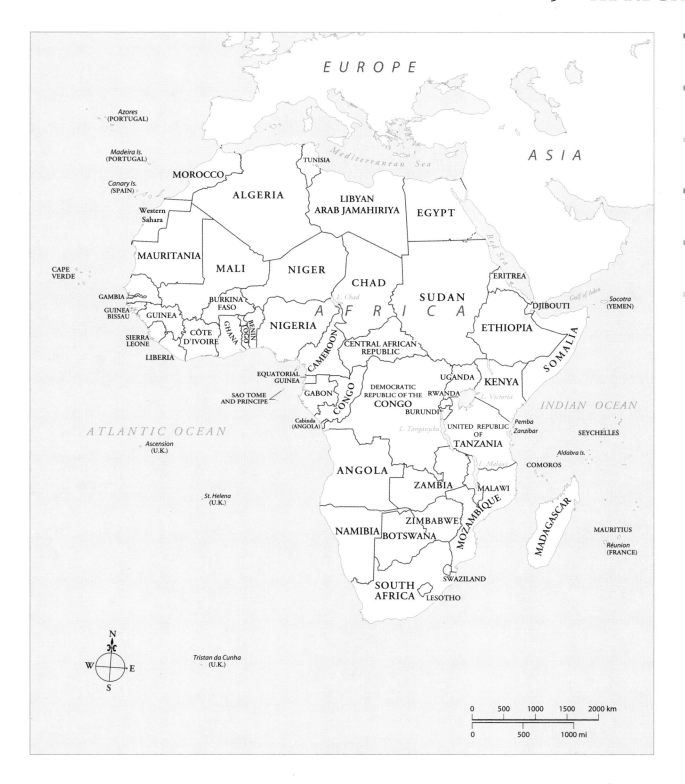

Africa, the cradle of human civilization, ranks, after Asia, as the second largest continent in the world. It consists of fifty-three sovereign states, totaling over one quarter of the member states of the United Nations. To understand Africa, one must appreciate its immense size and enormous diversity. With an area of 11.7 million square miles, it is bigger than Europe, China, the United States, India, Argentina, and New Zealand combined.[1] With a population of over 900 million, speaking over 1,000 languages, its peoples belong to different ethnic groups, each with its own language, culture, and way of life.

African countries vary in size, population, and resource endowment. For instance, Nigeria has 356,669 square miles, a population of over 123 million, 250 different ethno-linguistic groups, and considerable natural resources including petroleum, tin, columbite, iron, lead, zinc, and natural gas, while Gambia has only 4,361 square miles, slightly over 1 million people, and its only natural resource is fish. It is thus difficult to generalize about Africa. Nevertheless, amidst this diversity is an underlying African identity which binds the continent and its people through their unique history, values, and institutions.

In order to gain an understanding of current issues in Africa, one must first examine its past. Home to many civilizations, Africa boasts a rich and varied history, from the glories of ancient **Egypt** and the Ethiopian kingdom of Axum, to the medieval empires of **Benin, Ghana, Mali, Morocco,** and Songhay. Tragically, beginning in the fifteenth century, the Portuguese, joined by the Spanish, British, Dutch, French, and Arabs, began the inhuman traffic of slaves, which, from 1440 to 1870, transferred the productive labor of millions of Africans to the Americas. The international slave trade not only disrupted and devastated political and economic development in many parts of Africa, but also provided some of the human capital that fueled European trade and development. It also enriched the Americas.

The trans-Atlantic slave trade was soon supplanted by European colonialism, occasioned by European imperial rivalries; competition for Africa's resources; and expansionist pressures generated by capitalist economies seeking markets for European goods. Colonialism resulted in "massive exploitation of Africa in terms of resource depletion, labor exploitation, unfair taxation, lack of industrialization, the prohibition of inter-African trade, and the introduction of fragile dependent one-crop economies."[2] In addition, arbitrary colonial boundaries resulted in the creation of artificial states, subsuming several different ethno-linguistic groups under one political umbrella, while dividing one group among several states. This colonial legacy has exacerbated the task of nation-building in Africa, giving rise to post-independence territorial claims and counter-claims, sometimes resulting in inter-state and intra-state conflicts.

African resistance to colonial rule was coterminous with colonialism. It intensified after the Second World War and in 1960 alone, sixteen countries gained their independence. In May 1963, the Heads of State and Government of thirty-two independent African countries, excluding **South Africa**, assembled in Addis Ababa, **Ethiopia**, to inaugurate Africa's first continental organization: the Organization of African Unity (OAU), since transformed into the African Union (AU). Today, every single country in the continent is an independent sovereign state. Apartheid and white minority regimes have been eradicated and South Africa has emerged a free multi-ethnic and non-racial democracy. However, problems of economic development, peace and security persist. They will continue to challenge Africans and African leaders for years to come.

CONFLICT

Contests for territory, political power, or a dominating cultural ideology are currently the chief sources of contention in the continent.

TERRITORIAL DISPUTES

Many African countries battle to define or redefine exactly where their boundaries are drawn. **Eritrea** and **Ethiopia** have been in a war fought for territory that has been described as "nothing more than a few hectares of barren mountain and desert."[3] Its border, set almost 100 years earlier, was never clearly marked. Long before the fighting commenced, Eritrea felt hostile and insecure, firmly believing that Ethiopia intended to encroach on its territory. In 1997, a map issued in Ethiopia portrayed large areas of Eritrean land as belonging to the Ethiopian province of Tigray. Eritrea consequently claimed a need to protect its citizens in the region from foreign domination. However, Ethiopian Prime Minister Meles Zenawi responded that the map, commissioned by the Tigrayan province administration, did not truthfully represent Ethiopia's claims.

Nevertheless, he refused to elaborate on what those claims really were.

Despite efforts by the OAU and the United Nations, Eritrean troops continued to occupy Ethiopian soil and the matter remained unsettled. Eritrea agreed to the framework of a peace agreement and cease-fire drafted by the OAU in July of 1999; as of March 2000, Ethiopia had still not responded and fighting was taking place. In May 2000, in accordance with OAU demands, Eritrea withdrew from Ethiopian territory occupied after May 6, 1998, insisting, however, that the withdrawal did not amount to surrender but was in fact a tactical maneuver. On the other hand, Ethiopia did not withdraw entirely from Eritrean territory and continued to raid Eritrean villages. It was not until June 2000, that the two sides were participating in U.S.-led peace talks and fighting had ended.

Under the auspices of the Organization of African Unity, Ethiopia and Eritrea signed a cease-fire agreement in Algiers on June 18, 2000, and a Comprehensive Peace Agreement in December, providing, among other things, for an end to hostilities and the establishment of an independent Boundary Commission. On April 13, 2002, the Boundary Commission announced its decision on boundary delimitation. In accordance with the Algiers peace agreement, the decision is "final and binding." U.N. Secretary-General, Kofi Annan welcomed the decision as an important milestone in the peace process.

In **Western Sahara**, attempts to resolve a dispute over territory continue. On November 14, 1976, **Morocco** and **Mauritania** signed the Madrid Accords, dividing Western Saharan territory into two parts: Two thirds of the land was granted to Morocco and one third (the southern portion) to Mauritania. However, due to pressure from the Saharawi liberation movement (Frente POLISARIO), Mauritania abandoned its claims in 1979. Morocco subsequently assumed control of the forfeited region, resulting in conflicts between Morocco and the Frente POLISARIO. In 1988, the parties reached a Settlement Plan providing for a referendum to decide whether Western Sahara should be part of Morocco or an independent sovereign state. In 1991, the U.N.

Security Council set up the United Nations Mission for the Referendum in Western Sahara (MINURSO) to implement the plan. However, the referendum has yet to be held due to an impasse resulting from differences over the main provisions of the plan. On April 30, 2002, the Security Council extended the mandate of MINURSO until the end of July to consider the Secretary-General's report of February 19, 2002 proposing four options for the peace process (S/2002/178).

Under the first option, the United Nations would try to resume the implementation of the Settlement Plan even without requiring the agreement of Morocco and the Frente POLISARIO. This would require increasing the size of MINURSO. Under the second option, James A. Baker III, Personal Envoy of the Secretary-General, would try to revise the draft Framework Agreement by devolving authority to the inhabitants of Western Sahara, pending a subsequent referendum to determine their final status. In this case, the size of MINURSO could be reduced. As a third option, the parties would be invited, under the auspices of Mr. Baker, to explore their willingness to divide the territory. Their unwillingness or inability to reach a division by November 1, 2002, would require Mr. Baker to present a proposal for the division of the territory to the parties and the Security Council. Should the Council adopt this option, Mr. Baker's division of the territory would be non-negotiable. MINURSO could be maintained at its current level or even reduced. Under the fourth option, the Security Council could terminate MINURSO due to lack of progress, after eleven years and the expenditure of over U.S.$500 million.[4]

FIGHTING FOR CHANGE

Civil wars and rivalry among rebel groups advocating one or another form of change also plague the African continent. Various groups of rebels insistent on change contribute greatly to the rise of such conflicts. In the **Democratic Republic of Congo** (DRC), for example, disgruntled ethnic groups and dissatisfaction with the DRC's political voice in the international system have sparked conflict. On May 17, 1997, Laurent-Desire Kabila, a long-time rebel, named himself President of what was then Zaire (now the DRC). He made promises of democracy and international cooperation that appealed to the U.N. Security Council, which contemplated a DRC free of conflict, ethnic disputes, and rebellions. However, less than a year later, stability within the country dissolved, and on August 2, 1998, civil war broke out as rebel forces, backed by Rwanda and Uganda, took up arms against President Kabila's unlimited power. The war eventually drew in **Angola, Namibia,** and **Zimbabwe** on the side of the DRC. In July 1999, the combatants (Democratic Republic of Congo, Angola, Namibia, Zimbabwe, **Rwanda, Uganda,** and rebel groups) signed the Lusaka Ceasefire Agreement. To monitor the cease-fire, the U.N. Security Council deployed liaison personnel in August 1999, creating the U.N. Organization Mission in the Democratic Republic of Congo (known by its French acronym—MONUC) in November. In January 2001, President Laurent-Desire Kabila was assassinated by one of his bodyguards and was succeeded by his son, Joseph Kabila.

Despite repeated violations of the Lusaka Agreement, the Security Council, in November 2001, called for the withdrawal of all foreign troops and the disarmament, demobilization, and repatriation of armed combatants. The conflict had been fueled by the illegal exploitation of mineral resources in the DRC, including coltan, gold, diamonds, and cobalt. Inter-Congolese dialogue, designed to bring about a "new political dispensation," became bogged down despite the efforts of Sir Ketumile Masire, former president of **Botswana.** In an effort to rekindle the peace process and end the war in the DRC, the Security Council dispatched a delegation, led by the French ambassador to the Security Council, Jean-David Levitte, to visit the Great Lakes region from April 27 to May 7, 2002. The mission traveled to **South Africa,** the DRC, Angola, Uganda, **Tanzania, Burundi,** and Rwanda to urge all parties to the conflict to fulfill their obligations under the Lusaka Agreement, to expedite the withdrawal of foreign troops, and to facilitate the process of disarmament and demobilization.

Sierra Leone had been plagued by a civil war between the government and a rebel group, the Revolutionary United Front (RUF), since 1990. The army, which had been trying to defend the government against the RUF, eventually took over the government itself. In February 1995, the U.N. Secretary-General appointed a Special Envoy, Berhanu Dinka, who, in collaboration with the OAU and the Economic Community of West African States (ECOWAS), worked to negotiate a settlement of the conflict and return the country to civilian rule. Presidential elections were held in February 1996, and the army granted power to the winner, Alhaji Ahmad Tejan Kabbah. The RUF, having refused to participate in the elections, did not recognize the legitimacy of the election results.

President Kabbah committed his government to bringing peace to the country. Indeed, with the cooperation of Special Envoy Dinka, the parties signed a peace agreement in Abidjan in November 1996. The following year, Major Johnny Paul Koroma, commanding a group of dissatisfied army personnel and in alliance with the RUF, overthrew President Kabbah, forcing him into exile in neighboring Guinea. The Economic Community of West African States Cease-Fire Monitoring Group (ECOMOG) worked to suppress the rebellion and encourage negotiations. On March 10, 1998, President Kabbah returned to office and on June 5 the Security Council passed Resolution 1171, which imposed sanctions on members of the military junta. Koroma was forced into exile and later renounced his affiliation with the RUF.

On July 9, 1998, the U.N. established the United Nations Observer Mission in Sierra Leone (UNOMSIL), charged with monitoring the military, security, and human rights situation in the country. Its mandate was extended until June 13, 1999, by Security Council Resolution 1231. On July 7, 1999, after nine years of civil war, the contending factions signed the Lomé Peace Agreement. They pledged to end the conflict and institute a unified government. The agreement placed the RUF and the elected government on the same level, and Ahmed Foday Sankoh, the new leader of the RUF, was given the position of vice president, with immunity from all war crimes. When the UNOMSIL mandate expired in October 1999, the U.N. established a new peacekeeping mission, the United Nations Mission in Sierra Leone (UNAMSIL), to assist in implementing the Lomé Peace Agreement. Peacekeeping efforts received a devastating blow in May 2000, when the rebels took some 500 U.N. peacekeepers hostage, killing 11 of them, and appropriating a large cache of U.N. arms and ammunition. Shortly thereafter, Sankoh was captured. U.N. resolution 1299 of May 17, 2000, authorized the deployment of up to 13,000 troops, including observers, to Sierra Leone. After years of immense suffering, presidential and parliamentary elections took place on May 14, 2002 with the assistance of UNAMSIL, providing both security and logistical support. With 70 percent of the votes, Ahmed Tejan Kabbah was reelected president. His Sierra Leone People's Party won 83 out of the 112 contested parliamentary seats.[5]

ETHNIC STRIFE

Sometimes ethnic tensions act as a primary cause of war. However, ethnic identity is often hard to define. It may not be as simple as language, culture, or skin color, for many Africans who identify with one another speak multiple languages and have as many differing physical features. Most striking is the case of the Hutu and Tutsi tribes, who speak the same language, live in the same region, and have many of the same cultural traditions. Yet in **Rwanda** in 1994, Hutu elements of the country's armed forces and irregular Hutu militias killed hundreds of thousands of minority Tutsis and moderate Hutus, and raped and maimed countless others in a period of three months. The genocidal rampage ended only when the Tutsi-led Rwandan Patriotic Front defeated the forces of the Hutu government. Two million of the latter's supporters fled to neighboring countries, such as Zaire (now the **DRC**) and **Tanzania**; one million were internally displaced. Many have since returned home. Not unexpectedly, tensions continue among Tutsi and Hutu civilians.[6]

COMPETITION AMONG RIVAL POLITICAL FACTIONS

A struggle for independence is often followed by a battle for power among rival nationalist groups. Here lies another source of civil war, as **Angola's** post independence history makes only too clear. Angola's struggle for self-rule ended in November 1975, when it declared its independence from Portugal. Subsequent elections for a legislative assembly sparked a civil war among competing groups, chief among them, the Marxist-Leninist Popular Movement of Angola (MPLA) and the National Union for the Total Independence of Angola (UNITA). By 1976, the MPLA had gained control of the government; in 1979, José Eduardo dos Santos became president of the Popular Republic of Angola, but the war with UNITA continued. In 1991, after leading a transition to democracy, the MPLA government signed a cease-fire agreement with UNITA, the Biscesse Peace Accords. In free elections held under the agreement in 1992, dos Santos of the MPLA defeated UNITA leader Jonas Savimbi. UNITA, calling the elections rigged, resumed the fighting and managed to gain control of two thirds of Angola before reaching a stalemate with MPLA forces.

In November 1994, UNITA and the government signed the Lusaka Protocol, in which both sides agreed to lay down weapons and withdraw troops. Under this agreement, UNITA was to demobilize thousands of troops and relinquish all territories it had gained.

However, it soon became clear that UNITA had no intention of fully complying with the Lusaka Protocol. In August 1997, the United Nations imposed sanctions on UNITA. As the Angolan National Assembly put it, "Savimbi has made peace impossible, . . . criminally betraying the Angolan democratic regime."[7] Losing hope, the U.N. terminated its Observer Mission in Angola (MONUA) on February 26, 1999, and ended its peacekeeping role, although humanitarian assistance continued.

UNITA continued to terrorize tens of thousands of civilians, forcing them to leave their homes, despite the U.N.'s repeated urgings to abide by the terms of the Lusaka agreement. On October 15, 1999, the U.N. Security Council adopted Resolution 1268 setting up an office in Angola with the personnel necessary to explore measures for restoring peace, assisting the Angolan people in capacity-building (education, infrastructure) and with humanitarian aid, human rights promotion, and the coordination of other activities. U.N. Security Council Resolution 1295 (April 18, 2000) established a mechanism for monitoring and enforcing the sanctions against the rebels and for prohibiting the sale of diamonds from UNITA. The resolution also invited the Southern African Development Community (SADC) to take action to stop the diversion of fuel to UNITA.

Following the death of Jonas Savimbi, Angolan government officials and UNITA signed a Memorandum of Understanding on April 4, 2002, providing for a general cease-fire, thus marking a turning point in nearly three decades of civil war. In response to this "historic event," the United Council on May 17, 2002, temporarily suspended the travel restrictions it had imposed on UNITA. In keeping with the Memorandum, the United Nations is expected to "provide military observers, technical and material support, as well as technical expertise to the quartering, demilitarization and reintegration of UNITA military forces."

RELIGIOUS DIFFERENCES

Islamic movements in some African nations have sought to establish Islam as the state religion and remove all traces of Western liberalism. While the movements are not necessarily antidemocratic, some Western nations are concerned about the lack of democratic tradition in the Muslim world and about its history of authoritarian governments. **Algeria**, **Egypt**, **Nigeria**, and **Sudan** are among the countries in which Islamic fundamentalism has contributed to political and civil strife. Since the early 1980s, Sudanese rebel groups from the mostly Christian and animist South have been fighting successive governments in the Muslim-held north. In 2000, Sudan's government was run by the National Islamic Front (NIF), which

came to power by military coup and declared Sudan an Islamic state. Although the country has a history of multiparty politics, the NIF banned political parties and severely curtailed civil and political rights. The rebel groups, particularly the Sudan People's Liberation Army (SPLA), demanded greater autonomy for the South, the repeal of strict Islamic laws, and the establishment of a secular government. The Sudanese government had also restricted the distribution of food and medicine to peoples of the south already suffering by years of civil war and drought. A 1997 peace agreement negotiated with five southern leaders called for a referendum on the self-determination of the south. However, marginalized groups, such as the Nuba and Dinka peoples and rebels of the SPLA, were generally ignored.

The situation has been the reverse in Egypt where Islamic forces have rallied against a government that denied fundamentalists a role in the political process. President Hosni Mubarak has liberalized Egyptian politics to a modest degree and introduced moderate external policies. The government's approach to fundamentalism has been to reaffirm its own support for Islamic law while cracking down on Islamic extremists.

After **Algeria** gained its independence in 1962, the governing National Liberation Front (FLN) came under attack for its failure to institute an Islamic government and its tolerance of political pluralism. Faced with popular unrest, the FLN allowed multiparty elections in December 1991 in which the FIS (Islamic Salvation Front) was expected to win a parliamentary majority. The FLN immediately nullified the results; run-off elections, promised in 1992, were canceled and the FIS was outlawed. During most of the 1990s, the Algerian government was locked in an escalating struggle with the FIS, which had become a largely guerrilla movement that continued to launch attacks against security forces. The government, however, was also accused of contributing to the violence, by killing civilians in order to wipe out the rebels. The total number of Algerians killed between 1992 and the beginning of 1998 is estimated at 100,000[8]. A new president, Abdelaziz Bouteflika, was elected in April 1999, after his six rivals withdrew on the eve of the election alleging that the army, which controls politics in Algeria, was planning to rig the poll in favor of Bouteflika. Although the FIS officially disbanded in 2000, fighting continues in some areas of the country.

Religious differences do not always lead to political strife, however. For example, in **Senegal** and **Mali,** religious and secular leaders have maintained a mutually accommodating relationship in politics and society. The majority of Senegalese Muslims belong to the nonmilitant Sufi branch of Islam. Islam plays a role in all aspects of life—business, schools, government, and industry—as the heart of social organization. Religious leaders serve as a link between the state and the various elements of society. These leaders have formed alliances with wealthy Islamic countries to obtain support for social development programs.[9] **Cameroon** is peacefully divided between Islam and Christianity. Although Islam reached northern Cameroon in the first half of the twentieth century, most of the population adopted the religion only in the 1950s and 1960s, at about the same time as missionaries converted the south to Christianity. So far, this ideological difference has not caused political problems.

POLITICAL SYSTEMS

In a continent so divided by conflict, geography and ideology, how do nations manage to interact? Politics in Africa function much the way they do in other regions of the world. Leaders form coalitions and negotiate assistance and material aid from their neighbors; in return they go to the aid of their neighbors in times of need. For example, many East African states joined together to impose sanctions on **Burundi** after the military coup of 1996 in order to demonstrate their opposition to non-democratic changes in leadership. Political systems are in some cases based on the economic and social needs of the society and in others are made to serve the interests of only a few greedy warlords. After independence, some states became Marxist-Leninist or followed a socialist model. Until the 1990s, authoritarian systems abounded as some leaders sought to consolidate

and monopolize political power. Single-party rule kept some newly independent governments in control of state resources and helped to avoid the interethnic and interparty conflicts that often result from multiparty, competitive elections.

In other states, the military takes over the government from civilian regimes, by claiming that it will remain in power only long enough to organize multiparty elections. The military agrees it will then renounce power in favor of the duly elected president. This was the case in **Ghana** and **Nigeria** in 1979. Sometimes, however, the military simply formed its own political party and held elections in which its party's victory was assured. In some instances, military governments remained in power for many years.

In the late 1980s and 1990s, poor economic performance and increasing authoritarianism resulted in pressure for political liberalization and accountability from foreign donors and civil society. The Organization of African Unity asked twenty-eight authoritarian regimes in Africa to adopt more open and democratic practices, and eight countries held multiparty elections. By 1997, about three quarters of Africa was under one form or another of democratic rule mainly because the international community conditioned financial assistance on the expansion of human rights and democracy. Nevertheless, it is estimated that since the former colonies achieved independence, at least eighty violent changes of government have taken place in Africa.[10] Elections are often clouded with irregularities, and results are manipulated or simply ignored. Rulers in power often try to eliminate their competitors before elections can even be held. In the case of **Congo** (Brazzaville), President Pascal Lissouba attempted in 1997 to disarm the militia of the former president, Denis Sassou-Nguesso, in order to eliminate him as a rival in the upcoming elections. The militia fought back, and Sassou-Nguesso reinstated his dictatorship. In **Zambia,** President Patrick Chiluba amended the constitution prior to elections to require that only indigenous Zambians (both of whose parents are native Zambian) could run for office. The parents of his rival, Kenneth Kaunda, were allegedly Malawian, making Kaunda ineligible. In **Gambia,** President

Yaya Jammeh manipulated the constitution, gave insufficient time for preparation of the elections, used state resources for the promotion of his party, and monopolized press coverage.[11]

Sometimes, democratic elections do not necessarily equate to multiparty elections. Many countries are pluralistic states where voters are free to choose their leaders; others have only one political party to choose from. What happens after a leader attains power is another factor that complicates the politics of this ever-changing continent. According to a former minister in Congo, Henri Lopez, "It does not suffice to be elected democratically; you have to act accordingly."[12] All too often, unfortunately, that is not the case in Africa.

AFRICA'S HEALTH

HIV/AIDS

"AIDS is not an African problem alone . . . If we do not win in Africa, we are not going to win anywhere else." (U.N. Secretary General, Kofi Annan, at the Abuja Summit on AIDS in April 2001)[13]

Africa has the highest incidence of HIV/AIDS in the world. Of the estimated 40 million people living with the virus, 28.1 million, almost 70 percent, were in Africa. It is the leading cause of death in Sub-Saharan Africa. Killing about 2.3 million people in 2001, and infecting 3.4 million. AIDS kills more people each day than wars, famines, and floods combined. About 95 percent of the world's AIDS orphans are African. In parts of southern Africa, antenatal clinic data indicate HIV prevalence rates of over 30 percent. In **Swaziland,** HIV prevalence in 2000 ranged from 32.2 percent in urban areas to 34.5 percent in rural areas. In **Botswana,** the figures were 43.9 percent and 35.5 percent, respectively. In KwaZulu-Natal Province, **South Africa,** the HIV prevalence rate was 36.2 percent. In fact, it is reported that one out of every nine South Africans has the virus.[14]

AIDS is one of the biggest threats to Africa's development. The United Nations Economic Commission for Africa (UNECA) reports that:

In parts of Africa, AIDS is killing one in every three adults, making orphans out of every tenth child and decimating entire communities, directly affecting health and life expectancy, the labour force, and household security. Most deaths in young adults aged 25-45 are [sic] associated with AIDS. Since the start of the epidemic, some 12.1 million children have been orphaned in Africa, out of the global estimate of 13.2 million. Within the next ten years, it is projected that there will be 40 million AIDS orphans in Africa.[15]

In the continent, HIV/AIDS is largely a heterosexually transmitted disease. One way the disease spreads is through the commercial sex industry that has developed in many cities. Young girls are particularly vulnerable to contracting HIV, as cultural gender bias leaves them less power to refuse men sex. The infection rate among young women is several times higher than that for young men in a number of African countries. Other groups that are disproportionately affected by the disease are soldiers and children. Customs also contribute to the spread of the disease. In some cultures, men may marry more than one wife. Many of the women who contract HIV are of childbearing age and often pass the disease on to their children. Conflict further encourages transmission in hospitals and refugee camps among uprooted populations. With crude systems of tracking the disease, illiteracy, resistance to using condoms, the social stigma attached to the disease, inadequate blood-screening equipment, and insufficient budgetary allocations, Africa faces a steep uphill battle in containing HIV/AIDS infection. Furthermore, the teachers, health workers, and public servants needed to combat the disease through education, treatment, and research, are also among its victims.

The United Nations currently plays an active role in addressing HIV/AIDS. For the first time ever, the U.N. Security Council discussed the HIV/AIDS crisis in a meeting on January 10, 2000, presided over by U.S. Vice President Al

Gore. The Council recognized the effect that the population devastation has on the political and economic stability of Africa. Secretary-General Annan also addressed the group, saying the "impact of AIDS is no less destructive than that of warfare itself, and by some measures, far worse. Last year, AIDS killed about 10 times more people in Africa than [did] armed conflict."[16]

The Joint United Nations Programme on HIV/AIDS (UNAIDS) recently formed a partnership with African governments to confront the issue. The goal of UNAIDS is to garner international support in combating the AIDS crisis in Africa. The Second African Development Forum on AIDS: The Greatest Leadership Challenge, organized by UNECA in collaboration with UNAIDS, the OAU, and other partners in December 2000, adopted the African Consensus and Plan of Action: Leadership to Overcome HIV/AIDS, committing African leadership at the personal, community, national, regional, and international levels to the fight against HIV/AIDS and a continental strategy for the prevention, control, care, and treatment of people with the virus. In April 2001, a Special Summit of the OAU in Abuja, Nigeria, adopted a Declaration on HIV/AIDS, Tuberculosis and Other Related Infectious Diseases. Heads of state endorsed the African Consensus and Plan of Action, declared AIDS a state of emergency, and committed themselves to take personal responsibility and leadership in the fight against HIV/AIDS and other related infectious diseases. They pledged to allocate at least 15 percent of each country's annual budget to health matters.

As countries have witnessed the ruinous effects of HIV/AIDS, many have adopted successful campaigns on condom use and promoted sex education in schools and the commercial sex industry. In South Africa, condom distribution rose from 6 million in 1994 to 198 million in 1999. Nigeria launched a U.S.$240 million HIV/AIDS Emergency Action Plan in 2001. Nations such as **Kenya** and **Uganda** have managed to slow the infection rate. Uganda recorded an impressive decline in HIV prevalence among pregnant women in urban areas, from a high of 29.5 percent in 1992 to 11.25 percent in 2000.

In **Senegal**, an aggressive prevention campaign has led to a relatively low infection rate of less than 2 percent. Botswana became the first African country to provide antiretroviral drugs through the public health system. More than ten African countries now do so. Although international pharmaceutical companies have agreed to reduce the prices of antiretroviral drugs, they are still far too expensive for most patients. In a continent where more than half the population live on less than U.S.$1 a day, antiretroviral drugs, even at reduced prices, are beyond the reach of all but a handful of patients. Researchers estimate that fewer than 10,000 Africans have access to these drugs.[17] However, most agree that drugs alone cannot be the answer. There is a need to bring about behavioral change, strengthen political leadership, fight poverty, strengthen educational and public health systems, and ensure adequate aid to carry out the continent's health and development agendas.

Research efforts are under way to manufacture locally a vaccine against the African strain of the disease, which differs from that found in North America, where current vaccine research is concentrated. With 70 percent of the world's HIV/AIDS sufferers, African vaccine research receives only U.S.$41 million, a mere 1.6 percent of the U.S.$2.5 billion in research funding for the entire world. Furthermore, of the 30 HIV vaccine trials conducted globally since 1987, only two trials were held in Africa. African scientists, research agencies, and U.N. organizations, including UNAIDS and the WHO, met in Cape Town, South Africa, on June 3-4, 2002, to raise U.S.$233 million for the African AIDS Vaccine Program, as well as develop a plan of action for the next seven years. According to Peter Piot, Executive Director of UNAIDS, "a vaccine for Africa would be the best long-term preventive measure against AIDS."[18]

INFECTIOUS DISEASES

In addition to AIDS, poverty and social instability have fueled Africa's current health crisis, bringing about the reemergence of diseases once thought to have been eradicated. Across the continent, preventable diseases such as tuberculosis, hepatitis, malaria, river blindness (onchocerciasis), and cholera, have reappeared in pandemic proportions, leaving few people untouched. A recent report by the WHO indicates that there are over 300 million acute cases of malaria each year globally, resulting in more than one million deaths. About 90 percent of these deaths occur in Africa, mainly among children. The cost to Africa in lost GDP is estimated to be over U.S.$12 billion.[19]

In the same year, 1.7 million people died of tuberculosis. The U.N. Development Programme (UNDP) has partnered with the World Bank and seventy other donors to form the African Program for Onchocerciasis Control. It will treat 50 million people per year by its completion in 2007.

POPULATION GROWTH

Africa is currently experiencing an explosion in population growth that threatens to not only swamp its public services, including health care and education, but to also erode political and economic gains made by each government over the last decade. The continent's population is growing faster than that of any other region in the world and shows little sign of slowing down, even in the face of the HIV/AIDS epidemic. In 1990, Africa was home to 660 million people, a dramatic increase from its 210 million in 1960. The population is expected to double to 1.2 billion by the year 2015, placing immense pressures on this developing region.

Rapidly increasing fertility rates combined with a modest decline in mortality rates have induced this unprecedented population explosion, despite factors such as increased per capita income, greater access to education, urbanization, and a longer life expectancy. The latter trends are linked to declining population growth in many other areas of the world; in Africa, however, fertility rates have remained high for a number of reasons. In rural areas, children are needed to help with farm work and other everyday chores. Also, children are still seen as the best form of social security for aging adults, and in some areas the number of children serves as a status symbol.

When combined with early marriage and minimal contraception, these factors contribute to the population boom. Even in urban areas, where sex education and contraception are more prevalent, many observers find that men continue to want more offspring, whether or not they can support them.

The pressures on many nations' environments and economies have been increased by the migration of large groups of people attempting to avoid civil strife, natural disasters, and poverty. Sub-Saharan Africa, which includes many of the poorest nations in the world, is rapidly becoming urbanized. United Nations projections indicate that nearly one-half (49 percent) of sub-Saharan Africa's population will be urban by 2025. Refugees play a significant role in these changing demographics. According to the U.S. Committee for Refugees, in 1996 about 3.5 million of the 14.5 million refugees in the world were living in sub-Saharan Africa. Eight to ten million were considered internally displaced, meaning they had to leave their homes for political reasons or because of natural disasters but remained in their native country.[20]

The burden of supporting this massive boom has increased the pressure on resources that are already being depleted at an unusually rapid rate, leading to a severe intensification of current environmental problems. Fresh water is becoming increasingly scarce, and the disappearance of forests that meet demands for firewood and farmland exacerbates the desertification of the continent. Moreover, the prospects for food scarcity are alarming. Due to recent drought and floods, as

5.1 AFRICAN POPULATION ISSUES ON THE WEB

UNDP Population Information

http://www.un.org/popin/

Economic Commission on Africa (ECA)

http://www.uneca.org/

United Nations System-wide Special Initiative for Africa (UNSIA)

http://www.un.org/partners/civil_society/m-africa.htm

well as internal distribution problems, some African nations are again on the brink of famine. Many countries are attempting to shape their national policies along the lines suggested in the Program of Action developed by the International Conference on Population and Development (held in Cairo in 1994). In three follow-up meetings, most nations reported working hard to implement the programs necessary to deal with the impact of population growth on health care, family planning, empowerment of women, nongovernmental organization, and private-sector investment, among other areas. The UNDP, Economic Commission for Africa (ECA), and United Nations Special Initiative on Africa (UNSIA) are some of the U.N. agencies that have played a significant role in formulating solutions to these problems.

MOVING FORWARD

Despite numerous obstacles to social, political, and economic development, by 2002 certain countries had taken positive steps, and an increase in foreign investment in African industry suggested some optimism for the future. **Rwanda** and **Uganda** were proving that it is possible to rebuild after devastating dictatorships. **Namibia** and **Botswana** were free of conflict and seeing gradual improvements in their economies. Despite catastrophic flooding at the beginning of 2000, **Mozambique** showed a modest economic growth rate of 5 percent during the year. On May 29, 1999, **Nigeria** ended fifteen years of military rule when a democratically elected president, General Olusegun Obasanjo, was sworn in, replacing General Abdulsalami Abubakar. Obasanjo began his term as Nigeria faced its worst economic crisis since 1960, the year it declared its independence from Britain. Contributing to the crisis were low

oil prices, a binge of unbudgeted spending as the Abubakar regime came to an end, and a succession of military regimes before that, which had stolen billions of dollars in oil revenues. In May 2000, the UNDP's Mark Malloch Brown asserted that "Mozambique, Rwanda, Uganda, Nigeria and **South Africa** all provide good examples of development progress . . ." and that South Africa and Nigeria, the "linchpins of any African political and economic revival," are led by accountable, democratic governments. Like Mozambique, both countries overcame failures to galvanize broad-based consensus for change.[21]

South Africa, on June 2, 1999, held its second all-race national elections following the end of apartheid. In a landslide victory, Thabo Mbeki of the African National Congress (ANC) was elected president and immediately vowed to move ahead with a program of racial reconciliation and development. He was sworn in on June 16, as Nelson Mandela retired from his political career. Mbeki's political agenda includes the elimination of poverty, halting the spread of AIDS, job creation for blacks, and enforcing laws to protect the rights of all citizens, regardless of race, gender, or disability.

Advances in telecommunications and information technology have also changed the way nations interact. Ever more connected through telephone, computer, and communications infrastructure, citizens are learning about one another through the sharing of information across these networks. Many international organizations and corporations are investing large sums of money in this infrastructure, and it represents an opportunity for Africa to make rapid advances toward modernization, which should lead to improved education, health, and standards of living. However, it also represents an opportunity for a new kind of social control, or "neocolonialism," that Africans and their foreign partners could well be forced to resist.

The United Nations' role in Africa began after the Second World War, when the organization assumed trusteeship of the former German colonies that had been taken over by other European powers after World War I. The United Nations recognized the responsibility of the colonial powers for the welfare of the colonized peoples. Today, with 53 votes in the General Assembly, the African Group is the largest regional bloc in the United Nations. A decline in the social welfare of the African population, an increase in violence, and accusations that the U.N. has not done enough in the past to prevent or to alleviate conflict in the region have stimulated the organization's renewed commitment to the continent.

Within the United Nations, two bodies are working specifically to improve conditions in Africa. The United Nations Special Initiative on Africa (UNSIA) focuses on helping Africa help itself while securing U.N. support of Africa's efforts at sustainable development. This initiative brings together a number of different U.N. agencies and regional organizations to coordinate the implementation of the United Nations New Agenda for the Development of Africa (U.N.-NADAF). The goals of UNSIA include strengthening the peace-building mechanisms of the Organization of African Unity, now the African Union; promoting civil society; providing substantial debt relief; reforming health sectors as well as protecting the quality of food and preserving clean water and fresh soil; and reducing poverty. Annual regional meetings in Africa monitor progress toward the realization of these goals. Both UNSIA and U.N.-NADAF have strong support from U.N. agencies. As James Gustave Speth, former UNDP Administrator and co-chair of the initiative, said: "The Special Initiative represents the fulfillment of the goals and visions of the first U.N. Development Decade of the 1960s. It unites our strengths at every level, from that of

the village to that of international governmental cooperation. And we cannot fail, because we cannot afford to fail."

The Economic Commission for Africa (ECA), based in Addis Ababa, **Ethiopia,** has served as a regional branch of the United Nations since 1958. It is currently working to identify effective economic programs, find ways to increase technological development on the continent, and enhance the U.N.'s role in Africa. The ECA is the follow-up mechanism for all U.N. conferences, including the 1994 International Conference on Population and Development (Cairo) and the 1995 Fourth World Conference on Women (Beijing). "The Economic Commission for Africa remains optimistic about the future prospects of the continent. As a member of the United Nations family, and at the same time an integral part of the African institutional landscape, ECA is well placed to foster Africa's renaissance, both by enhancing the coherence and coordination of the U.N.'s work in Africa and by delivering core services," said K. Y. Amoako, an Under-Secretary-General of the United Nations and the Executive Secretary of the ECA. Both UNSIA and ECA work not only toward solving short-term issues that may vary from region to region on the continent but also toward fulfilling the long-term goals of the U.N.

PEACEKEEPING OPERATIONS

Since 1988, the majority of U.N. peacekeeping operations have been in Africa. MINURCA, the small Mission in the Central African Republic, whose mandate ended on February 15, 2000, has been called a resounding success. Where peacekeeping has not been successful, as in the case of **Somalia** or **Rwanda,** the failure was due to moving the peacekeeping operation in too quickly,

Rwandans who fled to Zaire returning home on Gisenyi-Ruhengeri Road, Rwanda, Great Lakes Region of Africa, November 1996. (UNHCR Photo: R. LeMoyne)

before conditions were favorable, or to a lack of support from U.N. members. In mid-2002, the U.N. had peacekeeping operations in four Africa countries: Democratic Republic of the Congo—MONUC, since December 1999; Ethiopia and Eritrea—UNMEE, since July 2000; Sierra Leone —UNAMSIL, since October 1999; and Western Sahara—MINURSO, since April 1991.

LANDMINES

Landmines kill more than 26,000 civilians every year, an estimated 8,000 to 10,000 of them children. These hidden weapons are used to block access to schools, hospitals, roads, and other locations where most often the victims are innocent civilians. In 1997, the Nobel Peace Prize was awarded to the International Campaign to Ban Land Mines, a coalition of more than 1,400 accredited NGOs (according to the Nongovernmental Organization Section of the U.N. Department of Public Information) in more than 90 countries. That campaign helped bring about the signing of the Convention on the Prohibition of Anti-Personnel Mines (or Ottawa Convention, also called the Mine Ban Treaty), which went into effect on March 1, 1999, prohibiting the use, production, stockpiling, and transfer of antipersonnel landmines. As of May 2002, 143 countries (not including the United States) had signed the treaty and 124 countries had ratified it.[22]

The United Nations Mine Action Service (UNMAS) is responsible for coordinating the mine-related activities of eleven U.N. departments and agencies. This includes gathering information about the current state of landmines in a country, recommendations for removal of old mines (demining), and publication of demining safety procedures and materials advocating mine bans. In 2001, UNMAS was active in **Chad, Eritrea, Ethiopia, Mozambique, Sierra Leone,** and northwest **Somalia,** assessing and monitoring land mine removal efforts. By the end of 2002, UNMAS will complete the installation of the Information Management System for Mine Action (IMSMA) in the **Democratic Republic of Congo, Sudan, Mauritania,** and **Guinea-Bissau.**[23]

HUMAN RIGHTS

An almost inevitable result of military conflict is the abuse of human rights. Human rights groups, such as Citizens for Peace, collect, organize, and distribute information on the human consequences of border conflicts. Special rapporteurs of the U.N. Commission on Human Rights and other experts are asked to monitor conditions in specific countries or look into particular human rights abuses.

For example, Olara Otunnu, the Special Representative of the Secretary-General, has traveled to several war-torn African countries. In May 2002, he visited **Angola** where "over 2 million children have been displaced, 100,000 separated from their families, 50,000 orphaned and tens of thousands injured by landmines." In camps, hospitals, and transit centers, he found children suffering from malnutrition, malaria, pneumonia, and other preventable diseases. More than 60 percent of Angola's children are unable to attend school.

Those who flee human rights abuses at home are not assured that their needs can be met by the agencies assigned to look after their welfare across the border. Camps east of **Western Sahara,** for instance, were established in 1975, when Western Sahara was divided under the rule of **Morocco** and **Mauritania.** More than twenty-five years later, the camps are still in use; hospital equipment is scarce, and there is often not enough medicine or food for the tens of thousands of Saharawis who have fled there.

In addition to monitoring and averting human rights violations, the United Nations has prosecuted those who have committed war crimes and atrocities such as genocide in **Rwanda,** as well as Rwandans who have committed such acts in neighboring countries from January 1 to December 21, 1994. On November 8, 1994, by Security Council Resolution 955, the U.N. established the International Criminal Tribunal for Rwanda (ICTR). The ICTR sentenced Jean Kambanda, former Prime Minister of Rwanda, to life imprisonment for six counts of genocide and crimes against humanity. (September 2, 1998).

AFRICA'S DEBT BURDEN

Among Africa's most crippling economic problems is its foreign debt. In 2001, Africa's debt was over U.S.$370 billion and rising, making the region the most heavily indebted in the world. Many African countries spend over 30 percent of their budget on debt servicing. Withdrawal of the colonial powers left the new African nations with weak economies that were based on the production of raw materials and agriculture. The colonial legacy also left Africa with only a rudimentary infrastructure. The economic turmoil of the 1970s brought woes for Africa as commodity prices fell and terms of trade deteriorated. Several African states received substantial loans that were spent in unwise investments, overly ambitious infrastructure projects, or the corrupt practices of politicians. Africa's external debt is especially troublesome because of its adverse effects on new investment and growth potential. Governments are being forced to divert large portions of their budgets into debt service and away from social and economic development benefits such as health care and education.

Africa continues to be heavily indebted to the World Bank and International Monetary Fund (IMF). To help Africa cope with its difficult economic situation, the World Bank introduced Structural Adjustment Programs (SAPs) in 1979.

Unfortunately, most SAPs have either had little effect or increased the debt burden. One reason for this is that they come with stringent conditions, including increased taxes, reductions in social programs (education, health care), devaluation of currency, high interest rates, and opening of trade barriers. Some African nations have achieved high growth rates in sectors such as GDP (gross domestic product) and export production but have yet to see a sizable decline in their debts. In fact, sub-Saharan Africa's external debt has increased by nearly 400 percent since the early 1980s, when many of the IMF and World Bank SAPs were first introduced in the region.

The United Nations rallied on behalf of poverty-stricken regions in 1996 by establishing a debt initiative for heavily indebted poor countries (HIPCs) aimed at reducing debt levels. Under this agreement, the poorest countries and those found to be facing an unsustainable debt situation were not held responsible for debt owed to multilateral creditors such as the World Bank. In exchange, they were to use the savings to initiate policies aimed at reducing poverty. **Uganda** was the first African nation to pass the eligibility review, and **Burkina Faso, Côte d'Ivoire, Ethiopia, Mali, Mauritania, Mozambique,** and **Tanzania** were also declared eligible for a share of U.S.$10.5 billion of debt relief. The enhanced HIPC Initiative was launched in October 1999, reducing the net present value (NPV) of debt to a maximum of 150 percent of exports or 250 percent of government revenue. In the 1996 initiative, the figures were 200-250 percent and 280 percent, respectively. As of May 2002, only four African countries, Burkina Faso, Mozambique, Tanzania, and Uganda, had reached the "completion point" under the enhanced framework. The following countries have reached the "decision point": **Benin, Cameroon, Chad, Gambia,** Ethiopia, **Ghana, Guinea, Guinea-Bissau, Madagascar, Malawi,** Mali, Mauritania, **Niger, Rwanda, São Tomé and Príncipe, Senegal, Sierra Leone,** and **Zambia.** In essence, these countries now receive some sort of debt relief. To add to the initiative, the countries of the G-7 decided in 1999 to cancel U.S.$130 billion of HIPC debt, but so far very little of that debt has actually been eliminated. Debt forgiveness and cancellation may be the only ways in which some nations in Africa can hope to alleviate the suffering of their populations and ensure sustainable economic policies.

AFRICA'S FUTURE

On October 9, 1999, the United Nations Development Programme launched NetAid, a new initiative that utilizes computer technology in its campaign for poverty reduction. Simultaneous rock concerts in various parts of the world were broadcast over the Internet to raise money and awareness for aid to Africa. NetAid has demonstrated to be one of the farthest-reaching partnerships the U.N. has ever formed with the private sector in its struggle against poverty in the developing world. On January 28, 2000, countries in Africa were the first to receive funds out of the U.S.$1.7 million that had been raised. One-half million dollars was earmarked for health and community projects in **Sudan** and **Somalia** and U.S.$30,000 for land mine awareness work in **Angola.**

Since billions of people in developing countries do not yet have computers, Internet access, or even electricity, the UNDP, along with many multinational organizations and corporations, is working to expand communications access through UNDP offices, churches, schools, and other central locations. The ECA helped in 1999 to launch a continent-wide effort to accelerate the use of information and communication technologies in Africa through the African Information Society Initiative (AISI). ECA's first African Development Forum of government, business, academic, and civil society leaders, in 1999, focused on the Information Age.

U.N. Secretary-General Kofi Annan, delivering the Godkin Lecture at Harvard University on April 24, 2002, spoke of a "new spirit of democratic empowerment throughout Africa—a spirit that can sustain belief in progress even in the most difficult times." According to Robert Bates:

> In 1995, 29 of Africa's 46 executives were selected in elections in which they faced rivals backed by an opposition party; only three had been so chosen in 1975. Similarly, in 1995, 35 of Africa's 46 states possessed legislatures chosen in competitive elections in which candidates faced rivals sponsored by an opposition party; in 1975, 24 of Africa's 46 states lacked any form of legislature.[24]

There is a growing determination among the citizenry to participate in decisions affecting their destiny. Societies are becoming more articulate and are demanding accountable and transparent leadership. Political liberalization has also brought about the emergence of a new generation of African leaders, determined to take charge of the economic and political development of their countries. At the regional level, the new leadership has manifested its vision of a new Africa by the creation of the New Partnership for Africa's Development (NEPAD); and the African Union (AU), which replaced the Organization of African Unity (OAU). In addition, coordination will continue through existing regional organizations.

NEW PARTNERSHIP FOR AFRICA'S DEVELOPMENT (NEPAD)

NEPAD is the result of two African initiatives: the Millennium Partnership for African Recovery Program developed by Thabo Mbeki of **South Africa,** Olusegun Obasanjo of **Nigeria,** and Abdelaziz Bouteflika of **Algeria;** and the Omega Plan, developed by Abdoulaye Wade of **Senegal.** At the Lusaka Summit in **Zambia,** both plans were merged to become the New African Initiative (NAI). On October 23, 2001, at the first meeting of the Implementation Committee of the New African Initiative in Abuja, Nigeria, NAI was renamed the New Partnership for Africa's Development (NEPAD) with Obasanjo as Chair and Bouteflika and Wade as Vice Chairs of the Implementation Committee.

Basically, NEPAD's objectives are to:

- Eradicate poverty in Africa;
- Promote accelerated growth and sustainable development;
- Halt Africa's marginalization; and
- Restore peace, security and stability in the continent.

To achieve these objectives, NEPAD calls for a new global partnership based on shared responsibility and mutual interest.

NEPAD has its headquarters in Pretoria, South Africa. Its structure makes it easy for it to deal with urgent economic and political matters requiring immediate attention. It is subordinate to the African Union, which must ratify its major decisions.

AFRICAN UNION (AU)

The Inaugural Summit of the African Union took place in July 2002, in Durban, **South Africa,** thus formally transforming Africa's regional organization, the Organization of African Unity (OAU), into the African Union (AU). This represents a serious undertaking to fulfill Africa's aspiration for economic and political unity and the restoration of peace and stability in the continent. The immediate impetus was the agreement by African leaders, during the OAU Algiers Summit in 1999, to Libyan leader Muammar Gaddafi's proposal to hold an Extra-ordinary Summit on strengthening Africa's continental organization in order to

5.2 THE NEW PARTNERSHIP FOR AFRICA'S DEVELOPMENT AT A GLANCE

WHAT IS NEPAD?

It is a holistic, comprehensive integrated strategic framework for the socio-economic development of Africa. The NEPAD document provides the vision for Africa, a statement of the problems facing the continent and a Programme of Action to resolve these problems in order to reach the vision.

PRIMARY OBJECTIVE

To eradicate poverty in Africa and to place African countries both individually and collectively on a path of sustainable growth and development, thus halting the marginalisation of Africa in the globalisation process.

PRIORITIES

- Peace and Security (management, prevention and resolution of conflict)
- Political Governance and Democracy
- Economic and Corporate Governance
- Human Resource Development
- Regional infrastructure
- Economic integration and intra-African trade
- Market Access and Agriculture
- Capital flows

(For detailed information on NEPAD visit www.nepad.org)

---

meet the challenges of the twenty-first century. Its genesis, however, goes back to the 1980 Lagos Plan of Action and the Lagos Final Act, the establishment of African Regional Economic Communities (RECs), and the 1991 Abuja Treaty establishing the African Economic Community. Several factors necessitated this transformation, including: the inadequacies of the OAU and its piecemeal approach to resolving Africa's intractable economic, political and security issues; the increasing use of regional integration to foster economic growth, as seen in the European Union (EU), the Association of Southeast Asian Nations (ASEAN), and the North American Free Trade Association (NAFTA); the challenges and opportunities created by globalization; the promotion of peace, security and stability as essential prerequisites for Africa's development and integration agenda; and the need for a strong organization endowed with the powers and resources to carry out its functions.

Unlike the OAU, which was essentially an inter-governmental organization, the AU provides for the participation of African peoples in the activities of the Union through such institutions as the African Parliament, the Court of Justice, and the Economic, Social and Cultural Council. It has the right to intervene in the domestic affairs of member states in grave circumstances such as war crimes, genocide, and crimes against humanity. Member states may also request Union intervention to restore peace and security. The Union can condemn and reject governments that come to power by unconstitutional means such as military coups. Such governments are not allowed to participate in Union activities. In contrast to the OAU's preoccupation with political emancipation, the African Union is chiefly concerned with economic development, through the speedy implementation of the Abuja Treaty and the promotion of peace and stability.

AFRICAN DEVELOPMENT BANK (ADB)

The African Development Bank (ADB) was established in 1963 and began operations in 1966. Its membership includes all African nations, plus 24 non-African states. The bank is financially stable but is plagued by poor management and internal conflicts, which reduce its effectiveness. In the late 1990s, the ADB gave little help to the African countries that were most in need of economic revival. This has led to questions concerning the bank's future and usefulness. The ADB group of development financing institutions includes the African Development Fund (ADF) and the Nigeria Trust Fund (NTF), which provide loans on concessionary terms, as well as the African Development Bank itself.

ECONOMIC COMMUNITY OF WEST AFRICAN STATES (ECOWAS)

The Economic Community of West African States (ECOWAS), established in 1975, is the main regional economic organization of West Africa. Its members are **Benin, Burkina Faso, Cape Verde, Côte d'Ivoire, Gambia, Ghana, Guinea, Guinea-Bissau, Liberia, Mali, Mauritania, Niger, Nigeria, Senegal, Sierra Leone,** and **Togo.** The purpose of this organization is to promote trade, cooperation, and self-reliance in West Africa. ECOWAS also aims to raise the standard of living of the people in its member countries, increase and maintain economic stability,improve relations among member countries, and contribute to the progress and development of Africa. Members have discussed establishing a common ECOWAS monetary unit to facilitate trade among themselves.

ECOWAS has been less effective than hoped due to the numerous other intergovernmental organizations operate in the region. However, in 1990, the body formed a Standing Mediation Committee to mediate conflicts between member states. In July 1990, ECOWAS ministers attempted to mediate the civil conflict in Liberia. ECOWAS then dispatched a Monitoring Group (ECOMOG) to try to bring about a cease-fire. In September 1990, ECOMOG failed to prevent the capture and killing of Liberian President Samuel Doe. In November of that year the protagonists agreed to a temporary cease-fire, and an interim president was installed by ECOMOG. Since elections in July 1997 and the completion of the United Nations Mission in Liberia that September, ECOMOG has played a role in defusing tensions in the capital.

SOUTHERN AFRICAN DEVELOPMENT COMMUNITY (SADC)

The Southern African Development Community (SADC) was originally established in 1979 to reduce the economic dependence of its member states on South Africa and, secondarily, to

A woman in Cross Roads, South Africa, preparing a meal. (UN Photo)

increase development. Its current member states are **Angola, Botswana, Lesotho, Malawi, Mozambique, Namibia, South Africa, Swaziland, Tanzania, Zambia,** and **Zimbabwe.** South Africa's admission after the fall of apartheid substantially shifted the focus of the organization. Currently the SADC's principal aim is to increase production, investment, and intraregional trade among members. Members are working toward a treaty to eliminate internal trade barriers and export subsidies within the region; once these conditions have been met, free movement of people would be permitted. The founding concern, to reduce dependence on South Africa, has not been abandoned. South Africa's economy is four times that of all other SADC members combined, and only 10 percent of its trade takes place within Africa. However, in order to achieve a fully integrated economic community, member states must build stronger economies and intraregional trade.

1. Ramsay, Jeffress F. *Global Studies: Africa.* 9th ed., Guilford Connecticut: McGraw-Hill/Dushkin, 4.

2. Khapoya, Vincent B., *The African Experience: An Introduction.* 2nd ed., New Jersey: Prentice-Hall, 144.

3. *The Economist,* June 5–11, 1999.

4. United Nations News Center. <http://www.un.org/News/Press/docs/2002/SC7384.doc.htm>

5. *Standard Times* (Freetown), May 27, 2002

6. Alvarez, Jose "Crimes of States/Crimes of Hate: Lessons from Rwanda." *Yale Journal of International Law,* vol. 24, summer 1999, 388.

7. *National Assembly Report.* Jan. 27, 1999.

8. Arab Net. <www.arab.net/arabview/articles/huweidi10.html>

9. Clark, Andrew. "Imperialism, Independence, and Islam in Senegal and Mali." *Africa Today,* vol. 46, 1999, nos. 3/4, 150-67.

10. Adedeji, A. ed., *Comprehending and Mastering African Conflicts: The Search for Sustainable Peace and Good Governance.* London: Zed Books in association with African Center for Development and Strategic Studies, 1999, 3.

11. Adejumobi, Said. "The Crisis of Elections and Democracy in Africa." *Africa Quarterly,* vol. 38, 1998, no. 2, 29-53.

12. Sundberg, Anne. "The Problem of Change and Reorganization of the One-party Dictatorship in Congo." *African Journal of Political Science,* vol. 4, 1999, no. 2, 181-213.

13. *Africa Recovery United Nations,* Vol. 15 No. 1-2, June 2001.

14. "AIDS Epidemic Update." UNAIDS. December 2001 <http://www.unaids.org/epidemic_update/report_dec01/index.html>.

15. "Background Information About the African Development Forum." United Nations Economic Commission for Africa. <http://www.uneca.org/>

16. United Nations, 10 Jan 2000 <http://www.un.org/>, U.N. Newservice, 10 Jan. 2000.

17. *African Recovery,* United Nations, June 2001, 10.

18. *BBC World News,* June 3, 2002.

19. *Rollback Malaria.* <www.rbm.who.int>

20. U.S. Committee for Refugees. <http://www.refugees.org/>.

21. United Nations Foundation. <http://www.unfoundation.org/unwire/archives/show_article.cfm?article=10824/>.

22. Geneva International Centre for Humanitarian Demining. <http://www.gichd.ch/>.

23. The United Nations Mine Action Service <http://www.mineaction,org>.

24. Bates, Robert H. "The Economic Bases of Democratization," in Richard Joseph ed., *State, Conflict, and Democracy in Africa.* Boulder, Colo.: Lynne Rienner Publishers, 1999, 91.

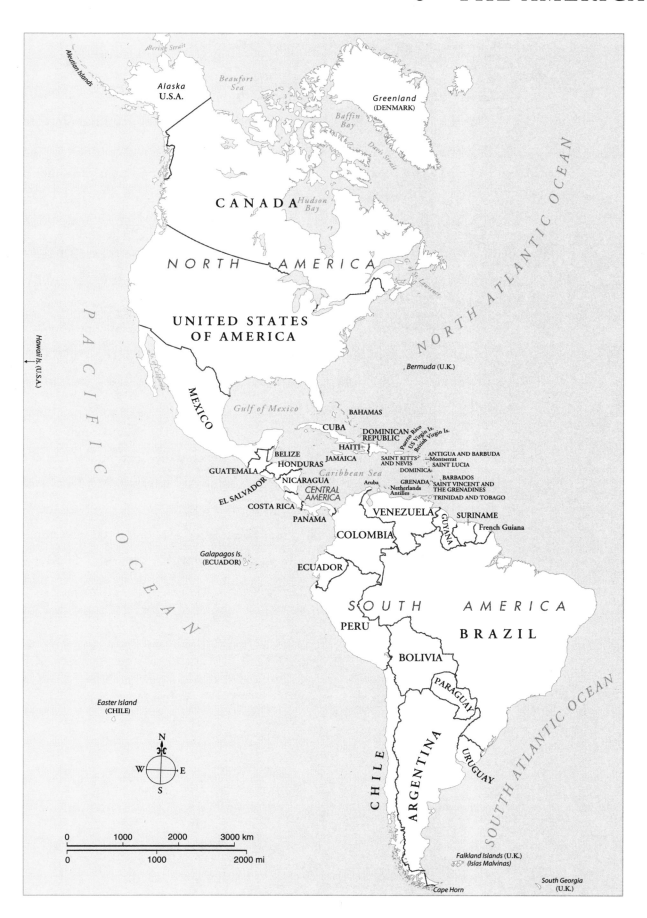

Comprised of thirty-five countries with citizens that speak as many languages, the Americas is a region that is diverse in population, culture, and resources. American history and diversity, past and present, are a combination of indigenous cultures and immigration from Europe, Africa, and Asia. The geographic region referred to as the Americas encompasses North, Central, and South America and the islands of the Caribbean Sea.

North America consists of Canada, Mexico, and the United States of America, while Central America is made up of Belize, Costa Rica, El Salvador, Guatemala, Honduras, Nicaragua, and Panama. Although Mexico is tied to North America by proximity as well as a variety of diplomatic and trade agreements, its culture and society more closely resemble those of the countries of Latin America. South America is commonly divided into three parts: the Andean region of Bolivia, Ecuador, Colombia, Peru, and Venezuela; the Southern Cone of Argentina, Chile, Paraguay, and Uruguay; and Brazil, the fifth-largest nation in the world.

The Caribbean region is a large belt of islands and island chains, many of which were once under the colonial rule of the British Empire or the United States. It is comprised of Antigua and Barbuda, the Bahamas, Barbados, Cuba, Dominica, the Dominican Republic, Grenada, Haiti, Jamaica, St. Kitts and Nevis, St. Lucia, St. Vincent and the Grenadines, and Trinidad and Tobago. It also includes Puerto Rico, which is a self-governing commonwealth in union with the United States; Guadeloupe, a territory of France; the British Virgin Islands; and the U.S. Virgin Islands.

The diversity of the Americas engenders a broad variety of issues and situations specific to its individual countries and sub-regions. International trade is a high priority for the entire hemisphere, and efforts to inaugurate trade agreements and strengthen existing ones continue to be important to economies of all sizes in the Americas. Other important issues include expanding the culture of democracy, controlling the demand for and supply of illegal drugs, promoting human rights, and implementing sustainable development practices.

AMERICAN TRADE

The governments of the Americas have negotiated twelve trade agreements since 1990 and are in the process of negotiating seven more. The largest and best known of these economic integration pacts is the North Atlantic Free Trade Agreement (NAFTA) between the **United States, Canada, and Mexico.** Other efforts at economic integration include MERCOSUR, the Andean Pact, and CARICOM.

The relative success of these and similar efforts led to a proposal for a Free Trade Area of the Americas (FTAA) in December 1994, when the heads of state of the thirty-four members of the Organization of American States (OAS) met in Miami, Florida, for the first Summit of the Americas. The negotiators committed their nations to complete bargaining for the FTAA by 2005.

On July 2, 1995, in Denver, Colorado, American trade ministers began negotiations on the establishment of the FTAA. They discussed market access, investment, standards of and technical barriers to trade, and customs procedures. The second meeting, in March 1996, in Cartagena, **Colombia,** achieved little except agreement on the need for expanded working groups to address such issues as government procurement, intellec-

tual property rights, and competition policy. A working group focused on small economies was established in the FTAA negotiations.

At the next meeting, held in May 1997 in Belo Horizonte, **Brazil,** the trade ministers affirmed their desire to complete FTAA negotiations by 2005. At the March 1998 meeting in San José, **Costa Rica,** members established a concrete organizational structure and adopted a set of general principles and objectives for the organization. At the second Summit of the Americas, in Santiago, **Chile,** in April 1998, the heads of state formally directed all ministers responsible for trade to officially begin negotiations for the FTAA; they again affirmed their commitment to conclude the negotiations no later than 2005.

The FTAA is unusual among trade pacts: No other trade agreement has included so many countries in such a short time, and no other region has as many preexisting trade agreements among its members. These characteristics, among others, distinguish the FTAA as an ambitious and bold initiative. In view of the diversity of the economies of the Americas and the economic uncertainty and turmoil of the 1990s, the slow pace of the FTAA process is understandable. In Latin America, where countries span the economic spectrum, a wide-ranging economic integration plan is difficult to formulate.

The fifth FTAA ministerial meeting took place in Toronto, Canada, at the end of 1999. Participants, building on the previous eighteen months of negotiations, discussed a course for the future and analyzed the social impacts of globalization not only on the economies of the FTAA countries, but also on the well-being of their citizens. For example, work programs to stimulate the involvement of civil society in the process drew attention. The work of the Negotiating Groups on Smaller Economies and the Committee of Government Representatives expanded, and a subcommittee on budget and administration was

According to a report released by the Inter-American Development Bank, about half of Latin America's children under the age of nine live in poverty. The Latin Americans most affected by poverty are indigenous people, women, children under eighteen, and those who are employed in agriculture. Children from families in any of the above groups are more vulnerable than the rest of the population to malnutrition, disease, abuse, abandonment, and illiteracy; and it doesn't end there. They are also more likely to face unemployment and low income later in life. According to Mauricio Diaz, director of the Honduran Social Forum on External Debt and Development (FOSDEH), a nongovernmental organization (NGO) in Honduras, "access to basic services should be equalized by concentrating on poorer populations."

Given the situation, the problem of exploitative child labor in Latin America is of desperate proportions. Nearly 30 million children work in areas such as agriculture or domestic labor, 15 million of them under the age of fifteen. Particularly distressing is the situation in Colombia. According to a report from the International Labor Organization, more than 1.5 million children in Colombia, nearly 19 percent of the child population, work at tasks that range from the production of drugs to prostitution. Only 26 percent of children have access to health services. In the Colombian province of Putumayo, the government's human rights office reports that almost 23 percent of the working population between the ages of five and eighteen is dedicated to harvesting coca for the production of cocaine.

created to strengthen financial management of the negotiations.

At the Toronto meeting, the executive secretary of the Economic Commission for Latin America and the Caribbean (ECLAC), Jose Antonio Ocampo, presented an assessment of the challenges facing the FTAA. Ocampo cited the importance of ensuring that "free trade and integration must go hand in hand with an effective, efficient, restructuring of production activities." He went on to say that in order to be successful, negotiations for the FTAA should include "mechanisms for restructuring uncompetitive sectors and firms, means of helping small and medium-size enterprises to participate in new trade flows on a competitive footing, and improvements in the physical and social infrastructure needed to back up dynamic economic activities."[1] To prevent an even wider divergence between rich and poor countries, especially within Latin America, participants called for a focus on human development (education, health care, job training) and for efforts to improve job creation in the formal sector and reduce the widening gaps between skilled and unskilled workers.

At the third Summit of the Americas meeting in Quebec City, Canada, in April 2001, the Trade Negotiations Committee presented the ministers with the first draft of the agreement. This was an important milestone in the negotiation process, but the goal remains to negotiate and reduce differences until a consensus is reached. At this point in the process, many experts see the 2005 deadline as unrealistic, as many issues remain to be resolved. However, it is important to view the achievements of the draft agreement: identification of options in areas of methods and measures for negotiating market access, adoption of a set of business facilitation measures, and an increase in technical assistance to create trade-related capabilities that have been reached by the thirty-four negotiating countries.[2]

The efforts to create the FTAA have strong political, strategic, and security dimensions as well as economic importance. In light of the terrorist activities of September 11, 2001, the importance of regional cooperation has increased. President George W. Bush addressed the OAS on January 1, 2002, stating that "the future of this hemisphere depends on the strength of three commitments: democracy, security, and market based development. These commitments are inseparable."[3]

DEMOCRATIZATION

Latin America has seen a slow shift away from its past of caudillo strongmen, military juntas, and revolving door regimes, toward constitutionally elected civilian governments. By the end of the last century, the majority of the region had experienced consecutive democratic elections. Unfortunately, honest and transparent elections do not guarantee that democratic institutions have become part of the social fabric of a country. True democracy exists in a climate that fosters co-equal executive, legislative, and judicial branches of government, tolerance of opposition views (both political and in the mass media), civilian control over the military, and public confidence and trust in the integrity of government institutions and leaders. Every effort must be made to strengthen democratic institutions (such as judicial propriety, fair elections, human rights) and civil society so that the economic ruin brought about by past authoritarian regimes can be made right.

The United Nations and other regional organizations have established programs for promoting democracy in nations that recently emerged from years of authoritarian rule. The Organization of American States (OAS) collaborates with member states to help strengthen democratic institutions in both government and civil society by supporting institutional consolidation and promoting cooperation. Among the specific priorities are strengthening the legislative branch of government and installing democratic values and practices in schools, political systems, and society at large, including participation in free and fair elections. To this end, the U.N. and other inter-governmental organizations participate in election monitoring in several countries in the Americas.

The role played by the international community in working toward consolidation of democracy has been most evident in Central America, particularly in **El Salvador** and **Haiti.** In El Salvador, the former rebels of the Frente Farabundo Martí para la Liberación Nacional (FMLN, Farabundo Marti National Liberation Front) laid down their weapons in exchange for recognition as a legal political party. After a 1991 military coup in Haiti, the international community cooperated in a mission to restore democratically elected President Jean-Bertrand Aristide to power. The mission was a success, but President Aristide returned in 1994 to face sporadic violence, civil unrest, and political corruption. The U.N. and OAS's goal is to strengthen Haiti's democracy by assisting in training the civilian police force, strengthening the country's democratic institutions, and fostering an active civil society.

HUMAN RIGHTS

Political violence, extra-judicial arrests, torture, and police brutality remain a challenge for governments in Latin America and for the international community at large. Human Rights Watch's *2002 World Report* cites **Argentina, Brazil, Chile, Colombia, Cuba, Guatemala, Haiti, Mexico, Peru,** and **Venezuela** for their poor human rights records. Many of the countries with the most serious crime problems are those in which law enforcement officers are known to have worked with criminal gangs; and problems such as police brutality, poor prison conditions, domestic violence, and labor rights abuses have largely gone unaddressed. These situations illustrate the enduring nature of authoritarian rule, not to mention the lack of accountability of public officials. Two important landmarks in Latin America's effort to achieve accountability for past human rights violations have been Chile's indictment of former dictator Augusto Pinochet and the Argentine judicial ruling that struck down the country's amnesty laws.[4]

HUMAN RIGHTS IN MEXICO

Mexico recently took steps to reform its institutions and adapt them to the demands of a modern democratic state governed by the rule of law. A national human rights commission was established in 1990. Since then, the national and state human right commissions have investigated numerous complaints, and to a large extent won the trust of the Mexican population. Improvements in the electoral system instituted by impartial regulatory bodies increased the confidence of voters in the electoral process. These reforms were first put to the test in the July 6, 1997 elections, which were noted for their competitiveness, transparency, and large voter turnout.

The Partido Revolucionario Institucional (PRI) had ruled for seventy consecutive years until the presidential elections of 2000, in which

In January 1999, the President of Haiti, Rene Preval, dissolved the National Assembly and following that, ruled by decree. Despite strong international and domestic pressure to hold legislative elections, Preval and the electoral council delayed them numerous times. Finally in May 2000, over 60 percent of Haiti's voters participated in the legislative election. Returns showed that the party led by former president Jean-Bertrand Aristide won a majority in the senate. These elections were cited by various international monitoring agencies as having serious irregularities, most notably in the counting of senate seats. Presidential elections were held in November 2000 though there was no correction of deficiencies revealed in the earlier legislative elections.

The political violence in Haiti has not lessened with the elections of 2000. The OAS maintains a special mission in Haiti. The most recent political violence occurred in December 2001 and, as a result, the OAS has created a Commission of Inquiry to examine the circumstances of such violence.

SOURCE

Organization of American States
<http://www.oas.org/>

---

opposition Partido de Acción Nacional (PAN) candidate Vicente Fox was elected. In November 2001, the Mexican National Human Rights Commission presented Fox with a study on the military's role in the disappearances of the 1970s. Fox ordered public access to the file, which represented the Mexican government's first official acknowledgment of responsibility for abuses, but did not name public officials suspected of being personally implicated.[5]

HUMAN RIGHTS IN CUBA

In 2001, an increasing number of **Cubans** were jailed for a range of peaceful activities that were deemed disrespectful or damaging to the state. Government-controlled courts in Cuba undermine the right to fair trial by failing to observe the few due process rights that are available to defendants under domestic law. The Cuban government relies more on short-term detentions, house arrest, travel restrictions, threats, surveillance, and other forms of harassment than criminal prosecution. Laws have been enacted that penalize "dangerousness" (el estado peligroso), including disseminating "enemy" propaganda, spreading "unauthorized news," and insulting dead heroes. The exercise of fundamental human rights of expression, association, assembly, and movement remain restricted by Cuban law. In 1999, the Cuban government declared international drug trafficking and the corruption of minors capital offenses, making more than 100 crimes punishable by death. In June 2001, Justice Minister Roberto Diaz Sotolong clarified that "for humanitarian reasons," Cuba preferred not to use capital punishment, but the existence of the penalty served as a warning to drug traffickers.[6]

Responses from the international community have varied. In the United Nations Commission on Human Rights, a resolution expressing concern over Cuban human rights practices passed by a narrow margin. The European Union, whose members accounted for about half of all foreign business ventures in Cuba, made further economic cooperation conditional on improvements in human rights. After Pope John Paul II's visit to Cuba in 1998, Latin American and Caribbean nations expanded official contact with Cuba (some restored diplomatic relations for the first time in decades). However, most nations failed to use this renewed dialogue to press for human rights protection.

The Cuban government regularly denies international NGOs access to the country. The International Committee of the Red Cross (ICRC) has not been allowed to conduct visits in Cuba since 1989, and Human Rights Watch has not been allowed to enter the country since 1995. In October 2001, Cuban exiles took advantage of a Belgian law that empowers its courts to hear crimes against humanity regardless of where they occurred, and filed suit against President Fidel Castro and other officials. The complaint describes torture and abuses suffered by political prisoners.[7] Human Rights Watch's *2001 World Report* revealed that in addition to those detained for political reasons, inmates who had committed common crimes were also subjected to abusive prison conditions.[8]

The **United States'** relationship with Cuba continues to be defined by a forty-plus-year trade embargo, which has yet to bring about the desired changes in Cuba's human rights record. The controversy surrounding Elian Gonzalez, the six-year old Cuban shipwreck survivor who was brought to the United States after the boat carrying him and his mother capsized when the two were attempting to flee Cuba, provided the first major impetus for Congressional efforts to relax the embargo. Elian Gonzalez was detained in the United States for seven months against the wishes of his Cuban father until the United States Supreme Court denied his Miami relatives' petition for asylum. Elian's return to Cuba provided a political victory for the Castro government and bolstered Cuban criticisms of United States policies, particularly the economic embargo. Opponents of the embargo maintained that its existence was responsible for encouraging illegal immigration of the kind that led to the death of Elian's mother, who was killed when the small boat she and Elian were fleeing Cuba in capsized off the coast of Florida.

After Hurricane Michelle devastated the island in November 2001, U.S. companies were allowed to sell food and medicines to Cuba, the first commercial transaction between the countries since the embargo was put in place in 1962.[9] In May 2002, President Bush announced an "Initiative for a New Cuba" in which he explained that "if Cuba's government takes all the necessary steps to ensure that the 2003 election [for the National Assembly] are certifiably free and fair and if Cuba also begins to adopt meaningful market-based reforms, then I will work with the U.S. Congress to ease the ban on trade and travel between our two countries." The initiative also includes the easing of restriction on humanitarian assistance, scholarships in the U.S. for Cuban students and professionals, and aid in modernizing Radio and TV Marti.[10]

Former U.S. President Jimmy Carter arrived in Cuba for a five-day visit in May 2002 as the highest-profile American ever to visit the Communist nation. Carter, who chairs The Carter Center in Atlanta, a non-governmental organization working for peace and health worldwide, described his visit as an effort to find common ground for fostering democracy in Cuba, in a May 23, 2000 *Washington Post* article he authored. The approach that the United States has historically championed includes restrictive visits between the two countries and the current economic embargo. Another approach, which Carter favors, involves providing maximum contact between the citizens of both nations, in hopes that Cuba may observe the advantages of a democratic society. Carter claimed, "The stagnant face-off has robbed our country of a chance to achieve our common goals." He blamed the polarization of Congressional efforts on politically influential Cuban immigrants allied with Washington administrations favoring the status quo and the increasing numbers of business and agricultural leaders allied with Congressional moderates for the alleviation of tensions. Furthermore, Carter's article stressed the need to avoid any sort of political or propaganda victory for each country as well as the importance of cultural exchanges between the nations in order to foster awareness about each nation's experience.

In the *Washington Post* article, Carter reported finding an unprecedented and unexpected degree of political freedom, especially in the media. The entire text of his speech calling for democracy was printed in *Granma*, the nation's official newspaper.[11]

HUMAN RIGHTS IN COLOMBIA

Governments and human rights groups have consistently cited **Colombia** for its serious human rights violations. Drug trafficking, abuses of authority, socioeconomic imbalances, and even land disputes have led to an increase of human rights abuses in the country. Armed conflict among paramilitary groups has created an atmosphere of fear and violence, and the government has been unsuccessful in stabilizing the situation. Such groups, working in some areas with the tolerance and open support of the armed forces, continued to subject civilians to violence, including selective killings and kidnappings. According to the Colombian Commission of Jurists, paramilitary organizations were considered responsible for 78 percent of the total number of human rights and international humanitarian law violations in Colombia in 1999. Investigators also linked soldiers engaged in military intelligence to a string of high-profile murders and death threats.

In the first ten months of 2001, the office of the Public Advocate in Colombia reported ninety-two massacres. As well, some 2,000 civilians and 1,500 combatants were reported killed and over 300,000 forced to flee from their homes.[12] Opinion polls showed that Colombians generally felt more insecure than in the past, partly because of a steady increase in kidnapping and extortion. More than eighty journalists and their coworkers have been murdered in Colombia since 1989, according to the Bogotá-based Foundation for Press Freedom. Many were victims of drug gangs and paramilitary forces. Violations of human rights and international humanitarian law continued to cause massive displacement.

According to the Grupo de Apoyo a Desplazados (GAD, Displaced Persons Support Group) in a 1999 Human Rights Watch report, an estimated 1.5 million Colombians have been displaced by political violence since 1985, making Colombia the country with the third largest internally displaced population in the world, after Sudan and Angola.

The office of the United Nations High Commissioner for Human Rights (UNHCHR) in Bogotá, Colombia, collects information; meets regularly with government officials, human rights groups, and victims of abuses; and lobbies continually for more robust human rights protections. In 1999, the U.N. High Commissioner for Human Rights, Mary Robinson, issued two strongly-worded statements condemning Colombia's human rights abuses, and the U.N. Human Rights Commission dedicated a full day of debate to Colombia, the second time the commission had focused special attention on the country, an indication of the seriousness of the situation.

6.3 U.N. Ranks Human Development in Latin America and the Caribbean

The *United Nations Human Development Report* has become a valuable source of data on the relative social and economic progress of countries. The 2001 *Report*, released by the United Nations Development Programme, provides important insight into the progress of development in many Latin American countries. Not surprisingly, the Human Development Index (HDI; the U.N. ranking system in the report, which takes into account life expectancy, literacy, and access to medical care, as well as economic indicators such as GDP) indicates that the richer countries in Latin America tend to rank higher on the overall development scale than the poorer ones. Delving deeper, it reveals that general economic indicators mask serious underlying inequalities.

Comparatively, Canada ranked third and the United States ranked sixth in the HDI rankings, while the highest ranking among Latin American countries was Argentina, at thirty-four.

However, it is Guatamela (108) and Haiti (134) that more accurately represent the poverty of the region. The report cited Latin American and Caribbean countries as having the highest levels of income inequality, revealing that in thirteen countries in the region, the poorest 10 percent lived on less than 1/20 of the income of the richest 10 percent. This inequality results in the suffering of millions.

Other indices in the report also present the international community with useful information. The Human Poverty Index (HPI) takes into account data on the unequal nature of development, gaps in income distribution, and the percentage of people without access to safe water and health services. Among industrialized countries, 100 percent of the population has access to adequate sanitation and essential drugs. In comparison, only 66 percent of Bolivia's people have access to adequate sanitation, and only 70 percent have access to

essential drugs. The report's findings for Haiti were even bleaker. Only 28 percent of the population have access to adequate sanitation while 30 percent have access to essential drugs.

In 2000, world leaders issued the Millennium Declaration, which, among other goals, called for halving the proportion of people in extreme poverty by 2015. Sadly, as the report notes, if this goal is achieved, 900 million people in the developing world will still live in extreme poverty.

SOURCE: "United Nations Human Development Report 2001: Making New Technologies Work for Human Development". United Nations Development Programme <http://hdr.undp.org/reports/global/2001/en/default.cfm>

Woman sorting newly harvested coffee beans on a farm in Haiti. (UN/DPI Photo)

In March 2001, U.S. Secretary of State Colin Powell announced to Congress that he would seek another $400 million for Colombia in fiscal year 2002 (nearly the same amount as 2000 and 2001). The bill approved by Congress contained strong conditions on human rights and no waiver authority concerning these conditions. In other words, the President cannot disregard human rights conditions if he finds "that to do so is in the national security interest,"[13] which had been lacking in previous legislation. In 2002, Congress once again imposed no waiver authority.

The peace talks between the Colombian government and rebel forces begun by President Andres Pastrana three years ago collapsed in February 2002, due to the failure of the rebel forces to negotiate seriously and the continued kidnappings and terrorist bombings. Colombians elected a new president, Alvaro Uribe Velez, on May 26, 2002. His campaign promised law, order, and authority. He proposes to provide security by doubling the number of police and salaried sol-

diers, organizing civilians to cooperate with security forces, and requiring private security guards to collaborate with police.[14]

WOMEN'S RIGHTS

Latin America and the Caribbean are marked by inequality: between nations, regions, and social classes, and also between men and women. Economic globalization has created a paradoxical situation for women's rights in the region. Although the issue began to draw attention in the late twentieth century, inequality between men and women increased on several fronts (unemployment and wage differentials), according to the Economic Commission for Latin America and the Caribbean (ECLAC).

At the eighth session of the Regional Conference on Women in Latin America and the Caribbean, held in Lima, Peru, in February 2000, the international community addressed many of

The sexual exploitation of children has reached alarming proportions in Central America. Although the sex trade is not new in the area (prostitution among children who live and work on the streets in Latin America has long been a result of the region's high level of poverty), the increase in tourism, along with other factors, has worsened the problem in recent years. Costa Rica's UNICEF director, Heimo Laakko-nen, calls it the "dark side of tourism." With the enforcement of stricter laws punishing those who solicit child prostitutes in traditional sex-trade destinations, chiefly Thailand and the Philippines, Central America's problem has become much more acute.

With many countries in Central America seeking to increase their tourist trade, Costa Rica, Guatemala, El Salvador, Nicaragua, and other countries are attracting greater numbers of men from all around the world looking for sex with children. Costa Rica, Central America's leading tourist destination, with one million visitors last year, is believed to have the region's most pronounced child prostitution problem.

the regional challenges facing women—such as the inclusion of women in "white collar" jobs in employment statistics, income disparities between men and women, and the devaluing of women's work in the informal sector—which have been ameliorated in some ways and worsened in others. ECLAC reported that "the context of exclusion [of women] that characterizes the global village is perhaps more evident than ever before."

Thanks to globalization, the region's labor market increased with respect to heterogeneity. Large multinational firms increased in number and small local enterprises felt the pressure of global competition. Given the position of women in Latin America and the Caribbean, opportunities for individual and collective development in the workforce are most affected by this change: in the 1990s, women in the region entered paid work en masse, yet most of the economically dependent adults were still women. Unemployment was higher for women than for men, and women were over-represented in low-skill, high-productivity positions. In addition, their income in the latter half of the 1990s was one-half that of men. Apart from a minority of highly educated women in stable and well-paid jobs, there has been no change in women's overall income curve.

There have been efforts to improve women's status in Latin America. Many nations have passed legislation supporting women's rights, and established official national women's organizations. Too often, however, such organizations have small budgets, are institutionally weak, receive scant attention from other government ministries, and are vulnerable to budget cuts when governments change. As a result, they have had difficulty in translating plans for equality into firm political commitments.

The Lima Consensus addressed many of these issues of inequality and incorporated the overall theme that resolution of the problem of women, as citizens and members of the labor force, cannot be separated from the overall need to humanize the economy and integrate economic policy with social policy on the basis of sustainable development. Other points included the need to strengthen democracy in the region, including women's rights to full and equal citizenship; to combat violence against women; and to recognize the social and economic contributions of unpaid work by women.

Representatives of Latin American and the Caribbean took the principles of the Lima Consensus to New York in June 2000 for the United Nations Special Session on the Follow-Up to the Fourth World Conference on Women (Beijing +5). In the final draft document, governments affirmed the Beijing Declaration and Platform for Action and, addressing many of the Lima Consensus points, agreed to further local, national, and international instruments aimed at eliminating violence against women, including marital rape and sexual abuse of women and girls, with "priority attention to be given to the protection of the human rights of women," including sexual and reproductive rights. Of particular interest to the Americas, was the declaration's agenda for the empowerment of women. It proclaimed that despite increased recognition of the gender dimensions of poverty, economic inequality between men and women is widening. Governments were called upon to respond by incorporating a gender perspective into socioeconomic policies toward poverty eradication, as well as creating safeguards against the uncertainties in women's work conditions associated with globalization.

TERRORISM

The worst international terrorist attack the world has ever seen occurred in the **United States** on September 11, 2001. Four separate airplanes were hijacked and used as human missiles; two crashed into the World Trade Center towers, which subsequently collapsed, in New York City; one was flown into the Pentagon in Arlington, Virginia; and the passengers on the final plane overpowered the hijackers and caused the plane to crash into a field in Pennsylvania, its intended target unknown. More than 3,000 persons, including rescue personnel and citizens of seventy-eight countries, perished in these attacks. Virtually every nation condemned the attacks and joined a U.S.-led coalition to fight terrorism diplomatically, economically, and militarily. Each of the nineteen hijackers belonged to the al-Qaida terrorist network and, as such, the first military targets were their training camps in Afghanistan. U.S. forces were eventually joined by those of fifty-five other countries.

The U.N. Security Council adopted three separate resolutions which "affirmed the right of self-defense, found terrorism to be a threat to peace and security, stressed the accountability of the supporter as well as the perpetrator of the acts, obliged member states to limit the ability of terrorists and terrorist organizations to operate internationally by freezing assets of terrorist affiliated persons and organizations and denying them safe haven." The General Assembly, as well as several regional organizations, strongly condemned the attacks and stressed the need for justice. The North Atlantic Council of NATO met on October 2, 2001, and determining that the attacks of September 11 were directed from abroad, regarded the attacks as an action covered by Article 5 of the Washington Treaty which states that an "armed attack on one or more of the Allies in Europe or North America shall be considered an attack against them all." On September 21, 2001, the OAS invoked the Inter-American Treaty of Reciprocal Assistance (Rio Treaty) to "maintain the peace and security of the continent."[15]

Notwithstanding the events of September 11, international terrorist attacks declined to 346 in 2001, down from 426 in 2000. Kidnapping remained one of the most persistent problems in the region. **Bolivia, Chile, Ecuador,** and **Peru** saw no attacks of international terrorism, but numerous incidents of domestic terrorism were reported. Ecuador's loosely controlled borders, weak financial controls, and widespread document fraud remain issues of concern. The number of domestic terrorist attacks in Peru (130 in 2001) has greatly increased over the past three years.[16]

As of September 2001, all three of **Colombia's** major illegal armed groups (FARC, Revolutionary Armed Forces of Colombia; ELN, National Liberation Army; AUC, United Self-Defense Forces of Colombia) had been designated by the U.S. as Foreign Terrorist Organizations. Some 3,500 murders were attributed to these groups. There were more kidnappings in Colombia than in any other country in the world in 2001. Colombia has attempted to broaden its capability to fight terrorism by "strengthening security forces, modernizing the penitentiary system, and expanding and improving civil and criminal investigation mechanisms."[17]

Abandoned street children eating garbage from a trash basket in São Paulo, Brazil. (UN/DPI Photo: Claudio Edinger)

Aside from longstanding differences on specific political issues, such as recognition of **Cuba**, there is general consensus in the Western Hemisphere on issues of international peace, security, and human development. On issues of sustainable development, the environment, human rights, the illicit drug trade, terrorism, and nuclear nonproliferation, for example, the nations of the region have generally worked together at the United Nations to achieve long-term solutions.

THE ILLICIT DRUG TRADE

Despite its attempts to stem the scourge, the Western Hemisphere continues to face the constant production of and traffic in illicit drugs. The region has experienced great suffering in both economic and human terms.

In ongoing efforts to raise awareness of the problem and to arrive at a consensus for action, the General Assembly held a Special Session on the World Drug Problem in June 1998. U.S. President Bill Clinton opened the conference by announcing his support for multilateral cooperation, but suggesting that some definitions be changed. Traditionally, countries have been labeled either drug suppliers or drug consumers. To bring an end to the illicit drug trade, President Clinton said, a worldwide problem must be acknowledged; it was not important to determine whether a nation is guilty of supply or demand in the epidemic.

Latin America representatives, of course, played a central role in the debate that followed. Representatives of the countries hardest hit by the drug trade called for increased financial, military, and social support. Transshipment countries such as **Mexico**, the **Bahamas**, and **Panama**, and producers of precursor products such as **Colombia**, **Peru**, and **Ecuador**, pledged renewed efforts to battle the world drug problem.

Several plans emerged from the three-day special session. A call for global cooperation in the arrest and prosecution of drug traffickers raised the issue of the compatibility of legal systems. One nation's strong anti-narcotics laws do not readily translate into those of another system of law, which becomes apparent when trans-boundary crimes occur or when issues of extradition arise. Participants in the conference accepted the scientific and economic basis for crop substitution. Replacing drug crops with asparagus, pineapples, and other "designer" vegetables or fruit crops, proponents of crop substitution contend, can void the common complaint that traditional crops (corn, cotton, coffee) do not compete financially. However, even if these exotic crops were planted, the major international financial institutions would be called upon to provide funding for more research on high-yield crops, and training and technical support for farmers who switched to alternative crops.

The most controversial idea discussed was that a reduced demand for illicit substances would significantly reduce drug supplies worldwide. Near the turn of the century, the money spent on reducing the drug trade focused on reducing supply; interdiction and preventing distribution were still the weapons of choice in the war on drugs. Alternatives gained prominence during the special session. The U.N. International Drug Control Programme and the World Health Organization (WHO) strongly recommended that more money be spent on education, in the belief that if anti-drug education were successful, it would decrease the actual demand for drugs, which would reduce the need for continued supply.

Although the special session focused on drug supply and demand, attention was also given to the byproducts of the drug trade, including money laundering and smuggling. Such corollaries impede the development of strong democratic institutions in Central and South America and present obstacles to a second regional priority of the United Nations and other intergovernmental bodies: good governance and the consolidation of democracy.

Following the special session, the United Nations Commission on Narcotic Drugs met in Vienna, Austria, in March 2000. In addition to discussing the world situation with regard to drug demand, supply, and trafficking, the commission decided to strengthen and elaborate the reporting mechanisms for all member states to provide the commission with national data on proscribed drug transactions. Topics of particular interest to the Americas included the dramatic increase of heroin in the United Started from 1992 onward (the number of heroin users rose from 68,000 to 325,000 in 1997). The focus for Latin America was on the supply and trafficking of narcotics, with particular emphasis on the drug trade in Colombia, Peru, and **Bolivia.** Illicit production of coca leaf remained relatively stable throughout the 1990s, leading to the potential global manufacture of an estimated 900 tons of cocaine in 1999. Colombia, where the most significant of cocaine seizures by international authorities took place, accounted for approximately two-thirds of the global production of coca. In Peru, eradication efforts, which the international community strengthened in the late 1990s, continued in 1999; on the other hand, large abandoned areas of former cultivation were reactivated in response to increases in the price of dried coca leaf. In Bolivia, despite a rise in the coca price, production seemed to have significantly declined.

Since these efforts took place, the United Nations Office for Drug Control and Crime Prevention (UNDCP) has overseen projects relating to the continued improvement of drug eradication. In Bolivia, a total of 26,000 hectares of illicit coca remain, mostly in the Chapare region. The current focus of the UNDCP is eliminating these remaining crops and creating alternative development of the land resources. At the same time, the agency has laid the groundwork for comprehensive training programs with the purpose of supplying jobs skills lying outside the realm of drug production and abuse to young people. Further-

more, the UNDCP statistic claiming a 50 percent decrease in Peruvian cocaine on the world markets by the end of 1999 has created the label, "The Peru Model." Peru's internal progress is linked to the strengthening of new and the revival of historic crops such as high quality Peruvian coffee, as well as the government's support of local farm organizations.[18]

However, Colombia continued to produce coca in 2001 despite efforts to stop trafficking.[19] Growing coca causes the destruction of millions of acres of rainforest, due to the fact that growers tend to abuse the chemicals used for growing such coca. These chemicals contaminate waterways, making the water system poisonous. Illegal substances such as kerosene, ethyl ether, sulfuric acid, potassium permanganate, acetone, lime, and carbide dumped into the ecosystem damage plants, rivers, and soil and expose animals and humans to contamination.[20]

Colombia is currently working with its armed forces to curb drug trafficking. The U.S. has been working with the government, providing military equipment and training for its forces. Over the past two years, the Colombian and U.S. governments have created a brigade comprised of 1,545 troops, and in 2001 trained 750 troops for a counternarcotics battalion. An aerial support group that tracks down drug smuggling planes was also formed. The Colombian National Police Antinarcotics Directorate (DIRAN) improved aerial support by adding a Huey helicopter fleet to the mission. In January 2001, there were approximately 15 Huey helicopters along with 33 UH-1N helicopters and two C-26 reconnaissance aircraft included in the mission. [21]

SUSTAINABLE DEVELOPMENT

At a conference held in November 1998 in Buenos Aires, **Argentina,** the parties to the U.N. Framework Convention on Climate Change agreed to a two-year plan for advancing the ambitious agenda outlined in the Kyoto Protocol. That protocol commits developed countries to reduce emission of greenhouse gases that most scientists believe cause global warming. The Buenos Aires conference demonstrated a significant breakthrough regarding developing countries' participation in international efforts to address climate change. Argentina became the first such country to announce its intention to set a binding emissions target for the 2008-2012 period. **Chile** advocated a stronger integration between national environmental policies and other public policies by governments across the region.

The World Summit on Sustainable Development met in Bali, Indonesia, in May 2002. Delegates met to discuss negotiations and to draft a plan on sustainable development governance. Sustainable development underscores the fact that human activity directly and indirectly affects economic and environmental health, locally and globally. Roberto Bissio, Director of the Instituto del Tercer Mundo of **Uruguay,** describes the current approach to this topic. "In the past few years…the concept of sustainable development introduces the environmental element in what was formerly thought of primarily as an economic concept."[22]

In that same month, the first World Ecotourism Summit was held in Quebec City, **Canada,** where the delegates focused on the importance of ecotourism dialogue and policy implementation for the alleviation of world poverty and environmental protection. The summit ultimately produced the Quebec Declaration on Ecotourism, intended for presentation to the United Nations World Summit in Johannesburg, South Africa in September 2002.[23]

Ecotourism plans involve the collaborative efforts of community members, nongovernmental organizations, government agencies, travel companies, and other stakeholders. While a common definition of the term "ecotourism" itself remains lacking, most definitions involve three general criteria: the provision of conservation measures, the inclusion of meaningful community participation, and the profitability and self-sustainability of such measures. Ecotourism's ambiguity has increased the need for ecotourism certification, particularly in the international institutions and national governments throughout the Americas. However, certification—formal documentation indicating compliance—itself becomes problematic owing to the infrastructure, coordination, and financial resources that are often lacking in the developing world as well as the world at large. During the Sustainable Development Web Conference of April 2002, participants submitted detailed essays describing institutional regulations such as tourism certification in **Brazil,** tourism legislation in **Venezuela,** and community tourism in **Ecuador.** Other nations reported the absence of necessary regulatory mechanisms in their institutions.[24]

Further progress in the separate areas of sustainable development stresses the need for educating consumers and professionals alike. Education fosters awareness, which in turn supports the increasing demand for socially and environmentally friendly products and services in global society. Specifically, the Internet has been targeted as the primary medium for educating the world's citizens. However, bridging the digital divide within developing countries, as well as among developed and developing countries, poses a significant challenge.

ECONOMIC DEVELOPMENT IN LATIN AMERICA AND THE CARIBBEAN

Latin America and the Caribbean have traditionally faced an extraordinary degree of instability in both finance and trade. There are drastic differences between sub-regions with respect to their economic problems. In the 1990s, economic stability in South America was threatened most by the Asian financial crisis and the devaluation of **Brazil's** currency. The stock markets in several countries, including **Argentina, Chile,** and Brazil, have demonstrated extreme vulnerability to international capital flow volatility. **Mexico** and Central America, on the other hand, took advantage of the expansion of the U.S. economy during that period to increase their exports. Parts of Central America and the Caribbean periodically suffer massive environmental degradation from natural disasters, such as hurricanes, which have a major but unpredictable impact on local economies. Such differences between sub-regions make regional and international solutions to economic problems exceedingly difficult to devise.

In 1994, the U.N. instituted a six-year Special Plan of Economic Cooperation to address economic crises in Latin America. The plan was implemented at the local level by government ministries and U.N. agencies, including the Economic Commission for Latin America and the Caribbean (ECLAC), the U.N. Development Programme (UNDP), and the World Bank. Projects addressed infrastructure development, emergency humanitarian relief, sustainable development, and private-sector development.

ECLAC also worked with Latin American governments and other U.N. agencies on economic development projects such as the joint ECLAC-UNDP program to promote technological innovations and competitiveness in the business sector. Together with the U.N.'s Food and Agriculture Organization (FAO), ECLAC improved the accessibility of land and created ways to make it available to small farmers in **Mexico** and **Brazil**. Argentina's National Institute of Statistics and Census joined ECLAC in a project to improve and strengthen the country's national statistical system. In **Paraguay,** the Central Bank and ECLAC cooperated on a project for the improvement of the country's national accounts system.

At the beginning of the twenty-first century, ECLAC presented its program of work for the next biennium. The commission took the occasion to sum up what it felt were the most complex challenges facing the region: social equity, development, and citizenship. ECLAC did note major advances in the region, including the correction of fiscal imbalances, reduction of inflation, reinforcement of regional economic integration, and an increase in government spending on social programs. However, the commission expressed concern that economic growth and the rise in productivity were insufficient, that the labor market had deteriorated in many countries, and that other forces came into play against the background of a long-term trend toward worsening patterns of wealth distribution.

Globalization and development were the main issues discussed during ECLAC's 29th session, held in Brasilia, Brazil, in 2002. The study proposed during the session involved examining globalization from an integral standpoint as as well as specific issues. By exploring the social, political, and cultural components of the global integration, the first part of the study focused on "the provision of global public goods, the correction of international asymmetries and the pursuit of a rights-based social agenda". The second part of the study focused on such areas as external vulnerability and macroeconomic policy, global trade, migration, and environmental sustainability.[25]

6.5 ARGENTINA IN TURMOIL

The Argentine people are experiencing an economic disaster unparalleled in their history. At the turn of the twentieth century, Argentina was an industrial and agriculturally rich society, boasting of a higher standard of living than that of France. In 1997, Argentina had one of the world's highest growth rates and low inflation due to a convertibility plan that pegged the peso to the U.S. dollar. Since then, the economy has gone into reverse. In December 2001, serious social protests and political chaos arose out of economic difficulties and as a result President Fernando de la Rua resigned. The country then went through four presidents in as many weeks.

The current economic situation in Argentina can be explained by several factors, none of which are exclusive; such as the fall in international prices, the growing public debt, the impact of devaluation of the Brazilian real, the appreciation of the dollar, and low tax collection. Once the service debt reached an unsustainable level, the International Monetary Fund (IMF) refused to release further loan disbursements until the government made the necessary policy changes. Negotiations are continuing. The government has floated the peso against the dollar, and temporary restrictive measures on financial institutions, such as a monthly cap on cash withdrawals and limitation on transfers of funds abroad, have been in place since December 2001.

The social repercussions of these actions have hit the Argentine people hard. Those who have bank accounts face restricted access, if any at all. People have taken to the street in protest of the government's policy and the unemployment rate continues to climb. Investors who were to potentially invest $66.4 billion in FDI for the 1999-2003 period are now taking a "wait-and-see" position due to the current climate of uncertainty.

CANADA IN THE UNITED NATIONS

At the heart of **Canada's** participation in the U.N. system is its commitment to strengthening the organization's ability to deal with economic and social issues. Canada has also maintained an extensive role in peacekeeping activities. No country has participated in more U.N.-sponsored observer, election, and truce-supervision operations. With thousands of Canadian soldiers serving under the United Nations flag around the world over the past forty-plus years, the government has been a strong supporter of preventive diplomacy and multilateral military action whenever necessary.

The U.N. is of prime importance to Canada's efforts to establish a clear and independent identity, and to make a sustained long-term impact on the evolution of world affairs. Canada is the seventh-largest contributor to the U.N. (providing 2.75 percent of the total budget). It has consistently paid its dues in full, on time, and without condition. In addition, Canada has not only participated in virtually every major U.N. peacekeeping operation, but it works with the organization on a vast array of issues affecting human security worldwide: antipersonnel land mines, small-arms traffic, children in armed conflict, and most recently, impunity of war criminals. Canada chaired the July 1998 negotiations that led to agreement on the statute of a permanent International Criminal Court in Rome. The country has also consistently worked through the U.N. toward resolution of a number of international challenges, including protection of civilians in armed conflict, child labor, arms control and disarmament, peacekeeping and peace building, and protection of the environment.

Canada views issues such as human rights, the environment, disarmament, and health as the forefront of the U.N.'s objectives. Canadian proposals for U.N. reform include: increasing the number of Security Council members, the enforcement of Article 19 of the U.N. Charter (members two years in arrears of dues payments should lose their voting rights), the creation of a U.N. rapid reaction force, strengthening of the U.N.'s Register of Conventional Arms, and the creation of a Sustainable Development Security Council, a U.N. body with the power to coordinate specialized agencies.[26]

THE UNITED STATES IN THE UNITED NATIONS

The strained relationship between the **United States** and the United Nations was eased by Congress' 1999 decision (through the Helms-Biden legislation) to pay the U.N. $926 million in back dues over the course of three years. The General Assembly subsequently agreed to reduce the level of U.S. payment to the U.N. regular budget and to a major and equitable reform of the U.N. peacekeeping operations assessment scale. Regardless, the U.S. continues to be the largest financial supporter of the U.N.

In the past two years, the U.S. has worked with the U.N. on recommendations on peacekeeping reform, human resources management reform, and improved audit, investigative, and inspection services. In addition to bureaucratic reduction and peacekeeping, the U.S.'s agenda in the U.N. includes containing the spread of weapons of mass destruction and the acknowledgment of AIDS as a global security issue.[27]

Attracting the world's attention, the hunger crisis in southern Africa has prompted action from donors around the world, including the United States' gift of 33,000 metric tons of maize, beans, and vegetable oil that arrived in Dar es Salaam, Tanzania, in May 2002. This action brought the United States' total contribution to the region to an estimated $36.6 million. Donations from the United States and other nations around the world are organized through the World Food Programme, the United Nation's front-line agency in the fight against global hunger.[28]

In April 2002, after a one-year absence, the United States rejoined the U.N.'s Commission on Human Rights, arguably the world's primary human rights body. The United States was elected by acclamation, or without a vote, owing to its membership in the Group of Western European and Other States, which had presented four candidates to fill four seats. (The other three nations elected by acclamation from this group were Australia, Germany, and Ireland.)[29]

In early May 2002, the United States formally withdrew its signature from the Rome Statute of the International Criminal Court, effectively freeing itself from any and all signatory obligations associated with passage of the statute. The U.S. government withdrew its year-and-a-half-old signature before ratification of the statute, citing concerns that the Court members would not be accountable for misconduct, as well as the Court's potential for politicization. Despite the United States' withdrawal, the Court's statute exceeded the required sixty ratifications from other nations and will come into being on July 1, 2002.[30] The vast majority of the international community has continued to stress that the ICC is essential for the prosecution of the serious human rights crimes described in its statute.

LATIN AMERICA IN THE UNITED NATIONS

One of the challenges facing Latin America is ensuring the current increase in democratic tendencies becomes a permanent element of the political systems of the region. In that context, Latin America has worked closely with the United Nations. All in all, the U.N. provided electoral assistance in more than a dozen countries in Latin America in the 1990s, in the hope of strengthening good governance and principles of democratic accountability. Although the situation in Central America improved in the late 1990s, the region continues to need long-term financial and technical support, and the U.N. will be a continuing presence in the new democracies for an undetermined but probably extended period.

In **Guatemala,** the U.N. mediated peace talks between the administration of President Alvaro Arzu and the rebel alliance and also monitored human rights abuses. A May 2002 U.N. mission in Guatemala expressed concern regarding the increased army budget that exceeded the amount agreed upon in the nation's peace accord.

Increased funds in this area may potentially divert funds from social development causes.[31] U.N. troops were stationed in **Haiti** throughout its difficult transition to democracy, and worked with the OAS to help restore elected leaders to power and promote democracy. In **El Salvador,** where human rights abuses have been a central feature of many conflicts, a U.N.-sponsored Commission on the Truth helped expose such abuses and recommended corrective action. The U.N. also supervised and organized national elections and assisted in recasting the institutions that resulted in functional government. U.N. experts visited the El Salvadorian and Panamanian governments to discuss combative measures against mercenary activities and terrorism.

Colombia took a major step towards democracy by holding a free presidential election in May 2002. The U.N. applauded this move and expects to soon observe the details of President-Elect Alvaro Uribe's new plans for U.N. involvement in helping to bring about peace in the nation.[32] This comes at a crucial time owing to a recent U.N. observation mission revealing Colombian paramilitary and rebel group activity responsible for scores of civilian deaths in the Medio Atrato region.[33]

U.N. SECURITY COUNCIL REFORM

Discussion of U.N. administrative and budgetary reforms often turns into a debate over expansion of the Security Council. The Council has fifteen members, of whom the **United States** is the only permanent member from the Americas. Many Latin American states have called for enlargement of the Security Council to allow better representation of each region. Besides the U.S., only two other representatives of the Americas are seated on the Security Council at any one time, each serving a two-year term as a nonpermanent, non-veto-wielding member. Many within the hemisphere have also called for a greater number of permanent seats on the Council, reduction or elimination of veto power, and greater representation of the developing world in general.

Historically, the development of regional organizations has played a major role in the Americas. Regional groups have addressed every field of concern, including international security, trade, education, and health.

ORGANIZATION OF AMERICAN STATES (OAS)

The Organization of American States, founded just three years after the United Nations, was created to promote peace and understanding within the Americas. The charter of the OAS was signed in Colombia in 1948 and entered into force in December 1951. The OAS's membership consists of the entire Western Hemisphere, with the exception of **Cuba**, whose membership was suspended in 1962 at the demand of the **United States. Canada** joined in 1990. The organization deals with the wide variety of economic, social, and political challenges that face the diverse economies, political systems, and cultures of the Americas.

The basic purposes of the OAS are to strengthen the peace and security of the two continents; to promote and consolidate representative democracy; to provide for common action on the part of member states in the event of aggression; to promote, by cooperative action, their economic, social, and cultural development; and to bring about an effective limitation of conventional weapons, making it possible to devote a majority of resources to the economic and social development of member states. OAS's work in the region is far-reaching. For example, the group has established electoral assistance programs in **Bolivia, Chile, Ecuador, Haiti, Peru,** and **Paraguay.** The OAS's relevance stems from its ability to adapt to a hemisphere in constant and rapid flux.

At the Summit of the Americas, held in Santiago, Chile, in April 1998, thirty-four heads of state met to discuss common problems and critical developments. Among the priorities established in the Santiago Plan of Action were education; preserving and strengthening democracy, justice, human rights, and civil society; the Free Trade Area of the Americas; improving telecommunications; promoting micro-enterprise; upholding labor rights; and implementing sustainable development practices. Resulting from the attacks on the United States of September 11, 2001, the organization's Inter-American Committee Against Terrorism strengthened its focus, resulting in the Resolution Strengthening Cooperation to Prevent, Combat, and Eliminate Terrorism.[34]

NORTH AMERICAN FREE TRADE AGREEMENT (NAFTA)

When the European Union first began to take shape in the 1960s, the nations of the Americas became interested in pursuing similar regional integration efforts. **Canada** and the **U.S.** first signed bilateral trade agreements in 1988, eliminating quotas, tariffs, and duties between the two countries. The North American Free Trade Agreement (NAFTA) of 1993, which emerged from the General Agreement on Tariffs and Trade (GATT) of 1947, brought **Mexico** into the process. Although the second phase of NAFTA's implementation drew much dissent in the United States, it was favorably received in Canada and Mexico. NAFTA removed all trade barriers and quotas among the three nations and made it much easier for companies to operate plants and factories across national borders. By joining more than 370 million people with a combined gross domestic product (GDP) of more than $6.4 trillion, NAFTA has become the second-largest world trading bloc, after the European Union. Eliminating trade barriers between these three countries has also benefitted U.S. agriculture. In 2000, more than one out of every four dollars earned by U.S. agricultural products was earned by exports in North America.[35]

However, NAFTA has also generated specific problems in the region. Because of the lowering of tariffs and the ease with which trade now flows, many feel that the agreement does more harm than good in the United States, to its labor force in particular. There has been concern over the number of jobs that have left the United States. U.S. industrial workers are more skilled than workers in other nations; they are also among the highest paid. Just across the border in Mexico, salaries are substantially lower, leading some companies to move their production plants south. This phenomenon is not unique to NAFTA: Many American companies have taken their production operations overseas and employ workers from South and East Asia at a fraction of American salaries.

Concerns about the negative effect of NAFTA on Mexico are easily identifiable. After the adoption of NAFTA, the industrialization and urbanization of Mexican cities and towns near its border with the United States increased. The process put stress on Mexican infrastructure, housing, education, and public health programs. On the economic side, there is strong evidence that large Mexican firms benefited from free trade while small and medium-size firms struggled under the strain of competition from U.S. companies.

SOUTH AMERICAN COMMON MARKET (MERCOSUR)

While North America's interregional trade relations focus on the North American Free Trade Agreement, South America has placed a majority of its resources and efforts into the South American Common Market (MERCOSUR, Mercado Común del Sur). The formal inauguration of the MERCOSUR integration process began on January 1, 1995. The process, initiated by **Argentina** and **Brazil** in 1986, came to include **Paraguay, Uruguay,** and two associate members, **Bolivia** and **Chile.** MERCOSUR is the third-largest trading bloc in the world after the EU and NAFTA; its

GDP exceeds $1 trillion and is growing at an average of 4 percent per year. The Treaty of Asunción, which provides the legal basis for MERCOSUR and was signed in 1991, established the goal of common-market status and will eventually allow free movement of goods, capital, labor, and services among the member states.

MERCOSUR made significant progress toward fixing a common external tariff (CET): By January 1, 1995, Brazil and Argentina had instituted such a tariff on approximately 85 percent of their tariff categories. Paraguay and Uruguay adopted that CET a year later. The organization hopes to reach a level at which it can institute a common currency and the regionalization of trade. In December 1995, MERCOSUR signed a framework treaty as the basis of future negotiations with the European Union. The EU and MERCOSUR opened formal negotiations to create a free trade zone before 2003. The meeting, in late 1999 in Brussels, brought together EU representatives and negotiators from all MERCOSUR members except Bolivia. In February 2000, however, Brazilian foreign minister Luiz Felipe Lampreia, acknowledged that MERCOSUR did have serious internal problems. Trade disputes between Brazil and Argentina regarding cotton exports proceeded to the World Trade Organization.

LATIN AMERICAN ECONOMIC SYSTEM (SELA)

The 1970s brought significant economic change to the Latin American region. Most economies there had begun to show signs of decline, and in 1975 representatives of several nations met to negotiate the Panama Convention, which established the Latin American Economic System (SELA), headquartered in Caracas, **Venezuela.** This regional intergovernmental organization's objectives include the promotion of common economic interests with third countries or in international arenas and cooperation among member states in support of economic and social development. The ultimate goal is to bring economic prosperity to the region through price protection of basic commodities and the creation and maintenance of export markets. While SELA works to help all Latin American and Caribbean states, several British Commonwealth nations are not members of the organization and do not enjoy its benefits.

The twenty-eight members of SELA are **Argentina, Bahamas, Barbados, Belize, Bolivia, Brazil, Colombia, Costa Rica, Cuba, Chile, Ecuador, Dominican Republic, El Salvador, Grenada, Guatemala, Guyana, Haiti, Honduras, Jamaica, Mexico, Nicaragua, Panama, Paraguay, Peru, Suriname, Trinidad and Tobago, Uruguay,** and **Venezuela.**

European Union, Latin American, and Caribbean heads of state met in Madrid, Spain in 2002 to formulate a bi-regional strategic partnership based on the Declaration and the Plan of Action adopted at the First Summit in Rio de Janeiro, Brazil in 1999. This partnership addressed political, economic, cultural, and social development between the two regions. Specifically, the political agenda involved strengthening the principles of the U.N. charter, encouraging and maintaining democracy, abiding by the principles of the Rome Statute of the International Criminal Court, combating terrorism, illicit drugs, and racism, as well as promoting gender equality, child welfare, HIV/AIDS prevention and education, and the preservation of human rights. The partnership also underscored guiding principles promoting economic growth, technological innovation and education, trade liberalization, sustainable development, and the adoption of the euro.[36]

CARIBBEAN COMMUNITY AND COMMON MARKET (CARICOM)

The Caribbean Community and Common Market (CARICOM) took effect under the Treaty of Chaguaramas on August 1, 1973 at a conference in Trinidad. CARICOM's members are the small island nations of **Antigua and Barbuda, Bahamas, Barbados, Belize, Dominica, Grenada, Guyana, Jamaica, Montserrat, St. Kitts and Nevis, St. Lucia, St. Vincent and the Grenadines, Suriname,** and **Trinidad and Tobago.** Several states have observer status, including Aruba, Bermuda, the British Virgin Islands, the Cayman Islands, Dominican Republic, Haiti, the Netherlands Antilles, Puerto Rico, and Turks and Caicos Islands. Associate members are **Colombia, Mexico,** and **Venezuela.**

Among CARICOM's objectives are the strengthening and coordination of economic and trade relations among member states in order to accelerate balanced development; the continued integration of economic activities such as transborder trade among members, the benefits of which will be equally shared, taking into account the need to provide special opportunities for less developed countries (LDCs); and the achievement of greater economic independence and strength vis-à-vis other states and regional organizations.

The Caribbean Community and the Southern African Development Community (SADC) took a step toward closer cooperation when high-level officials from the two regional groups met in Kingston, **Jamaica** in April 2000. After sharing information on recent political and economic developments in their respective regions, the delegations agreed to establish a framework for closer cooperation and collaboration on issues being addressed in the international arena.

The meeting identified a significant new area for cooperation: disaster preparedness and mitigation. At the request of the SADC, which is trying to develop a regional mechanism for this work, the CARICOM delegation outlined the structure and operations of the Caribbean Disaster Emergency Relief Agency (CDERA). The delegation agreed to give urgent consideration to ways of supporting the SADC effort.

ANDEAN COMMUNITY

The Andean Community (CAN, Comunidad Andina), a subregional organization made up of **Bolivia, Colombia, Ecuador, Peru,** and **Venezuela,** was created to achieve goals similar to those of MERCOSUR. The regional organization promotes a political process for economic integration as well as general economic, financial, and commercial cooperation. The beginnings of CAN date back to 1969 when the Cartagena Agreement, also known as the Andean Pact, was signed with the purpose of creating a customs union within a period of ten years.

Since its creation, CAN has achieved many of its economic integration goals, including creating a free trade area (which Peru is gradually joining). Leaders of CAN member countries have also called for the coordination of social, political, cultural, and security initiatives. Recently, in June 2002, CAN foreign ministers approved the Andean Charter for Peace and Security, which outlines the principles for creating a Community policy on security in the subregion.[37]

1. "Ministerial Meeting for the Free Trade Areas of the Americas." Press Centre, Economic Commission for Latin America and the Caribbean. November 4, 1999. <http://www.eclac.org/cgizbin/getProd.asp?xml=/prensa/noticias/discursos/6/656/P656.xml&xsl=/prensa/tpli/p4f.xsl&base=/prensa/tpl-i/topbottom.xsl> (June 27, 2002).

2. "The FTAA, the OAS and the New Pact in the Americas." Trade Unit, Organization of American States. February 2001. <http://sice.oas.org/tunit/STAFF_ARTICLE/jmsx_pact_e.asp> (May 27, 2002).

3. "Latin American Trade Policies in 2002 and Beyond: Diagnosis and Prognosis." Organization of American States Undated. <http://sice.oas.org/tunit/STAFF_ARTICLE/jmsx_diagnosis_e.asp> (May 27, 2002).

4. "Americas Overview." Human Rights Watch World Report 2002. Undated. <http://www.hrw.org/wr2k2/americas.html> (May 28, 2002).

5. Ibid.

6. "Cuba." Human Rights Watch 2002 World Report: Cuba. Undated. <http://www.hrw.org/wr2k2/print.cgi?americas5.html> (May 28, 2002).

7. Ibid.

8. Ibid.

9. "Assembly Calls for End to United States Embargo Against Cuba." United Nations. June 11, 2002. <http://www.un.org/News/Press/docs/2001/ga9979.doc.htm> (November 11, 2001).

10. "President Bush Announces Initiative for a New Cuba." U.S. Department of State. May 20, 2002. <http://www.state.gov/p/wha/rls/rm/10321.htm> (May 27, 2002).

11 "Openings to Cuba: We Must Find a Common Ground." *Washington Post Online.* May 23, 2002. <http://www.washingtonpost.com/wp-dyn/articles/A2094-2002May23.html> (June 11, 2002).

12. Human Rights Watch, World Report 2002: Colombia. Undated.<http://www.hrw.org/wr2k2/print.cgi?americas4.html> (May 28, 2002).

13. "Relevant Excerpts from Conference Report on H.R. 2506, the Foreign Operations Appropriations Bill (with Annotations)." December 21, 2001. <http://www.ciponline.org/colombia/121901.htm> (June 11, 2002).

14. "A Fearful Legacy." *The Economist.* May 24, 2002. <http://www.economist.com/agenda/PrinterFriendly.cfm?Story_ID=1147698>

15. "Patterns of Global Terrorism, Appendix H: Multinational Response to September 11." Office of the Coordinator for Counterterrorism, U.S. Department of State. May 21, 2002.<http://www.state.gov/s/ct/rls/pgtrpt/2001/html/10264,htm> (May 27, 2002).

16. Ibid.

17. Ibid.

18. "UNDCP Projects in Peru," UNODCCP. Undated. <http://www.undcp.org/peru/projects.html> (June 11, 2002).

19. "Statement of Explanation for Colombia Drug Certification." U.S. Department of State. March 2, 2001. <http://usinfo.state.gov> (June 7, 2002).

20. "Environmental Consequences of the Illicit Coca Trade." U.S. Department of State, Bureau for the International Narcotics and Law Enforcement Affairs. June 28, 2001. <http://usinfo.state.gov> (June 7, 2002).

21. "The Americas." U.S. Department of State. Undated. <http://usinfo.state.gov> (June 7, 2002).

22. "The World Summit on Sustainable Development." Linkages. June 8, 2002. <http://www.iisd.ca/linkages/2002/pc4> (June 11, 2002).

23. "U.N. Hails Forum's Declaration Defining Basis for Ecotourism Development." U.N. News Centre. May 23, 2002. <http://www0.un.org/apps/news/story.asp?NewsID=3766&Cr=ecotourism&Cr1=> (June 11, 2002).

24. "Sustainable Development of Ecotourism Conference." Planeta.com. June 1, 2002. < http://www.planeta.com/ecotravel/tour/2002ecotourismreport.html> (June 11, 2002).

25. "Globalization and Development." Economic Commission for Latin America and the

Caribbean. Undated. <http://www.eclac.org/cgibin/getProd.asp?xml=/publicaciones/xml/0/10030/P10030.xml&xsl=/tpl-i/p9f.xsl&base=\tpl-i\top-bottom.xsl> (June 11, 2002).

26. "Canadian Priorities for United Nations Reform: Proposals for Policy Changes by the United Nations and the Government of Canada." UNA-Canada. Undated. <http://www.unac.org/en/link_learn/fact_sheets/process.asp> (May 27, 2002).

27. "Factsheet: U.S. Support for the United Nations." U.S. Permanent Mission to the U.N. February 2002. <http://www.un.int/usa/fact9.htm> (June 11, 2002).

28. "United States Donation to World Food Programme Arrives in Southern Africa." U.N. News Centre. May 28, 2002. <http://www0.un.org/apps/news/story.asp?NewsID=3786&Cr=wfp&Cr1=africa> (June 11, 2002).

29. "15 Members Elected to U.N.'s Key Rights Panel; U.S. is Back After Year's Absence." U.N. News Centre. April 29, 2002. <http://www0.un.org/apps/news/story.asp?NewsID=3524&Cr=rights&Cr1=commission> (June 11, 2002).

30. "Annan Regrets U.S. Decision Not to Ratify International Criminal Court Statute." U.N. News Centre. May 8, 2002. <http://www0.un.org/apps/news/story.asp?NewsID=3624&Cr=icc&Cr1=court> (June 11, 2002).

31. "Guatemala: U.N. Mission Voices Concern Over Increase in Army Budget." U.N. News Centre. May 17, 2002. <http://www0.un.org/apps/news/story.asp?NewsID=3706&Cr=minugua&Cr1=> (June 11, 2002).

32. "U.N. Welcomes Colombian's Resolve In Electing Candidate of Their Choice." U.N. News Centre. May 28, 2002. <http://www0.un.org/apps/news/story.asp?NewsID=3788&Cr=colombia&Cr1=> (June 11, 2002).

33. "Colombia: U.N. Report Blames FARC and Paramilitary Groups for Civilian Deaths." U.N. News Centre. May 22, 2002. <http://www0.un.org/apps/news/story.asp?NewsID=3744&Cr=colombia&Cr1=> (June 11, 2002).

34. "Inter-American Committee Against Terrorism." Organization of American States. Undated. <http://www.oas.org/OASpage/eng/Latestnews.htm> (June 11, 2002).

35. "North American Free Trade Agreement." FAS Online. July 2001. <http://ffas.usda.gov/info/factsheets/nafta.html> (June 11, 2002).

36. "Latin American Economic System." Undated. <http://www.sela.org> (June 11, 2002).

37. Andean Community. Undated. < http://www.comunidadandina.org/ingles/who.htm> (June 26, 2002).

Additional Source: Robert T. Buckman. *Latin America 2000.* 34th ed. (West Virginia: Styker-Post Publications, 2000).

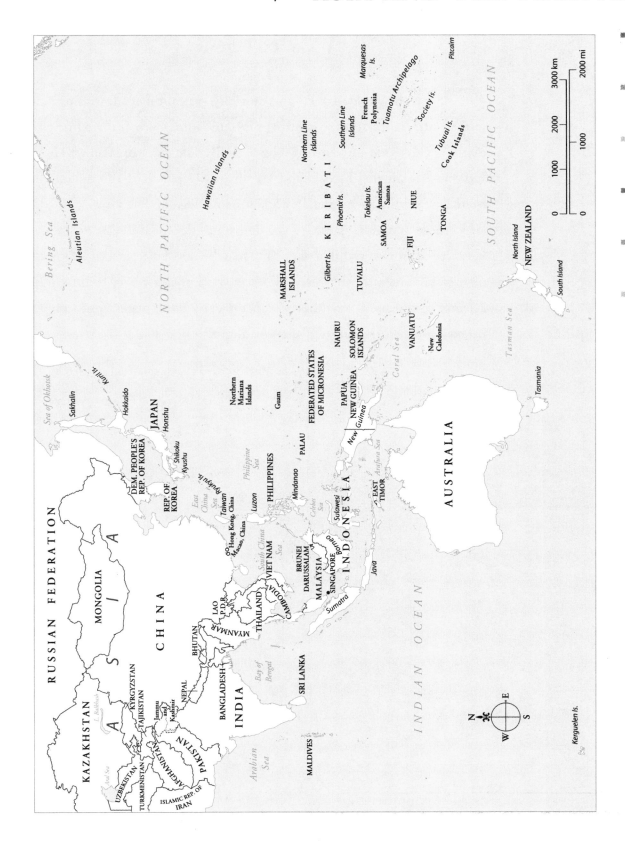

Asia is the world's largest and most diverse continent. Encompassing over 30 percent of the earth's land area, the continent is home to more than three fifths of the world's population. The world's five major religions—Buddhism, Christianity, Hinduism, Islam, and Judaism—originated in Asia and are all widely practiced throughout the region. Asia is more a geographic term than a homogeneous region. The Greeks were among the earliest Westerners to use the name Asia to designate the lands situated to the east of their homeland. It is also believed that the name may be derived from the Assyrian word *asu,* meaning "east." Linguistically, Asia embraces most major non-African language families. An attempt to capture the richness and complexity of the region must only be made through kaleidoscopic lenses; no single lens or monochrome will do.

The painful events of September 11, 2001, brought in their aftermath a renewed military emphasis and stability of focus to Asia. The future of the region will be determined by prosperity based on the rule of law, fairness in trade relations, and increased sensitivity on the part of international bodies in bridging the gaps between the developed and developing worlds. Security in the region will come through sustained engagement by the world through preventive diplomacy, constructive dialogue, and the control of the spread of nuclear weapons; and political stability will come via transitions to more people-focused governments.

CONFLICTS IN ASIA

In Asia, disputes over territory, legitimacy, sovereignty, and self-government continue to threaten peace and prosperity. Governments tussle over disputed territories; governments claim sovereignty over other governments; regions and provinces within a country fight for autonomy and independence. Asia is still plagued with a variety of international and internal disputes, some of which are explosive in nature. Difficulties in resolving the conflicts arise from the vagueness of international law and the lack of an existing framework to address such disputes. Furthermore, territory and political authority are two concepts that are strongly linked with nationalism and the definition of a modern nation-state. Nationalism here refers to political nationalism, for example, an Indian asserting "I am an Indian," belonging to the politically and territorially defined country called India, as opposed to asserting that he or she is a Hindu or a Muslim, or speaks Sanskrit or English. Moreover, the anti-terrorism campaign has also called into question the difficulty of defining what is a legitimate struggle for statehood and what is obtrusive

armed interference by a neighboring state. Conflicts over territory and political authority in Asia can be categorized into six groups:

- Civil war;
- Border disputes between two countries;
- Territory claimed by two or more countries;
- Self-government movements within a state;
- Sovereignty dispute between two governments; and
- Armed interference in neighboring countries' affairs.

Some disputes are a combination of more than one type of conflict. Because there is no institution of international law that has the power to make and enforce settlements of disputes single-handedly between nations, civil unrest, wars, and military standoffs, such as the current standoff between **India** and **Pakistan,** are the likely results of these conflicts. These conflicts are unresolved largely due to lack of investment by both the international community and the nations involved.

CIVIL WARS

Civil wars--battles within nations for control of the government--have been common across the world and throughout history. In **Afghanistan,** a slightly brighter chapter has started that offers a ray of hope for a nation ravaged by civil war for over two decades. A new interim government under the leadership of Chairman Hamid Karzai, a moderate Afghanistani Pasthun leader who has studied in the United States and **India,** has taken office. The new administration consists primarily of erstwhile opposition Northern Alliance leaders who fought against the Taliban with the support of Iran, Russia, India, and the Central Asian republics. The Taliban (literally, students of knowledge) were a group of ethnic Pashtun students studying in a *madarassa* (a local religious school for the poor). However, they studied a particularly skewered and limited interpretation of Islam, and in the mid-1990s with the help of the **Pakistani** government and intelligence services, took over the Afghani capital, Kabul, and soon thereafter controlled most of the country. They were very parochial in their thinking and banned all forms of entertainment including listening to music and flying kites. The Taliban government, largely due to American involvement and international pressure resulting in the withdrawal of military and other support by Pakistan, was defeated in the fall of 2002 by a U.S.-led military coalition. Fighting is still currently occuring in some provinces of Eastern Afghanistan. **Tajikistan,** the poorest and most fragile country in the Central Asian region, has become a crucial ally of the U.S. in its war against terrorism. It has received U.S.$3 million from the U.S. in relief aid following a very serious drought that hit the nation in 2000. In 1997, the government and opposition leaders signed a peace treaty that ended a five-year civil war. Fortunately, the peace treaty has been successful so far, and has survived shocks such as the April 2001 assassination of Deputy Interior Minister Khabib Sanginov.[1]

BORDER DISPUTES BETWEEN TWO COUNTRIES

During the past several decades, many countries in Asia have brokered or attempted to broker bilateral agreements and compromises resolving historic boundary disputes. In December 1999, **China** and **Vietnam** signed a long-awaited bilateral treaty on the land border between the two countries. The China-Vietnam border stretches over 1,100 kilometers and was the cause of a brief but bloody border war in 1979. China and Vietnam resumed diplomatic relations in 1991 and have since tried to resolve their land and maritime border disputes. China, however, continues to have boundary disputes with **India** over two small sections of their border, with Russia over parts of its northern border despite a 1997 agreement,

with **Tajikistan** over most of their border, and with **North Korea** over a 33-kilometer section of their border. China and India made some progress during Indian Foreign Minister Jaswant Singh's visit to China in the spring of 2002, during which both sides exchanged maps and agreed to ongoing consultations aimed at a resolution of the border dispute.

TERRITORIES CLAIMED BY TWO OR MORE COUNTRIES

In Asia, the post-colonial independence movement and the post-World War II reinstatement of governments that had been in exile created many territories claimed by two or more parties, especially island chains. The Spratly Islands, in the South China Sea, are the focus of conflict for no fewer than six governments. This chain of uninhabited islands contains potentially large-scale suboceanic oil deposits. The strategic importance of the sea lanes and pressure from multinational oil companies further complicate the territorial dispute. In March 2000, however, the Association of South East Asian Nations (ASEAN) and **China** agreed to a common "code of conduct," paving the way for eventual resolution of the conflict. Another example of a dispute in this category is the conflict between **India** and **Pakistan** over the state of **Jammu and Kashmir.** India and Pakistan had a much-ballyhooed bilateral summit in summer of 2001 in Agra, India, site of the Taj Mahal. Intensive settlement talks were unsuccessful and even failed to produce a joint statement.

SELF-GOVERNMENT MOVEMENTS
WITHIN A STATE

Movements for autonomy and independence (in the form of an autonomous region or a separate, independent state) may be based on four claims:

* The right to equality and nondiscrimination;
* The right of minorities to preserve and develop their own culture;
* The right of indigenous populations to preserve their traditions, as well as their special rights to land and its natural resources; and
* The right of peoples to self-determination.

At the heart of this debate is a conflict between a state's territorial integrity and a people's right to full independence and secession. The anti-terror campaign has further polarized this debate due to fears of state heavy-handedness and maligning of genuine independence movements. The ethnic and cultural diversity present in Asian countries further complicates this type of conflict. The situations in **Tibet** and **East Timor** are two contrasting examples of conflicts in this category. Tibet remains under Chinese control, defined as part of mainland **China**, while East Timor has recently transitioned from a U.N.-supervised transitional regime to a democratic regime under the formerly imprisoned guerilla leader Xanana Gusmao (*see* "Asia and the United Nations").

SOVEREIGNTY DISPUTES BETWEEN
TWO GOVERNMENTS

In Asia, the current disputes over **Chinese** and **Korean** sovereignty can be classified in this category. Both Beijing and Taipei claim to be the legitimate governments of China. Beijing also claims sovereignty over **Taiwan**, regarding the island as a "renegade" province. Taiwan, on the other hand, relinquished its territorial claim over the mainland in 1993 and is temporarily suspended in the status quo.

China's economic ties with the U.S. have continued to improve; however, due to a crisis over a U.S. spy plane shot down in April 2002 over the South China Sea,[2] and separately, an increased influence of Taiwan on the U.S. government, relations between the two countries have strained slightly. The Taiwanese population, though, has not reached a consensus on whether to support reunification or independence. Taipei's official policy is that reunification with the mainland will be considered as soon as the mainland is democratic and egalitarian enough for reunification to occur. Beijing continues to threaten the island with a military invasion to discourage Taipei from declaring independence.

The conflict on the **Korean** Peninsula is similar, but with a few major differences. Following World War II, the Korean Peninsula was divided into two countries. The communist North and the democratic South have remained officially at war, with the 1953 armistice creating the Demilitarized Zone (DMZ). Both Koreas support eventual reunification, however North Korea maintains a territorial claim over the entire peninsula. Korea, in short, is a "divided nation," much like Germany prior to reunification. Pyongyang and Seoul have separate U.N. delegations, and most of the international community has diplomatic ties with both countries.

In early June 1999, North and South Korea agreed to hold vice minister-level talks to discuss an exchange of visits of separated families in return for South Korean aid to North Korea. The talks stalled later that month when the countries' navies exchanged gunfire in the Yellow Sea after a North Korean torpedo boat entered South Korean waters. North Korea's test firing of missiles further strained South Korean president Kim Dae Jung's "Sunshine Policy" of engagement. Despite continuing economic aid from Seoul, the capital of the South, to alleviate the famine in the North, relations remained chilly. On June 12, 2000, Presidents Kim Dae Jung and Kim Jong Il grabbed international headlines with a historic inter-Korea summit in Pyongyang, the capital of North Korea, raising the hope of reunification in the near future. South Korea's interest in aiding North Korea, and reuniting, has continued energetically.

The recent branding by U.S. President George W. Bush of North Korea, along with Iran and Iraq, as part of an "axis of evil," has hurt relations slightly between the U.S. and North Korea. They have not, however, worsened North-South Korean relations in any significant way.

ARMED INTERFERENCE IN NEIGHBORING COUNTRIES' AFFAIRS

From 1989 onwards, and with the defeat of the Soviet army, **Pakistan** kept up an active intelligence and military support network for militia and fundamentalist groups in **Afghanistan.** During this time, it also engaged in a strategy of armed infiltration and interference in **Indian-administered Kashmir.** In late September and early October 2001, due to U.S. pressure, Pakistan dropped its support of the Taliban and officially minimized its activities in Afghanistan. In early January 2002, owing to Indian and U.S. pressure, Pakistani President Pervez Musharraf announced a reversal of course towards India and a decision to stand firm against terrorist networks involved in fighting in Kashmir. A real and transparent crackdown remains to be seen.

POLITICAL CHANGE IN ASIA

In the post-World War II era, the developing world's most dynamic efforts on behalf of political stability occurred in Asia. In East Asia, the world's largest communist state, **China,** has emerged as a global economic and political force. **Japan,** weakened in the early 1990s by years of recession and government corruption, rose once again, leading the recovery from the financial crisis. Under Prime Minister Junichiro Koizumi, Japan has shown cautious optimism about becoming stronger economically. In South Asia, **India** claims its place as the world's largest democracy, a large consumer market, and one of the region's strongest information technology players. Throughout the region, 2001 was a year of political change. The future of the region's political systems rests upon the outcomes of upcoming elections and referendums, transitions in leadership, and the growing dominance of regional powers.

ELECTIONS AND REFERENDUMS

In 1999, **Australia** voted to retain the British monarch as head of state rather than declare a republic with a president as head of state. Surprisingly, Prime Minister John Howard advocated a "no" vote. The failed vote for a republic was the result of disagreement on the form of the republic. Many wanted a direct vote, rather than delegating parliament to choose the president. The referendum has left the nation monarchist in form but republican in spirit. Australia has continued on that route into 2002. However, it must be noted that although the British monarch is still the head of state, the title is merely ceremonial.

In June 1999, **South Korea's** President Kim Dae Jung's Millennium Democratic Party (MDP), formerly the National Congress for New Politics Party, lost the parliamentary by-elections in Seoul, giving the opposition Grand National Party (GNP) a greater number of seats in the National Assembly. In the April 2000 general election, the Grand National Party took control of the Assembly, with the ruling MDP winning 115 seats to the GNP's 133. In September 2001, the South Korea cabinet quit and left the government in disarray. The economic crisis and low projections for growth lurked behind this weighty political crisis. In a special election held in October, the opposition Grand National Party won all three of the available parliamentary seats. President Kim, whose term ends in 2003, took responsibility for the loss and stepped down as leader of the Millennium Democratic Party.

Women politicians have always held leadership positions in Asian politics, in fact more so than their Western counterparts. In **Bangladesh,** confrontation between the ruling and opposition parties and the two women who lead them--Prime Minister Sheikh Hasina Wajed and opposition leader Begum Khaleda Zia—led to a hotly contested election, held in October 2001, that Begum Zia won with a two thirds majority. Begum Zia's election, as feared by many regional analysts, has been accompanied by increased intolerance towards Hindu minorities in Bangladesh, and an overall radicalization of Bangladesh in general. Bangladesh's largest Islamic party, Jamaat-i-Islami, has vowed to turn the country into an Islamic republic, introducing Koranic laws to replace the constitution. Soon after President Zia's election, a wave of migration of Hindu Bangladeshis into the Indian state of West Bengal took place due to religious persecution. **Sri Lankan** President Chandrika Kumaratunga was reelected in December 1999, despite a failed assassination attempt three days prior to election day. In February 2002, the government of newly elected Prime Minister Ranil Wickremesinghe agreed to a truce with the Tamil separatist leader Velupillai Prabhakaran, which was brokered with the help of the Norwegian government. At the time of this writing, a fragile peace was holding and future talks were expected to take place between the Singhalese majority government and the rebel forces, known as the Liberation Tigers of Tamil Eelam (LTTE).

THE ROAD TOWARD STABILITY IN ASIA

In **Myanmar** (formerly known as Burma), the ruling military government continued to consolidate its grip on power, clamping down on the opposition National League for Democracy (NLD) and its leader, Nobel Peace Prize laureate Aung San Suu Kyi, who was released from house arrest in mid-2002 due to Western pressure. Although the NLD is withering under heavy pressure from the military, the freeing of Aung Kyi may lead to some political change.

In April 1999, **Cambodia** was admitted as the newest member of ASEAN. With the coalition government formed in November 1998 still intact, Cambodia is beginning a long road of development. The government of Prime Minister Hun Sen announced plans in late 2001 to turn thirty-six houses of former Khmer Rouge leaders in the group's last stronghold of Anlong Veng, a frontier town near the Thai border, into a museum to attract more tourists to the country. Eighty percent of the country's 5.2 million registered voters turned out in the first election for local leaders, held in February 2002. The election was for heads of 1,621 communes to replace appointed officials, some of whom had held their jobs for more than twenty years.

In recent years, **Vietnam** has been successful in reestablishing and improving relations with major world powers. In 1995, U.S.-Vietnamese relations were normalized with the reopening of the U.S. embassy in Hanoi. On December 31, 1999, Prime Minister Phan Van Khai signed a Sino-Vietnamese treaty with China, ending a decades-long border conflict. In June 2001, Nguyen Van An was unanimously nominated by the Politburo to become Chairman of the National Assembly and was elected on June 28, 2001, replacing Nong Duc Manh, who was promoted to the top job as head of the Communist Party. Some progress followed, such as the approval by the increasingly influential National Assembly of a constitutional amendment that gives it the power to hold no-confidence votes and to dismiss government leaders, including the president and prime minister.

On November 30, 1999, **Malaysian** Prime Minister Mahathir Mohamad was elected to a fifth term. A growing opposition, however, comprised of Islamic fundamentalists and supporters of former deputy Prime Minister Anwar Ibrahim, threatens the ruling National Front coalition. Ibrahim was sentenced to six years in jail after being convicted of abuse of power. Interestingly, in August 2001, more than 2,000 ethnic Chinese community leaders pledged their support for Prime Minister Mahathir Mohamad. With his support among ethnic Malays slipping, backing from the Chinese is increasingly important for the prime minister to remain in power.

Indonesia underwent a significant change in leadership. Following the conflict in **East Timor,** the quirky, moderate Muslim leader Abdurrahman Wahid was elected president on October 20, 1999, replacing former President B.J. Habibie. In July 2001, Parliament removed Mr. Wahid and replaced him with Mrs. Megawati Sukarnoputri. A majority of parliamentary factions endorsed a plan to shift from a complex two-step electoral formula to a new system of direct presidential elections. Lawmakers said they expected the plan to be adopted in time for the next election, in 2004.

On October 12, 1999, a bloodless coup ousted former **Pakistani** Prime Minister Nawaz Sharif

7.2 SELECTED CONFLICTS IN ASIA

SPRATLY ISLANDS

Type of conflict: Disputed territory claimed by various countries

Parties involved: Brunei, China, Malaysia, Philippines, Taiwan, and Vietnam

Summary of conflict: China, Taiwan, and Vietnam each claim all of the disputed island chain called the Spratly Islands. Malaysia and the Philippines claim several but not all of the islands. Brunei claims one submerged reef. China and Taiwan assert the same historical claim that the islands have been Chinese territory since ancient times. In 1933, the French colonial authorities in Vietnam established the first effective administration over the islands, leading the South Vietnamese government to assert its claim in 1957. The government of the unified Vietnam subsequently took over the claims. Between 1939 and 1945, Japan occupied the islands, turning them into submarine bases. A Filipino national discovered several of the islands in 1947, claimed ownership, and then transferred his claims to the Philippines government in 1971. The more recent claims of Malaysia and Brunei are based on the extension of their continental shelf.

Current situation: A military conflict between China and the Philippines nearly erupted in February 1995, after the Philippines discovered Chinese-built concrete structures on a reef claimed by the Philippines. In March 2000, ASEAN and China agreed to a common "code of conduct" for disputed territorial claims in the South China Sea. It governed handling disputes; ways to enhance contacts and confidence; fields of cooperation covering marine, environmental protection, and scientific research; and continued talks to conclude the document. According to the Chinese delegation, however, the agreement would not be concluded in the foreseeable future. The "code of conduct" has, de facto, become an agreement by concerned countries to "not talk about the conflict."

SRI LANKA

Type of conflict: Civil war

Parties involved: The government of Sri Lanka and the Liberation Tigers of Tamil Eelam (LTTE)

Summary of conflict: Ceylon, a former British colony, became independent in 1948 and was renamed the Republic of Sri Lanka in 1972. Communal violence directed mainly at the country's Tamil population broke out eleven years later, sparking a separatist war in the northern and eastern provinces, which continued into the new millennium. Participants in the Tamil uprising, led by the Liberation Tigers of Tamil Eelam (LTTE), have been accused of terrorist acts, including the assassination of former Premier Ranasinghe Premadasa in 1988; numerous suicide bombings; and an attempt to assassinate President Chandrika Kumaratunga in December 1999. In 1995, President Kumaratunga offered the LTTE a generous devolution package as an alternative to separate statehood and achieved a temporary truce. The ceasefire held for 100 days, but the rebels bombed a Colombo market in August 1995 and a prolonged military campaign ensued.

Current situation: Sri Lankan Ranil Wickremasinghe, with help of the government of Norway, has been on a mission to achieve peace in the embattled island country. Several peace initiatives and ceasefire announcements by both sides have produced hope for peace. The Prime Minister recently visited Jaffna, an area in Sri Lanka formerly considered too dangerous for the Prime Minister to travel to. As of this writing, Ranil Wickemasinghe has gone to India to garner support from the Indians in an attempt to sustain the peace process.

TIBET

Type of conflict: Self-government movement

Parties involved: China and the Tibetan Government in Exile

Summary of conflict: In October 1950, China's People's Liberation Army (PLA) invaded Tibet. The fourteenth Dalai Lama, leader of a theocratic society, was forced to sign a seventeen-point agreement recognizing China's sovereign claim to Tibet. In the following years, China imposed state communist policies of collectivization, socialist transformation, and Han (the Chinese ethnic majority) settlement on Tibet. In 1959, in an uprising in Lhasa, the people declared Tibetan independence. The PLA subdued the revolt. The Dalai Lama fled to India, where he established the Tibetan Government in Exile. Since then, the Dalai Lama has campaigned internationally for Tibetan self-determination. Accusations of human rights abuses by the Chinese government in Tibet and support from international celebrities placed Tibet high on the international agenda in the late 1990s. The Government in Exile bases its claim to self-rule on cultural, religious, and social distinctness. The Dalai Lama asserts that the Chinese government is a repressive regime that denies Tibetans the rights of a people and culture; Tibetan self-rule must be granted in order to preserve the Tibetan people and their right of self-determination. According to Beijing, China's claim over Tibet is based on conquest and territorial integrity; Tibet is a domestic matter, and any international involvement would be a violation of China's sovereignty and rights as a nation.

Current situation: Sino-Tibetan relations remain at a standstill. Beijing is adamant in its stance, fearing that any loosening in Chinese control of Tibet may spur self-government movements in other parts of western China, such as Xinjiang. Relations between the Dalai Lama and Beijing were further strained in January 2000 by the defection of the Karmapa Lama (selected by Beijing in 1992) to the Dalai Lama's camp in India.

(Sources follow on page 110.)

and his government. Army chief Pervez Musharraf established a new regime, and its cabinet was sworn in on November 6, 1999. Since then, General Musharraf has consolidated his position further, and in June 2001 also assumed the presidency by asking the figurehead president, Rafiq Tarar, to step down. Since September 2001, he has had to become a reluctant U.S. ally and severed ties with the Taliban under enormous pressure.

EMERGING REGIONAL POWERS: CHINA, INDIA, AND JAPAN

The future of **China's** domestic politics will rest on the change in leadership at the Sixteenth National People's Congress in 2003, when President Jiang is constitutionally obliged to step down as head of state. The man to watch will be his successor, Vice President Hu Jintao. Interestingly, Hu will also take over Jiang's more crucial post as Communist Party Chief, preventing the country from heading for another Deng Xiaoping-style gerontocracy. To foreign and domestic scholars, Mr. Hu is a political cipher. Even by the secretive standards of Beijing politics, his personal leanings are largely unrevealed on the great issues of the day, including the pace of political change at home and China's ultimate goals abroad.

On July 1, 1997, **Hong Kong** reverted to Chinese rule after nearly a century of British colonial administration. Beijing's next, and most cherished, reunification goal is **Taiwan.** Chinese foreign relations, however, reached a low point in 1999. In March, U.S. allegations of Chinese spying on nuclear secrets began to emerge. The greatest damage to Sino-American ties occurred on May 7, 1999, when U.S./NATO planes acciden-

Security Council Unanimously Adopts Wide-Ranging Anti-Terrorism Resolution 1373, Acts to Counter Financing of Terrorist Activities, September 28, 2001. (UN/DPI Photo)

tally bombed the Chinese embassy in Belgrade, killing three people. On July 22, 1999, Beijing outlawed the Falun Gong, a group of members that engage in spiritual practices similar to yoga. In April 2001, a major row between the two countries occurred when Chinese fighter jet pilots downed a U.S. spy plane. The row ended with the 24-person U.S. crew returned harmless, but China refused to allow the U.S. plane to fly over its borders, citing national pride as the reason. The plane was disassembled and returned to the U.S. in boxes. The U.S. government's problems with China have had wider repercussions in that they have led to a political climate much more favorable to closer relationships with India on the part of the U.S. As one expert put it: "One of the least-noted changes in the Bush administration's policy toward Asia has been its approach to India. India's large size, its increasingly dynamic economy, its nuclear capability, and its determination to play a greater role in international affairs outside the subcontinent make it increasingly relevant to U.S. policy in the Asia-Pacific region."[3]

The greatest threat to the future of China, however, is the change in Taiwanese domestic politics.[4] On March 19, 2000, Taiwan elected a new president. In the week before Taiwan's election, Beijing issued a stream of threats about the possibility of an invasion if a pro-independence candidate were elected. Undeterred by the threats, Taiwanese voters elected the pro-independence, Democratic Progressive Party candidate Chen Shui-bian as their new president, ending more than half a century of Nationalist rule. Chen has agreed to refrain from declaring outright independence for the time being. Soon after the election, riots erupted in the streets of Taipei, leading to the resignation of President Lee Tenghui as head of the Nationalist Party. Chen called for a "peace summit" with China in a move interpreted as a conciliatory gesture toward Beijing. Jiang Zemin spurned Chen's overtures, demanding that Taiwan recognize its position as part of China as a precondition for talks. Chen has rejected such a precondition. Taiwan remains a thorny issue between China and the U.S., with the U.S. continuing arms trade and export to Taiwan and China wanting to integrate Taiwan into the mainland.[5]

In **India** in March 1998, the Hindu revivalist Bharatiya Janata Party (BJP) formed a coalition government headed by Atal Behari Vajpayee. During the following year, the BJP-led coalition faced increasing opposition from the Congress Party, rejuvenated by its new leader, Sonia Gandhi, the widow of former prime minister Rajiv Gandhi. The Vajpayee government fell in April 1999, after only thirteen months in office, when Jayalalitha Jayaram, leader of the All-India Party, withdrew her party's support. In May 1999, war nearly erupted with **Pakistan** in Kargil, a region in the Indian-administered part of the disputed state of **Jammu** and **Kashmir.** By July, it was evident that India had regained its positions and prevailed in Kargil. The incumbent government's deft handling of the war and wartime diplomacy boosted Vajpayee's popularity leading into the fall elections.

In the October 1999 elections, the BJP-led eighteen-party National Democratic Alliance (NDA) won 296 seats in the new 545-member lower house of parliament. The main opposition Congress Party won only 112 seats, its lowest tally in its 52-year existence. The new government led by Vajpayee called for unilateral cease-fires in Jammu and Kashmir, then in a surprise move, invited General Musharraf of Pakistan to India for talks. Although the talks failed, the diplomatic initiative won Vajpayee much recognition in the international community as a man of peace. After September 11, 2001, the Indian government, known for taking the most non-controversial position diplomatically, again surprised everyone by pledging support immediately for the U.S. war on terrorism. In early 2002, a year after a very successful rehabilitation program in the Indian state of Gujarat following the massive 6.9 earthquake in January 2001, Gujarat again appeared in the news. Hindu-Muslim riots started after a train car full of Hindus was burned down by a religious mob. However, the days thereafter saw brutal atrocities committed on Muslims in Gujarat, with the state government and police acting many times as silent witnesses. Tensions, although less intense, have continued with many Muslims still not being able to return to their homes. These recent communal riots in the state of Gujarat in India, and tensions with Pakistan over terrorism in Kashmir, have proven to be a test for Vajpayee's government.

The conservative Liberal Democratic Party (LDP) has ruled **Japan** nearly continuously since 1955. However, the future of Japan, and of the LDP-led coalition government, depends on the resolution of several domestic issues, including economic recovery and restructuring of the country's corporate and financial systems. Japan, still the world's second largest economy, continues to be in the doldrums.

In April 2001, Junichiro Koizumi became the new prime minister after winning support from the ruling coalition. Heightened fears about a possible threat to security from **North Korea** have led to the passage of guidelines that include plans for starting joint research with the U.S. on a missile-defense system, increasing spending on the military for the first time in three years, and plans for launching four spy satellites. The defense guidelines were the first upgrade in the U.S.-Japan security alliance since 1978.

FINANCIAL HEALTH: RECOVERING FROM THE CRISIS, AND AFTER

Between 1970 and 1997, many Asian countries experienced unprecedented economic growth. **Hong Kong, Korea, Singapore,** and **Taiwan** were labeled high-performing Asian economies (HPAEs) and newly industrialized economies (NIEs). What made the growth unusual was the combination of high per capita income growth, low-income inequality, and high productivity growth. Many economists attributed the so-called Asian Miracle to rapid capital accumulation and pragmatic government intervention in industrial policies. A combination of other factors, including high domestic savings rates, good primary and secondary education, long-term technocratic planning, dynamic agricultural sectors, close government-business links, and the introduction of new technologies, are also believed to have contributed to the region's growth.[6]

Somewhere between 1997 and 1998, optimism and sustained economic prosperity suddenly halted. What began as a currency crisis in **Thailand** during the summer of 1997 quickly evolved into one of the greatest financial collapses since the 1929 Great Depression. The crisis exposed a surprising vulnerability on the part of many Asian economies to regional crisis contagion. The collapse of the Thai currency, the *baht,* spread throughout the region, causing a massive loss of funds from domestic financial markets. Drastically falling exchange rates and heavy drops in the stock market led to stunted growth and a recession. In 1998, the Southeast Asian region suffered a 10.5 percent drop in real GDP growth, and the East Asian region experienced a 5.5 percent decrease in growth. Only **India,** with its gradual opening of the economy and rapid remedial measures, was able to escape the worse effects of the crises. However, broadly speaking, the region has witnessed severe economic, political, and social damage caused by the economic meltdown. As an immediate international response to the crisis, a number of rescue packages with an attached major reform agenda from the International Monetary Fund (IMF), the World Bank, and the Asian Development Bank were produced for the countries in trouble. The effectiveness of these remedies and reforms, however, has been questioned.[7]

According to the Asian Development Bank (ADB), the recovery has been driven by increased industrial sector activity and improved agricultural sector performance. Economist Paul Krugman attributed the recovery to government reimposed monetary stability. With the exception of the Hong Kong dollar and Chinese *yuan,* all regional currencies had to be devalued due to the unsustainable current account deficits that resulted from capital flight. The future of the East Asian economies and the sustainability of the recent recovery will depend upon the region's progress in restructuring its financial sectors.

In **South Korea,** the government restored confidence in the banking sector by pumping in more than U.S.$45 billion for recapitalization of banks and by selling bankrupt banks, such as Seoul Bank, to foreign firms. When Daewoo, the country's second-largest *chaebol* (the Korean word for the large domestically owned conglomerates that have dominated Korean industries since the 1960s), was declared insolvent in the summer of 1999, the government took over the group and arranged the sale of its individual units. The only guarantee against another crisis in Korea is economic restructuring.

In **Hong Kong**, the stock and futures exchanges merged on March 6, 2000 into a single entity, the Hong Kong Exchanges and Clearing Limited (HKEx). The IMF has recognized Singapore, along with South Korea, Hong Kong, and Taiwan, the four Asian tigers, as developed countries since 1997.

China and India's relatively closed financial markets have insulated their economies from the effects of the crisis. The explosive growth rate China experienced in the 1980s has tapered off due to the diminishing effects of expansionary public expenditure policies. The key long-term challenge facing the government is to implement structural reforms in state-owned enterprises and the banking sector, improve the overall legal framework governing the economy, and increase domestic demand. Also crucial to China's economic future are trade reforms. In 1999 and early 2000, China's trade agenda was dominated by its efforts to join the World Trade Organization (WTO). China's 14-year-long quest to join the WTO was sidetracked in April 1999 when U.S. President Bill Clinton rejected a U.S.-China agreement for China's WTO membership. In November 2000, a last-minute deal between China and the U.S. was reached. In the past year, China succeeded in signing all 135 required bilateral agreements, and in November 2001, with much fanfare, China's entry into the WTO was announced. This event provides a major impetus for trade-related economic growth in China.

Taiwan's recovery is mainly due to a rapid increase in exports to other Asian economies, most notably mainland China. The government is currently attempting to accelerate trade reforms in order to satisfy requirements to join the WTO. Taiwan's membership was only to be considered once China had entered the WTO. However,

with China achieving entry in early 2002, Taiwan too was awarded entry into the WTO.

In **Malaysia**, Prime Minister Mahathir Mohamed imposed capital controls and restrictions on the movement of foreign investment funds, pegging the exchange rate to the U.S. dollar. The controls increased stability, allowed interest rates to fall, and decreased the current account deficit by making exports relatively cheaper. Malaysia, turning down IMF support, has surprisingly looked good in its recovery and has raised questions about the IMF's role in economic rescue and reconstruction programs. **Indonesia**, with the help of the IMF, undertook an ambitious reform program aimed at restoring sound health to the banking system. Restructurings of banking systems, however, were marred by the political turmoil caused by **East Timor** and by a major bank embezzlement scandal. The **Philippines** maintained macroeconomic stability by scrambling to secure more than U.S.$1.8 billion in loans to cover the budget deficit in 1999. In Thailand, after two full years of contraction, the economy showed the first signs of recovery during the first quarter of 1999. The government's fiscal stimulus program and a more relaxed monetary policy also contributed to Thailand's economic growth.

After suffering its longest recession ever, the **Japanese** economy posted a 7.9 percent growth rate in the first three months of 2000. Mergers rather than breakups have dominated the news. E-commerce has also played a major role. According to the government, while overall retail sales fell 4.4 percent in 1998, Internet-based sales doubled. Junichiro Koizumi became Japan's prime minister in early 2000 on promises of economic growth and reform. The future economic health of the region depends upon the pace of reform.

Population growth, along with the manner of demographical development, is one phenomenon that not only threatens to place severe restraints on Asia's public services but also provides evidence of the region's political and economic gains over the past few decades. According to its 2001 census, **India** has become the second country after **China** to have a population of over one bil-

7.3 GROWTH RATE OF GDP OF ASIAN AND PACIFIC COUNTRIES (EXPRESSED AS A %)

DMC	1995	1996	1997	1998	1999	2000
Afghanistan	•	•	•	•	•	
Azerbaijan	−11.8	1.3	8.8	10.6	7.4	11.4
Bangladesh	4.9	4.6	5.4	5.2	4.9	5.9
Bhutan	7.4	6.0	7.3	5.5	5.9	6.1
Cambodia	8.4	3.5	3.7	1.5	6.9	5.4
China, People's Rep. of	10.5*	9.6*	8.8*	7.8*	7.1*	8.0
Cook Islands	−4.4	−0.1	−3.9	−3.2	5.8	9.8
Fiji Islands	2.5	3.1	−0.9	1.4	9.6	−9.3
Hong Kong, China	3.9	4.5	5.0	−5.3	3.0	10.5
India	4.2	8.1	4.8	6.6	6.4	5.2
Indonesia	8.2	7.8	4.7	−13.1	0.8	4.8
Kazakhstan	−8.2	0.8	1.3	−1.7	3.0	9.0
Kiribati	3.5	4.3	1.0	7.3	2.3*	−3.8
Korea, Rep. of	8.9	6.7	5.0	−6.7	10.9	8.8
Kyrgyz Republic	−5.2	6.9	9.9	2.0	3.8	5.2
Lao, PDR	7.0	6.9	6.9	4.0	7.3	5.7
Malaysia	9.8	10.0	7.3	−7.4	6.1	8.3
Maldives	7.8	8.8	11.2	7.9	8.5	5.6
Marshall Islands	9.8	−15.9	−9.4	1.1	0.1	−0.9
Micronesia, Fed. States of	3.5	−1.5	−4.8	−1.7	1.3	2.5
Mongolia	6.3	2.4	4.0	3.5	3.2	1.1
Myanmar	6.9	6.4	5.7	5.8	10.9	•
Nauru	•	•	•	•	•	•
Nepal	3.5	5.3	5.0	3.0	4.4	5.8
Pakistan	5.1	5.0	1.2	1.2	3.7	4.4
Papua New Guinea	−3.3	7.7	−3.9	−3.8	7.6	0.8
Philippines	4.7	5.8	5.2	−0.6	3.4	4.0
Samoa	6.4	11.6	0.8	2.5	3.1	7.3
Singapore	8.0	7.6	8.5	0.1	5.9	9.9
Solomon Islands	13.1	2.5	−1.0	0.8	−1.4	−14.5
Sri Lanka	5.5	3.8*	6.4	4.7	4.3	6.0
Taipei, China	6.4	6.1	6.7	4.6	5.4	6.0
Tajikistan	−12.5*	−4.4*	1.7*	5.3*	3.7*	5.0
Thailand	9.3	5.9	−1.4	−10.8	4.2*	4.4
Tonga	3.2	−0.2	0.6	2.5	4.6	6.2
Turkmenistan	−7.2*	−6.7*	−11.4*	7.0*	16.0*	17.0
Tuvalu	−5.0	10.3	3.5	14.9	3.0*	3.0
Uzbekistan	−0.9	1.7	5.2	4.3	4.3	4.0
Vanuatu	0.0	2.5	1.5	2.2	−2.5	2.8
Vietnam	9.5	9.3	8.2	5.8	4.8	6.8

SOURCE: ADB, Asian Development Outlook 2001.
<http://www.adb.org/Documents/Books/Key_Indicators/2001/default.asp>

lion. With a child born every two seconds, India is expected to overtake China in population, home to 1.25 billion people, by 2012. Half of the world's population lives in Asia and a third of it in China and India alone. Six of the ten most populated countries in the world are located in Asia.[8] However, population growth must be understood in context. A more useful indicator to look at is the breakdown of the population in terms of age groups. The comparison between the 1990 and 2000 population breakdowns show an increasing age 65+ population that will put more strain on already strained Asian public services.[9]

In 2000, to face this challenge more effectively, India adopted a National Population Policy which states that in the short run, it will meet the contraception and health care needs of every citizen; in the medium run by 2010, bring the fertility rate to replacement levels; and by 2045 arrive at a stable population. However, to be successful, the policies must focus on the four major states with high population growth, namely Bihar, Uttar Pradesh, Rajasthan, and Madhya Pradesh. The newly appointed National Commission on Population will advise the government on the implementation of this policy. China is now seeing the effects of its family planning policies, most notably the one-child policy that began in 1980. The one-child policy made it illegal for parents to have more than one child. The success of that policy is questionable, however, as it has not been applied universally, especially in rural areas where ethnic minorities are allowed two or three children. Reports of forced abortions and other such human rights abuses have also called into question the ethicality of the policy. Starting in 2000, Beijing relaxed its policy in urban areas such as Beijing and Shanghai, where couples are now allowed to have two children. China's population is still growing as the effects of birth control take more than one generation to feed through fully; population growth in China is not expected to go into reverse until after 2050.

Elsewhere in Asia, development in population control and family planning continues. Ending a 40-year ban, the **Japanese** government now allows the sale of the contraceptive pill. **Pakistan,** meanwhile, has launched a poster and television advertising campaign to cut a 2.6 percent annual rise in population. In many parts of Asia, women are having fewer children due to improved education and health care, along with increased access to family planning. Still, the highest rates of growth are occurring in poorer countries, further widening the gap between developing and developed countries. Also, there are fears that the Asian financial crisis has reversed the gains made in the region--smaller family size, higher living standards, and improvements in the status of women--during the last three decades of the twentieth century, especially in Southeast Asia. Along with the population time bomb is another problem working in the opposite direction: HIV/AIDS.[10] The virus has begun to spread throughout the region, with the U.N. estimating that over seven million Asians are HIV-positive and that half of the new infections are in the 15-to-24-year-old age group.[11]

HUMAN RIGHTS

Conflict in Asia has resulted in a massive refugee problem for the region. In Afghanistan, hundreds of thousands were displaced following the U.S.-led attacks last fall. Large populations of internally displaced people also exist in **Sri Lanka, Myanmar,** and **India.** More than 100,000 Burmese refugees arrived in other Asian countries, including **Thailand** and **Bangladesh.**

At the U.N. World Conference Against Racism in September 2001, Asian activists succeeded in getting international coverage on their campaign against caste discrimination.[12] Human rights groups were shocked when the Commission on Human Rights failed to issue a resolution condemning China for its human rights violations when convening in April 2002. Various human rights groups, including Human Rights Watch, have criticized China for its arbitrary arrests and executions, suppression of free speech, and censorship of the media.[13]

7.4 ASIA AND THE INTERNET

The digital divide between the urban and rural, and between the developed and developing worlds continues to be a problem. Nowhere is this more interestingly being explored than in India, Asia's software giant and the biggest exporter of technical human capital. The Indian scene is bubbling with Internet cafes and kiosks at every street corner although office and home connectivity, while easily attainable, is still painfully slow. Over the last two years, projects to lay fiber optic lines across the country have been undertaken. But illiteracy in villages poses a great problem to usability of computers and knowledge access on the Internet. To confront that, scientists from the Indian Institute of Science in Bangalore have recently invented something called the Simputer. The Simputer, short for simple computer, is a graphics and audio based computer with vernacular languages and symbols that is beginning to revolutionize the way villages' access to content on the Internet will occur. It is based on natural userfaces utilizing sight, touch, and audio. It is priced at only U.S.$200, roughly, which is divisible among villagers through distributed Smartcards.

India is moving fast and focusing on software and technology as the driving engine for the growth of its economy. Governments in the region are now exploring new industrial policies in high-tech manufacturing and construction of cyberports. The Internet-user population in Asia, excluding Japan, rose to 21.8 million by the end of 1999, from 12.9 million the previous year. The volume of e-commerce in the region almost tripled, to U.S.$2.2 billion. The implications of an increasingly dominant Internet scene go beyond the economy. The unregulated freedom of communication the Internet provides has already brought about major changes in Asia's political life. The university network in Indonesia provided students with a potent tool for organizing protests against the regime of former President Suharto. The Internet later mobilized support for referendums in East Timor and Aceh. In China, the Internet emerged as a potentially unsettling political tool. On April 25, 1999, Beijing witnessed a gathering of 10,000 supporters of a semi-religious exercise group called Falun Gong. The protesters' sudden appearance shocked Beijing, causing the government to ban the group. The group was able to organize such a demonstration in part through the Internet, which by 1999 had reached over two million Chinese. China's exiled dissidents and pro-Tibetan supporters also took to the Web in their efforts to carry their messages inside the country and around the world. It was not a one-sided game. Increasingly cyber-savvy Chinese agents fought back by knocking out offending Web sites. Officials in China also claim to have the means to wage cyber-wars with enemies by hacking into government sites. Taiwan responded by creating an information-warfare unit. India, long known as a software giant, collaborated with the U.S. post-September 11, 2001 in providing the U.S.-led international coalition against terrorism with anti-cyberterrorism and Internet experts. During the 1960s, export-led growth launched the Asian economic miracle. Perhaps during this decade, Internet-led growth will catapult the entire Asian-Pacific region into another economic miracle.

SOURCES

"Asia Yearbook 2000" *Far Eastern Economic Review* December 1999.

Charlesworth, Peter. "Rebuilding Asia" *Business Week* 24 November 1999: 68.

"Economic Analysis and Research Division" *Asian Development Outlook* 1999 Update.

Oxford, England: Asian Development Bank, 1999.

Mathew, K.M., ed. "Science Scan 2001." *Manorama Yearbook 2002.* Kottayam, India: 2002.

PEACEKEEPING MISSIONS IN ASIA

Since 1948, there have been a total of 49 U.N. peacekeeping missions worldwide, with approximately one fifth occurring in Asia. Completed missions include peacekeeping operations in **Afghanistan** (UNGOMAP), **Cambodia** (UNAMIC and UNTAC), **India/Pakistan** border (UNIPOPM), **West New Guinea** (UNSF), and **Tajikstan** (UNMOT). The U.N.'s current peacekeeping operations in Asia are the United Nations Military Observer Group in India and Pakistan (UNMOGIP) and the United Nations Mission in Support of East Timor (UNMISET). In 1949, the United Military Observer Group in India and Pakistan (UNMOGIP) was created to supervise the cease-fire between India and Pakistan in the state of **Jammu** and **Kashmir**. Since renewed hostilities broke out in late 1971, UNMOGIP has monitored the cease-fire called for by the Security Council. The United Nations Mission in Support of East Timor (UNIMISET), created in May 2002, was established to provide assistance to the new country for a period of two and a half years, replacing UNAMET, the U.N. Mission in East Timor..

EAST TIMOR

Violence and civil unrest in **East Timor** in the last few years reignited several controversial and conflicting issues that have plagued international and domestic politics since the beginning of the modern era: the rights of peoples to self-determination, self-government, and secession; the territorial integrity and legitimacy of sovereign states; and the appropriateness of foreign intervention in a state's domestic politics. Do minorities and peoples in a sovereign state have the right to self-rule? If so, does that infringe upon the sovereign rights of the state? If a government refuses to grant autonomy or self-rule, does the interna-

tional community have the right to intervene? The East Timor conflict called into question all three of these issues. Its consequences were felt across the world. The conflict led to the fall from power of **Indonesian** President B.J. Habibie. **Australia,** the main contributor to the peacekeeping operation, faced a U.S.$1.7 billion debt burden and soured relations with Jakarta. ASEAN's failure to react created skepticism about the regional organization's potential ability as a political cooperative community. Finally, an independent East Timor has many implications for similar autonomous or indigenous movements in other areas across the region (Tibet and Xinjiang in **China,** Jammu and Kashmir in India/Pakistan, aboriginal movements in Australia, and other provinces in Indonesia facing ethnic conflicts).

The modern history of the conflict in East Timor starts in 1945. Upon **Japan's** surrender at the end of World War II, **Indonesia** declared independence from the Netherlands on August 17, 1945, and East Timor remained under Portuguese colonial rule. In 1960, the General Assembly added East Timor to the list of Non-Self-Governing Territories. Fourteen years later, in 1974, Portugal sought to establish a provisional government and a popular assembly to determine the status of East Timor. Civil war broke out between those who favored independence and those who advocated integration with Indonesia. Unable to control the situation, Portugal withdrew. Indonesia then intervened militarily and later integrated East Timor as its twenty-seventh province. The United Nations never recognized this integration, and both the Security Council and the General Assembly called for Indonesia's withdrawal.

Beginning in 1982, at the request of the General Assembly, successive Secretaries-General held regular talks with Indonesia and Portugal aimed at resolving the status of the territory. During this time, reports of Indonesian brutality, unequal

development, corruption, and unemployment reinforced East Timorese resistance to rule from Jakarta. In June 1998, Indonesia proposed a limited autonomy for East Timor within Indonesia. In light of this proposal, the talks made rapid progress and resulted in a series of agreements between Indonesia and Portugal, signed in New York on May 5, 1999. The two governments entrusted the U.N. Secretary-General with organizing and conducting a "popular consultation" in order to ascertain whether the East Timorese people accepted or rejected a special autonomy for East Timor within the unitary Republic of Indonesia. On June 11, 1999, the Security Coun-

cil established the United Nations Mission in East Timor (UNAMET). The May 5 agreements stipulated that, after the vote, UNAMET would oversee a transition period pending implementation of the decision of the East Timorese people.

On August 30, 1999, 98 percent of registered voters went to the polls and decided by a margin of 78.5 to 21.5 percent to reject the proposed autonomy and begin a process of transition toward independence. Following the announcement of the result, pro-integration militias, at times with the support of elements of the Indonesian security forces, launched a campaign of violence, looting, and arson throughout the entire

Returnees from West Timor to East Timor aboard a bus heading to the Dili Stadium transit center, 1999. (UN/UNHCR Photo: F. Pagetti)

territory. The Indonesian authorities did not respond effectively to the violence, despite clear commitments made under the May 5 agreements. Many East Timorese were killed and as many as 500,000 were displaced from their homes, about half leaving the territory.

In response to pressure from the international community to meet its responsibility to maintain security and order in the territory, President Habibie agreed on September 12, 1999, to accept the offer of assistance from the international community. The Security Council then authorized a multinational force (INTERFET) under a unified command structure headed by Australia to restore peace and security in East Timor, to protect and support UNAMET in carrying out its tasks, and, within force capabilities, to facilitate humanitarian assistance operations. The multinational force consisted of 8,000 peacekeepers, of whom Australians numbered about 5,000.

Following the outbreak of violence, the Indonesian armed forces and police began to withdraw from the territory, eventually leaving completely. Indonesian administrative officials also left. In September 1999, Indonesia and Portugal, at a meeting with the United Nations, reiterated their agreement for the transfer of authority in East Timor to the United Nations. They also agreed that ad hoc measures were required to fill the gap created by the early departure of the Indonesian civil authorities. UNAMET reestablished its headquarters in Dili, the provincial capital of East Timor, and immediately began efforts to restore the mission's logistical capacity.

On October 20, 1999, Abdurrahman Wahid was elected as Indonesia's fourth president, replacing B.J. Habibie. On October 25, the Security Council established the United Nations Transitional Administration in East Timor (UNTAET), an integrated, multidimensional peacekeeping operation fully responsible for the administration of East Timor during its transition to independence. UNTAET has overall responsibility for the administration of East Timor and is empowered to exercise all legislative and executive authority, including the administration of justice.

UNTAET's mandate consists of the following elements:

- To provide security and maintain law and order throughout the territory of East Timor;
- To establish an effective administration;
- To assist in the development of civil and social services;
- To ensure the coordination and delivery of humanitarian assistance, rehabilitation, and development assistance;
- To support capacity-building for self-government; and
- To assist in the establishment of conditions for sustainable development.

UNTAET has taken a number of steps toward meeting the objectives outlined in Security Council Resolution 1272, but the challenge remains formidable. One of UNTAET's major tasks is to seek urgent funding for economic development, which would promote social stability in East Timor. In December 1999, UNTAET created a local newspaper agency. In January 2000, the U.S. dollar was designated as the official East Timorese currency. On the military front, in February 2000, INTERFET began handing over the command of its operation to the 11,000-strong UNTAET. In March 2000, the first customs and tax system was established to provide the territory with much-needed revenue.

A National Consultative Council was established to ensure the participation of the East Timorese people in the decision-making process during the period of the transitional administration in East Timor. The fifteen-member committee, which the U.N. consults on all decisions, was designed to roughly mirror the results of East Timor's referendum. The Council comprises seven pro-independence East Timorese leaders and three pro-autonomy figures. They are joined by one representative from the influential Roman Catholic Church and four UNTAET representatives, including its head, Sergio Vieira de Mello.

Over the past year, UNTAET provided the administration for East Timor while aiding it on the route to becoming a sovereign nation. The tough uphill climb culminated in a cautious but jubilant celebration on May 20, 2002, when power was transferred to a democratic, locally elected government by U.N. Secretary General Kofi Annan. Several heads of state, including former U.S. President Bill Clinton, attended the event. Most significantly, the current President of Indonesia, Megawati Sukarno, was present and welcomed East Timor as an independent neighbor.[14]

JAMMU AND KASHMIR

In August 1947, **India,** under the leadership of Gandhi, won independence from Britain. Under the plan of partition of India into India and **Pakistan,** provided for by the Indian Independence Act of 1947, the state of **Jammu** and **Kashmir** (widely referred to as "Kashmir") was free to adhere to either India or Pakistan. Kashmir's undecided status became a matter of dispute between the two countries and fighting broke out later that year. In January 1948, the Security Council adopted Resolution 39, establishing the United Nations Commission for India and Pakistan (UNCIP) to investigate and mediate the dispute. In July 1949, India and Pakistan signed the Karachi Agreement establishing a cease-fire line to be supervised by observers. On March 30, 1951, following the termination of UNCIP, the Security Council decided to create the United Nations Military Observer Group in India and Pakistan (UNMOGIP) to succeed UNCIP. UNMOGIP continued to supervise the cease-fire in Kashmir. UNMOGIP's functions were to observe strict adherence to the cease-fire, investigate cease-fire violation complaints lodged by both parties, and to report its findings to the Secretary-General and to each party.

At the end of 1971, hostilities again broke out between India and Pakistan. When a cease-fire came into effect, a number of positions on both sides of the 1949 cease-fire line had changed hands. In July 1972, India and Pakistan signed an agreement defining a Line of Control in Kashmir, which, except for a few minor deviations, followed virtually the same course as the cease-fire line established by the Karachi Agreement. India took the position that the mandate of UNMOGIP had lapsed, as it related specifically to the cease-fire line under the Karachi Agreement. Pakistan, however, did not accept this position. Given the disagreement between the two parties about UNMOGIP's mandate and functions, the Secretary-General's position has been that UNMOGIP can be terminated only by a decision of the Security Council. The military authorities of Pakistan have continued to lodge complaints with UNMOGIP about cease-fire violations. The military authorities of India have lodged no complaints since January 1972 and have restricted the activities of the U.N. observers on the Indian side of the Line of Control.

Jammu and Kashmir continues to be a source of friction between the two countries. In May 1999, another war over territory nearly erupted when Pakistan-backed insurgents and Pakistani troops occupied mountain heights in Kargil, a district inside the Indian-administered area of Jammu and Kashmir. On May 27, 1999, Pakistan shot down two Indian fighter jets and an outbreak of violence ensued. By mid-July, faced with mounting military losses and intense international pressure, Pakistan's then Prime Minister Nawaz Sharif agreed to back down. After the October 1999 military coup in Pakistan, the hijacking of an Indian Airlines flight by Pakistani nationals, and with the growing nuclear buildup in the two countries, tensions between India and Pakistan reached new heights. Jammu and Kashmir remains a focus of international concern.

In July 2001, President Musharraf and Prime Minister Vajpayee met in Agra, India, for talks, however no significant progress was made. In December of that year, militants attacked the Indian parliament, killing nine other people before being killed themselves. 2002 has been a particularly volatile year in the ongoing dispute. Approximately 100 hundred people were killed in gunfire in the first half of the year, including several women and children.[15]

SECURITY COUNCIL REFORM

Since 1945, there has been only one adjustment to the Security Council's membership, increasing the number of non-permanent seats from five to ten. Critics assert that the Security Council must expand its permanent members to include **India,** a democratic and powerful regional voice, and **Japan,** which provides significant monetary contributions to the U.N. Other critics argue that the current veto arrangement has prevented the Security Council from developing the system of global security envisaged in the U.N. Charter. The composition of the Security Council no longer reflects the present-day international scene and balance of power. Proposals to reform the Security Council address two main problems: the first involving structure, the second involving the issue of the veto. Asian member states have been highly vocal in calling for Security Council reform. Industrialized nations such as Japan have sought permanent seats to reflect their global economic power. For example, Japan pays 18 percent of the U.N. budget, the second largest share. The United States pays 25 percent, Germany 9 percent, France 6.5 percent, and the other three perma-

nent members of the Security Council pay a combined total of 10 percent.

Larger developing nations such as India have sought permanent representation on the basis of their potential economic power. India is the world's largest democracy and will soon overtake **China** in terms of population. Other developing countries have argued that additional Southern permanent seats are vital to strike a North-South balance. Many small and medium-sized states have challenged the legitimacy of permanent seats and the veto rather than trying to add to the number of countries that have them. Without general consensus on what aspects of the Security Council should be reformed and without the support of the five permanent members, Security Council reform does not appear to be very near. With China's veto power, and with Japan and India campaigning for permanent seats, the Asian members may play a very crucial role in deciding the future of the Security Council.[16]

Security Council President Wang Yingfan of China (right) with U.N. Secretary-General Kofi Annan; United Nations, New York; May 4, 2000. (UN/DPI Photo: Eskinder Debebe

The greatest threat to regional stability and prosperity in Asia is conflict between its regional powers. Existing territorial disputes, volatile rhetoric, and extensive weaponisation in **China, India, North Korea,** and **Pakistan** are cause for grave concern. Bilateral security arrangements with Western powers no longer provide adequate security and deterrence. Recovering from the financial crisis, the regional economy finds itself facing increasing competition from the rest of the world. In other areas of the world, countries are building regional organizations—from free trade areas and security umbrellas to supranational governments—to reap the benefits of cooperation, coordination, and economies of scale. In Asia, however, the economic and political disparities among nations complicate the establishment of an overarching regional forum. The Association of Southeast Asian Nations (ASEAN) is the region's only cooperative security framework, but its effectiveness has been called into question by the organization's failure to conduct cooperative peacekeeping operations in **East Timor.**

ASSOCIATION OF SOUTHEAST ASIAN NATIONS (ASEAN)

Indonesia, Malaysia, Philippines, Singapore, and **Thailand** signed the 1967 Bangkok Declaration, forming the first and most successful regional organization in Asia. ASEAN comprises ten countries (the original five plus **Brunei, Cambodia, Laos, Myanmar,** and **Vietnam**) with a combined population of nearly 500 million people. Originally created as a response to communist advances in Indochina, ASEAN evolved into a diverse organization whose members range from tiny, prosperous nations such as Singapore to large, poorer nations such as Vietnam. In April 1999, the founders' dream of an organization embracing all ten Southeast Asian countries was

fulfilled when Cambodia officially became a member.

According to the organization's charter, ASEAN's principal aims are to accelerate mutually beneficial economic growth and to promote regional peace and stability. ASEAN operates by consensus: its members must unanimously agree on all policies. Summits are held every three years; the most recent was the December 1998 Hanoi Summit. ASEAN operates at the ministerial level; the principal policy-making event is the annual ASEAN Ministerial Meeting (AMM). The AMM is immediately followed by the Post-Ministerial Conference (PMC), at which ASEAN members meet with their "dialogue partners": **Australia,** Canada, China, the European Union, **India, Japan, Korea, New Zealand,** Russia, the United States, and the United Nations Development Programme.

In 1992, the organization launched a scheme for an ASEAN Free Trade Area (AFTA) whose strategic objective is to increase the ASEAN region's competitive advantage as a single production unit by eliminating tariff barriers among the member countries. At the 1995 Bangkok Summit, the heads of government set a timetable for the realization of AFTA in ten years. The ASEAN Regional Forum (ARF) was established in 1994. This annual meeting between ASEAN and other members of the international community has become an increasingly important in the promotion of open dialogue on political and security cooperation in the region.

The effectiveness of the organization as a political and security framework, however, was called into question during the **East Timor** crisis. The nations of Southeast Asia, unable to raise forces to conduct an ASEAN peacekeeping operation, were passive as Australia led an intervention force into the former Portuguese colony. In meeting two tasks it has set for itself, developing a regional free-trade area and building an effective framework for regional security, ASEAN and its future depend on how the organization addresses two main concerns: its members' disparate economies and their dissimilar governing styles.[17]

ASIA-PACIFIC ECONOMIC COOPERATION (APEC)

APEC was established in 1989 in response to the growing interdependence among Asia-Pacific economies. Its goal is to advance Asia-Pacific economic dynamism and a sense of community. The twenty-plus APEC members include **Australia, Brunei**, Canada, **China, Indonesia, Japan, Korea, Malaysia**, Mexico, **New Zealand, Philippines, Singapore, Taiwan, Thailand**, the United States, and **Vietnam**. Initially focused largely on exchanges of views and project-based initiatives, APEC has since evolved into a forum of greater substance and higher purpose: to build the Asia-Pacific community by achieving economic growth and equitable development through trade and economic cooperation. Since 1993, APEC ministers and heads of government have gathered annually for informal summits to discuss the economic developments of the previous year and to propose new initiatives. In 1994, the organization announced the goal of free and open trade and investment in the region by 2010 for developed-member economies and by 2020 for developing-member economies.

SOUTH ASIAN ASSOCIATION FOR REGIONAL COOPERATION (SAARC)

SAARC, made up of **Bangladesh, Bhutan, India, Maldives, Nepal, Pakistan**, and **Sri Lanka**, was established in 1985 at a summit held in Dhaka, Bangladesh. The organization's main goal is to promote peace, cooperation, and economic and social progress in South Asia. Since its inception, SAARC has given priority to cooperation in agriculture, rural development, science and technology, health, population control, and combating narcotics and terrorism.

The group signed the SAARC Preferential Trading Agreement (SAPTA) in 1993, which will gradually reduce and eventually eliminate tariff barriers through bilateral and multilateral initiatives. In 1999, SAARC launched a development fund with three aims: identification and development of projects, institutional and human-resource development, and social and infrastructure development projects. SAARC's potential as a regional organization is vast, but many problems result from its member states' internal and external conflicts, rigid economic policies, and inefficient and corrupt bureaucracies. In late 2001, SAARC countries met again to discuss progress on economic and other fronts, but India and Pakistan used the SAARC forum as a podium for attacking one another. However, a joint statement denouncing terrorism in all its forms was agreed upon.

ASIAN DEVELOPMENT BANK (ADB)

Founded by 31 states in 1966, the Asian Development Bank (ADB) in 2002 had 60 member countries, of which 43 were within the region and 17 outside. The Bank, based in Manila, is a multilateral development-finance institution, giving special attention to the needs of the smaller or less developed countries and priority to regional and national projects. Its principal functions are to extend loans to developing member countries and to provide advisory services and technical assistance for the preparation and execution of development projects. The ADB's five strategic development objectives are economic growth, reducing poverty, supporting human development, improving the status of women, and protecting the environment.

The Bank extends loans, using its Asian Development Fund (ADF), designed to provide loans on concessional terms to those developing member countries (DMCs) that have a low per capita gross national product (GNP) and limited debt-repayment capacity. The ADF is a regularized donor fund financed by nonborrowing members and other donors. The Bank currently lends to 28 ADF borrowers; the size of the ADF is estimated to be U.S.$6.3 billion.

In November 1999, the ADB and the World Bank jointly organized the Manila Social Forum, a gathering of more than 250 policy makers. The participants reviewed the issues of global labor markets, promoting reduction of urban and rural poverty, and building social protection programs. The Bank played an important role in the region's recovery from the financial crisis, providing responsible loans to member countries, gathering vital statistics, and coordinating recovery policies. The future of the Bank depends on its ability to gain self-sufficiency. It plans to achieve self-sufficiency—an ADF that is not funded by donations—by 2012.

PACIFIC ISLANDS FORUM

The Pacific Islands Forum, formerly known as the South Pacific Forum, represents the heads of government of all independent and self-governing Pacific Island countries—**Cook Islands, Fiji, Kiribati, Marshall Islands, Micronesia, Nauru, Niue, Palau, Papua New Guinea, Samoa, Solomon Islands, Tonga, Tuvalu, and Vanuatu**—as well as **Australia** and **New Zealand.** Since 1971 it has provided its sixteen member nations the opportunity to express their joint political views and to cooperate on issues of political and economic concern. Heads of government meet once a year, followed by a post-Forum dialogue meeting with the foreign ministers and Forum's dialogue partners.

At the Forum Ministers Meeting in June 1999 in Fiji, member states adopted the Melanesian Spearhead Group (MSG) Trade Agreement, which calls for the establishment of a regional free trade agreement. At the October 1999 forum in Koror, Palau, the heads of government agreed to establish the South Pacific Free Trade Agreement (SPFTA), to go into effect in early 2012. Although Australia and New Zealand are excluded from SPFTA, it may merge with the free trade area that already exists between the two countries. It was also agreed that the organization's name would be changed to the Pacific Islands Forum in 2001.

1. Mathew, K.M ed. *Manorama Yearbook 2002,* (Kottayam, Malayala 2002)

2. Mathew, K.M. ed. "Cold War over South China Sea," *Manorama Yearbook 2002.*

3. Miles, James "The World in 2000: China's Many Troubles," *The Economist.* Dec. 1999, p. 37.

4. Chinoy, Mike "Taiwan President-Elect Calls for Peace, Shares Plunge Amid Political Uncertainty," CNN. 19 20 March 2000 <http://www.cnn.com/2000/ASIANOW/east/03/19/taiwan.election.03/index.html>.

5. "The East Asian Miracle: Economics Growth and Public Policy" *The World Bank.* 1995.

6. Goldstein, Morris, *The Asian Financial Crisis: Causes, Cures, and Systemic Implications* (Washington, D.C.: Institute for International Economics, 1998); Griffith-Jones, Stephany, Jacques Cailloux, and Stephan Pfaffenzeller, *The East Asian Financial Crisis: A Reflection on Its Causes, Consequences, and Policy Implications* (Brighton, England: Institute of Development Studies, 1998); Jones, David Martin, and Mike Smith, "Tigers Ready to Roar?" *The World Today* (October 1999, pp. 17-18); Van Hoa, Tran, *The Asia Crisis: The Cures, their Effectiveness, and the Prospects After* (New York, St. Martin's Press, 2000).

7. "Science Scan 2001" *Manorama Yearbook 2002.*

8. *Asia Yearbook 2000.* (Hong Kong: Far Eastern Economic Review, December 1999); Charlesworth, Peter, "Rebuilding Asia" (Business Week, November 24, 1999, p. 68); Economic Analysis and Research Division, Asian Development Outlook 1999 Update (Oxford: Asian Development Bank, 1999).

9. "Country Sources: UN Demographic Yearbook 1998", UN Statistical Yearbook for the Asia and the Pacific 2000, and UN World Population Prospects, the 1998 Revision

10. Source: Country Sources—ESCAP, SYCAP 1999; WB, World Bank Indicators 2000 CD-ROM; UN World Population Prospects, The 2000 Revision; South Pacific Commission, Pacific Island Populations Revised Edition 1998 <http://www.adb.org/Documents/Books/Key_Indicators/2001/rt03_ki2001.xls>.

11. "Know About AIDS" *Manorama Yearbook 2002.*

(Notes continue on page 110)

12. "Human Rights Watch World Report 2002". Human Rights Watch. <www.hrw/wr2k2asia. htmll>

13. "China: United Nations Fails to Act". Human Rights Watch. www.hw.org/press.2002/04/ choma041002.htm *Asia Yearbook 2000* p. 66-69.

14. *Asia Yearbook 2000,* p. 68.

15. "Timeline: Conflict over Kashmir" CNN. <www.asia.cnn.com/2002/worldasiapcf/south/05/ 24/kashmir.timeline/index.html

16. "Tajikistan Election Watch," CNN. 27 February 2000 <http://cnn.com/WORLD/election.watch/ asiapcf/tajikistan.html>

17. United Nations. <http://www.un.org/Overview/ unmember.html>

Box 7.1 Sources

"China cautions India over apparent defection of religious leader." CNN. 12 January 2000. 12 June 2002. <www.cnn.com/2000/ASIANOW/ east/01/12/china.karmapa.01/index.html>

Chung, Chien-peng. "The Spratlys and Other South China Sea Disputes." *Journal of Social, Political, and Economic Studies* spring 1999: 17-36.

"Code for Sea Disputes Takes Shape." Bangkok Post March 16, 2000.

Feldman, Harvey. *Taiwan and the United Nations.* Stanford, Calif.: Hoover Institution, 1995.

Lapidoth, Ruth. *Autonomy: Flexible Solutions to Ethnic Conflicts.* Washington, D.C.: United States Institute of Peace, 1996.

Liu, Juliana."Sri Lankan PM to lobby for trade and peace plan in India." *Reuters: Asia* 9 June 2002. 10 June 2002. <http://asia.reuters.com/news_article.jhtml;jsessionid= U1BRT2RFTPCR0CRBAE0CFFAKEEATGIW D?type=topnews&StoryID=1066503>

Mathew, K.M., ed. "People and Events" and "World Panorama." *Manorama Yearbook 2002* Kottayam, India, 2002.

Roth, Brad, *Governmental Legitimacy in International Law.* Oxford, England: Clarendon Press, 1999. Taiwan Security Research <www.taiwansecurity. org>

Van Walt van Praag, Michael. *The Status of Tibet.* Boulder, Colo.: Westview Press, 1987.

Wippman, David. *International Law and Ethnic Conflict.* Ithaca, N.Y.: Cornell University Press, 1998.

Yang, Philip. "Taiwan's Legal Status: Going Beyond the Unification-Independence Dichotomy." *CSIS Seminar on Cross-Strait Relations at the Turn of the Century.* Washington, D.C.: September 21, 1999.

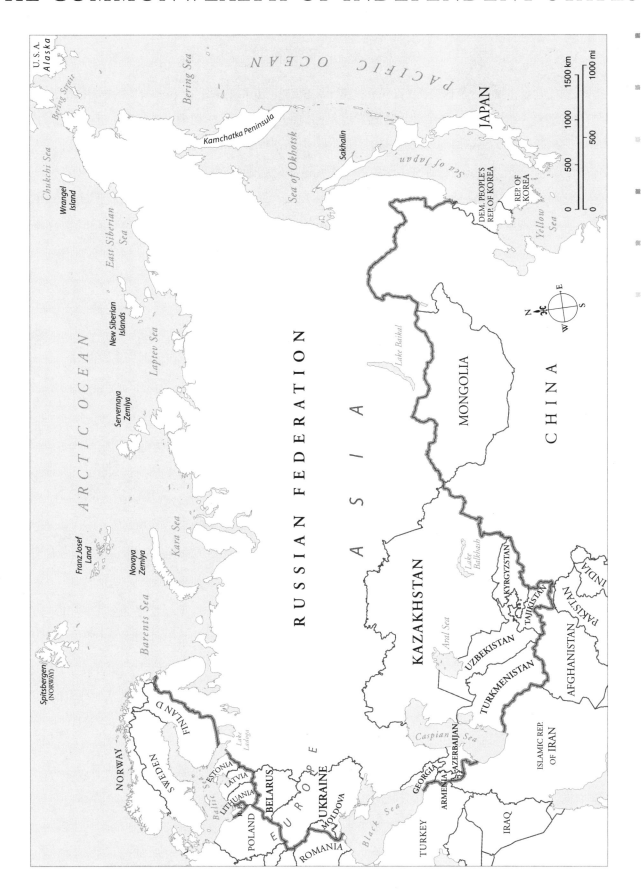

After the collapse of the Soviet Union, twelve out of fifteen former Soviet Republics came together in 1991 to form the Commonwealth of Independent States (CIS) in order to preserve economic, military, and strategic ties which are essential to their stability. The states that make up the union are Belarus, Ukraine, and Moldova in Europe; Georgia, Armenia, and Azerbaijan in the Caucasus; Turkmenistan, Uzbekistan, Kazakhstan, Tajikistan, and Kyrgyzstan in Central Asia. At the center of the newly created republics is Russia, which has retained its global status as a world power as the successor to the Soviet Union.

Considering the enormous expanse of territory once occupied by the Soviet Union and the diversity of the ethnic composition of each of the fifteen former Soviet republics, the 1991 transition from one state into fifteen newly independent entities was remarkably peaceful. Although ethnic conflicts did erupt in several states, they were not directly related to the unplanned collapse of the Union of Soviet Socialist Republics (USSR). The gradual evaporation of Mikhail Gorbachev's power, the failed putsch of the Communist Party in August 1991, and general public discontent with the Soviet regime all contributed to the dismantling of the USSR.

The formation of the new states known as the **Russian Federation** has raised key issues concerning the federation's role in the region and of national sovereignty, citizenship, and regional cooperation. The states once united under Soviet rule differ drastically from one another in ideology, ethnicity, political structures, economic resources, military capabilities, and foreign policy preferences. The task of coordinating the often conflicting policies of individual states has been difficult. A decade after the collapse of the Soviet Union, the states in the region still face major economic and political challenges. The transition from communism to democracy has been fraught with complexities and problems, among them a stagnating economy, political instability, widespread corruption, a flawed legal system, and ethnic conflicts.

POST-COLD WAR INTEGRATION

The collapse of the Soviet Union left fifteen newly independent states sharing a centrally planned economy; common currency, communication, and transportation systems; and an economic authority still concentrated in Moscow.

Politically, each of the fifteen states now faced the challenge of redefining its national identity and its citizenship policies. No less important, was the fact that none of these states had clearly defined boundaries, and most had no independent army to defend their territory. The new states had all been politically and economically dependent on Russia prior to the collapse of the Soviet Union, and independence brought the necessity of creating political and economic institutions without external aid. While most states were eager to establish themselves as sovereign entities free of Soviet control, many wished to create a regional organization that would facilitate the transition from communism to democracy. Some of the leaders of the new states felt that the establishment of a regional organization would be crucial to maintaining post-Soviet regional order.

The groundwork for the creation of the Commonwealth of Independent States (CIS) was laid at Minsk, **Belarus,** on December 8, 1991, with the signing of the Minsk Agreement (also known as the Belovezh Accords) by Belarus, Russia, and **Ukraine.** The CIS addressed the anxieties of the newly independent states about existing and potential political instability, economic challenges, and ethnic conflicts. The CIS was also the only means of integrating the newly independent states that Russia strongly advocated.

The CIS derived from Gorbachev's State Council and originally consisted of the Council of Heads of State and the Council of Heads of Government. The first meeting, held in Moscow, Russia, in February 1992, focused primarily on the role of Russia in the region. With the exception of Ukraine, all the members in attendance were willing to grant Russia the status of legal successor of the Soviet Union. However, today, the CIS states' fears of Russian domination in the region remain a focal issue, partly as a result of Russia's strong advocacy of the CIS and partly because of the former Soviet republics' political

8.1 THE COMMONWEALTH OF INDEPENDENT STATES

ARMENIA
Capital: Yerevan
Chief of state: Robert Kocharian
Territory: 29,800 sq. km
Population: 3,798,500
Currency: dram

AZERBAIJAN
Capital: Baku
Chief of state: Heydar Aliyev
Territory: 86,600 sq. km
Population: 7,700,000
Currency: manat

BELARUS
Capital: Minsk
Chief of state: Aleksandr Lukashenko
Territory: 207,600 sq. km
Population: 10,226,800
Currency: Belarussian ruble

GEORGIA
Capital: Tbilisi
Chief of state: Eduard Shevardnadze
Territory: 69,700 sq. km
Population: 5,445,000
Currency: lari

KAZAKHSTAN
Capital: Astana
Chief of state: Nursultan Nazarbayev
Territory: 2,724,900 sq. km
Population: 15,491,300
Currency: tenge

KYRGYZSTAN
Capital: Bishkek
Chief of state: Askar Akaev
Territory: 199,900 sq. km
Population: 4,729,600
Currency: som

MOLDOVA
Capital: Chisinau
Chief of state: Vladimir Voronin
Territory: 33,800 sq. km
Population: 3,648,300
Currency: lei

RUSSIA
Capital: Moscow
Chief of state: Vladimir Putin
Territory: 17,075,400 sq. km
Population: 146,700,000
Currency: ruble

TAJIKISTAN
Capital: Dushanbe
Chief of state: Emomali Rakhmonov
Territory: 143,100 sq. km
Population: 6,164,000
Currency: Tajik ruble

TURKMENISTAN
Capital: Ashgabat
Chief of state: Saparmurat Niyazov
Territory: 491,200 sq. km
Population: 4,990,000
Currency: manat

UKRAINE
Capital: Kyiv
Chief of state: Leonid Kuchma
Territory: 603,700 sq. km
Population: 50,090,900
Currency: hryvnia

UZBEKISTAN
Capital: Tashkent
Chief of state: Islam Karimov
Territory: 447,400 sq. km
Population: 24,232,000
Currency: Uzbek som

SOURCES: Inter-State Statistical Committee of the CIS, as published on website <http://www.unece.org/> and reprinted in Martha Brill Olcott, Anders Aslund, and Sherman W. Garnett, *Getting It Wrong: Regional Cooperation and the Commonwealth of Independent States* (New York: Carnegie Endowment for International Peace, 1999).

U.S. Department of State. <www.state.gov>

8.2 THE PROCESS OF INTEGRATION

1991

December 8	Belarus, Russia, and Ukraine sign the Minsk Agreement (also known as the Belovezh Accords) on the creation of the CIS.
December 13	Kazakhstan, Kyrgyzstan, Tajikistan, Turkmenistan, and Uzbekistan express their desire to join the CIS.
December 21	The five Central Asian states, as well as Armenia, Azerbaijan, and Moldova, join the CIS.

1992

January 16	CIS members discuss military affairs and agree to coordinate CIS foreign policy.
February 14	Member states sign an agreement to regulate trade and economic cooperation and declare the ruble to be the sole monetary unit of the CIS.
March 13	CIS members agree on joint responsibility for repaying the Soviet debt.
March 20	Member states sign the Declaration of the Non-Use of Force or Threat of Force in Relations Among CIS Members, Agreement of Groups of Military Observers and Collective Peacekeeping Forces, and Agreement on the Joint Command of the Border Troops.

1993

January 3–4	Central Asian Union is created.
January 22	CIS Inter-State Bank is created.
September 24	Initial conception of an Economic Union, which provides for the free flow of commodities, capital, and workforce among member states; also coordinates budget, tax, and foreign economic policy.
December 24	Implementation of Economic Union begins.

1995

January 28	Customs Union is created.
February 10	Member states sign agreement stating they will not use political, economic, or military pressure on each other to achieve domestic or foreign policy goals.

1997

October 10	Azerbaijan, Georgia, Moldova, and Ukraine join to form GUAM to address issues of regional security and to create a transport route for Caspian oil.

1999

February	By decision of the Interstate Council of four countries (Belarus, Kazakhstan, Kyrgyzstan, Russia), the Republic of Tajikistan is recognized as a participant in Customs Union, enjoying full rights.
April 25	Uzbekistan joins GUAM as its fifth member, creating GUUAM.

2000

January 25	Decision is made to discuss problems of combating international terrorism in light of the results of the OSCE Istanbul Summit. A report is analyzed on implementation of the interstate program of joint measures for struggle against organized crime and other kinds of dangerous crime on the territory of CIS member states for the period up to 2000.
June 20–21	CIS Council of Heads of States adopts plan-schedule of implementation of proposals on establishment and functioning of the free trade zone and the plan of measures for realization of the program of actions for development of the Commonwealth of Independent States for the period up to 2005.
November 30–December 1	During the Minsk summit, a final decision on launching a full-range activity of the CIS Anti-Terrorist Center is taken. The heads of government adopt the provisions on this body, which will execute its activity making use of the capacity of the specialized anti-terrorist units of CIS security organs and specialized agencies.

2001

May 31	The meeting of the Council endorses a prospective plan of development of military cooperation between CIS member states for the period up to 2005. It stipulates framing of legal, information, and analytical documents on cooperation in the military and political spheres, military and technical spheres, peace-making activity, and humanitarian sphere.
November 29–30	At a meeting of the Council, held in Moscow, an agreement is signed on coordination of actions in the area of licensing of educational activity, attesting and accrediting educational establishments of the Commonwealth's countries. Interstate program adopted for implementation of the concept of establishment of a single (common) educational space of the CIS. Heads of CIS states proclaim their support for the U.S.-led anti-terror coalition.

SOURCES: Martha Brill Olcott, Anders Aslund, and Sherman W. Garnett, *Getting It Wrong: Regional Cooperation and the Commonwealth of Independent States* (New York: Carnegie Endowment for International Peace, 1999) 243–48.

Russian News Network <http://www.russiannewsnetwork.com/cis2.html>

Executive Committee of the Commonwealth of the Independent States <http://www.cis.minsk.by/english/meet_cis.htm>

and economic dependence on Russia prior to the collapse of the Soviet Union.

One of the main goals of the CIS has been to provide member states with the opportunity to coordinate their foreign and security policies. The Commonwealth is also seen as a viable vehicle for the establishment of a regional economic union, comparable to the European Union. Such a common economic union would allow member states to have a common customs policy. Another of its major goals is the distribution of the former Soviet Union's assets, particularly its military hardware. Some of the other goals on the agenda are joint efforts to protect the environment, regulation of migration policies, development of joint communications networks, and detection and punishment of organized crime.

The CIS has failed to achieve many of these goals, and has yet to meet the challenge of integrating and coordinating the foreign, economic, and security policies of its member states. Although most leaders of the member states support integration through the CIS, each wants to retain control over the state's domestic and foreign policies and gives priority to issues that best serve the national interest of that individual state. Because of the lack of agreement on the role of the CIS and on the coordination of policies, the Commonwealth of Independent States has proven to be an effective avenue of communication between member states rather than a viable decision-making organization.

DEMOCRATIZATION AND POLITICAL STABILITY

The transition to democracy for each of the states in the CIS has been fraught with problems, some of which are inherent in all transitional states, others of which are unique to each country's chosen path to democratization. The domestic structures of CIS states differ dramatically. While some are clearly committed to adhering to liberal democratic norms, most are reluctant to abandon autocratic practices. Government corruption, inefficient economic reforms, and unfair elections are common in the region.

The turmoil in **Russia** has led to serious political instability. The financial crisis of 1998, and the erratic administration of President Boris Yeltsin, followed by his resignation in December 1999, increased public discontent with the government and led to further political and ideological fragmentation. Numerous terrorist attacks in 1999 raised fears of organized opposition and increasing social unrest. Vladimir Putin, elected president in March 2000, has been determined to strengthen Russia both politically and economically and resolved to redefine Russia's role in the CIS. In 2001, Putin made a move toward reform by appointing a number of progressive cabinet members.[1] The president specifically committed himself to improving Russia's economic and legal systems in his 2002 state of the nation address.[2] His position has been strengthened even further after meeting with American President George W. Bush. Both heads of state signed a declaration in Moscow on May 24, 2002 agreeing on mutual cooperation in key military and strategic areas.

In the **Armenian** government, internal divisions are prevalent, based largely on disagreement among the country's leaders on the policies to be adopted in the Nagorno-Karabakh conflict with **Azerbaijan** (*see* Ethnic Conflicts). The first elected president of the Republic of Armenia, Levon Ter-Petrossian, was forced to resign when he showed signs of willingness to negotiate a peace agreement with the government of Azerbaijan. In October 1999, a group of gunmen set stability and progress back by entering the parliament building, killing Armenia's prime minister and other leading politicians, and holding the other cabinet members hostage. Armenian President Kocharian remained in charge. The militarization of politics needs to be addressed and a resolution to the Nagorno-Karabakh conflict reached if Armenia is to avoid similar setbacks in the future. Armenian and Azeri Presidents favor a peaceful solution to the conflict, which has proved to be devastating to both nations. Yet, no major steps have been taken toward achieving a concrete peace agreement.

Azerbaijan has been among the CIS nations least willing to cooperate internationally or to

8.3 Turmoil in Russia

A decade after the dissolution of the Soviet Union and the end of the Cold War, Russia has remained a key player in shaping global politics. However, despite its advantageous location between Asia and Europe, it remains plagued by political and economic instability.

The largest country in the world in land area adopted its constitution on December 12, 1993. In the transition from communism to democracy, Russia experienced difficulties in moving from its old centrally planned economy to a modern market economy. The new government introduced numerous structural reform initiatives, but they advanced slowly. The development level of small businesses decreased and agricultural land reform stalled. In December 1997, the Russian Central Bank let interest rates rise sharply. The nation's cumulative debt in 1998 was estimated at $135 billion.

President Boris Yeltsin, once hailed as the guarantor of stability and economic success, was by that time battling physical illness and waning political authority. On May 12, 1999, Yeltsin fired his popular prime minister, Yevgeny Primakov, marking his third firing of a prime minister in three months. Primakov was officially dismissed because of the country's slow pace of economic change, but his supporters in Russia's lower parliamentary body, the Duma, said it was because he had publicly questioned Yeltsin. The day of the prime minister's firing, the Duma urged Yeltsin to resign, deeming him incapable of leading Russia into a better future. Members of the Duma attempted to begin impeachment hearings on five counts, including one accusing him of beginning a violent civil war in the province of Chechnya in 1994. The motion failed, however, and Yeltsin replaced Primakov with Sergei Stepashin, former deputy prime minister, stating that a change in government would quicken the pace of reform in Russia.

It was Russia's civilian population that suffered the most under these conditions of political and economic instability. In 1999, the government owed 77 billion rubles to its employees, and even major companies had been forced to resort to barter. Yeltsin pledged that economic reform would improve the people's way of life, but, instead, thousands of Russians waited months to be paid their wages. Experts blamed the situation on corruption and the lack

of an economic safety net. The Asian economic crisis also had a major effect on the country by decreasing the demand for its exports and damaging the confidence of international investors. Many people worried that Russia's problems could create political instability in neighboring countries such as Ukraine and Belarus, and negatively impact the international economy. Despite President Yeltsin's resignation in December 1999 and the appointment of Acting President Vladimir Putin, few were hopeful that there would be any major changes in the government. Russia's newly emerged middle class welcomed the birth of a free market, and then had to watch helplessly as the country fell into political and economic ruin.

Relations between Russia and the West were strained by the Kosovo crisis, during which Russia viewed NATO's actions in the Balkans as a direct challenge to its national interests and security. Serbian President Slobodan Milosevic saw this deteriorating relationship as a chance to deal with the Kosovo situation on his own terms. Experts have predicted that Russia will strike a closer rapport with China as a direct result of the opposition it experienced in the Balkan crisis. Such an alliance between China and Russia would create a reason for the West to take both countries seriously.

Because of its location, Europe is especially vulnerable to Russia's actions. Russia took advantage of that vulnerability to extract concessions from Western countries that were eager to prevent a Sino-Russian alliance of any kind. On June 18, 1999, Russian and U.S. defense and foreign ministers drew up the Helsinki Agreement, which made general arrangements regarding Russian peacekeepers in Kosovo. Despite the agreement, Russia remained dissatisfied with its lack of political control over peacekeeping troops. Russian troops were under the separate command of Colonel General Viktor M. Zavarzin, but questions concerning their location and whose orders they should follow delayed the arrival of additional Russian troops in the Kosovar capital of Pristina.

Russia is a country physically and historically too vast to be ignored in the international arena; despite its turbulent economy and constant crises, it remains a key factor in global politics. It is an important part of Europe

because of its borders with Finland, Latvia, and Poland, among others. It has a wide base of natural resources, including deposits of oil, natural gas, and coal.

Russia will have several pressing issues to confront in the near future: Most important, it must solve its domestic economic crisis to appease its frustrated and suffering population. It cannot rely solely on Western loans, aid, and investments to solve its financial problems. The crisis in Kosovo brought to light the massive scale of ideological and political differences between Russia and the West. Russia established itself as strictly opposed to the way NATO handled the situation in Kosovo; its growing relationship with China was a direct result of that stance. What remained a certainty was that any political action taken by Russia would affect the rest of the world.

After the September 11 attacks on the World Trade Center and Pentagon, Russia's relationship with the West, particularly the United States, significantly improved. President Putin publicly voiced his support for U.S. efforts to eradicate world terrorism. Putin and U.S. President George W. Bush affirmed a growing cooperation, which includes intelligence shared between the two countries. After a meeting between the two presidents on May 24-26 in Moscow and St. Petersburg, several important agreements were signed. This marked a new stage in military, economic, and strategic cooperation between the United States and Russia. In addition, a new level of understanding was reached between Russia and NATO after both sides agreed to hold a joint summit meeting of NATO and Russia in May 2002. (Russia stands on the same level with other member states, although it does not have veto power when it comes to the decision-making process.) Russian interest in fighting terrorism stems from protecting its own stability, which is threatened by radical Islamic groups in the Caucasus and Central Asia. Before the U.S. intervention into Afghanistan, Russia actively financed and armed the Northern Alliance against the Taliban. Currently, Russia has an interest in making sure that Central Asian energy reserves, and especially the gas pipeline through Turkmenistan, remain under Russian influence.

Source: "All Smiles, For Now." The Economist 15 December 2001.

reform its autocratic domestic policies. Questions about the health and political longevity of President Heydar Aliyev have added to concerns about the nation's political stability. Mr. Aliyev, a longtime leader of Azerbaijan in the Soviet period, returned to power in 1993 and has commanded the political scene thereafter. He imposed political stability after dealing with a succession of attempted coups, dominating the cabinet and parliament with autocratic, authoritarian rule. The president won a five-year term in the October 1998 election with no real contest. Foreign policy under Aliyev has been largely pro-Western, and the nation's relations with Russia suffer because of Russia's consistent support of Armenia in the conflict over the Nagorno-Karabakh enclave. The conflict remains unresolved, and currently the Armenians still run a separate administration there, but major hostilities have not erupted since 1994. Several informal steps toward reconciliation have been taken in the form of dialogue without any concrete results.

In **Kazakhstan**, with poverty and social ills widespread, the risk of unrest is high; lack of organized opposition, however, has meant that the government will likely stay in power. Political parties supporting President Nursultan Nazarbayev won the December 1998 elections, further strengthening his control over all aspects of government. Continued Russian aid and economic support of Kazakhstan are essential to its survival and development as a sovereign state. Many in the Kazakh government fear a resurgence of nationalist and communist factions whose revisionist territorial claims could threaten Kazakh sovereignty. Recently, popular dissatisfaction with the despotic regime has triggered a more active opposition movement within the country. Nazarbaev's repressive policies toward his political opponents have been criticized by the Western community.[3]

The situation in **Kyrgyzstan** appears similar to that in Kazakhstan, insofar as President Askar Akayev has ruled the nation with an iron hand, adeptly blocking reform. Nevertheless, Kyrgyzstan remains one of the most democratic republics in Central Asia. Recently, political repression

greatly increased, as the opposition became more active after a drastic increase of Western presence in the country. With the deployment of U.S. and other Allied troops to the country in the campaign to eradicate terrorism, the government has adopted harsher methods of quelling growing unrest within the country.[4]

Although at the beginning of the millennium **Tajikistan** faced critical tests of its viability and integrity as a state, its leadership appears to lean toward cooperation and reconciliation. Armed groups with or without a political agenda are still in a position to create instability, and the central government remains weak. However, the prospects of the government and the main opposition group, the United Tajik Opposition (UTO), to work together in a coalition and jointly deal with occasional outbreaks of fighting are encouraging. External relations remain strained. Relations with **Uzbekistan** are poor, and the Tajik government is on the lookout for signs of an Uzbek-backed rebellion. Tajikistan's southern neighbor, Afghanistan, is clearly a long-term concern. As Uzbekistan is no longer an ally, Tajikistan's already strong relationship with Russia has become more important than ever. Russia maintains a large military presence, with some 20,000 troops in the country. Iran's position in Tajikistan has considerably strengthened: It continues to rely on its cultural and linguistic ties with the Tajiks, the crucial role it played in achieving the 1997 peace accord, its close relationship with the UTO, and the provision of modest but increasing credit. Tajikistan has proved to be a worthy ally of the United States in the war on terrorism. It has begun to receive much more economic and social aid from the West in order to secure its stability and to help it fight a growing traffic in narcotics from Afghanistan.[5]

Regionalism has been a divisive force within Uzbekistan. President Islam Abdughanievich Karimov has dealt with regionalist tendencies by appointing local governors, whom he then swiftly ousted to ensure that one official would not become too powerful. This policy did little to strengthen popular support for the president, who was perceived as trying to thwart popular power and deny the populace the leaders they would choose; regionalist ties were thus reinforced. Bomb attacks in the capital and tension with Tajikistan and other states in the region have exacerbated the situation by damaging Uzbekistan's image of relative domestic stability. In addition, the nation's position vis-à-vis Russia has worsened. Uzbekistan's sponsorship of the uprising in northern Tajikistan in November 1998 signaled an increase in overt Uzbek intervention in Tajikistan; its hope was ultimately to supplant Russia, Tajikistan's most important patron. Russian military and logistical support for the Tajik government in the crisis was a warning to Uzbekistan not to become too ambitious. Uzbekistan's relations with the other Central Asian republics were complicated by economic disputes. Nevertheless, Uzbekistan belongs to the Organization of the Islamic Conference (OIC) and the Economic Cooperation Organization (composed of five Central Asian countries: Afghanistan, Azerbaijan, Iran, Pakistan, and Turkey). It was a founding member of the Central Asian Union, formed with Kazakhstan and Kyrgyzstan and joined in March 1998 by Tajikistan. Although Uzbekistan is considered to be one of the most dictatorial Central Asian republics, it demonstrated its commitment to fighting terrorism on the side of the Allies by allowing the U.S. to use its military bases for operations in Afghanistan. Throughout the 1990s, Uzbekistan was a battleground between the government and one of the most dangerous terrorist organizations, the Islamic Movement of Uzbekistan (IMU). Allied military operations in Afghanistan greatly strengthened the government of Islam Karimov and greatly weakened Uzbekistan's Islamic fundamentalist opposition.[6]

Moldova was initially shaken by several ethnic conflicts as a result of an ineffective parliament and the lack of a viable constitution. A major conflict developed in the early 1990s after Moldova gained its independence. A Russian minority began to demand recognition in the region called Transnistria, which led to the development of an armed conflict involving separatists, Russian troops, and Moldavian troops. Moldova has sought a peaceful resolution of the conflict in the Transnistria region by working with Romania, **Ukraine**, and Russia; by calling for international mediation; and by cooperating with the Organization for Security and Cooperation in Europe (OSCE) and U.N. fact-finding and observer missions. Another conflict, involving Gagauz separatists, was diffused by the granting of local autonomy in 1994. In 2000, Parliament passed a decree declaring Moldova a Parliamentary Republic. However, Parliament initially failed three times to elect a new president. The acting president dissolved the parliament and called for new parliamentary elections in order to facilitate the election process. In February 2001, the popular elections, deemed free and fair by international observers, led to Communist domination of the parliament with 71 out of 101 seats. Communist leader Vladimir Voronin became the president, but continued with democratic reforms, including privatization of government-controlled industries and strengthening ties with the West.[7]

HUMAN RIGHTS

The transition to democracy in the CIS has been marked by serious human rights violations in all the states, though to varying degrees. Atrocities by **Russian** troops in Chechnya continue to be a major concern among the international community. Indiscriminate targeting of civilians and summary executions of alleged Chechen collaborationists are widespread. As a result of a prolonged military campaign, nearly 500,000 refugees fled the war zone. The conduct of the Russian military continues to outrage human rights activists, even though, in April 2002, the U.N. Commission on Human Rights failed to condemn the abuses by a narrow margin, because of many abstentions and the opposition of such states as Cuba and Iran. The lack of a legal system to prosecute human rights violations and the absence of accountability are commonplace. In regard to **Belarus**, the U.N. Committee Against Torture has expressed its grave concern about numerous "continuous allegations of torture and other cruel, inhuman and degrading punishment or treatment, committed by officials of the State party [Belarus] or with their acquiescence, particularly affecting political opponents of the Government and peaceful demonstrators, and including disappearances, beatings and other actions."[8] Persecution of religious minorities and police brutality often take place in **Georgia**, **Armenia**, and **Turkmenistan**. Repression of political opposition and free press is associated with Belarus, **Turkmenistan**, **Kyrgyzstan**, and **Azerbaijan**. Recently, concern has been voiced about the **Russian** government's appropriation of independent TV stations in 2001, such as NTV and TV-6, which may eventually lead to a crackdown on the country's free press.[9] Corruption contributes to illegitimate activities such as trafficking in women in **Russia**, Belarus, and **Ukraine**. In addition, it is evident that many CIS states do not have an adequate legal framework to prosecute human rights abuses. On the practical level, even if there are legal tools that can be used to protect the individual rights of citizens, enforcement mechanisms are greatly flawed due to factors ranging from corruption in the justice system to lack of power over enforcement mechanisms such as the police, which must be used in order to bring violators of human rights to justice. Although the United Nations, the United States, and the European Union criticize CIS members for their human rights violations, they do not consider them to be of primary importance in their relations and often do not place significant emphasis on the human rights issue.[10]

REGIONAL SECURITY

In many cases what is in the national interest of an individual state conflicts with the choices and preferences dictated by CIS institutions. For example, the question of how to enlarge the North Atlantic Treaty Organization (NATO) has hampered attempts to coordinate the CIS states' foreign policies. While **Belarus** supports **Russia's** objection to NATO expansion, most other member states of the CIS do not have a vested interest in NATO and thus have not included this issue on their foreign policy agendas. The political

leadership in **Ukraine,** on the other hand, is not only supportive of NATO expansion, but also hopes that Ukraine will eventually join the alliance.

From the inception of the CIS, the establishment of an integrated security structure has been at the top of the agenda. Russian interests are a crucial factor in the security arrangements that have been set up in the region. Russia considers an integrated CIS security structure a means to ensure that member states will not join alliances directed against Russia or any of the other CIS members. The security structure of the CIS was at first pluralistic and fragmented, largely as a result of Russia's weakness and the lack of consensus among member states. Each of the newly independent states tries to minimize its dependence on Russia. States that seek to cooperate with Russia on security issues do so to satisfy their own security needs rather than to contribute to the creation of a common regional security arrangement. As a result, most states in the region have formed independent bilateral or multilateral security arrangements.

Armenia has been a strong supporter of an integrated CIS security structure, in large measure because of its need for military aid in the Nagorno-Karabakh conflict with **Azerbaijan.** Russia provides Armenia with considerable diplomatic and military aid, both unilaterally and in conjunction with the United States and France under the OSCE-sponsored Minsk Group, a diplomatic forum whose goal is to reach a settlement of that conflict.[11] Armenia's cooperation with Russia and its willingness to establish close bilateral ties with that country are a means to ensure support and obtain aid in the face of a security threat from Azerbaijan and an economic threat from its western neighbor Turkey.

Kazakhstan has developed a close alliance with Russia after the collapse of the Soviet Union and is Russia's main strategic ally in Central Asia. Russia maintains a military presence in the country and has unrestricted access to major military and aeronautic facilities, along with natural resources such as gas. The 1992 Treaty on Friendship, Cooperation, and Mutual Assistance legalized Russian military presence in Kazakhstan.[12] Russia's interest there was primarily based on the strategic importance of the space center at Baikonur, as well as other test and military sites. Kazakhstan, in turn, benefits greatly from Russian aid in the buildup and training of its own military.

Belarus began cooperating with Russia on security issues immediately after the collapse of the Soviet Union. Although Belarus did not enter into a formal military alliance with Russia, claiming a policy of neutrality, it clearly supports Russian policies, particularly in regard to NATO expansion. In January 1995, Russia and Belarus signed an agreement to arrange for joint air defense and military-industrial cooperation. There was also considerable debate between the leaders of the two countries on establishing a viable common defense policy.[13] But at this time, the response from NATO and Western Europe that joint military action might trigger makes this unlikely or impossible.

Georgia committed itself to support the United States in its efforts to combat terrorism and began close military cooperation in the wake of September 11. During early 2002, the United States deployed several hundred military experts and significantly increased its aid to Georgia in order to combat regional terrorism. This should contribute to stability in the Caucasus, which is troubled by conflicts in Abhazia, South Osetia, and Chechnya.

Russia has a strong interest in cooperating with the Central Asian states, such as **Tajikistan, Kyrgyzstan,** and **Uzbekistan,** in order to counteract a thriving narcotics trade that has reportedly increased since the fall of the Taliban. In order to maintain the stability that was once threatened by the Uzbek Fundamentalist Islamic guerrillas who are funded by the illicit drug trade, Russia placed 12,000 troops in Tajikistan. The United Nations Office for Drug Control and Crime Prevention (UNODCCP) also funds the Tajik state Drug Control Agency (although not fully, due to lack of European support) in order to help fight the lucrative and dangerous drug trade.[14]

As part of the War on Terrorism campaign, the United States has actively fostered military and intelligence cooperation among the Central Asian states. This has led to a significant influx of U.S. funds into the region, which has helped to stabilize the region and improve its infrastructure.

ECONOMIC STAGNATION

When the Commonwealth of Independent States was formed, its leaders were preoccupied with state building, political instability, and ethnic problems. As a result, they did little to address the economics problem. High inflation rates, decreasing production, and Soviet-style state price-fixing drove the new states' economies into decline. The Declaration on the Coordination of Economic Policy, issued on December 8, 1991, set forth an agenda for negotiating economic integration.[15] However, the document was not binding and thus did not help to determine how CIS economic institutions would actually function.

The states' economic dependence on Russia and on each other after the collapse of the Soviet Union magnified the need to create a viable economic structure in the CIS. Russia was a source of currency, energy, and raw materials. Whereas Russia could considerably harm any one of the CIS states by blockading oil or gas pipelines, none of those states had similar leverage over the Russian economy.

Trade among CIS countries continued to be based on Soviet-style bilateral agreements. In September 1993, several CIS government leaders met to discuss the possibility of creating a mechanism that would lead to a full economic union resembling the European Union.[16] However, the meeting failed to accomplish its goals, and only an outline of an economic organization was proposed. In 2000, more than sixty economic institutions existed within the CIS. They closely resembled Soviet institutions in their style and structure. Although attempts were made to work out multilateral agreements that would foster closer economic cooperation among the CIS states, none came into force.

Political considerations rather than market forces have often guided economic cooperation

8.4 Putin's Vision of a New CIS and Stronger Russia

During the time he was Acting President, Vladimir Putin used the January 24-25, 2000 CIS Summit in Moscow to redefine the role of Russia vis-à-vis its close neighbors, and transform the CIS from a weak organization into a strong regional arrangement. The member states' lack of consensus on its role resulted in a fractured view of the largest regional organization in the post-Soviet area. Armenia, Kyrgyzstan, and Tajikistan always viewed the CIS as a means to ensure Russian support in the military domain. Russia and Belarus used the organization to maintain control over the region. Moldova, Kazakhstan, Turkmenistan, and Ukraine cooperated only minimally with Russia, largely for economic reasons. Azerbaijan and Georgia, who were the last to join the CIS, were reluctant to cooperate on many occasions and tried to undermine Russia's power in the region.

President Putin has made it clear that he will not tolerate member states' attempts to undermine Russia's hegemonic role in the region or the importance of the CIS; he sees a potential alliance of CIS member states with NATO or the European Union (EU) as a means to erode the possibility of the CIS becoming a viable, cohesive organization. Putin's main goal is to ensure that CIS member states are committed to cooperating with Russia, and to deter actions that would undermine Russian domination. His assertiveness rests largely on the assumption that most of the CIS member states are reluctant to withdraw from the organization

because of their political, military, or economic dependence on Russia. Azerbaijan and Georgia have posed the greatest threat to the CIS because of their increasingly strong relations with Turkey, plans to establish oil pipelines, and quiet support for the Chechens in the war with Russia.

Putin's assertiveness is not limited to the strengthening of the CIS alone. He has also demonstrated a willingness to reactivate Soviet-style relationships with foreign countries. Whereas the Yeltsin administration had abandoned diplomatic and economic ties with its Soviet-era allies, Putin is determined to rekindle relations with some of those states. The Treaty on Friendship, Good-Neighbor Relations and Cooperation, signed in North Korea in February 2000, was a clear attempt to reassert Russian influence in that region.

Relations with Vietnam are also likely to be rekindled. Vietnam's mineral resources and proximity to trading routes make it a valuable trading partner for Russia. Vietnam is also strategically important to Russia because it acts as a coordinator between Russia and the Association of Southeast Asian Nations (ASEAN).

Russia views the strengthening of relations with these states as a means to increase its power in relation to the West, particularly the United States. Although Europe and the United States claimed that IMF loans to Russia would be withheld if Russia did not rectify its behavior in

Chechnya, the Putin administration seems to have ceased playing by international rules. In the face of political instability and a stagnating economy, the new administration sees these methods of regional and global engagement as a means to assert Russia's national interests.

Since Putin took office, Russia has undergone significant regulatory changes that allow private businesses and in particular natural resources-based corporations to thrive and contend with their Western counterparts. Russia's corporate tax of 24 percent is one of the world's lowest, while Russian firms are moving toward corporate transparency and are trying to observe international accounting standards, pay regular dividends, and protect minority stockholders' rights. Russian economic tycoons, or "oligarchs," have strengthened their grip over natural resources, such as oil, gas, and heavy and precious metals, and have continuously expanded their influence over the neighboring republics. Thus, with improving economic ties between Russia and its neighbors come close political ties. Russian influence on its neighbors' economies via the corporate sector allow it to uphold its dominant status among the CIS states.

Sources: Martha Brill Olcott, "Reforming Russia's Tycoons." *Foreign Policy* May/June 2002."

Reinventing the CIS: Putin Takes the Helm." *Weekly Global Intelligence Update* 8 February 2000. <statfor.com>

---

and decisions about intra-CIS trade. For example, Russia offers access to natural gas resources at lower prices to countries that maintain a close relationship with Russia than to countries that challenge its domination in the region or directly oppose its interests. Russia had aided the economies of CIS member states after the collapse of the Soviet Union but eventually had to curtail its support due to its own economic stagnation, particularly after the Russian financial crisis of 1998. While most Soviet-style restrictions were later lifted, others, such as the poor payments system and the lack of adequate financing,

continue to hamper the growth of interstate trade.

The Russian financial crisis of 1998 had dire consequences for the economies of all CIS member countries. After the crisis, foreigners were reluctant to invest not only in Russia, but also in other CIS economies. The process of large-scale privatization, on which the CIS countries had embarked as part of their economic reform policy was hampered by the lack of foreign investment, as well as by widespread corruption. As a result, CIS governments were forced to implement more rigorous fiscal policies. The situation was further exacerbated by the collapse of the Russian market, which caused a drastic decline in exports to Russia.

Unilateral protectionist acts by CIS countries intensified due to the 1998 Russian economic crisis, causing the overall interstate trade to drop. Although CIS countries attempted to create a free trade zone and an effective customs union, they made no progress in solving the dire economic problems facing them. The absence of a coherent mechanism to spurn economic integration in the region had negative consequences on Western perceptions of CIS member states. Most members that had expressed a desire to join the World Trade Organization (WTO) weakened their candidacy by implementing unilateral protectionist policies and by failing to implement effective economic reforms, such as trade liberalization. However, after President Putin expressed Russia's full support for the United States in the War on Terrorism and signed a joint declaration with President George W. Bush, which marked the beginning of a new stage in mutual cooperation between the two states on several levels, Russia's chances to join the WTO greatly increased. Russia now seeks to increase its output of oil to the U.S. in order to present a viable alternative to OPEC, further improving its relationship with the West and spurring continued economic growth.[17]

ETHNIC CONFLICTS

Under the Soviet regime, ethnicity was almost never politicized, largely because of the government's strong desire to unify all of the republics under the umbrella of the Soviet empire. With the collapse of the Soviet Union, many of those republics began to declare their independence, and national sovereignty and identity became key issues facing the newly independent states. Almost none of these states had ever had clearly defined boundaries, and the various ethnic groups within a given state had been united by Soviet policies, such as a mandatory **Russian** educational system and the imposition of Russian as the second official language. Ethnic sentiments inevitably became acute as states began to redefine their respective national identities and, in some cases, to express their reluctance to accept the boundaries that had been drawn under the Soviet regime. Ethnic conflicts in Nagorno-Karabakh, Georgia, and Chechnya had a serious impact not only on the CIS region, but also on the relationship of the CIS countries with Russia and the West.

NAGORNO-KARABAKH

The dispute between **Armenia** and **Azerbaijan** over the Nagorno-Karabakh, an enclave located in southwest Azerbaijan, along the Iranian and Armenian borders, began even before the collapse of the Soviet Union. In 1988, regular mass demonstrations demanding unification with Armenia were held in Nagorno-Karabakh. In February of the same year, Mikhail Gorbachev promised to review the status of Karabakh, but failed to do so. The situation was exacerbated by continued mass protest in Armenia and the decision of the Nagorno-Karabakh Supreme Soviet to secede from Azerbaijan. In 1989, Azerbaijan imposed the first of a series of blockades of food, fuel, and goods bound for Armenia and Nagorno-Karabakh. A referendum held on December 10, 1991 resulted in the declaration of independence of the Nagorno-Karabakh Republic in January of the following year.

This conflict had considerable strategic importance in the CIS region. Russia continues to supply Armenia with military aid to assist the country in its dispute with Azerbaijan, while the latter has sought help from Turkey and the West. Turkey has declined to aid Azerbaijan on several occasions, citing opposition from its NATO allies. The West adopted measures to help resolve the conflict in the enclave: The Conference on Security and Cooperation in Europe (CSCE) began to conduct negotiations to mediate the conflict in 1992. CSCE peacekeeping forces were deployed in the region on several occasions. In January 1993, the European Parliament passed a resolution stating that the Azerbaijani blockade of Armenia and Nagorno-Karabakh was a violation of human rights. The U.N. Security Council also

8.5 Ethnic Composition of Former Soviet States in 1989

ARMENIA
Armenian	93%
Azeri	3%
Russian	2%
Other	2%

AZERBAIJAN
Azeri	82.7%
Armenian	5.6%
Russian	5.6%
Dagestani	3.2%
Other	2.9%

BELARUS
Belarusian	77.9%
Russian	13.2%
Polish	4.1%
Ukrainian	2.9%
Other	1.9%

ESTONIA
Estonian	61.5%
Russian	30.3%
Ukrainian	3.2%
Other	5.0%

GEORGIA
Georgian	70.1%
Armenian	8.1%
Russian	6.3%
Azeri	5.7%
Ossetian	3.0%
Abkhaz	1.8%
Other	5.0%

KAZAKHSTAN
Kazakh	41.9%
Russian	37.0%
Ukrainian	5.2%
German	4.7%
Uzbek	2.1%
Tatar	2.0%
Other	7.1%

KYRGYZSTAN
Kyrgyz	52.4%
Russian	21.5%
Uzbek	12.9%
Ukrainian	2.5%
German	2.4%
Other	8.3%

LATVIA
Latvian	51.7%
Russian	33.8%
Belarusian	4.5%
Ukrainian	3.4%
Polish	2.3%
Other	4.2%

LITHUANIA
Lithuanian	80.1%
Russian	8.6%
Polish	7.7%
Other	3.6%

MOLDOVA
Moldovan/Romanian	64.5%
Ukrainian	13.8%
Russian	13.0%
Gagauz	3.5%
Bulgarian	2.0%
Other	3.2%

RUSSIA
Russian	81.5%
Tatar	3.8%
Ukrainian	3.0%
Chuvash	1.2%
Dagestani	1.2%
Other	9.3%

TAJIKISTAN
Tajik	64.9%
Uzbek	25.0%
Russian	3.5%
Other	6.6%

TURKMENISTAN
Turkmen	73.3%
Russian	9.8%
Uzbek	9.0%
Kazakh	2.0%
Other	5.9%

UKRAINE
Ukrainian	73.0%
Russian	22.0%
Kazakh	4.1%
Other	5.0%

UZBEKISTAN
Uzbek	71.4%
Russian	8.3%
Tajik	4.7%
Tatar	2.4%
Karakalpak	2.1%
Other	7.0%

SOURCE: Ian Bremmer and Ray Taras, eds., *New States, New Politics: Building the Post-Soviet Nations* (Cambridge: Cambridge University Press, 1997), 48, 706–07; reprinted in Martha Brill Olcott, Anders Aslund, and Sherman W. Garnett, *Getting It Wrong: Regional Cooperation and the Commonwealth of Independent States* (New York: Carnegie Endowment for International Peace, 1999), 15.

undertook to help mediate the conflict through the adoption in February 1993 of a resolution calling for immediate cessation of hostilities, unimpeded access for international humanitarian aid to the region, and the eventual deployment of a peacekeeping force in the region. Currently, the situation is relatively peaceful, but remains unresolved. The presidents of both countries have expressed their willingness to find a peaceful solution to the conflict. Yet, no formal agreements have been signed.

GEORGIA-ABKHAZIA

The conflict in Abkhazia began early in 1992, when the local authorities attempted to secede from the Republic of **Georgia.** Georgia's first president, Zviad K. Gamsakhurdia, was a Georgian nationalist who eventually institutionalized ethnic Georgian nationalism as the only legitimate political force in Georgia. Those nationalist policies led to the formation of armed factions and, consequently, a civil war with the deployment of Georgian troops in Abkhazia in the summer of 1992. Representatives of the Republic of Georgia, Abkhazia, and **Russia** agreed on a ceasefire in Moscow in September 1993. The agreement ensured that the territorial integrity of Georgia would be preserved, a peace settlement would be reached by the end of the year, prisoners would be exchanged, and illegal armed groups would be disarmed. The agreement, although promising, was never fully implemented.

The cease-fire collapsed only a month later, and the fighting resumed. In May of the following year, the U.N. Secretary-General appointed a Special Envoy for Georgia in hopes of establishing a new cease-fire. That month, another agreement on the separation of forces and a cease-fire was reached in Moscow. The Security Council, which had established the U.N. Observer Mission in Georgia (UNOMIG) by resolution 858 (1993), now required the mission to monitor the implementation of the cease-fire agreement and to observe the operation of the CIS peacekeeping forces stationed in the conflict area.

Although Russian involvement helped to bring about cease-fires in Abkhazia after 1994, Russia was unwilling or unable to exert its influence further to resolve the conflict. Russia's relationship with Georgia stalemated after Georgia's initial refusal to join the CIS at its inception and its explicit reluctance to maintain close ties with Russia. Georgia's foreign policy since independence had been oriented toward the West. However, the internal instability caused by ethnic conflicts and the ensuing economic crisis became major impediments to establishing close contacts with NATO and other Western organizations. The current relationship between Abkhazia and Georgia remains tense, although the two sides met in January 2002 and agreed on protocol involving the Kodori Valley.

CHECHNYA

In 1991, Chechnya, a breakaway republic of Russia, declared its independence. Russia tried to regain control of the region by force three years later, and the war continued until 1996. In 1999, a new campaign was launched by Russia in response to alleged Chechen terrorist acts and increased rebel activity. Chechnya considered itself independent, however, and demonstrated its determination to assert that status by holding internationally monitored elections. Russia attacked again, claiming to fight terrorism and accusing Chechen groups of three bombings in Moscow. Russia's attempt to reassert its military and political power in the region took the form of systematic destruction of Chechen communications and infrastructure systems and the continued presence of its troops.

The conflict was not only devastating for the region but also attracted international attention. Russian soldiers harmed civilians and failed to observe their obligation, outlined in the Geneva convention, to focus their attacks on Chechen combat forces. Human rights groups documented three large-scale massacres by Russian forces. The Russian forces' killings of civilians and arrests of Chechen men and women caused more than 200,000 Chechens to flee their homes. These refugees faced great difficulties in obtaining shelter, food, and other essentials. Russia failed to stop abuses by its forces in the region. Not only did the authorities fail to monitor, deter, or punish human rights abuses by their troops; when confronted by the West, they denied such abuses.

The current situation in Chechnya remains deplorable. Day-to-day skirmishes between the rebels and Russian forces continue. Chechen rebels often rely on hit-and-run incursions into Russian held territory, as well as terrorist acts that target both civilians and combatants. Recently, Russia stepped up its campaign and began to comb through various regions in Chechnya. In May 2002, Russian forces heavily bombarded Chechen strongholds from the air and with artillery. As the fighting intensifies, a diplomatic solution to the conflict remains unachievable.[18]

NUCLEAR WEAPONS AND RUSSIA

With the collapse of the Soviet Union and the end of the Cold War, **Russia** vowed not to use its massive nuclear weapons arsenal as a first-strike capability. Its national security doctrine thereafter was based largely on economic incentives to maintain positive cooperative relations with the developed Western countries, and to create sound financial structures in post-Soviet Russia.

In January 2000, Acting President Vladimir Putin announced the reversal of Russia's prior decision not to use nuclear weapons as a first-strike capability. This announcement adversely affected Russia's role in the CIS and the country's relationship with the West. Putin's reversal of the nuclear weapons policy signaled the reluctance of the new administration to base its national security preferences on economic priorities and stressed its determination to form a new national security doctrine. The policies implemented by the United States in Iraq and Kosovo starkly contrasted the foreign policy preferences of the Russian Federation. The Russian leadership perceived the actions of the West as an attempt to undermine Russia's status as a major world power.

Following the 1998 financial crisis, economic relations with the West deteriorated considerably, making nuclear capability Russia's only means of reasserting itself in the international arena. Russia's reassertion of its nuclear capability was also a reminder to the West, particularly the United States, that Russia is the only country in the world with enough nuclear weapons to conduct a preemptive nuclear strike against the U.S. President Putin's announcement compelled U.S. policymakers to consider Russia's preferences and possible responses to U.S. foreign policy. His decision was crucial primarily because Russia was at a great disadvantage in conventional forces. Although it was unlikely that Russia would use its nuclear weapons to retaliate against a decision by the United States to conduct a foreign policy agenda comparable to that used in Kosovo, such an outcome was not implausible. That may have made it less likely that Russia would again be treated with the indifference to its views exhibited by the U.S. during the crisis in Kosovo.

Russia's new national security doctrine prompted other CIS countries to give up their nuclear armaments, leaving Russia the only former Soviet republic in possession of such weapons. Russia's willingness to use its nuclear arsenal threatened not only the West but also states such as **Georgia,** which had adopted a pro-Western foreign policy and benefited from U.S. aid. The United States was forced to reconsider its foreign policy in the CIS region: In Chechnya, for example, Russia could perceive U.S. aid as a threat to its national security and might, therefore, consider using its nuclear weapons.

START I, a treaty between Russia and United States that came into force on December 5, 1994, requires reductions in strategic offensive arms to 6,000 accountable warheads on each side as of December 4, 2001. All parties to the Treaty have been successful in meeting the Treaty's reduction requirements. On April 14, 2000, the Russian Duma approved the START II Treaty and the START II Protocol, and on May 5, President Putin signed the ratification document. In ratifying the START II Treaty, the Russian Duma passed a federal law containing a number of conditions. Among them is a requirement that the United States ratify the START II Protocol before the START II Treaty can come into force. Under START II, which was signed by the United States and Russia on January 3, 1993, all heavy ICBMs and MIRVed ICBMs must be eliminated from each side's deployed forces. In January 1996, the U.S. Senate gave its advice and consent to ratification of the START II Treaty. At the Helsinki summit on March 21, 1997, Presidents Clinton and Yeltsin made a Joint Statement on Parameters on Future Reductions in Nuclear Forces, according to which the parties pledged to launch negotiations on START III immediately after START II entered into force. Basic elements outlined by the two presidents at the time included:

- Lower aggregate levels of 2,000-2,500 strategic nuclear warheads—80 percent below the Cold War peak—for each of the parties;
- Transparency measures related to strategic nuclear warheads inventories and the destruction of strategic nuclear warheads;

- Exploration of possible measures relating to nuclear long-range sea-launched cruise missiles and tactical nuclear systems, including confidence-building and transparency measures;
- Early deactivation of all strategic nuclear delivery vehicles to be eliminated under START II by December 31, 2003, by removing nuclear warheads or taking other jointly agreed steps.[19]

On May 24, 2002, Presidents Vladimir Putin and George W. Bush signed an official agreement that obliges the two sides to cut the number of standing nuclear warheads down to 1,700 or 2,200 in the next ten years. This event marked an important step in mutual cooperation between the two nuclear powers.[20]

8.6 RUSSIAN REFORMS UNDER PRESIDENT PUTIN

Under President Putin, Russia has:

- Offered extensive support in the global campaign against terrorism: information-sharing, overflight clearance for U.S. aircraft, and search and rescue assistance. Contrary to what many Western analysts would have predicted, President Putin has posed no objections to the stationing of U.S. forces in Central Asia or a U.S. Train and Equip program for Georgia to fight terrorism.

- Accepted the U.S.'s offer of parallel reductions in operationally deployed nuclear warheads to the lowest levels in decades: down to between 1,700 and 2,200.

- Accepted the U.S.'s decision to move beyond the ABM Treaty and demonstrated more openness to its arguments on missile defense.

- Opened the way to a closer NATO-Russia working relationship, and dropped past

strong Russian objections to NATO enlargement.

- Coordinated with the U.S. and closely supported its position on the Middle East.

- Announced the closing of Russia's massive intelligence facility at Lourdes, Cuba and withdrawal from the Cam Ranh naval base in Vietnam.

- Cooperated with the U.S. in the Balkans as it continues efforts to promote a lasting settlement and stable, democratic development.

- Maintained a dialogue with the U.S. on Iraq, opening the way for U.N. Security Council agreement on a Goods Review List to streamline and make more effective sanctions against the Iraqi regime.

- Sustained oil production despite pressure from OPEC to make cuts and boost prices, thus helping to sustain a moderate global price.

- Recognized that small- and medium-size enterprises (SMEs) are a key source of growth and employment, and has publicly committed to create conditions that allow SMEs to flourish, many spurred by American training or American partners.

- Welcomed joint ventures and other investments by non-Russian firms. Although foreign direct investment (FDI) in Russia is proportionately low compared to many other countries, it is beginning to grow, and American firms account for the leading share, 35 percent, of total cumulative FDI.

SOURCE: "United States State Department Country Report: Russia." U.S. Department of State. <www.state.gov>

The Commonwealth of Independent States and the United Nations

PEACEKEEPING OPERATIONS

GEORGIA

The presence of the U.N. Observer Mission in **Georgia** (UNOMIG) has not prevented violations of a cease-fire between the Georgian government and the ethnic Abkhaz minority. The twenty-three nation U.N. force has monitored and assisted the collective peacekeeping forces of the Commonwealth of Independent States, composed mostly of **Russian** troops, who were locally believed to secretly support the Abkhaz secessionists. From 1994 through 2000, Moscow, at Georgia's invitation, stationed roughly 8,000 soldiers in the country.

The conflict's strategic location and intensity gained it international attention. The suggested pipelines to transport Caspian Sea oil reserves motivated U.N. member states to continue paying $1.55 million a month to maintain UNOMIG from 1993 on.

Nearly half a million people (Chechens, Georgians, Ingush, Ossetians, and Russians) were displaced during the conflict. The security situation continued to deteriorate, international personnel were targeted for robbery, there were numerous assassination attempts on the Georgian president, and aid workers were constantly harassed. Despite the UNOMIG presence and Russian-centered diplomatic efforts to mediate the conflict and achieve a sustainable peace, there was no significant move toward reconciliation.

The Chief Military Observer of the Mission chaired meetings of a joint fact-finding group established on January 19, 2000. It includes representatives of the CIS peacekeeping force, as well as of the Georgian and Abkhaz sides. The UNOMIG engineering and construction program in support of the Mission's operational needs is also continuing. Cooperation between UNOMIG and the CIS peacekeeping force remains very close. Criminality and lawlessness continue to be major destabilizing factors, placing in jeopardy the overall security situation. Complaints about terrorizing and intimidation by armed groups have repeatedly been lodged by the local population in both sectors. Repeated violations of the Agreement on a Ceasefire and Separation of Forces of May 14, 1994 and restrictions on the freedom of movement of UNOMIG continue. On January 31, 2002, the Security Council, by its resolution 1393, extended the mandate of UNOMIG until July 31, 2002. It also decided to review the mandate if the CIS peacekeeping force was not extended by February 15, 2002, noting that the Georgian authorities had agreed on January 31, 2002 to extend that mandate until the end of July 2002. The situation remains unresolved.[25]

TAJIKISTAN

Since early 1993, the armed insurgency of opposition forces, in particular from across the Tajik-Afghan border, continued to destabilize **Tajikistan.** In addition to the Tajik armed forces, **Russian** border forces, with the approval of the Tajik government, were deployed along the border to repel infiltration. The Commonwealth of Independent States deployed a peacekeeping force within the country. By resolution 968 (December 16, 1994), the Security Council established the U.N. Mission of Observers in Tajikistan (UNMOT).

On June 27, 1997, in Moscow, President Emomali Rakhmonov; Sayed Abdullo Nuri, leader of the United Tajik Opposition (UTO); and Mr. Gerd Merrem, then Special Representative of the United Nations Secretary-General, signed the General Agreement on the Establishment of Peace and National Accord in Tajikistan and the Moscow Protocol. The signing of the agreement and the subsequent convening of the Commission on National Reconciliation

launched a period of transition. The parties requested United Nations assistance in the implementation of the agreement. The Security Council, by its resolution 1138 of November 14, 1997, expanded the mandate of UNMOT.

The peace process was, however, disrupted by violence and made only slow progress. Intense fighting continued in 2000, and assaults against aid workers, U.N. personnel, civilians, and soldiers alike resulted in tightened funding from wearying donor nations. Nevertheless, Tajikistan's first multiparty elections were held in spring 2000, and UNMOT's mandate was terminated on May 15, 2000, with the U.N. Security Council officially stating that UNMOT had accomplished all of its assigned tasks.

The delegation of Kazakhstan at the fifty-third session of the General Assembly on September 28, 1998 in New York. (UN/DPI Photo: Evan Schneider)

Regional Organizations in the Commonwealth of Independent States

CIS countries have formed several bilateral and multilateral regional organizations to achieve some of the goals that underly the commonwealth's formation. These new regional organizations appear to be successful in providing the states with an opportunity to articulate their national interests.

RUSSIAN-BELARUSSIAN INTEGRATION

Russia and Belarus have achieved the most successful bilateral integration in the region. Unlike most newly independent states, Belarus neither had a strongly developed national identity nor wished to assert its newfound independence. The reluctance of its government to implement effective economic and political reforms, combined with the country's economic dependence on Russia, made active integration with Russia a high priority for Belarus.

The Belarussian government's first steps towards integration were economic agreements, such as a January 1994 agreement on a monetary union. This economic link between Russia and Belarus was inherently problematic because of the stagnation of the Belarussian economy, the country's dependence on Russia for monetary and economic assistance, and the high cost of such a relationship for Russia. The Russian government recognized that, economically, Belarus had considerably more to gain from this union than Russia and therefore required that Belarus implement economic reforms as a prerequisite to economic cooperation and integration. While the general public in Belarus widely supported integrationist policies, the Belarussian elite feared absorption by Russia. The issue of national sovereignty and the extent to which the two countries were willing to integrate economic, monetary, and domestic policies remained to be resolved.

The administration of Belarussian president Alexander Grigorievich Lukashenko strongly advocated integration. In 1996, President Lukashenko and his Russian counterpart, Boris Yeltsin, signed an agreement to create a Russian-Belarussian commonwealth. This was followed by a resolution to upgrade the relationship to a union in 1997. In December of the following year, representatives signed a treaty establishing equal rights and treatment for citizens of the two countries.[21] Although both governments contemplated and discussed further integration into a united state, the growing sense of sovereignty in Belarus and the high costs further integration would entail for Russia have hampered the active pursuit of such policies.

Despite Lukashenko's unpopularity, he was reelected to the presidency in September 2001 in a contest that his chief challenger called fraudulent. The Russian media, which for the most part supported Lukashenko, was said to have greatly influenced the outcome of the election. Lukashenko has remained a vigorous proponent of stronger ties with Russia, while President Putin tends to distance himself publicly from the autocratic Belarussian leader.[22]

THE CUSTOMS UNION

When it became clear that economic integration in the Commonwealth of Independent States would be a slow process, some of the states decided to form a customs union. The September 1993 treaty on the Conception of an Economic Union signed by CIS member states had not succeeded in providing a viable trade area and customs union. Belarus, Kazakhstan, and Russia were the first to form a customs union, in 1995. In January 1996, the CIS heads of government advised that the customs union be extended to include all CIS member states, but only Kyrgyzstan joined the the new organization. In March 1996, the four countries signed the Agreement on Increased Integration in the Economic and Humanitarian

Spheres, which became the founding document of the Customs Union. Membership was declared temporarily closed.

Tajikistan was allowed to apply in 1998 and joined the union a year later. As CIS states already had free trade within the region under the CIS Free Trade Agreement, free trade did not constitute an incentive for other CIS states to join the organization. The Customs Union was concerned primarily with establishing common import and export tariffs. The four member states agreed on a tariff that would be based on that of Russia. However, each state eventually proposed modifications to the existing tariff, and the organization then split over the issue of tariff rates.

Normally a customs union is expected to apply to the World Trade Organization (WTO) as a single entity, but Belarus, Kazakhstan, and Russia all submitted separate applications to the organization. Kyrgyzstan joined the World Trade Organization in 1998 and is required to abide by the laws and obligations of the WTO regardless of its commitment to the Customs Union.

Russia is currently in the process of negotiating terms of accession to the WTO. By the end of 1999 it had completed ten working party meetings. It tabled its initial services market access offer in October 1999 and has conducted negotiations on its goods market access offer. These offers contain Russia's proposed commitments to maximum tariff rates and the opening of Russian markets to foreign providers of services.[23]

In addition to disagreements on tariffs and ambitions to join the WTO, the Customs Union lacked efficient institutions to establish the principles by which the organization would be guided. Russia's tariff, which was considerably higher than those of other CIS states, was a major impediment to more states joining the organization.

Despite the existence of a customs union, a practical constraint remains: widespread corruption at member country borders on the part of underpaid customs authorities. In Russia, for instance, the country's 58,000 customs officials receive average salaries of $50-100 a month.[24]

THE CENTRAL ASIAN ECONOMIC COMMUNITY

The inter-republic working group established in June 1990 was the first attempt to unify the Central Asian states through economic and political integration. The first meeting focused on the management of the region's water resources and hydroelectric systems. In January 1993, the Central Asian states signed a communiqué agreeing to establish diplomatic relations. They also negotiated the creation of embassies, an inter-republic coordinating council, and a Central Asian economic market.

In July 1994, **Kazakhstan, Kyrgyzstan,** and **Uzbekistan** took the first step to formalize their union, calling for the creation of an interstate bank, the Central Asian Bank for Cooperation and Development. The leaders of the Central Asian states did not wish to undermine the CIS or replace it; instead, they considered the Central Asian Economic Community a mechanism for furthering integration within their immediate region. **Tajikistan** became an observer in the Central Asian Economic Community in 1995 and joined in July 1998. The organization, besides providing its members with an important forum for negotiations, extended beyond the economic realm to other issues, such as security relations within the region. In 1995, Kazakhstan, Kyrgyzstan, and Uzbekistan formed the Central Asian Battalion, a NATO-sponsored cooperative security arrangement.

The unfolding civil war in Tajikistan made Central Asian states more susceptible to Russian influence and increasingly dependent on Russian support, just when they were trying to curtail this dependence. Another problem was **Turkmenistan's** reluctance to join the Central Asian Economic Community on the ground of preserving its neutrality. The organization lacked coherence as a result of some persisting restrictions on trade among the countries, considerable differences in the economic strategies pursued by the member states, price controls, varying standards of living, and price differentials created by the variability in living standards. Also troublesome was the growing narcotics trade in the region,

which members of the community had little success in addressing. One of the priorities of the community's agenda was the issue of the uneven distribution of natural resources, such as gas, oil, and freshwater, throughout the region. A Central Asian Heads of State Summit, held in Ashgabat, Turkmenistan, on April 8, 1999, in conjunction with the International Fund for Saving the Aral Sea, addressed the problem of the Aral Sea as part of a larger scheme to improve the Central Asian water management system.

As long as the countries in the region remain economically competitive with one another, these and other problems are likely to persist. While the Central Asian Economic Community has provided its member states with an effective forum for the negotiation of security issues, the organization has yet to foster economic cooperation in Central Asia and economic growth for individual states as well as for the region as a whole.

Chechnyans displaced inside Chechnya were provided with food rations and non-food items, consisting of mattresses, blankets plastic sheeting and a cooking set upon returning. Grozny, Chechnya, Russia; 1997. (UN/UNHCR Photo: T.Bolstad)

1. "The President's Ear." *The Economist*. 16 February 2002.

2. Ulyanov, Nikolai and Yevgeny Yevdokimov. "Vladimir Putin Opens State of the Nation Speech with the Rare High Notes of His Address." *Russian Observer / National Information Service Online Magazine*. April 18, 2002. <http://www.russianobserver.com/stories/02/04/18/1020/15172.html> (June 9, 2002).

3. "A Challenge to the President." *The Economist*. 26 January 2002.

4. "Country Reports on Human Rights Practices—2001: Kyrgyz Republic." U.S. Department of State Bureau of Democracy, Human Rights, and Labor. March 4, 2002. <http://www.state.gov/g/drl/rls/hrrpt/2001/eur/8276.htm> (June 9, 2002).

5. "Patterns of Global Terrorism 2001: Eurasia Overview." Office of the Coordinator for Counterterrorism, U.S. Department of State. May 21, 2002. <http://www.state.gov/s/ct/rls/pgtrpt/2001/html/10239.htm> (June 9, 2002)

6. "Terrorism: Question & Answers—Uzbekistan." Council on Foreign Relations. <http://www.terrorismanswers.com/coalition/uzbekistan.html> (June 9, 2002)

7. "Background Note: Moldova." Bureau of European and Eurasian Affairs, U.S. Department of State. October 2001. <http://www.state.gov/r/pa/ei/bgn/5357.htm> (June 9, 2002).

8. "Third Periodic Reports of States Parties United Nations Office of the High Commissioner for Human Rights." Convention against Torture and Other Cruel, Inhuman or Degrading Treatment or Punishment. April 27, 2000. <http://www.unhchr.ch/tbs/doc.nsf/(Symbol)/d9860c282a210b1ac125697a004c3ea7?Opendocument> (June 9, 2002).

9. "Russian Media: Blank Screens." *The Economist*. 26 January 2002.

10. Information taken from "U.S. Department Country Reports" U.S. Department of State <http://www.state.gov/countries/ and Human Rights Watch http://www.hrw.org/> (June 9, 2002).

11. Olcott, Martha Brill, Anders Aslund, and Sherman W. Garnett, *Getting It Wrong: Regional Cooperation and the Commonwealth of Independent States* (New York: Carnegie Endowment for International Peace, 1999), p. 101.

12. Ibid., p. 97.

13. Ibid., p. 100.

14. "ODCCP Projects in Central Asia." United Nations Office for Drug Control and Crime Prevention. <http://www.undcp.org/uzbekistan/projects.html> (June 9, 2002)

15. Olcott et al., p. 37.

16. Ibid., p. 41.

17. "Vladimir Putin's Long, Hard Haul." *The Economist*. May 18, 2002.

18. Radio Svoboda (Russian). <http://www.svoboda.org/> (June 9, 2002).

19. "Background Note: Russia." Bureau of European and Eurasian Affairs, U.S. Department of State. November 2001. <http://www.state.gov/r/pa/ei/bgn/3183.htm> (June 9, 2002)

20. Radio Svoboda. <www.svoboda.org> (June 9, 2002).

21. Olcott et al., p. 174.

22. "Vladimir Putin's Long, Hard Haul."

23. "Background Note: Russia." Bureau of European and Eurasian Affairs, U.S. Department of State, November 2001. <http://www.state.gov/r/pa/ei/bgn/3183.htm> (June 9, 2002).

24. "Border Bore" *The Economist*. December 15, 2001.

25. "Georgia—UNOMIG: Background." United Nations Department of Public Information, Peace and Security Section. <http://www.un.org/Depts/DPKO/Missions/unomig/unomigB.htm> (June 9, 2002).

* FORMER YUGOSLAV REPUBLIC OF MACEDONIA

The geographic region referred to as Europe stretches from the middle of the Atlantic Ocean in the West to the Caucuses Mountains in the East, and from the North Pole to the coast of Africa in the South. The climate of this region is as varied as its geography, including arctic and sub-arctic climates in Iceland and Scandinavia, temperate climates across much of central Europe, and mild-Mediterranean climates around the Sea of the same name.

Although once considered a separate continent, today, most geographers consider the European Peninsula to simply be a distinct cultural region of a single continent known as Eurasia. Within this region there are several important geographic and cultural groupings. The "Nordic" countries are Denmark, Finland, Norway, Sweden, and Iceland. The "BeNeLux" countries are an acronym for Belgium, the Netherlands, and Luxembourg, which are wedged between the two largest states of "Western" Europe, France and Germany. Germany is also sometimes grouped with its fellow "Germanic" countries of Austria, Liechtenstein, and Switzerland. Likewise, Ireland and the United Kingdom share a common "Anglophone" heritage. Similar economic conditions, however, unite the "Iberian" countries of Spain and Portugal with Italy, Malta, and Greece in "Southern" Europe, whereas Andorra, the Holy See, Monaco, and San Marino share a common status as "City-States" in modern Europe. Finally, since the end of the Cold War in 1989, these states of "Western" Europe have been joined by many of the states of Eastern Europe. These include the "Baltics," Estonia, Latvia, and Lithuania; the "Balkans," Albania, Bosnia-Herzegovia, Croatia, the Former Yugoslav Republic of Macedonia, Slovenia, and Serbia and Montenegro; as well as Bulgaria, the Czech Republic, Hungary, Poland, Romania, and Slovakia. Finally, this region also includes the Republic of Moldova, the Russian Federation, and Ukraine, which will be considered in the chapter on the Commonwealth of Independent States (CIS), as well as the divided island of Cyprus and Turkey, which will also be examined in the Middle East chapter.

As the twenty-first century dawns, "Europe" is becoming ever more synonymous with the "European Union"—a new and different sort of political entity. Unlike other regional organizations, the European Union {EU) has come to dominate economic life on the European sub-continent, and its influence in various areas of politics and foreign affairs continues to increase. In addition to debating the future size and role of the European Union, there are other pressing issues in this region. In the world's most densely populated region, sustainable development and the environment remain near the top of the agenda. Work also remains towards the goal of protection of human rights in the region, particularly regarding the treatment of ethnic minorities. Finally, despite being perhaps the most peaceful region in the world today, Europe has several outstanding peace and security issues. In particular, many of the countries in the Balkan Peninsula remain on the edge of armed conflict, while in Western Europe the threat of terrorism is now more serious than ever.

RECENT ELECTIONS[1]

A number of elections have recently made headlines across Europe. In the **United Kingdom,**[2] Tony Blair's Labour Party was reelected in the summer of 2001 by a very large margin.[3] Blair has promised to use the momentum from the election to hold and win a nationwide referendum on joining the Euro Area (see page 140) later in his term.[4]

Meanwhile, in **France,** the field of presidential candidates included far more left-leaning candidates than right-leaning candidates, allowing the anti-immigration, nationalist candidate Jean-Marie Le Pen to join the centre-right Jacques Chirac as one of the top two finishers in the first round of the 2002 presidential election.[5] Many

French voters were horrified that a candidate who was both isolationist and perceived to harbor racist sentiments did so well, and thus gave Chirac an astonishing 82 percent of the vote in the second round. Chirac now has a five-year term as president (after a recent constitutional amendment) and parliamentary elections are due in France in June 2002.[6]

In **The Netherlands,**[7] a spring 2002 election was marred by the assassination of the socially liberal, but anti-immigration, candidate Pim Fortuyn by left-wing extremists.[8] Nevertheless, the political party he had named after himself placed a strong second to the centre-right Christian Democrats, thus giving the country its first right-wing government in eight years. [9]

Elsewhere, in **Italy,**[10] voters overlooked serious ethical charges[11] against Silvio Berlusconi to elect his centre-right coalition in late 2001. In **Portugal,**[12] the centre-right ousted the ruling Socialists by the narrowest of margins.[13] The same was true in Scandinavia, where Social Democrat governments were ousted in both **Denmark** and **Norway**[14] in favor of the centre-right in late 2001, with elections due in **Sweden** in 2002.[15] Finally, in late 2002, a close parliamentary election (which determines the Chancellor as well) is expected in **Germany.** The 2002 election in **Slovakia** will also be closely watched, as many Western nations fear a return to power of former Communist leader Vladimir Meciar.[16]

INTEGRATION:
THE EUROPEAN UNION

During its cautious beginnings, the European Union was designed to foster economic and political cooperation after the Second World War. The EU has now become an organization affecting almost every aspect of European life.[17] Currently on the verge of nearly doubling its membership to

9.1
OUTSIDE THE EU

Although this section focuses on the EU and its applicant members, the European region also includes a few states that are neither EU members nor formal applicants, but are also covered here:

Albania, Andorra, Bosnia and Herzegovina, Croatia, Former Yugoslav Republic of Macedonia, the Holy See, Iceland, Liechtenstein, Monaco, Norway, San Marino, Serbia and Montenegro, Switzerland.

9.2
EU MEMBERS
(DATE OF ENTRY)

Austria (1994)
Belgium (1952)
Denmark (1973)
Finland (1994)
France (1952)
Germany (1952)
Greece (1981)
Ireland (1973)
Italy (1952)
Luxembourg (1952)
Netherlands (1952)
Portugal (1986)
Spain (1986)
Sweden (1994)
United Kingdom (1973)

include states from Eastern and Southern Europe, the EU now faces questions about its ultimate purpose. In particular, the introduction of the new "euro" currency has presented special economic challenges, while proposals for common defense and foreign policies promise new challenges of their own.[18]

HISTORY[19]

After World War II, the desire to secure a lasting peace dominated all plans for Europe's future. The European Coal and Steel Community (ECSC) pooled its member countries' basic war-making materials, coal and steel, in the hope that closer economic ties would eventually make war impossible. In 1957, the six member countries (**Belgium, France, Italy, Luxembourg, The Netherlands,** and **West Germany**) signed the Treaty of Rome, which complemented the ECSC with organizations seeking to institute a general common market among member states and an atomic energy pool. By 1965, these multilateral institutions were known as The European Community (EC).

The end of the Cold War in 1989 accelerated the drive for integration among the members of the EC. The reunification of Germany meant that that country now represented 27 percent of the EC's GDP and 25 percent of its population. This posed some uncomfortable political problems, as the core of the EC had so far been a partnership of "equals" between France and West Germany. France suddenly saw its relative power and economic might being eclipsed by Germany.[20] Also, Germany was very conscious of its past, and thus very anxious about any perceived threats felt by its neighbors.[21] Consequently both sides had an incentive for further integration—the Germans in order to legitimize their newfound power without the perceived stain of nationalism, and the French and others to tie rising German power to the institutions of the EC, where it might be checked by other European states.

These interests led to the 1991 signing of the Treaty on European Union in Maastricht, The Netherlands. Also known as the Maastricht Treaty, it came into force in 1993, changing the

name of the EC to European Union (EU) in order to emphasize the closer relationship among members that changes to the organization would foster. In addition, the Maastricht Treaty set Europe on the road to a single currency, the euro, which began public circulation in 2001. Finally, Maastricht established the four main bodies of the EU: the Council of Ministers, the European Parliament, the European Court of Justice, and the European Commission.

Of these, the Council of Ministers is the main negotiating forum. Here, nationally appointed representatives of member states legislate for the Union, set its political objectives, and coordinate national policies. Legislation formulated by the Council is legally binding on member states and comes under the jurisdiction of the European Court of Justice. The European Commission, meanwhile, has three distinct roles: initiator of proposals for legislation, guardian of treaties, and executor of Union policies and international trade relationships. The role of the directly elected European Parliament, however, is primarily advisory, although it does include supervisory and budgetary duties.

Today, the EU is active in a wide range of policy areas, from creation of a single European market among its member states, whereby the free movement of goods, services, labor, and capital is ensured, to the framing of agricultural and commercial policies. As the organ responsible for the common commercial policy of its members, the Commission participates as an individual entity in such forums as the World Trade Organization (WTO). The EU also played a key role in mediation efforts to bring peace to the former Yugoslavia, and is today the largest humanitarian donor to victims of that conflict. The growing importance of the EU itself, as an institution, in foreign affairs is underscored by the presence of official EU delegations in more than 100 countries, including an observer mission at the U. N.

"EVER CLOSER UNION"

No three words are more controversial in Europe than "ever closer union," from the founding

Treaty of Rome, which continues to define the rationale behind the EU even today. But what does "ever closer union" mean? Is it closer cooperation among individual nation-states, as the **United Kingdom** argues? Or does it imply the future existence of a federal United States of Europe, as **Germany's** foreign minister, Joschka Fischer, argues? At the time of this writing, a European Constitutional Convention[22] was underway to attempt to redefine the future meaning and purpose of the European Union.[23] The results of the convention promise to shape the direction of European integration for at least the next half-century.[24]

EXPANSION[25]

The 1957 Treaty of Rome stipulated that membership in the European Economic Community was open to all democratic and peace-loving states in Europe prepared to accept the legal standards of the Community.[26] With the demise of the Communist Bloc, however, the European Union is now confronted with ·the challenge of nearly doubling its membership through new applicant states. In large part to address these challenges, the EU member states recently

signed the Treaty of Nice, which is designed to reform EU institutions to accommodate the influx of new members. One of the most important of these reforms is instituting majority voting in EU institutions. The Treaty of Nice will not go into effect, however, until it is ratified by all member states, which in **Ireland** requires approval in a popular referendum. As of this writing, Irish voters had narrowly rejected the Treaty of Nice in a referendum, but the government was planning to resubmit the treaty to voters in 2002.[27]

Once an applicant state has been accepted to begin negotiating entry into the European Union, it must pass an enormous amount of EU legislation—nearly 80,000 pages worth—or negotiate agreements with the EU that supplement the areas of EU legislation not passed. This can be difficult, as there are many risks for both sides of the EU expansion. As an example, one of the primary concerns of the EU members is that they will be flooded by poor workers from Central and Eastern Europe who will be willing to settle for low wages and drive down salaries.[28] On the other side, some of the applicant countries, particularly Poland,[29] worry that investors from wealthy Western European countries will buy up land in their own countries. Thus, some interim agreement

A partial view of a meeting of the European Coal Organization, May 13, 1947, Geneva, Switzerland. (UN Photo)

Once accepted as a
formal candidate for
admission to the EU,
a long period of
negotiations begins
before admission can
be completed. Here is
the status of all of the
formally recognized
candidates for
admission to the EU.

**Negotiations on Pace
for Admission in
2004-2005:**

Cyprus
Czech Republic
Estonia
Hungary
Latvia
Lithuania
Malta
Poland
Slovakia
Slovenia

**Negotiations on Pace
for Admission in
2007-2008:**

Bulgaria
Romania

**Negotiations Not
Yet Begun:**

Turkey

limiting worker and capital flows between new and old EU Members will be necessary and, indeed, is currently under negotiation.

Another thorny issue is the European Common Agricultural Policy (CAP), which pays large amounts of direct-payment subsidies to European farmers.[30] If the CAP were extended as is to the new applicant countries, which are far poorer and more agricultural than the current EU members, the EU would quickly be bankrupted. Yet, the farmers in current EU member countries are unwilling to give up their subsidies, while at the same time the new applicant countries are unwilling to enter the European Union without full equality with other EU members. Despite grumblings from some countries, particularly the **Czech Republic** and **Estonia,** regarding the compromises required to conclude these negotiations, the EU is widely expected to complete negotiations with ten applicant states by the end of 2002 for membership in 2004 or 2005.

Most observers currently expect the EU to admit a class of ten applicant states all at once in 2004 or 2005, due to sensitive political considerations. After all, it would be politically difficult, for instance, to admit only the most Westernized Baltic state, Estonia, and not its neighbors, Lithuania and Latvia.[31] Likewise, it would be difficult to admit the Czech Republic, but not its former partner, **Slovakia,** despite lingering concerns about the state of democracy in the latter country. Furthermore, **Greece** has threatened to veto the admission of any new members if **Cyprus** is not included among them. In addition, **Turkey** has threatened to make the operations of North Atlantic Treaty Oranization (NATO) difficult if Cyprus is admitted prior to the reunification of Cyprus with the Turkish Republic of Northern Cyprus.[32] (NATO is a consensus-based organization that requires unanimous consent for all decisions, which permits even one nation to hold up any decision within NATO for any reason.)

ECONOMIC AND MONETARY UNION

On January 1, 2002, the European Union introduced "euro" notes and coins into public circula-
tion, thereby bringing about true monetary union for the euro area members. This launch was very successful, producing only minor economic disruptions. Although euros have been available for transactions between financial institutions since 1999, the introduction of hard currency notes and coins truly made the euro a reality for the 312 million Europeans in the twelve euro area countries. Despite the success of introducing some 14 billion bank notes and another 50 billion coins, in what the European Central Bank called "the biggest logistical exercise in peacetime,"[33] the euro continues to present challenges for the future. Among these are the addition of new members, the future of the Stability Pact on which the euro is based, and the possibility of future crises.

If there was a dark cloud in the launch of the euro, it was that three of the EU members chose not to participate in the Monetary Union, namely **Denmark, Sweden,** and most notably, the **United Kingdom.** All three countries have said that they will consider joining the Monetary Union in the future, but none of them appear ready to do so in the near future. (All new applicants to the European Union, however, are required to adopt the euro.)

Another potential trouble spot is that in order to harmonize their economies before adopting a common currency, the euro area members agreed to a Stability Pact that was designed to prevent one euro area member from causing an economic crisis for all of the euro area members. The Stability Pact requires member countries to keep their budget deficits under 3 percent of GDP, or else face serious fines. The Pact was tested almost immediately in early 2002, however, as both **Germany** and **Portugal's** budget deficits began to approach the 3 percent limit. Although Pact guidelines called for the issuing of a formal warning to both countries about the size of their deficits, no warning was issued, as the EU did not want to embarrass Germany (the Euro Area's largest and most powerful member), nor could it be seen as chastising a small country (Portugal) and giving a free pass to a large country (Germany). As of this writing, it was unclear whether either country will broach the limits in 2002, and if so, if either will be assessed fines. Already, some

9.4 European Union Timeline

1951 Treaty of Paris establishing European Steel and Coal Community (ESCC) signed by Belgium, France, Italy, Luxembourg, The Netherlands, and West Germany

1957 European Economic Community (EEC) and Euratom formed by Treaty of Rome

1963 Application of U.K. for membership vetoed by France

1965 EEC, Euratom, and ESCC merged to form the European Community (EC)

1968 EC Free Trade Area begins

1973 Denmark, Ireland, and the U.K. join the EC

1981 Greece joins the EC

1985 "Single European Act" marks first reform of EC institutions to accommodate expansion in membership

1986 Spain and Portugal join the EC

1989 Collapse of Berlin Wall marks end of Cold War

1990 East Germany merges with West Germany; United Germany now largest EC member

1991 Maastricht Treaty, second reform of the EC and committing the EC to monetary union, is signed

1993 The European Union (EU) replaces the EC

1994 Austria, Finland, and Sweden join the EU

1995 Schengen Agreement creates open borders for six countries (now ten)

1996 Amsterdam Treaty marks third reform of EU Institutions

1999 Euro is introduced by eleven countries for use in financial transactions

2000 Treaty of Nice, fourth reform of EU institutions, signed (not yet in effect)

2000 Charter of Fundamental Rights of the European Union informally adopted at Nice

2001 Greece adopts the euro

2002 Euro notes and coins enter public circulation

2002 European Union Constitutional Convention begins

---

economists have called for scrapping the Stability Pact altogether, despite the possible consequences in lost prestige and confidence in the euro. For now, though, all countries claim to be fully committed to the Stability Pact, and are currently in full compliance. [34]

The greatest risk of the euro experiment, however, is that the member countries have given up control over monetary policy to the EU's European Central Bank (ECB). Ordinarily, a national central bank raises interest rates when the economy is growing to help prevent inflation, and lowers interest rates when the economy is slowing down to promote economic growth. Yet if one country of the Euro Area is growing rapidly while another is slowing down, the ECB will have to choose one policy or the other, which creates the potential for conflict. In the meantime, the benefits of membership include the ability to easily compare prices across borders and to more easily attract foreign investment into what is now the world's second largest currency area (after the US$).

A Common Foreign Policy

Traditionally, European foreign affairs have remained the preserve of individual states. However, with ratification of the treaties of Maastricht and Amsterdam, which contain mandates for common foreign, security, social, and commercial policies, a more "European" policy on global issues is emerging.

Under article J(3) of the 1997 Amsterdam Treaty, the European Council defines the principles and general guidelines for the Common Foreign and Security Policy (CFSP) and decides on common strategies to be implemented by the Union in fields in which the member states have important common interests. Although some Europeans who are strongly in favor of fast integration have proposed consolidated European foreign representation into a single European Foreign Ministry, with single European embassies and foreign representation, the EU member states so far seem unwilling to give up the ability to have an independent foreign policy.

Perhaps the most significant development on this front has been the authorization of a 60,000-strong European Rapid Reaction Force

12 Euro Area
Members:

Austria
Belgium
Finland
France
Germany
Greece
Ireland
Italy
Luxembourg
Netherlands
Portugal
Spain

Non-Euro Member
Countries Also Making
"National" Euros:

Holy See
Monaco
San Marino

Other Countries and
Areas Using the Euro:

Andorra
Kosovo
Montenegro

(EuroForce), due to begin operations in 2003. The impetus for this authorization was a result of the **Kosovo** Crisis, during which the Europeans were embarrassed by their inability to intervene on behalf of the Kosovars, and were instead forced to call upon the U.S. to lead the operation.

The mission of the EuroForce as currently established, however, does not include such "peacemaking" activities, but instead authorizes what are known as the Petersburg Tasks (after the hotel in **Germany** where they were defined), which are primarily oriented towards peacekeeping and humanitarian relief. Many European policymakers, however, consider it the first step towards getting the EU involved, in the words of one European General, in "the war-fighting game."[35] For the moment, however, the EuroForce is somewhat limited by the objections of **Turkey**, which is nervous about the EuroForce (of which it is not a member) undermining NATO (of which it is a member). Since NATO is the premier defense organization in the world, the EuroForce will be heavily reliant upon it for logistics and support that would be too expensive and impractical to duplicate. Although, the EuroForce is currently limited to missions that NATO chooses not to undertake, many Europeans envision a close EuroForce-NATO partnership in the future.

At present, however, the EuroForce also faces the major challenge of achieving adequate funding. In the fall of 2001, *The Economist* noted that "the EU, although it has 375m people compared with America's 280m, spends only about 57 percent of what America does on defense. What is more, it does not get value for money. Its members too often duplicate each other's work. Many European armies are long on undeployable conscripts and short on crack troops. NATO reckons the Europeans have only a tenth of the readily deployable forces available to the Americans."[36] Clearly, the creation of EuroForce is but one bold step on the way to true independent defense for Europe.

SUSTAINABLE DEVELOPMENT[37]

Over two hundred years ago, Europe was the birthplace of the Industrial Revolution. As such, Europeans have first-hand knowledge of the long-term consequences of irresponsible industrial development. Moreover, Europe now faces the post-Cold War task of cleaning up the unparalleled devastation wrought by state-planned communist economies in the twentieth century. Thus, today the nations of Europe are arguably the foremost international advocates of environmental responsibility. For many of them, protection of the environment both at home and abroad is an important foreign policy priority.

The hottest buzzword in this area right now is "sustainable development," the process of creating economic growth that does not harm the environment. Not all economic growth necessarily has the same impact on the environment, and as Eastern Europe's experience with communism demonstrated, it is possible for irresponsible economic growth to devastate the natural environment. Thus, the goal of sustainable development is to find ways of producing rapid economic growth while also safeguarding the health of the environment.

The Amsterdam Treaty stresses that all EU members, present and future, must address environmental concerns within their borders. Furthermore, it acknowledges that sustainable development should be treated not as a theory but as a system to which all governments and citizens must adhere to, in order to ensure that future generations will enjoy an Earth that is capable of fulfilling their needs.

In 2000, the EU drafted the Sixth Action Programme, which is designed to guide European environmental policy into the twenty-first century. The new guidelines stress the need for all governments of the EU to make sustainable development a higher priority. It was clear that the EU felt that one main issue must be brought to the fore: cooperation between governments and people. The organization believes that each of its members' governments has a duty to involve them in every aspect of the process.

Most recently, another major issue in this vein

for the European Union has been the Kyoto Treaty, which proposed to require industrialized nations to undertake aggressive mandatory limits on their emissions of greenhouse gases. European Union members have been almost unanimous in their condemnation of the United States' decision to reject this treaty. Although they all pledged to carry on with meeting the Treaty's obligations without the United States, it is unclear that they will be willing to undertake the high costs of meeting these obligations without the world's largest emitter of greenhouse gases also participating. Although the U. S. has proposed some compromises, such as placing limits on developing countries as well and issuing "credits" for measures taken to reduce greenhouse gases that are already in the atmosphere, the EU considers them to be inadequate, and continues to push for mandatory cuts on emissions by all industrialized nations.

HUMAN RIGHTS

Europe has a long and storied tradition of promoting democracy and human rights. Indeed, the history of democracy itself was written from classical Athens and Rome, the first parliaments of **Iceland** and **Switzerland,** the U.K.'s Magna Carta and the French revolutionaries' Declaration of the Rights of Man. Today Europe participates in a wide variety of organizations dedicated to the defense of Human Rights, including the U. N. Commission on Human Rights, the European Union, the Council of Europe, and the Organization for Security and Cooperation in Europe.[38]

THE EUROPEAN UNION

In order to apply for membership in the European Union, applicant states are required to meet exacting standards of protection for human rights and democracy. The EU emphasizes, however, that primary accountability for the protection and promotion of human rights lies with EU member states themselves. In particular, **Turkey's** application to become the first predominantly Muslim member of the European Union has been

held up, according to the organization, largely due to concerns about its human rights record. Areas of the EU's concern include Turkey's continued use of the death penalty (which is considered by Europeans to be a serious human rights violation) and the continued role of the military in interfering with the country's democracy. Also troubling for the EU is Turkey's treatment of its minorities, particularly the Kurds, who live predominantly in the southeast of the country and are forbidden by the Turkish government to use their language and practice certain cultural traditions.

At the Nice Summit, held in **Italy** at the end of 2000, the European Union adopted a comprehensive Charter of Fundamental Rights of the European Union which identifies a broad array of human rights that are to be guaranteed to all European citizens. In particular, this document is important (and controversial) in that it extends the concept of human rights beyond the political rights that are familiar to certain countries, such as the United States, to include a wide variety of economic and social rights. As of this writing, the legal status of the Charter is pending on the outcome of the currently ongoing European Constitutional Convention.

THE COUNCIL OF EUROPE

The Council of Europe has more than forty members, including all current EU countries and applicants. It was founded in 1949, and its core document is the European Convention on Human Rights (Convention for the Protection of Human Rights and Fundamental Freedoms, CPRHFF), which ensures the protection of basic human rights and liberties. Each member state of the Council of Europe ratified the convention, which went into force in 1953. Furthermore, Article 6(1) of the Treaty of European Union states that the EU must respect the fundamental rights guaranteed by the CPRHFF. The convention established the European Commission of Human Rights and the European Court of Human Rights, the latter of which deals with the petitions of individuals and interstate cases. The Court has become somewhat controversial in

9.8 Web Resources on Human Rights

U.N. Commissioner for Human Rights

http://www.unhchr.ch

Charter of Fundamental Rights of the European Union

http://www.europarl.eu.int/charter/default_en.htm

Council of Europe—Human Rights Web

http://humanrights.coe.int

European Commission on Human Rights

http://dhcommhr/coe.int

European Court of Human Rights

http://echr.coe.int

Office for Democratic Institutions and Human Rights

http://www.osce.org/odihr

recent years, due to concerns that its ability to hear the petitions of individuals who have exhausted domestic legal recourses might undermine national sovereignty.

ORGANIZATION FOR SECURITY AND COOPERATION IN EUROPE

The Organization for Security and Cooperation in Europe (OSCE) consists of every nation of Europe and the former Soviet Union, as well as the United States and Canada. The OSCE's primary work includes election-monitoring and some conflict resolution. Also important is the OSCE's Office for Democratic Institutions and Human Rights (ODIHR), based in Warsaw, **Poland**, which promotes human rights and democratization. The OSCE High Commissioner for National Minorities attempts to reduce tensions in the early stages of disagreements among national minorities and alerts the OSCE to possible conflicts.

9.9 THE ROMA

One of the most pressing human rights issues in Europe is the treatment of minorities. As a people without a country of their own, the treatment of the Roma is of particular concern in this regard. In Central and Eastern Europe, they comprise between 5 and 12 percent of the population. Living among the relatively poor countries of Europe, the Roma often rank as the most economically disadvantaged ethnic group within EU applicant countries. The conundrum of an ethnic minority living at developing world poverty levels, particularly as soon-to-be citizens of the European Union, is a problem that must be solved.

The popular name of the Roma, Gypsy, comes from the once common misconception that these people originated in Egypt. Rather, it is

believed they descended from migrants from India in the eleventh century. Moreover, despite the stereotypical image of wandering nomads with covered Medieval wagons, the Roma, many of whom perished in Nazi concentration camps in the Second World War, have for the most part given up the nomadic lifestyle. Today, they tend to live in slums outside the major cities of Europe.

In response to ethnic persecution across Europe, the Roma have traditionally been a dispersed people lacking cohesion, and many adopted a nomadic lifestyle that lasted for centuries. The legacy of this is that today there is almost no Roma national identity larger than the family or clan, making infighting among

the Roma peoples even more common than cooperation to solve their problems.

And the problems are many. In some countries, nearly 75 percent of orphans and nearly 60 percent of the prison inmates are Roma, despite being only a tenth of the population. Moreover, while 40 percent of Europe's Roma are children, one third of those Roma children never attend any school, and only one in a thousand ever attend college or university. Thus, an entire generation is growing up without education, without jobs, and without future leaders. Clearly, if Europe wants to reverse the effects of centuries of ethnic persecution, it must find a way to make a better life for its six million Roma.

Members of the European Union share very similar agendas and views at the United Nations, and often speak and vote as a bloc. Enticed by the prospects of joining the EU, Eastern European countries are increasingly following the Union's lead, diverging only on issues of overwhelmingly domestic concern. Likewise, many non-EU members or applicants have cooperated closely with the EU on matters of foreign policy, especially in international organizations like the U.N. The region's primary concerns include peacekeeping, global disarmament, sustainable development, assistance to economies in transition, human rights, humanitarian assistance, and security issues (particularly the conflict in the Balkans).

INTERNATIONAL CRIMINAL TRIBUNAL FOR THE FORMER YUGOSLAVIA (ICTY)

The International Criminal Tribunal for the former Yugoslavia (ICTY) is situated in The Hague, **Netherlands.**[39] Established by Security Council Resolution 827 on May 25, 1993, its mandate is to prosecute individuals who are responsible for serious violations of international humanitarian law committed since 1991 in the territory of the former Yugoslavia.[40] The ICTY has the authority to issue arrest warrants for persons who may be in any state's jurisdiction. Under its statute, the tribunal is able to prosecute four types of offenses:

- Genocide (Article 4). Acts with intent to destroy, in whole or in part, a national, ethnic, social, or religious group;
- Crimes against humanity (Article 5). Crimes include murder, enslavement, imprisonment, torture, and rape, committed in armed conflict against any civilian population;

- Grave breaches of the 1949 Geneva Conventions (Article 2). Acts include willful killing, torture, appropriation of property, deportation, and hostage-taking;
- Violations of the laws or customs of war (Article 3). Acts include unjustified destruction of towns, plunder of property, use of poisonous weapons, and willful damage to religious, charitable, or arts institutions.

WELCOME, SWITZERLAND

For decades, one of the great anachronisms of the United Nations system has been that the U.N. has maintained a close working relationship with **Switzerland,** one of the few countries in the world that has declined U.N. membership. With its long history of neutrality, Switzerland had always been concerned that the obligations of the U.N. Charter might require it to take sides in international conflicts at the directive of the U.N. Security Council, such as by participating in sanctions against Iraq or being called to the collective defense of a country, as in the case of the Republic of Korea during the Korean War. On March 3, 2002, however, Swiss voters narrowly decided that the benefits of membership outweighed the risks and approved a decision to join the World Body.[43] The U.N. Security Council and General Assembly are expected to easily approve Switzerland's application for membership in the fall of 2002. The accession of Switzerland will mean that there are only a few small corners of the globe that are not represented by full membership in the U.N., most notably Taiwan, the Holy See, the Palestinian Authority Territories, Kosovo, and Northern Cyprus.

SECURITY ISSUES IN EUROPE

CYPRUS

One of Europe's most intractable disputes involves the divided island of **Cyprus.** In 1960, three years after independence from the **U.K.,** the **Greek Cypriot** government proposed constitutional changes that would have ended power-sharing with the Turkish Cypriot minority. After rioting broke out in response, the United Nations Peacekeeping Force in Cyprus (UNFICYP) was established by Security Council Resolution 186, on March 4, 1964. In 1974, a coup by Greek Cypriots threatened to merge the island with **Greece.** Within days, **Turkey** invaded the predominantly **Turkish Cypriot** northern portion of the island to protect the Turkish Cypriots. UNFICYP's mandate was extended to maintain a buffer zone between the Turkish Cypriot forces and the Cyprus National Guard along what is now known as the Green Line, after the color used to draw it on the map. In 1983, peace talks broke down and the northern portion of the island declared independence as the Turkish Republic of Northern Cyprus (TRNC). Currently, only Turkey, which maintains 35,000 troops in the TRNC, recognizes its independence.[44] As of this writing, many observers believe that U.N.-sponsored peace talks are near a breakthrough that might finally bring lasting peace to this divided island.[45]

CROATIA

The United Nations Mission of Observers in Prevlaka (UNMOP) was first deployed in October 1992 to monitor the strategic Prevlaka Peninsula, which was disputed by **Croatia** and the Federal Republic of Yugoslavia (now **Serbia** and **Montenegro.**) By resolution 1038, the Security Council extended its mandate in January 1996 to help decrease tensions in the area. On December 13, 1999, the Secretary-General submitted a report to the Security Council that welcomed the confirmed withdrawal of Yugoslav military forces from the U.N. demilitarized zone. The continuing absence of Croatian troops has sparked hope of improving the UNMOP operation. Negotiations on the political level are still needed, however.

BOSNIA-HERZEGOVINA

The United Nations Mission in **Bosnia-Herzegovina** (UNMIBH) was established on December 21, 1995, by Security Council Resolution 1035. The operation is composed of the United Nations International Police Task Force (IPTF) and a U.N. civilian office for the territory of Bosnia and Herzegovina. It was initially authorized for one year, under the peace agreement signed on December 14, 1995, by the leaders of Bosnia and Herzegovina, Croatia, and the Federal Republic of Yugoslavia. The operation worked to implement the peace agreement through humanitarian relief, monitoring, and economic reconstruction.

KOSOVO

The United Nations Interim Administration in **Kosovo** (U. N. Mission in Kosovo, UNMIK) was established on June 10, 1999, under Security Council Resolution 1244. It serves as the transitional government and works with community leaders and citizens. UNMIK, the first operation of its type, concentrates on four key functions: humanitarian assistance under the UNHCR, civil administration, democratization and institution building under the OSCE, and economic development under the EU. The Kosovo-UNMIK Joint Interim Administrative Structure (JIAS), set up in December 1999, established shared responsibility between UNMIK and the Kosovar people. This mission has been a unique success story for the U.N. and Europe, as making Kosovo essentially a U.N. protectorate has managed to bring peace to the area.[46] The most outstanding difficulty in the peace process, however, seems to be that the Kosovars appear ever more unwilling to reunify with **Serbia,** thus necessitating difficult negotiations on the final status of Kosovo in the future.[47]

FORMER YUGOSLAV REPUBLIC OF MACEDONIA (FYR MACEDONIA)

Since **Greece** fears that any independent country by the name of Macedonia may someday seek to acquire the neighboring Greek province of Macedonia, the small country formed from the former Yugoslav republic of Macedonia has only able to gain diplomatic recognition under the awkward name of the **Former Yugoslav Republic of Macedonia** (FYR Macedonia).[48]

Much more serious than debates about the length of its name has been the recent infiltration of Kosovar rebels into the Northern FYR Macedonia, in an attempt to incite Macedonian Albanians to violence.[49] NATO took a lead in

resolving this conflict by brokering a settlement between the government of FYR Macedonia and representatives of the ethnic Albanian minority.[50] In addition, NATO continues to carry out a number of missions in the country, including peacekeeping and the disarming of rebel forces.[51]

MONTENEGRO

Montenegro is the only former Yugoslav Republic and one of only two areas in the former Yugoslavia that remains joined with **Serbia** (the other being the autonomous region of Vojvodina, a predominantly Hungarian enclave of Serbia in the North, just as **Kosovo** was a predominantly Albanian enclave of Serbia in the South). Many observers have worried that the next Balkan war would ensue over an attempt of Montenegro to secede and reestablish the independence it once held briefly in the early twentieth century, possibly as a result of a Montenegrin vote on independence that was scheduled for the summer of 2002. These fears were allayed, however, in March 2002 when the EU brokered a deal in which Montenegro canceled the vote in exchange for greater autonomy in a new federation with Serbia that replaced "Yugoslavia" with the new country of **"Serbia and Montenegro."**[52] Since Montenegro has a large Serbian minority, which promised to make the scheduled vote on independence very close, this deal appears to benefit both sides.

NORTHERN IRELAND

Despite occasional lapses into communal violence, the **Northern Ireland** peace plan appears to be well underway. The **United Kingdom** has chosen to resolve this conflict primarily on a bilateral basis with representatives of the various Northern Irish communities, the **Republic of Ireland,** and occasional mediation from the United States. The U.N. has not been actively involved in settling this dispute.

BASQUE

The Basques are a minority who live on the northern coast of **Spain**[53] and a small corner of **France** near the Spanish border.[54] The terrorist activities of the ETA (Basque Fatherland and Liberty Group), a militant group that advocates independence for the Basques, however, have made the situation a violent one.[55] Currently, the Basque region enjoys a high degree of autonomy within Spain, and the majority of Spain's Basques are satisfied with this arrangement, considering themselves to be both Basques and Spaniards. As such, Spain has sought resolution of the terrorist crisis primarily on a unilateral basis.

STRAITS OF GIBRALTAR

Various accidents of history have made the political map around the Straits of Gibraltar unusually complex.[56] The **United Kingdom** owns a small enclave around the Rock of Gibraltar, the residents of which overwhelmingly prefer to remain British citizens.[57] **Spain,** for its part, has two enclaves of its own, Ceuta and Melilla, on the coast of Morocco.[58] Although Spain regularly presses for negotiations to gain control of Gibraltar, and Morocco does the same for Ceuta and Melilla, a formal hand-over of any of the territories continues to appear unlikely.[59]

EUROPE AND SECURITY COUNCIL REFORM

Security Council reform remains one of the most important issues for Europe at the U.N., if for no other reason than that in almost all proposals, Europe stands to gain at least one new permanent Security Council member in **Germany.**[41] Not all European countries are excited by this prospect, however, particularly **Italy,** which still considers itself to be a major European power and does not want to be the last "major European power" without a veto.[42] Of course, plans to give permanent Security Council membership to Germany and Japan have circulated for a decade now with little signs of progress. Many developing nations think that the permanent membership of the Security Council currently reflects the world as it was in 1945, and that adding Germany and Japan would simply make the membership a reflection of the world in 1939, which would not, in their minds, represent progress. This stalemate has led some observers to float a radical long-term proposal for Security Council reform, suggesting that if the EU were ever to truly adopt a single, common foreign policy, all EU member states could be represented by a single permanent member. This would then open the way for adding permanent members from the developing world without making the total number of permanent members unwieldy.

Some of the most important international organizations that are active in this region, including the EU, the Council of Europe, the Organization for Security and Cooperation in Europe, and of course, the United Nations, have already been dealt with extensively in this chapter. A notable exception has been the North Atlantic Treaty Organization (NATO).

NORTH ATLANTIC TREATY ORGANIZATION (NATO)

The North Atlantic Treaty Organization (NATO) is the keystone of the European security architecture. Created in 1949 by the North Atlantic Treaty (also referred to as the Treaty of Washington), it is a defensive alliance based on political and military cooperation. NATO was established in accordance with article 51 of the United Nations Charter, which provides for the right of U.N. Members to collective self-defense. As stated in the treaty's preamble, NATO members are committed to safeguarding the freedom, common heritage, and civilization of their people, through observance of the principles of democracy, individual liberty, and the rule of law.[60]

NATO decisions are made on the basis of consensus of all member nations. It is a multinational, intergovernmental association of free and independent states and has no supranational authority or independent policy-making function. Hence, NATO can implement a decision only if every member state agrees to it. The organization's objectives are primarily political, with an emphasis on shared defense planning and military cooperation, but also encompass economic, scientific, environmental, and other relevant fields.[61]

NATO supported U. N. peacekeeping efforts in the former Yugoslavia beginning in 1992 and, continued with the conclusion of the Dayton Peace Accords which brought peace to **Bosnia-Herzegovina** in 1995. Under the Dayton accords, NATO has led both the Implementation Force (IFOR) and the Stabilization Force (SFOR).

This involvement in peacekeeping was the first step in the evolution of NATO from an alliance designed to protect Western Europe from Warsaw Pact forces storming through the Fulsa Gap in Germany to a NATO that is designed to engage in peacekeeping and security missions throughout the North Atlantic. The true revolution, however, occurred when NATO embraced a policy now known as the Clinton Doctrine to become militarily involved in the situation in Kosovo.

For nearly two centuries, peace in Europe was based on the "Westphalian doctrine", which states that sovereign states do not get involved in the internal affairs of other sovereign states.[62] Yet, when the **Republic of Serbia** (part of the Federal Republic of Yugoslavia) began persecuting its Albanian minority in **Kosovo** (as part of a broader campaign against Albanian rebels), many Western governments felt compelled to act to protect innocent Albanian citizens from violence and violations of their human rights. The matter was brought before the U. N. Security Council, but the Council was unable to reach agreement on a plan of action.

At this point, U. S. President Bill Clinton, at the urging of European allies, proposed a new policy. Although never formally articulated, the policy adopted by NATO was based on the principle that "the nations of the free world will intervene on the behalf of basic human rights in other countries, when they have the opportunity to do so." This revolutionized centuries of thinking in foreign policy, in that for the first time, the nations of the West formally declared that sovereignty is not an inviolable concept. Moreover, the intervention in Kosovo created a new identity for NATO as an organization that could intervene in conflicts, due to its inherent nature as an associa-

9.11 WHO IS IN NATO?

Belgium
Canada
Czech Republic
Denmark
France
Germany
Greece
Hungary
Iceland
Italy
Luxembourg
Netherlands
Norway
Poland
Portugal
Spain
Turkey
United Kingdom
United States

When the North Atlantic Treaty (which formed NATO) was crafted at the end of the Second World War, the intention of the framers was to ensure the commitment of the United States to the defense of Western Europe in the event of an attack by the forces of the Warsaw Pact through the words of Article 5 that "an armed attack against one or more . . . . shall be considered an attack against . . . all." Yet, this Article was first activated not to bring the United States to the defense of Europe, but to bring Europe to the defense of the United States following the terrorist attacks of September 11. The commitment of NATO has been more than symbolic. For several months after the attacks,

NATO planes flew air defense patrols over American cities, and the special forces of several NATO members, including the U.K., France, Germany, Denmark, Norway, and The Netherlands, have fought alongside U.S. forces on the ground in Afghanistan. In addition, all NATO members, as well as almost all aspiring NATO members, have provided logistical support and the right-of-use to both territory and airspace.

As America prepares to continue its war on terrorism against what President George W. Bush has called "the axis of evil" of Iraq, Iran, and North Korea (DPRK), the reaction has

been mixed. The strongest support has come from countries that either have historically strong ties to the United States, such as the U.K.; countries that confront their own terrorist threat, such as Spain; and countries that are trying to get the United States' blessing to join NATO, such as those in Central and Eastern Europe. Nevertheless, across all of Europe, there is not nearly as much support for the war on terrorism as there is in the United States. In general, Europeans prefer to view themselves as a "voice of reason" on the subject, urging caution, prudence, and appropriate action before going along with any military action.

tion of free and democratic nations, in places where the United Nations is unable to act.

After waging a successful military campaign against Serbia, NATO paved the way for the United Nations and the EU to take greater control of and responsibility for peacekeeping in Kosovo. Moreover, NATO has remained committed to the area through its leading role in preventing another Balkan war in the **FYR Macedonia**. It remains to be seen, however, how this new identity will apply to conflicts in the future.

PARTNERSHIP FOR PEACE

The Partnership for Peace is a consultative body wherein NATO cooperates with its former Cold War enemies. It is designed to promote understanding and cooperation among members on issues of mutual interest, such as conflict resolution and military training and preparedness. In addition, membership in the Partnership for Peace has paved the way to NATO membership for three current members: **Poland, Hungary,** and the **Czech Republic**

At the time of this writing, NATO was sched-

uled to convene for a major summit in Prague, to be held in November 2002, at which it is expected to invite a number of members of the Partnership for Peace to become full members of the Alliance. Most observers currently anticipate that NATO will make a historic invitation of membership to at least three former Soviet Republics: **Estonia, Latvia,** and **Lithuania.**[63] Additionally, **Slovenia** is considered almost certain to be invited, with the applications of **Slovakia, Romania,** and **Bulgaria** under strong consideration as well.[64]

Paving the way for this expansion is an agreement signed in March 2002 to create a NATO-Russia Partnership Council in which NATO can coordinate policy with Russia on matters of common interest. The Partnership Council is advisory in nature only, and has no authority to limit the independence of NATO members to take independent decisions. Nevertheless, the Council is a historic opportunity for cooperation between the former enemies, and carries the promise of a future of lasting peace for the European region.[65]

1. For complete election information on any country, visit <http://www.electionworld.org> or <http://www.electionguide.org>

2. "Survey: United Kingdom." *The Economist.* 4 November 1999. <http://www.economist.com/surveys/showsurvey.cfm?issue=19991106> (30 May 2002).

3. "Blair Storms to UK Poll Triumph." CNN.com. June 8 2001. <http://www.cnn.com/2001/WORLD/europe/06/07/uk.election.03/> (30 May 2002).

4. "Vote 2001." BBC News. 14 August 2001. <http://news.bbc.co.uk/vote2001/default.stm> (30 May 2002).

5. "After the Cataclysm." *The Economist.* 27 April 2002.

6. "Chirac Wins by a Landslide." BBC News. 5 May 5 2002. http://news.bbc.co.uk/hi/english/world/europe/newsid_1969000/1969649.stm > (30 May 2002).

7. "Survey: The Netherlands." *The Economist.* 2 May 2002 <http://www.economist.com/surveys/showsurvey.cfm?issue=20020504> (30 May 2002).

8. "Netherlands Decides 2002." CNN.com. Undated. <http://www.cnn.com/SPECIALS/2002/dutch.election/> (30 May 2002).

9. "A Wind of Change in the Netherlands—and Across Europe." *The Economist.* 18 May 2002.

10. "Survey: Italy." *The Economist.* 5 July 2001. <http://www.economist.com/surveys/showsurvey.cfm?issue=20010707> (30 May 2002).

11. "An Italian Story." *The Economist.* 28 April 2001.

12. "Survey: Portugal." *The Economist.* 30 November 2000. <http://www.economist.com/surveys/showsurvey.cfm?issue=20001202> (30 May 2002).

13. "Mandate for an Odd Couple." *The Economist.* 23 March 2002.

14. "Danish Prime Minister Resigns." CNN.com. 21 November 2001. <http://europe.cnn.com/2001/WORLD/europe/11/21/denmark.result> (30 May 2002).

15. "Survey: The Nordic Countries." *The Economist.* 21 January 1999. <http://www.economist.com/surveys/showsurvey.cfm?issue=19990123> (30 May 2002).

16. "The Menace of Vladimir Meciar." *The Economist.* 26 January 2002.

17. "Inside Europe: Your Guide to Life Inside the European Union." BBC.co.uk. Undated. <http://news.bbc.co.uk/hi/english/static/in_depth/europ/2001/inside_europe/default.stm> (30 May 2002).

18. "Survey: Europe." *The Economist.* 21 October 1999. <http://www.economist.com/surveys/showsurvey.cfm?issue=19991023> (30 May 2002).

19. "European Union Timeline." European Union Center, University System of Georgia. Undated. <http://www.inta.gatech.edu/eucenter/resources/eu_timeline.html> (30 May 2002).

20. "Survey: France." *The Economist.* 3 June 1999. <http://www.economist.com/surveys/showsurvey.cfm?issue=19990605> (30 May 2002).

21. "Survey: Germany." *The Economist.* 4 February 1999 (30 May 2002).<http://www.economist.com/surveys/showsurvey.cfm?issue=19990206> (30 May 2002).

22. "Our Constitution for Europe." *The Economist.* 28 October 2001.

23. "The Latest Battle for the Continent's New Shape." *The Economist.* 8 December 2001.

24. "Back to Basics." *The Economist.* 22 July 2000.

25. "Survey: European Union Enlargement." *The Economist* 17 May 2001.<http://www.economist.com/surveys/showsurvey.cfm?issue=20010519> (30 May 2002).

26. "European Union Expands Eastward: 2002." Radio Free Europe / Radio Liberty. Undated. <http://www.rferl.org/nca/special/euexpands/> (30 May 2002).

27. "Could Everything Now Go Horribly Wrong?" *The Economist.* 16 June 2001.

28. "A Whiff of Veto in the Air?" *The Economist.* 1 December 2001.

29. "Survey: Poland." *The Economist.* 25 October 2001. <http://www.economist.com/surveys/showsurvey.cfm?issue=20011027> (30 May 2002).

30. "The Angry Farmers." *The Economist.* 9 February 2002. <http://www.economist.com/displayStory.cfm?Story_ID=976063> (30 May 2002).

31. "Knocking at the Clubhouse Door." *The Economist.* September 1 2001.

32. "Crisis Ahead." *The Economist.* 8 September 2001.

33. "Crisp and Even: The History of Paper Money." *The Economist.* 22 December 2001.

34. "Promises, Promises, Fudge, Fudge." *The Economist.* 16 February 2002.

35. "If Only Words Were Guns," *The Economist.* 24 November 2001.

36. Ibid.

37. For more information, see "European Union Strategy for Sustainable Development" on The European Union On-Line at <http://europa.eu.int/comm/environment/eussd/ and the Earth Summit 2002 website at <http://www.earthsummit2002.org/>

38. "Uphill Struggle for Europe's Roma." BBC.co.uk. 10 September 2001. <http://news.bbc.co.uk/hi/english/world/europe/newsid_1536000/1536442.stm> (30 May 2002).

39. "At a Glance: Hague Tribunal." BBC.co.uk. 3 July 2001. <http://news.bbc.co.uk/hi/english/world/europe/newsid_1418000/1418304.stm> (30 May 2002).

40. "One Brought to Justice, Many at Large." *The Economist.* 9 February 2002.

41. "Security Council Reform: Germany's Position." Permanent Mission of Germany to the United Nations." Undated. <http://www.germanyinfo.org/UN/un_reform.htm> (30 May 2002).

42. "Italy and the Security Council." Permanent Mission of Italy to the United Nations. Undated. <http://www.italyun.org/sc.html> (30 May 2002).

43. "Just a Toe Across the Line." *The Economist.* 9 March 2002.

44. "Timeline: Cyprus." BBC.co.uk. 20 February 2002.<http://news.bbc.co.uk/hi/english/world/europe/newsid_1021000/1021835.stm> (30 May 2002).

45. "Breakthrough?" *The Economist.* 25 May 2002.

46. "A Ghastly Job." *The Economist.* 26 January 2002.

47. "Kosovo: An Uneasy Peace." BBC.co.uk. Undated.<http://news.bbc.co.uk/hi/english/static/kosovo_fact_files/default.stm> (30 May 2002).

48. "Slav, or Not?" *The Economist.* 18 August 2001.

49. "Better and Worse: Macedonia and Kosovo." *The Economist* 17 November 2001.

50. "Will the Doves Really Fly?" *The Economist.* 18 August 2001.

51. "No Outside Police? No Peace." *The Economist.* 15 September 2001.

52. "Bye-bye, Yugoslavia?" *The Economist.* 23 March 2002.

53. "Survey: Spain." *The Economist.* 23 November 2000. <http://www.economist.com/surveys/showsurvey.cfm?issue=20001125> (30 May 2002).

54. "Proud Basques Defend Ancient Culture." BBC.co.uk. 6 December 1999. <http://news.bbc.co.uk/hi/english/world/europe/newsid_548000/548545.stm> (30 May 2002).

55. "No End, and Not Much Hope of One." *The Economist.* 30 March 2002.

56. "Will the Rock Be Rolled Over?" *The Economist.* 17 November 2001.

57. "True Brits." *The Economist.* 11 May 2002.

58. "Gibraltar in Reverse?" *The Economist.* 23 February 2002.

59. "Chilly in the West, Warmer in the East." *The Economist.* 25 May 2002.

60. "Survey: NATO." *The Economist.* 22 April 1999. <http://www.economist.com/surveys/showsurvey.cfm?issue=19990424> (30 May 2002).

61. Editorial. "Stay Together, Fight Together." *The Economist.* 4 May 2002.

62. Correll, John T. "The Doctrine of Intervention." *Air Force Magazine.* February 2000. <http://www.afa.org/magazine/editorial/02edit00_print.html> (30 May 2002).

63 "A Moment of Truth." *The Economist.* 2 May 2002.

64. "A Nastase Shock for NATO?" *The Economist.* 4 April 2002.

65. Richburg, Keith B. "NATO, Russia Form sLimited Partnership." WashingtonPost.com. 29 May 2002. <http://www.washingtonpost.com/wp-dyn/articles/A23560-2002May28.html> (30 May 2002).

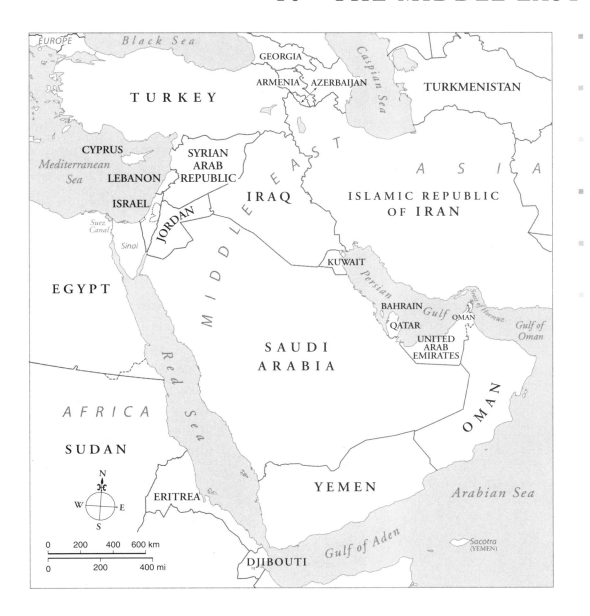

The Middle East, often referred to as the cradle of civilization, has a rich history that dates back to some of the earliest civilizations in the world, including Ancient Egypt and Mesopotamia. It is the birthplace of all three of the world's monotheistic religions: Judaism, Christianity, and Islam. Geographically, the Middle East comprises an area that spans Northeast Africa and Southeast Asia. Dominated by desert, the region is extremely dry and often falls victim to drought.

The region is made up of approximately two dozen countries, including: Algeria, Bahrain, Comoros, Djibouti, Egypt, Israel and the disputed territories, Iran, Iraq, Jordan, Kuwait, Lebanon, Libya, Mauritania, Morocco, Oman, Qatar, Saudi Arabia, Somalia, Sudan, Syria, Tunisia, Turkey, the United Arab Emirates, and Yemen.

In the twentieth century, the Middle East experienced the end of European colonialism, the birth of Arab nationalism, and the rise of modern nation-states. Israel, formed in 1948, represents an anomaly in the Middle East as the only Jewish state in a predominantly Muslim region. Today the Middle East faces challenges in exercising its rights to self-determination, while struggling to shape its identities as a conservative, authoritarian, and Muslim region in a world that is at war with extremism, seeking liberal and free markets and democratic ideals as a common goal for people around the world. Political instability has led to many challenges to the governments of the Middle East. A crisis of power has arisen as a result of the Arab loss of the war of 1967 to Israel, the rise of radical Islam, the Gulf War, the failure of negotiations regarding a Palestinian state, and the occupation of Palestinian territories. Although regional organizations have addressed these issues of instability, peace continues to elude the region which contributes to its economic problems.

ECONOMIC POLICY AND DEMOGRAPHICS

Economic growth has been on the rise in the Middle East, but disproportionate demographic pressures, such as high rates of population growth, remain a major threat. In 2000, 58 percent of the Middle East was urbanized; that proportion is expected to increase to 70 percent by 2015. Urbanization brings social needs that require sustained economic growth. At the turn of the millennium, the region had one of the highest youth demographics; 40 percent of the population of the Middle East was under the age of fourteen. This significantly high number of non-wage earners has weakened the Gross Domestic Product (GDP) of countries in the region.

The region has an enormous supply of petroleum, holding a substantial percentage of the world's reserves. Eight of the eleven members of the Organization of the Petroleum Exporting Countries (OPEC), an organization of developing countries that rely on oil as their main supply of revenue, are located in the Middle East.[1] The

10.1 DEMOGRAPHIC SAMPLING OF THE MIDDLE EAST*

Country	Population Density (1999)	Human Development Index	Population Growth Rate % (1999)	Population (1999) (millions)
Iraq	133	.586	2.8	22.5
Libya	7	.756	2.5	5.0
Oman	30	.725	3.9	2.5
Saudi Arabia	25	.740	3.0	20.9
Syria	224	.663	2.8	16.0
Yemen	80	.449	2.9	16.4

*All figures from the Population Information Program.

A bulldozer crushes bodies of 500 kg bombs designed for use as chemical weapons, Iraq. (UN/DPI Photo)

to fund its health care services but recently considered imposing a mandatory health insurance program for the six million expatriates who live and work in the country.

Syria has taken steps to open its economy to the international community by allowing private banks to operate in the country. Foreign investment and a more liberal trade policy are two steps that Syria has proposed to ease its relations with the West. However, problems persist as Syria's free trade zones only comprise a part of the country and it is uncertain whether the restricted zones will deter private banks from entering. Syria has proposed a free trade agreement with all Arab countries and, additionally, a possible trade agreement with the European Union by 2004. The main point of contention between the international community and Syria is the transportation of Iraqi oil into the country. Although both Iraq and Syria have claimed that this transportation of oil was to test a 1950s-era pipe, this violation of the international sanctions has put Syria's relations with the rest of the world in jeopardy.[3]

Middle East is so heavily dependent on income from energy exports that few nations will voluntarily limit their export revenues, and whether the Middle East will act as a stable supplier of oil and gas exports at market-driven prices remains a critical question. This remains uncertain in the midst of internal conflicts and economic stagnancy. Both war and sanctions have limited exports of key oil countries such as **Iran, Iraq,** and **Libya.** The question also remains as to whether the Middle East can finance the energy development it needs without more privatization and significantly higher rates of foreign investment.[2]

The Middle East is currently experiencing a unique phenomenon in which expatriate populations live in most of the region and are the majority of the national workforce. The majority of the indigenous people receive government-supported assistance. Due to the indigenous populations' increasing size, many nations, especially members of the Gulf Cooperative Council (GCC), have implemented wide-ranging economic reforms. **Saudi Arabia,** for instance, has used petrodollars

NARCOTICS TRAFFICKING

Iran, currently experiencing drug abuse among its people, now also serves as part of a smuggling route that traffickers use to peddle drugs produced in Afghanistan and Pakistan for sale in the West.[4] **Morocco** is the largest exporter of hashish as well as a provider of harder drugs such as cocaine and Ecstasy. The World Customs Organization has stated that Morocco supplies 70 percent of Europe's hashish. The drug trade has become so large in Morocco that it blatantly challenges the Moroccan government's authority. The French newspaper *Le Monde* has even accused the Moroccan monarchy of corruption and involvement in the drug trade. Luring workers away from their jobs, the drug trade in Morocco has succeeded in damaging the Moroccan economy as well as creating social instability.[5]

WATER SCARCITY

The Middle East is one of the driest regions of the world, desperately in need of water to sustain its population. Water-scarcity places a significant strain on the economies and social development of countries in the region.[6] Water is the single most important natural resource to the rural sections, and the scarcity of it is likely to become the region's most binding constraint on agricultural production in the twenty-first century.[7] While nearly 90 percent of the available water is used in the agricultural sector, the demand for water has sharply increased in urban sectors as a result of population growth, increases in household income, and irrigation development.[8] The region also lacks institutional mechanisms and policies to reallocate water to the cities and toward specific, higher-value uses.[9]

For example, the Gulf nations lack water policies to conserve, preserve, or manage its use and measures to minimize sewage waste. Water is commonly wasted, as there is often little or no charge for its use. **Saudi Arabia,** the **United Arab Emirates,** and **Kuwait** drain their aquifers, import high volumes of water, and desalinate water. This water is often inefficiently used, leading to significant waste. While the desalination plants turn seawater into safe drinking water and have become cheaper, they are also bound to become incapable of meeting increasing water demands in the near future.[10] Without efficient governing and managing of water resources, from the private or public sector, Arab nations of the Gulf will potentially run out of all natural sources of water and be completely dependent upon outside nations for their water needs.

The water resource situation in the region is becoming progressively bleaker due to droughts of higher frequency and longer duration. Droughts have affected almost every country in the region over the past decade and have seriously impacted development in several countries. Some countries in the Middle East are taking steps to secure its water supplies. **Jordan** has taken measures to improve its water supply system in the capital city, Amman. It is the first governorate

to refurbish and replace its dilapidated water networks.[11]

Turkey is in the process of building dams on the Euphrates and Tigris Rivers to regulate the flow of water and increase its water capacity for growing consumption uses. This, however, poses problems with some neighboring countries because it will give Turkey control over water that reaches **Iraq** and **Syria.** Critics of the plan also question Turkey's "lawful or natural rights" to the Euphrates and Tigris Rivers. Both Syria and Iraq are calling on the international community, including the International Law Commission and International Court of Justice, to resolve this potential conflict.[12]

The Second World Water Forum addressed the issue of scarcity at The Hague in March 2000. However, the most important "water decision" taken at the global level is possibly the International Development Target set by the U.N. Millennium Assembly in October 2000, which sets out to "halve the proportion of people who suffer from hunger and are unable to reach or to afford safe drinking water resources." The December 2001 International Freshwater conference also focused on water as the key to sustainable development.[13] The U.N.'s Agenda 21 outlines a program to protect the quality and supply of freshwater resources, and offers approaches for the development, management, and use of water sources.[14] In anticipation of the Johannesburg Summit in September 2002, Secretary-General Kofi Annan listed water and sanitation as "one of five key areas where concrete results can be obtained." Countries of the region must make efforts to conserve and manage water cooperatively in order to avoid further war and poverty.[15]

RADICAL ISLAM AS A POLITICAL FORCE

The astonishing influence of the rise to power of Islam after 700 A.D. continues to play an integral role in all aspects of life in the Middle East. From the Arabian Peninsula arose an empire that in its heyday stretched from the Atlantic coast of Africa to the Philippines in the Pacific. Islam in the sixth century succeeded in uniting a predominantly tribal society into a unified political force and thus its political rebirth is not surprising. The perceived failure of the Arab Middle East to consolidate political stability and gain complete independence from the West contributed greatly to the resurgence of political Islam in the region.

The Iranian Revolution in 1979 heralded a new political phase in the Middle East. An Islamic resurgence was at hand, seemingly led by **Iran;** the U.S. hostage crisis in Tehran signaled the rise of radical Islamic groups hostile to Western interests. Although the extremist element of Islam does not characterize the majority of Muslims throughout the world, the rise of Islam has affected many areas of Middle Eastern society. Radical Islamic groups today represent a challenge to many Middle Eastern governments. The use of Islamic symbolism has become highly important to opposition groups both moderate and radical.

The Muslim Brotherhood in **Egypt** represents one of the main opposition groups; its influence is felt in **Jordan** and it holds much local power in **Algeria.** This Muslim organization has been working for an Islamic state in Egypt since its 1928 inception and has flourished in more liberal democratic states. The success of the *jihad* (holy war) movement against the Soviet Union in Afghanistan during the 1980s demonstrated that influence of certain radical Islamic groups. The failure of Arab governments to seriously address the Palestinian plight has added to the popularity of Islamic opposition groups as a viable alternative to Arab nationalism. During the post-Gulf War period, two major attacks took place on U.S. interests in the Middle East, both of which have been linked to radical Islamic groups: the bombing of the Khobar Towers in **Saudi Arabia** on June 25, 1996, and the bombing of the USS Cole in **Yemen** on October 12, 2000. Sixteen people were convicted for the Khobar Towers bombing of which fourteen were discovered to have been members of the radical Islamic group Hezbollah. These attacks demonstrate the grave threat that radical Islamic groups pose to stability in the Middle East.[16]

TERRORISM

While many of these radical Islamic groups are considered terrorists by the majority of the international community, some countries, including **Syria** and **Lebanon,** consider Hezbollah, among other groups, to be resistance fighters at war with their occupiers—**Israel,** rather than terrorists. During 2001, Israeli military forces killed more than two-dozen suspected terrorists. Some attacks at Israelis were thwarted, but violence continued within the West Bank and Gaza strip, killing almost 200 Israelis and over 500 Palestinians for the year.[17] The struggle for peace talks continues between Israel and **Palestine** with frequent suicide bombings in Israeli civilian areas, and Israeli military raids of villages and refugee camps. The cycle of violence between Israel and Palestine is the epicenter of international tension as countries of the Middle East and North Africa (MENA) region continue to condemn Israeli occupation and simultaneously renounce terrorism.

Terrorist activity and planning were carried out in great detail throughout many countries of the MENA region. Almost all of the MENA countries also took steps to fight against terrorism in the aftermath of the September 11 attacks in the United States. Many Middle East governments agreed to U.N. resolutions that froze financial assets tied to possible terrorists or terror organizations. Other security measures included publicly condemning terrorist attacks, increasing security for high-risk targets, and arresting members of terrorist cells.[18]

RELIGIOUS STRIFE AND THE CREATION OF THE ORGANIZATION OF THE ISLAMIC CONFERENCE

In 1957, after an attempted Israeli arson attack on the Al Aqsa mosque in Jerusalem, the U.N. established The Organization of the Islamic Conference (OIC). In response to this attack, the OIC pledged to defend the rights of Muslims throughout the Middle East and the world. The world's Muslim population is approximately one billion, which is one fifth of the human race and clearly represents the international scope within which the OIC operates. The Al Aqsa mosque is the third most sacred site in Islam and its attempted destruction caused great concern in the Muslim Word. The OIC consists of 57 representatives from different member states, meeting three times a year to address issues specific to Muslims. OIC conferences have dealt with priorities such as the liberation of the Palestinian people and Islamic values emphasizing human dignity, development, and equality. The OIC has recently condemned acts of terrorism in the name of Islam as un-Islamic and seeks open constructive debate between the Middle East and the West. Originally established in Morocco, its headquarters were moved in the 1990s to Jeddah, **Saudi Arabia.**[19] The OIC also works for the establishment of a Palestinian state where it eventually hopes to establish its headquarters. Although the OIC holds little political power, its importance lies primarily in human development by regularly defending the religious and cultural rights of Muslims throughout the world.[20]

ISRAEL AND THE ARAB WORLD

On May 14, 1948, **Israel** proclaimed its independence and became a nation-state. Since then, Israel's relations with its Arab neighbors have been strained and generally hostile, aside from a close military alliance established with **Turkey** in 1996. War broke in 1967, following Israel's invasion of the Sinai Peninsula. Israel's military strength and the rapid Arab defeat created a great shock in the region. In addition, during the 1967 war Israel invaded East Jerusalem, unifying the city, contrary to U.N. General Assembly Resolution 303 of December 9, 1949, which held that the city should be placed under a permanent international regime. Jerusalem remains highly contested and will continue to be a central problem in any future peace initiatives.

The region has been plagued with widespread instability in the region following the 1967 war. Relations between Israel and its neighbors have been hostile for more than fifty years, as the Arab states do not recognize Israel's sovereignty and wish to see the creation of a Palestinian state. **Syria** and Israel have been involved in a dispute over Israeli settlements in the Golan Heights that borders between Israel and Syria. As a prelude to the '67 war, Syria attacked Israeli water supplies and mounted sniper attacks on Jewish settlements, which were declared to be infringing on Syria. The United Nations Truce and Supervision Organization (UNTSO) was the first peacekeeping mission to be deployed in the region after the Arab-Israeli war, monitoring the cease-fire in the Suez Canal area and Golan Heights. In 2000, UNTSO continued assisting and cooperating with the U.N. Disengagement Observer Force (UNDOF) on the Golan Heights in the Israel-Syria sector and with UNIFIL in the Israel-Lebanon sector. UNTSO was also present in the **Egypt**-Israel sector in the Sinai.

After peace talks between Israel and Syria broke off in 1996, Israeli Prime Minister Ehud Barak resumed them in 1999 only to fail in the attaining resumption of normal diplomatic relations. Israel's refusal to withdraw from the Golan Heights region and the September 2000 *intifada,* or Palestinian rebellion, resulted in a suspension of all peace talks between Israel and Syria.

Syria has made recent efforts to open doors to a limited amount of foreign investment, as well as increase diplomatic efforts. In October 2001, the U.N. elected Syria to a two-year term as a nonpermanent member of the U.N. Security Council. However, Syria still lacks any formal peace agreements with Israel.[21]

Lebanon also lacks peace agreements with Israel. Lebanon's internal balance was fractured in 1975 due to an influx of Palestinian refugees from Israel, which led to a civil war between Lebanese Christians and Palestinian Muslims. Syria tried unsuccessfully to stop the fighting by sending a sizeable military force but, since 1975, has still kept a sizable military presence in Lebanon. On March 11, 1978, a PLO commando attack in Israel led to an Israeli invasion of Lebanon, which sought to expel Palestinian forces. Three years after this invasion, Israel set up a nine-mile "safety zone" between Israel and Lebanon to prevent any future hostile incursions. In June 1982, Israel forces invaded Lebanon again and advanced to

1948 Following more than fifty years of attempting to create a Jewish homeland, Jewish settlers proclaim the state of Israel. Neighboring Arab countries attack in response. Approximately 700,000 Palestinian refugees leave or are driven out of Israel, becoming refugees in nearby Arab states.

June 5, 1967 Israel launches preemptive strike against Egyptian, Syrian, and Jordanian troops amassed on its borders in preparation for an attack against Israel, commencing the Six-Day War. The Sinai Peninsula and Gaza Strip are captured from Egypt, the Golan Heights from Syria, and the West Bank and East Jerusalem from Jordan.

October 6, 1973 Egypt and Syria launch attacks against Israeli forces in Sinai and Golan Heights on the day of Yom Kippur.

March–June 1978 Israel invades southern Lebanon to protect its northern border from repeated incursions.

September 1978 Egypt and Israel sign the Camp David accords, returning Sinai Peninsula to Egypt in return for peace and normalization.

June 6, 1982 Israel reinvades Lebanon to drive out the Palestine Liberation Organization (PLO).

December 9, 1987 Palestinian *intifada* (uprising) against Israeli rule starts in West Bank and Gaza.

October 1991 Madrid Peace Conference with Israel, Syria, Jordan, Lebanon, and the Palestinians in attendance. Jordanian-Israeli and Syrian-Israeli peace negotiation tracks are opened.

January 1993 Secret Israeli-PLO talks in Oslo begin.

September 13, 1993 PLO Chairman Yasser Arafat and Israeli Prime Minister Yitzhak Rabin sign Declaration of Principles.

May 4, 1994 Israel and PLO reach agreement on initial implementation of Oslo Accords. Israeli military withdraws from 60 percent of Gaza Strip and from West Bank town of Jericho. A five-year period of confidence-building begins, during which a permanent resolution is to be negotiated on Jerusalem, settlements, Palestinian refugees, and sovereignty.

July 1, 1994 Arafat returns to Gaza and assumes position as head of the new Palestinian National Authority (PNA).

October 26, 1994 Israel-Jordan peace treaty is signed.

September 28, 1995 Arafat and Rabin sign Oslo II and expand Palestinian self-rule in West Bank and Gaza, allowing for Palestinian elections.

November 4, 1995 Prime Minister Yitzhak Rabin is assassinated.

November 1995–March 1996 Israeli Prime Minister Shimon Peres takes major steps for peace deal with Syria.

April 11, 1996 Israel begins a 17-day bombardment of Lebanon, Operation Grapes of Wrath. Lebanese Hezbollah guerrillas fire Katyusha rockets at populated areas of northern Israel.

April 18, 1996 Israel shells a U.N. compound at Qana, killing approximately 100 out of 800 civilians sheltered there.

May 29, 1996 Binyamin Netanyahu elected prime minister of Israel.

January 17, 1997 Israel hands over 80 percent of Hebron to the Palestinian National Authority.

October 23, 1998 Netanyahu signs the Wye River Memorandum outlining further Israeli withdrawal from West Bank.

May 18, 1999 Ehud Barak elected prime minster of Israel.

September 5, 1999 Israelis and Palestinians sign revised deal based on Wye River accord.

November 8, 1999 Final-status talks resume between Israel and Palestinians.

December 6, 1999 Final-status talks stall when Palestinians withdraw in protest over the building of new Jewish settlements in West Bank. Barak responds by announcing a freeze in the addition of 1,800 more houses to Jewish settlements around Jerusalem.

December 15, 1999 Barak meets with Syrian officials for high-level talks.

February 3, 2000 As summit between Barak and PNA President Yasser Arafat stalls over disagreement on promised Israeli withdrawal from West Bank under revised Wye River accord.

February 13, 2000 Final-status negotiations between Israel and Palestinians are deadlocked; the deadline for a framework agreement is missed.

May 22, 2000 Israel withdraws from southern Lebanon.

June 1, 2000 United Nations Security Council votes unanimously to extend Golan Heights observer force.

July 27, 2000 Renewed Palestinian-Israeli negotiations, under the auspices of U.S. President Bill Clinton, make some headway but again reach an impasse, particularly over Jerusalem.

February 6, 2001 Upon being elected prime minister of Israel, Ariel Sharon speaks of a new path to peace and security.

February 20, 2001 Barak quits as leader of the Labor party and refuses to serve in Sharon's government.

April 5, 2001 Israel strikes Syrian targets. Syrian army radar positions hit as Israel accuses Hezbollah terrorist group of operating under Syrian military.

September 26, 2001 Arafat and Israeli Foreign Minister Shimon Peres agree on a truce and on measures to make the ceasefire permanent.

October 16, 2001 Israeli Tourist Minister, Rehavam Zeev, is shot dead in a Jerusalem hotel.

March 28, 2002 Israel attacks Arafat's compound in Ramallah. Bulldozers and thirty tanks surround Arafat's headquarters, holding him captive.

April 15, 2002 U.S. Secretary of State Colin Powell spends three hours in peace talks with Arafat. Talks with the Palestinian leader focus on securing a ceasefire after three week-long Israeli military action in West Bank

May 30, 2002 Arafat, under pressure for reform, signs the Palestinian Basic Law that was passed in 1997 by the Palestinian Legislative Council (PLC).

June 10, 2002 Israel surrounds Arafat's headquarters in Ramallah again at the start of talks between U.S. President George W. Bush and Israeli Prime Minister Ariel Sharon in Washington.

Beirut, the capital, in order "to install a friendly regime and destroy Mr. Arafat's Palestinian Liberation Organization," which would "help persuade Palestinians to accept Israeli rule in the West Bank and Gaza Strip."[22] The Security Council authorized the U.N. Interim Force in Lebanon (UNFIL) to observe the withdrawal of Israeli forces and their allies, the South Lebanese Army.

After twenty-two years of occupation, the Israeli military withdrew troops from the South and Bekaa Valley in May 2000. However, both Syria and Lebanon are appealing to the United Nations, claiming that Israel has not completely withdrawn, and still occupies the Sheba Farms area of the Golan Heights. Israeli air strikes on Syrian radar sites in Lebanon, and repeated military strikes between Hezbollah forces and Israeli troops, have continued despite a decrease in the level of violence along the temporary Israel-Lebanon border.[23] Syria recognizes groups such as Hezbollah and others as legitimate "resistance fighters" against Israel and not "terrorists." Syria and Lebanon do not agree with Israel's definition of terrorism, and like other Arab countries, have called for a U.N.-sponsored conference to "address the underlying causes of terrorism."[24]

ISRAEL AND PALESTINE

In 1993, **Israel** and the **Palestinians** signed the Oslo Agreement, which appeared to be a promising step towards lasting peace. The agreement set forth a timetable for the incremental withdrawal of Israeli forces from the occupied territories and addressed a future Palestinian state. At its core, the Oslo Agreement looked to address the most pressing issues between both sides, Palestinian recognition of Israel and its security needs and the establishment of a Palestinian state. Peace talks made great gains under Israeli leaders Shimon Peres and Yitkzhak Rabin, but under Israeli leader Binyamin Netanyahu the Oslo peace initiative floundered. Continued violence by rogue Palestinian groups led to an Israeli withdrawal from talks, and Netanyahu accused Palestinian National Authority Chairman Yasser Arafat of failing to stop acts of violence. In 1998, the United States attempted to breathe new life into the peace process with the Wye River Memorandum which called for a significant Israeli military redeployment as well as calling upon the Palestinian authorities to combat terrorist organizations. The election of Prime Minister Ehud Barak in early 1999 revived the peace process again. Barak, a former soldier turned politician, renewed hopes for peace in the region with promises of a military withdrawal from the West Bank and Gaza. In addition, Barak withdrew troops from **Lebanon**, negotiated a peace deal with **Syria** involving the return of the Golan Heights, and resumed negotiations with the Palestinians. Israel's failure to withdraw from the West Bank and the continued establishment of settlements led to the ultimate failure of the peace talks.

The current *intifada* commenced in the final days of September 2000 when the massive police presence outside of a mosque led to stone throwing and shooting into the crowd. The result: deaths and injuries. Within two days, Israel launched a military assault. The U.S. response was to close an arms deal requested previously that provided Israel with 35 Black Hawk helicopters, 70 engines, spare parts, training equipment, and logistical items. Britain too closed an arms deal. The Israeli air fleet, army defense capacities, and general Israeli aims were all strengthened. The U.N. response was a Security Council resolution that called upon Israel to "abide scrupulously by its legal obligations under the fourth Geneva Convention." The vote on the resolution was 14 to 0, with 1 abstention by the United States.

Jerusalem remained an obstacle to the negotiations and a harsh point of contention between both sides. The 1947 U.N. partition plan would have made Jerusalem an international city. After the 1948 war, the city was divided between Israel and **Jordan**; Israel captured East Jerusalem after the Six-Day War in 1967. Barak ruled out Israel's withdrawal to the 1967 border, dismantling of settlements in the occupied territories, and the right of return for the Palestinian Diaspora. The Israelis insisted that a united Jerusalem will remain their eternal capital; the Palestinians contended that the eastern half of Jerusalem, site of the Al-Aqsa mosque and Dome of the Rock,

both sacred sites in Islam, is to be the capital of their new state. Although various options for mutual control have been drawn up, many on both sides feel that compromise on many issues will not meet the requirements for a lasting peace.

The election of Ariel Sharon on February 7, 2001, and the resignation of Ehud Barak signaled an all-time low in the peace process. Palestinians saw Sharon as representing a loss in the campaign for statehood and independence. However, on March 12, 2002 the Security Council approved a resolution that focused on a vision of a separate Palestinian state. The resolution was submitted by the United States and fell short of addressing Israel as an occupying power.[25] That, however, was contained within a letter to Sharon from Kofi Annan expressing concern that Israel's "illegal occupations," mixed with the particular use of military tactics, had come to "resemble all out conventional warfare."[26] These fears were further realized on March 29, 2002, when Israeli forces

invaded Ramallah and began a military campaign to destroy terrorist groups throughout the West Bank. The Israeli military campaign came in response to a wave of suicide bombings during the March Passover celebrations. Israel surrounded Yasser Arafat's compound, effectively holding him hostage, and destroyed the Palestinian security force headquarters.

Fighting in the West Bank between the Israeli military and Palestinian militia groups drew sharp criticism from the U.N. and parts of the international community. The U.S. has attempted to demand an Israeli withdrawal but Israel has thus far defied international calls, stating that it will withdraw when it has completed its operation. The success of Israel's current military mission is questionable as today Palestinian suicide bombings and terrorist acts continue to afflict Israel, but as yet, the international community has refrained from direct action in the region.

The Middle East was the scene of the first U.N. Authorized international military coalition, formed to liberate **Kuwait** from **Iraqi** occupation. The region currently hosts four peacekeeping operations, including the United Nations Truce Supervision Observation (UNITSO), the U.N.'s first peacekeeping operation, created in 1948 to monitor the truce in Palestine.[27]

ENFORCEMENT OF SECURITY AND SANCTIONS

Iraq has engaged in various wars in the past few decades, with the most debilitating being the drawn-out eight-year **Iran-Iraq** War, from 1980 to 1988. The war took many lives, and depleted resources that otherwise could have gone toward economic development. The ensuing effect on the economy was one of economic downturn. Morale in the country also dropped and, after the war, Hussein was more concerned with solidifying his authoritarian position as head of state than with economic concerns, devoting most of his time and the country's few remaining resources towards such solidification. Insufficient infrastructure also discouraged economic growth and impeded development within Iraq.[28]

Soon thereafter, Iraq invaded **Kuwait** in August 1990. The invasion led to the Gulf War, as other countries stepped in to help to protect Kuwait and, potentially, **Saudi Arabia's** oil resources from being seized by Iraq.[29] This war further depleted Iraq's energy and resources and destroyed the little remaining infrastructure necessary for development. A bombing campaign in 1998, which dropped more than 300 cruise missiles and hundreds of bombs aimed at potential targets building weapons of mass destruction (WMD), further contributed to destabilization of the country and its ability to produce weapons.[30]

Iraq was recognized internationally as a threat to world security, as demonstrated by the invasion of Kuwait. Newly knowledgeable about its possession of weaponry, the United States decided to take measures it hoped would topple Hussein's regime and dismantle Iraq's potential for WMD and their delivery systems. The United Nations Special Commission on Iraq (UNSCOM) was formed to inspect Iraq and last reported in 1998 that Iraq was "free of nuclear weapons and missiles, almost free of chemical weapons, and questionable regarding biological weapons," before the teams was thrown out of Iraq by Saddam Hussein. In December 1999, the Security Council voted to replace UNSCOM with the United Nations Monitoring, Verification, and Inspection Commission (UNMOVIC).

The U.N. imposed economic sanctions on Iraq that cut off trade and access to the funds required for infrastructure repair and gave weapons inspections monitors authority to seek out and destroy real and potential WMD. U.S. armed forces led a series of low-level air bombings that destroyed structures capable of producing WMD and other targets essential to destabilizing Iraq.[31] The sanctions have had a significant impact on children and the poor, limiting access to food, water, and essential supplies. Debt and deprivation are common, because unemployment and inflation have reduced a family's purchasing power.[32] Another result of the sanctions has been the creation of a huge black market that has made it even more difficult to stabilize the economy. Most of the money Iraq has received from oil and other casual trading has been diverted towards military and intelligence budgets to keep Hussein in power. In fact, most evidence points to his regime's strength and potential to begin building WMD again that could be used directly against Iraqi opponents, or passed on to terrorist groups.[33]

An attempt to improve the conditions of the poor has resulted, however, as the international

August 2, 1990
Iraq invades Kuwait.

August 6, 1990
United Nations imposes economic sanctions on Iraq.

February 21, 1991
International military coalition liberates Kuwait from Iraqi occupation.

April 3, 1991
U.N. Security Council passes Resolution 687, opening way for inspections and destruction of Iraqi weapons of mass destruction.

April 19, 1991
Security Council authorizes establishment of United Nations Special Commission (UNSCOM).

June 9, 1991
UNSCOM commences weapons inspections.

June 17, 1991
S/RES/699; confirms that UNSCOM and the International Atomic Energy Agency (IAEA) have continuing authority to conduct activities.

August 15, 1991
S/RES/707; demands that Iraq provide without further delay, full, final, and complete disclosures of its proscribed weapons and programs, as required by Resolution 687 (1991).

October 11, 1991
S/RES/715; approves the plans for ongoing monitoring and verification submitted by U.N. Secretary-General (S/22871/Rev.l) and the Director General of the IAEA (S/22872/Rev.1). The Commission's plan also establishes that Iraq shall "accept unconditionally the inspectors and all other personnel designated by the Special Commission."

January 1993
Iraq violates no-fly zone.

October 15, 1994
S/RES/949; demands that Iraq "cooperate fully" with UNSCOM and that it withdraw all

military units deployed in southern Iraq to their original positions. Iraq thereafter withdraws its forces and resumes its work with the Commission.

November 1995
Jordan intercepts large shipment of missile guidance components en route to Iraq.

March 27, 1996
S/RES/1051; approves export-import monitoring mechanism for Iraq and demands that Iraq unconditionally meet all its obligations under the mechanism and cooperate fully with the Special Commission and IAEA Director General.

June 12, 1996
S/RES/1060; terms Iraq's actions a clear violation of the provisions of Council's resolutions; also demands that Iraq grant immediate and unrestricted access to all sites designated for inspection by UNSCOM.

June 21, 1997
S/RES/1115; condemns Iraq's actions and demands that Iraq allow UNSCOM team immediate, unconditional, and unrestricted access to any sites for inspection and to officials for interviews by UNSCOM. Council also calls for additional report on Iraq's cooperation with the commission and suspends periodic sanctions reviews.

October 23, 1997
S/RES/1134; demands that Iraq cooperate fully with the Special Commission, continues suspension of periodic sanctions reviews, and foreshadows additional sanctions pending a further report on Iraq's cooperation with UNSCOM.

November 13, 1997
Iraq demands the removal of United States members of UNSCOM team.

March 2, 1998
S/RES/1154; endorses the provisions of the Memorandum of Understanding (MOU).

August 5, 1998
Iraq refuses to comply with UNSCOM until sanctions are lifted.

September 9, 1998
S/RES/1194; unanimously condemns Iraq's decision to suspend cooperation with UNSCOM, terming the actions a totally unacceptable contravention of Iraq's obligations; demands Iraq rescind its decision and decides not to conduct the 60-day sanctions reviews until Iraq does so and the Commission reports to the Council that it is satisfied it has been able to exercise full range of activities, including inspections.

October 31, 1998
Iraq halts cooperation with UNSCOM.

November 5, 1998
S/RES/1205; unanimously condemns Iraq's actions and demands that Iraq immediately and unconditionally rescind its decisions of August 5 and October 31.

November 14, 1998
Iraq commences export of oil under oil-for-food plan.

December 16, 1998
Air strikes by United States and United Kingdom against Iraqi military targets commence.

December 17, 1999
Security Council adopts Resolution 1284 replacing UNSCOM with United Nations Monitoring Verification and Inspection Commission (UNMOVIC).

March 31, 2000
S/RES/1293; increases allocation for spare parts and equipment for Iraq by $300 million.

October 2000
Iraq resumes domestic passenger flights, the first since the 1991 Gulf War. Commercial air links re-established with Russia, Ireland, and Middle East.

November 2000
Iraqi Deputy Prime Minister Tariq Aziz rejects new weapons inspection proposals.

December 1, 2000
Iraq temporarily halts oil exports after the United Nations rejects its request that buyers pay a 50-cent-a-barrel surcharge into an Iraqi bank account not controlled by the U.N.

February 2001
Britain and the United States carry out bombing raids to try to disable Iraq's air defense network. The bombings have little international support.

May 2001
Saddam Hussein's son Qusay elected to the leadership of the ruling Baath Party, fueling speculation that he's being groomed to succeed his father.

January 2002
Iraq invites a U.N. human rights expert to visit for the first time since envoys were banned from the country in 1992.

April 2002
Iraq issues a 30-day oil embargo as a result of Israeli military action in West Bank and threatens to lengthen embargo until a full withdrawal takes place.

community has tried to keep the regime in check. Various NGOs and U.N. agencies provide humanitarian drops frequently. The U.N. also sponsors the Oil-for-Food program, which provides aid to Iraq in exchange for limited oil exports. These aid programs have had limited success. Hussein exploits these programs to his political advantage by manipulating its exports and imports to strengthen trade in Iraq's favor, and suspending and reducing oil supply to influence U.N. decision-making. Hussein, in an effort to keep his position as the absolute ruler of Iraq, continues to devote most of the country's few resources to the army and police networks, whose main priority is the elimination of threats to the regime.[34]

The latest efforts on the part of the U.N. are revised sanctions. In July 2002, the Security Council's shift in policy took effect to ease the sanction's harsh effects on civilians, based on ongoing U.N. Security Council supervision of Iraq's oil exports and revenues, and includes vigorous inspections of any and all commerce. The new measures will allow more consumer goods into Iraq and continue to restrict items that could be used for military purposes.[35]

The revised sanctions are intended to increase pressure on Hussein to allow inspectors back into Iraq by making it harder for him to claim that ordinary Iraqis are being unduly punished by the sanctions. In further efforts to restart weapons monitoring, U.S. Under-Secretary for Arms Control and International Security John Bolton has publicly accused Iraq, among other countries, of "developing, producing, and stockpiling biological warfare agents and weapons," thereby hoping to increase international pressure. The Security Council is also working to persuade Hussein's government to allow weapons inspectors to return in an effort to lift the sanctions and destroy WMD that Iraq might still have. The U.N. is taking diplomatic measures to avoid increased hostilities between Iraq and the rest of world. The United States has accused Hussein of harboring terrorists, and is alone among the fifteen Security Council members in leaning toward a military campaign to remove Hussein from power.[36] The challenges posed by Iraq and Saddam Hussein continue to provoke serious debate among policymakers and are one of the central concerns in the Middle East.

HUMAN RIGHTS

Human rights abuses in the Middle East continue on a daily basis with deliberate and arbitrary killings of civilians, torture, and hostage-taking afflicting the population. Governments and their military commit many of these atrocities. Torture and ill treatment by security forces, police, and other state authorities were common violations and found in most countries of the region. Prisoners of conscience are regularly incarcerated, people "disappear" or go unaccounted for, arbi-

10.4 THE U.N. AND PALESTINE'S REFUGEES

The United Nations Relief and Works Agency (UNRWA) was established by the General Assembly in 1949 to provide relief to Palestinian refugees. UNRWA provides food, clothing, shelter, education, health care, and other social services to over 3.9 million refugees.

According to UNRWA, a Palestinian refugee is a person whose normal place of residence was Palestine between the June 1946 and May 1948 and lost both their home means of livelihood due to the 1948 Arab-Israeli conflict. (This definition also extends to descendants of individuals who became refugees in 1948.) Refugees in the Middle East generally live in camps in Syria, Jordan, Lebanon, the West Bank, or the Gaza Strip, or in cities and villages around the camps.

UNRWA has accomplished several achievements since its creation, including:

* Repairing and renovating hundreds of shelters for refugee families;

* Providing access to free elementary and preparatory education for all Palestinian refugee children;

* Significantly lowering in infant mortality rates among refugees in Gaza; and

* Initiating microenterprise programs in the West Bank and the Gaza Strip.

SOURCE: United Nations Relief Works Agency http://www.un.org/unrwa/index.html

trary arrests are made, and detention without trial is common.[37]

Debates over human rights continue between the United Nations and Middle East countries. Diplomats from **Saudi Arabia** recently met with the United Nations Committee Against Torture to defend their use of flogging and amputation of limbs as fair corporal punishments that are part of Shariah, the Islamic legal code derived from the Koran. Other Islamic countries including **Libya** and **Iran** also argue that Shariah falls outside the jurisdiction of international treaties.[38] Saudi Arabia continues to implement the death penalty and arrests of suspected political and religious activists, including hundreds of demonstrators arrested following protests against Israel's military attacks on Palestinian territories. The Saudi Government keeps secret the number of those detained and the conditions under which they are held.

The various Middle East regional organizations exist primarily to promote economic cooperation, improve political stability, reinforce military cooperation, and achieve social and cultural development among the peoples of the region. The countries have formed the following organizations: the League of Arab States (Arab League), the Council of Arab Economic Unity (CAEU), the Organization of the Islamic Conference (OIC), and the Gulf Cooperative Council (GCC).

LEAGUE OF ARAB STATES (ARAB LEAGUE)

The League of Arab States, established in 1945, was created to foster economic, political, and military cooperation. The original member states were **Egypt, Iraq, Jordan, Lebanon, Saudi Arabia, Syria,** and **Yemen.** Though **Palestine** is not a state, it is a charter member with full status and a vote in the league.

The League structure consists of a council, special committees, and a permanent secretariat based in Cairo. In addition to its original member states, the League is composed of **Algeria, Bahrain, Comoros, Djibouti, Kuwait, Libya, Mauritania, Morocco, Oman, Qatar, Somalia, Sudan, Tunisia,** and the **United Arab Emirates.**

COUNCIL OF ARAB ECONOMIC UNITY (CAEU)

Established on June 3, 1957, by a resolution of the Arab Economic Council of the Arab League, CAEU promotes economic integration and social development among its members. Its membership consists of **Egypt, Iraq, Jordan, Kuwait, Libya, Mauritania,** the **Palestine Liberation Organization, Somalia, Syria, Sudan,** the **United Arab Emirates,** and **Yemen.** The council has sponsored the creation of a number of Arab joint companies and specialized trade federations aimed at enabling Arab firms to compete in new business sectors. An agreement within the council established the Arab Common Market among Iraq, Jordan, Egypt, and Syria in 1964; it was later joined by Libya, Mauritania, and Yemen.

ORGANIZATION OF THE ISLAMIC CONFERENCE (OIC)

The OIC has fifty-seven member states. The conference is composed of foreign ministers, a secretary general, and subgroups; its purpose is to further political, cultural, economic, and social cooperation between member states and other countries.

The organization was established in **Morocco** on September 25, 1969, after the Al-Aqsa Mosque in Jerusalem was set ablaze on August 21, 1969. Its general secretariat is temporarily housed in Saudi Arabia. (See page 158 for more information.)

GULF COOPERATION COUNCIL (GCC)

With Iran encroaching on the smaller Gulf States, the GCC was established in 1981 by **Bahrain, Kuwait, Oman, Qatar, Saudi Arabia,** and the **United Arab Emirates** (UAE) to promote stability and economic cooperation among Gulf nations. In 1991, the GCC joined with **Egypt** and **Syria** to create a regional peacekeeping force, which aided the liberation of Kuwait. In 2001, leaders of the members states met in Muscat, Oman, to discuss plans for creating a future customs union and common currency.

In March 1991 a special mission was sent to Kuwait to survey the loss of civilians, and infrastructural and environmental damage during the Iraqi occupation. (UN/DPI Photo: John Isaac)

1. "About OPEC." Organization of Petroleum Exporting Countries. Undated.<http://www.opec.org> (June 8, 2002).

2. Cordesman, Anthony. "Geopolitics and Energy in the Middle East." Center for Strategic & International Studies. September 15, 1999. <http://www.csis.org/mideast/reports/MEenergy.html> (June 10, 2002).

3. "Syria Profile." Energy Information Administration. February 2002. <http://www.eia.doe.gov/emeu/cabs/syria.html> (June 11, 2002).

4. "Six Die in Iranian Drugs Haul." BBC News. April 29, 2002. <http://news.bbc.co.uk/hi/english/world/middle_east/newsid_1958000/1958037.stm> (June 7, 2002).

5. Ketterer, James. "Networks of Discontent in Northern Morocco: Drugs, Opposition and Urban Unrest." The Middle East Research Project, *Middle East Report* 218. Spring 2001. <http://www.merip.org/mer/mer218/218_ketterer.html> (June 11, 2002).

6. "World Bank MENA Regional Brief." The World Bank Group. September 27, 2001. <http://P:\!units\mnavp\rcu\informationbriefs\mena&worldbank-01-RegionalBreif.DOC> (May 21, 2002).

7. "MENA Rural Development." The World Bank Group. Undated. <http://lnweb18.worldbank.org/mna/mena.nsf> (May 21, 2002).

8. Alavian, Vahid and Ssatoru Ueda. "Regional Water Initiative Program." World Bank Group. February 2002. <http://www.worldbank.org/MNA-Water> (May 21, 2002).

9. "MENA Urban Water & Sanitation." World Bank Group. Undated. <http://lnweb18.worldbank.org/mna/mena.nsf> (May 21, 2002).

10. Johnson, James. "Problems on the Peninsula."

The Princeton Tory. March 2002. <http://www.
princeton.edu/~tory/Articles/301/peninsula.htm>
(May 21, 2002).

11. Dalal, Khalid. "$65m USAID grant to Improve
Water Supply System." *Jordan Times* on Middle
East News Online. <http://www.middleeastwire.
com> (May 21, 2002).

12. "Water Issues between Turkey, Syria, and Iraq."
Embassy of the Republic of Turkey. Undated.
<http://www.turkey.org/groupc/Water/
CONTENTS.HTM> (May 23, 2002).

13. Willem, Alexander. "No Water No Future: A
Water Focus for Johannesburg." May 2002.
<http://www.johannesburgsummit.org> (May 23,
2002).

14. "Agenda 21." United Nations Sustainable Development. October 8, 1999.
<http://www.un.org/esa/sustdev/agenda21text.
htm> (May 24, 2002).

15. "U.N. Secretary-General Names Five Key Areas
where Johannesburg Summit Makes a Real Difference." Johannesburg 2002 What's New. May
14, 2002. <http://www.johannesburgsummit.
org/html/whats_new/whatsnew.html> (May 25,
2002).

16. Esposito, John L. *The Islamic Threat, Myth or
Reality.* (New York: Oxford University Press,
1992)

17. "Patterns of Global Terrorism—2001." U.S.
Department of State. May 21, 2002. <http://
www.state.gov/www/global/terrorism/annual_
reports.html> (May 26, 2002).

18. Ibid.

19. Organization of the Islamic Conference.
<http://www.oic-oci.org>.

20. "In Depth, World, Israel and the Palestinians."
British Broadcasting Corporation.
<http://www.news.bbc.co.uk>.

21. "Background Note: Syria." U.S. Department of
State. February 2002. <http:// www.state.gov/
www/background_notes/syria_0499_bgn.html>
(May 26, 2002).

22. "Background Note: Lebanon." U.S. Department
of State. February 2002. <http://dosfan.lib.uic.
edu/ERC/bgnotes/nea/lebanon9401.html> (May
26, 2002).

23. Ibid.

24. "Patterns of Global Terrorism." U.S. Department
of State. <http://www.state.gov/www/global/
terrorism/annual_reports.html>.

25. "Resolution 1397." United Nations Security
Council. March 12, 2002.
<http://www.un.org/Docs/scres/2002/res1397e.p
df> (May 4, 2002).

26. Pisik, Betsy. "Annan's letter criticizes Israel."
Washington Times. March 19, 2002.
<http://www.washtimes.com> (June 5, 2002).

27. "Current Peacekeeping Operations". United
Nations Peacekeeping Operations.
<http://www.un.org/Depts/DPKO/Missions/unts
o/body_untso.htm>

28. Arnove, Anthony, ed. *Iraq Under Siege: The Deadly Impact of Sanctions and War.* (Cambridge, MA:
South End Press, 2000).

29. PBS. *The Gulf War.* 1996. <http://www.pbs.org/
wgbh/pages/frontline/gulf>.

30. Smith, Sharon. "Building the Movement to End
Sanctions." A. Arnove (Ed.), *Iraq Under Siege:
The Deadly Impact of Sanctions and War.*
(Cambridge, MA: South End Press, 2000), 185-
198.

31. Bennis, Phyllis. "The Failure of U.S. Policy
Toward Iraq and Proposed Alternatives." *Middle
East Policy* (September 2001), 101-109.

32. Hoskins, Eric. "The Impact of Sanctions: A Study
of UNICEF'S Perspective." UNICEF Office of
Emergency Programmes. February 1998.
<http://www.unicef.org/emerg/Sanctions.html>
(November 18, 2001).

33. Bennis 101-109

34. Alkadiri, Raad. "The Iraqi Klondike: Oil and
Regional Trade." *Middle East Report,* vol. 220.
(2001) 30-35.

35. Sengupta, Somini. "U.N. Broadens List of Products Iraq Can Import." *New York Times.* May 15,
2002. <http://www.nytimes.com>.

36. Sengupta, Somini. "Security Council Tries to Ease
Tensions Between U.S. and Iraq." *New York
Times.* May 23, 2002. <http://www.nytimes
.com>.

37. "Middle East and North Africa Highlights of
Amnesty International Report 2002." Amnesty
International. April 2002.
<http://www.amnesty.org> (May 26, 2002).

38. Olson, Elizabeth, "Fair Penalties or Torture? U.N.
at Odds With Saudis." *New York Times.* May 19,
2002. <http://www.nytimes.com> (May 27,
2002).

AAIB Arab-African International Bank

ACABQ Advisory Committee on Administrative and Budgetary Questions

ACDA Arms Control and Disarmament Agency

ACS The Association of Caribbean States

ADB, AsDB Asian Development Bank

ADL Armistice demarcation line

AEC African Economic Community

AfDB African Development Bank

AFTA Association of Southeast Asian Nations (ASEAN) Free Trade Area

AIDS Acquired Immune-Deficiency Syndrome

ALADI Association Latinoamericana de Integracion

ANZUS Australia, New Zealand, and United States Pact

AOL Area of Limitation

AOO Area of operation

AOR Area of responsibility

AOS Area of separation

AOSIS Alliance of Small Island States

AP mine Antipersonnel mine

APEC Asia Pacific Economic Cooperation

ASEAN Association of Southeast Asian Nations

ASEM Asia-Europe Meeting

AU African Union

CACE Central African Customs and Economic Union

CACM Central American Common Market

CAEU Council of Arab Economic Unity

CARICOM Caribbean Community and Common Market

CAU Central Asian Union

CCPCJ Commission on Crime Prevention and Criminal Justice

C.D. Conference on Disarmament

CDB Caribbean Development Bank

CDP Committee on Development Planning

CEAU Committee on Economic Arab Unity

CFL Cease-fire line

CGAP Consultative Group to Assist the Poorest

CGIAR Consultative Group for International Agricultural Research

CHR Commission on Human Rights

CIDA Canadian International Development Agency

CIS Commonwealth of Independent States

CND Commission on Narcotic Drugs

COE Council of Europe

COMESA Common Market for East and Southern Africa

COPUOS Commission on the Peaceful Uses of Outer Space

CSD Commission on Sustainable Development

CSTD Commission on Science and Technology for Development

CSW Commission on the Status of Women

CTBT The Comprehensive Nuclear Test-Ban-Treaty

CWC Chemical Weapons Convention

DAC Development Assistance Committee

DMZ Demilitarized zone

DP Displaced person

DPKO Department of Peacekeeping Operations

ECA Economic Commission for Africa

ECE Economic Commission for Europe

ECLAC Economic Commission for Latin America

ECOMOG Economic Community of West African States Cease-Fire Monitoring Group

ECOSOC Economic and Social Council

ECOWAS Economic Community of West African States

ECSC European Coal and Steel Community

EFTA European Free Trade Association

ESCAP Economic and Social Commission for Asia and the Pacific

ESCWA Economic and Social Commission for Western Asia

EU European Union

FAO Food and Agriculture Organization

FSU Former Soviet Union

FTA Free trade area

G-3 Latin American Group of Three

G-7 Group of Seven

G-8 Group of Eight

G.A. General Assembly (United Nations)

GATT General Agreement on Tariffs and Trade

GDP gross domestic product

GNP gross national product

H.Q. Headquarters

HIPCs Heavily Indebted Poor Countries

HKSAR Hong Kong Special Administrative Region

HNS host nation support

IADB Inter-American Development Bank

IAEA International Atomic Energy Agency

IBRD International Bank for Reconstruction

ICAO International Civil Aviation Organization

ICC International Criminal Court

ICJ International Court of Justice

ICTR International Criminal Tribunal for Rwanda

ICTY International Criminal Tribunal for the Former Yugoslavia

IDA International Development Association

IFAD International Fund for Agricultural Development

IFC International Finance Corporation

IFOR Implementation Force: Yugoslavia

IGO intergovernmental organization

ILC International Law Commission

ILO International Labor Organization

IMF International Monetary Fund

INSTRAW United Nations International Research and Training Institute for the Advancement of Women

INTERPOL International Criminal Police Organization

JCIT Joint Committee for Investment and Trade

JTF joint task force

LAC Latin American and Caribbean Region

LAES Latin American Economic System

LAS League of Arab States

LDC Less-Developed Country

MAP Millennium Partnership for African Recovery Program

MERCOSUR South American Common Market

MIA missing in action

MICIVIH OAS International Civilian Mission in Haiti

MIGA The Multilateral Investment Guarantee Agency

MINUGUA United Nations Mission for the Verification of Human Rights to Guatemala

MINURCA United Nations Verification Mission in the Central African Republic

MINURSO United Nations Mission for the Referendum in Western Sahara

MFN most favored nation

MONUA United Nations Observer Mission in Angola

MONUC United Nations Organization Mission in the Democratic Republic of Congo

MOU Memorandum of Understanding

MP Montreal Protocol

MRTA Tupac Amaru Revolutionary Movement

MSG Melanesian Spearhead Group

NAFTA North American Free Trade Agreement

NAI New African Initiative

NAM Non-Aligned Movement

NATO North Atlantic Treaty Organization

NEPAD New Partnership for Africa's Development

NGO non-governmental organization

NPT Nuclear Non-Proliferation Treaty

OAS Organization of American States

OAU Organization of African Unity

ODS Ozone-depleting substances

OECD Organization for Economic Cooperation and Development

OECF Overseas Economic Cooperation Fund (Japan)

OECS Organization of Eastern Caribbean States

OIC Organization of the Islamic Conference

OPANAL Agency for the Prohibition of Nuclear Weapons

OSCE Organization for Security and Cooperation in Europe

PAHO Pan-American Health Organization

P.K. peacekeeping

PKO peacekeeping operation

PLO Palestinian Liberation Organization

RDF rapid-deployment force

RRF rapid-reaction force

ROE rules of engagement

SAARC South Asian Association for Regional Development

SADC Southern African Development Committee

SAP Structural Adjustment Program/Policy

SAPTA SAARC Preferential Trading Agreement

S.C. Security Council

SCITECH Commission on Science and Technology

SEATO Southeast Asian Treaty Organization

SECAL Sector adjustment loan

SFOR Stabilization Force: Yugoslavia

START I, II Strategic Arms Reduction Treaty

T.C. Trusteeship Council

UDHR Universal Declaration of Human Rights

UNA-USA United Nations Association of the United States of America

UNAIDS Joint United Nations Program

UNAMIC United Nations Advance Mission in Cambodia

UNAMIR United Nations Assistance Mission for Rwanda

UNAMSIL United Nations Mission in Sierra Leone

UNCED United Nations Conference on the Environment and Development

UNCHS United Nations Center for Human Settlements

UNCIP United Nations Commission for India and Pakistan

UNCITRAL United Nations Commission on International Trade Law

UNCND United Nations Commission on Narcotic Drugs

UNCTAD United Nations Conference on Trade and Development

UNDCP United Nations International Drug Control Program

UNDP United Nations Development Program

UNDRO United Nations Disaster Relief Organization

UNECA United Nations Economic Commission for Africa

UNEP United Nations Environment Program

UNESCO United Nations Educational, Scientific and Cultural Organization

UNFPA United Nations Population Fund

UNHCHR United Nations High Commissioner for Human Rights

UNHCR United Nations High Commissioner for Refugees

UNICEF United Nations Children's Fund

UNIDO United Nations Industrial Development Organization

UNIFEM United Nations Development Fund for Women

UNIPOM United Nations India-Pakistan Observation Mission

UNITAR United Nations Institute for Training and Research

UNMISET United Nations Mission of Support in East Timor

UNMOGIP United Nations Military Observer Group in India and Pakistan

UNMOT United Nations Mission of Observers in Tajikistan

U.N.-NADAF United Nations New Agenda for the Development of Africa

UNOG United Nations Office in Geneva

UNOMIG United Nations Observer Mission in Georgia

UNOMSIL United Nations Observer Mission in Sierra Leone

UNOMUR United Nations Observer Mission for Uganda-Rwanda

UNPROFOR United Nations Protection Force

UNRWA United Nations Relief and Works Agency for Palestine Refugees in the Near East

UNSCOM United Nations Special Commission for Iraq

UNSF United Nations Security Force in West New Guinea

UNSIA United Nations Special Initiative on Africa

UNTAC United Nations Transitional Authority in Cambodia

UNTAET United Nations Transitional Authority in East Timor

WAEC West African Economic Community

WEU Western European Union

WFC World Food Council

WFP World Food Programme

WFUNA World Federation of United Nations Associations

WHO World Health Organization

abolish To annul; put an end to. Implies absolute destruction, having its root in the Latin word "*absolere*," meaning to destroy utterly. Applies particularly to things of a permanent nature, such as institutions and customs; for example the abolition of slavery.

acclamation An overwhelmingly affirmative vote. If no opposition is indicated, the resolution or other item of business passes "by acclamation".

accord A diplomatic agreement that does not have the same binding force as a treaty but is often treated as such, e.g., the Camp David Accord signed by Israel and Egypt in 1978.

Acquired Immune-Deficiency Syndrome (AIDS) A disease that destroys the immune system of the human body. The disease was first diagnosed in 1979 in the United States, and incidence increased dramatically after its identification, with a death rate of about 40%. Extensive research into social and physical contacts among victims has sought to aid medical determination of the cause and transmission of the disease.

act of state The actions of a government for which no individual can be held accountable.

activism A doctrine or practice that emphasizes direct, vigorous action, especially in support of or in opposition to one side of a controversial issue.

ad hoc For a specific purpose; for a single case only.

administration The management of institutional or governmental affairs; a term for the government itself and its policy-makers, as in "the Clinton administration".

aegis Any power or influence that protects or shields. Nations take part in peacekeeping operations under the aegis of the United Nations.

African Development Bank (AfDB) The institution provides financing through direct loans to African member states to cover the foreign exchange costs incurred in Bank-approved development projects in those countries. Fifty-three African countries are members and ordinarily receive loans. The African Development Bank comprises the AFDB as well as the African Development Fund and the Nigeria Trust Fund. The Bank was established in August 1963 (it began operations in July 1966), with headquarters in Abidjan, Côte d'Ivoire. The members are: Algeria, Angola, Benin, Botswana, Burkina Faso, Burundi, Cameroon, Cape Verde, Central African Republic, Chad, Comoros, Democratic Republic of Congo, Republic of the Congo, Côte d'Ivoire, Djibouti, Egypt, Equatorial Guinea, Eritrea, Ethiopia, Gabon, Gambia, Ghana, Guinea, Guinea-Bissau, Kenya, Lesotho, Liberia, Libya, Madagascar, Malawi, Mali, Mauritania, Mauritius, Morocco, Mozambique, Namibia, Niger, Nigeria, Rwanda, Sao Tome and Principe, Senegal, Seychelles, Sierra Leone, Somalia, South Africa, Sudan, Swaziland, Tanzania, Togo, Tunisia, Uganda, Zambia, and Zimbabwe. The non-regional members are Argentina, Austria, Belgium, Brazil, Canada, China, Denmark, Finland, France, Germany, India, Italy, Japan, South Korea, Kuwait, Netherlands, Norway, Portugal, Saudi Arabia, Spain, Sweden, Switzerland, UAE, U.K., and U.S.

African Economic Community (AEC) This group seeks to promote economic, social, and cultural development and the integration of African economies. The member states of the Organization of African Unity (OAU) are signatories to the AEC.

African Union (AU) Formerly known as the Organization of African Unity (OAU). Founded in May 1963 with 32 African countries, the organization has since grown to 53 members. It aims to further African unity and solidarity, to coordinate political, economic, cultural, scientific, and defense policies; and to eliminate colonialism in Africa. Members include: Algeria, Angola, Benin, Botswana, Burkina Faso, Burundi, Cameroon, Cape Verde, Central Africa Republic, Chad, Comoros, Congo, Côte d'Ivoire, Egypt, Equatorial Guinea, Ethiopia, Gabon, Gambia, Ghana, Guinea, Guinea-Bissau, Kenya, Lesotho, Liberia, Libya, Madagascar, Malawi, Mali, Mauritania, Mauritius, Morocco, Mozambique, Namibia, Niger, Nigeria, Rwanda, Sao Tome and Principe, Senegal, Seychelles, Sierra Leone, Somalia, Sudan, Swaziland, Tanzania, Togo, Tunisia, Uganda, Zaire, Zambia, and Zimbabwe. AU headquarters are in Addis Ababa, Ethiopia.

agenda A list of things to be done or dealt with.

aggregate demand The total demand for goods and services in an economy, including demands for consumer goods and investment goods, the demands of local and central government, and the demands of other countries for exports.

aggregate supply The total supply of goods and services in an economy, including imports and exports that are available to meet aggregate demand.

aggression An act of force; belligerent actions by one state against another. Iraq committed an act of aggression when it invaded Kuwait in 1990.

agitation In a political sense, it refers to keeping an issue or a debate constantly before the public (e.g., agitation for reform). Usually used to refer to opposition to the status quo.

air logistic support Airplane landings or air drops for the purpose of supply, movement of personnel, evacuation of casualties, and recovery of equipment and vehicles.

air strike Refers to bombing attacks against any tactical or strategic target and, as such, should be distinguished from close air support, which involves protecting friendly troops on the ground against attack and striking directly at the immediate source of threat.

airlift The carrying of troops and equipment over large distances by air to bring them into crisis areas rapidly.

allegiance Loyalty to a principle, a leader, or a country, as in the "Pledge of Allegiance".

alliance A union for joint action of various powers or states in international relations, such as the alliance of the European powers and the United States against Germany and its allies during World War II.

Alliance of Small Island States (AOSIS) This is a coalition of 42 small island states in all regions of the world that share common objectives on environmental and sustainable development matters. It has formed a partnership with two nongovernmental organizations: Counterpart International and EarthVoice International. AOSIS members are: American Samoa, Antigua and Barbuda, Bahamas, Barbados, Belize, Cape Verde, Comoros, Cook Islands, Cuba, Cyprus, Dominica, Federated States of Micronesia, Fiji, Grenada, Guam, Guinea-Bissau, Guyana, Jamaica, Kiribati, Maldives, Malta, Marshall Islands, Mauritius, Nauru, Netherlands Antilles, Niue, Palau, Papua New Guinea, Samoa, Sao Tome and Principe, Seychelles, Singapore, Solomon Islands, St. Kitts and Nevis, St. Lucia, St. Vincent and the Grenadines, Suriname, Tonga, Trinidad and Tobago, Tuvalu, U.S. Virgin Islands, and Vanuatu.

ambassador The highest rank of diplomatic representatives sent by one government to another. Prior to the development of modern communication, ambassadors were frequently entrusted with extensive plenary powers. They have since tended, however, to become spokesmen of their foreign offices, and rarely does an ambassador enjoy extensive discretion. An ambassador's personality may play an important part in making the views of his government understood, and her firsthand knowledge of the country to which she is accredited may enable her to influence her government's policy decisively.

ammunition Projectiles fired from weapons, such as bullets, together with the charges that propel them; or thrown, such as grenades.

amnesty A state pardon of political or other offenders, usually as a group. Amnesties are often used as a gesture of political reconciliation. In 1990, the ruling Sandinistas in Nicaragua declared an amnesty for over a thousand political prisoners as a prelude to a general election. Amnesties are sometimes granted after a change of government or regime.

anarchy The absence of a government, a state of lawlessness or political disorder owing to the absence of a government authority.

annexation A formal act whereby a state proclaims its sovereignty over territory outside its domain. Unlike secession, whereby territory is given or sold by a treaty, annexation is a unilateral act made effective by actual possession and legitimated by general recognition. It is frequently preceded by conquest and military occupation—an illegal use of force that is condemned in the Charter of the United Nations.

Andean Pact The agreement was reached in Cartagena, Colombia, on May 26, 1969, by Bolivia, Chile, Colombia, Ecuador, and Peru (Venezuela joined in 1974 and Chile withdrew in 1978). The main goal of the Andean Pact is to promote balanced growth among the members and to accelerate growth through economic integration.

anti-personnel mines Landmines intended to injure or kill soldiers also pose an enormous danger for the civilian population (in Cambodia, Afghanistan, and Angola, for example).

appeasement The policy of giving in to the demands of a hostile or dangerous power in an attempt to prevent trouble.

Arab-African International Bank (AAIB) This pan-Arab consortium was incorporated in 1964 as a self-governing autonomous entity of the Ministry of Finance of Kuwait and the Central Bank of Egypt; each holds 49.37% of the Bank's shares. AAIB headquarters are in Cairo, Egypt. A New York branch of the AAIB was established in 1981 to facilitate the financing of trade between North America and the Middle East.

arbitrage A business operation involving the purchase of foreign exchange, gold, financial securities, or commodities in one market and their almost simultaneous sale in another market, in order to profit from price differentials existing between the markets. In less-developed countries arbitrage can consist of the buying and selling of commodities in different villages within the country; in highly developed countries the term generally refers to international operations involving foreign exchange rates, short-term interest rates, prices of gold, and prices of securities.

arbitration A legal method of settling disputes between parties outside ordinary court procedures by deferring to a mutually agreed-upon third party with the authority to make a legally binding decision.

area of limitation of armaments An area established beyond a buffer zone; the usual arrangement is for the two sides to agree on equal numbers of small, lightly armed forces in the areas immediately adjacent to the buffer zone.

area of operation (AOO) That portion of an area of conflict necessary for the conduct of a peacekeeping operation.

aristocracy Government by a small privileged class; a government in which power is vested in a minority consisting of those believed to be best qualified.

armistice The ending of hostilities, as in the armistice of November 1918, which marked the end of World War I.

armistice demarcation line (ADL) A boundary line that the parties to an armistice agreement have accepted; it usually becomes a de facto border.

Arms Control and Disarmament Agency (ACDA) This independent agency within the U.S. State Department. ACDA participates in interagency working groups that discuss export license applications requiring dispute resolution. ACDA is interested in dual-use license applications from a non-proliferation perspective and is concerned with the proliferation of missiles, chemical and biological weapons, and nuclear weapons. ACDA's positions need not be consonant with those of the State Department. The Director is the principal arms control advisor to the Secretary of State, the President, and the NSC on conventional arms transfers, commercial sales of munitions; nuclear, chemical, and biological warfare; East-West military munitions issues; CoCom, and negotiating MOUs with the Third World on strategic trade.

ASEAN Free Trade Area (AFTA) Its objective is to increase the Association of Southeast Asian Nations' (ASEAN) competitive advantage as a single production unit by eliminating tariff barriers among the member countries.

Asia–Europe Meeting Held on March 1–2, 1996, the first summit ever between Asia and Europe brought to Thailand leaders from two continents, representing 25 countries and the European Commission. The members are: Brunei, China, Indonesia, Japan, South Korea, Malaysia, Philippines, Singapore, Thailand, Vietnam, Austria, Belgium, Denmark, Finland, France, Germany, Greece, Ireland, Italy, Luxembourg, Netherlands, Portugal, Spain, Sweden, United Kingdom, and the president of the European Commission The second summit was held in London, and the third in Seoul.

Asia Pacific Economic Cooperation (APEC) Established in November 1989, this informal grouping of Asian countries provides a forum for ministerial-level discussion of a broad range of economic issues. APEC includes six ASEAN countries—Brunei, Indonesia, Malaysia, Philippines, Singapore, and Thailand—plus Australia, Canada, China, Hong Kong, Japan, New Zealand, South Korea, Taiwan, and the United States.

Asian Development Bank (ADB) This multilateral development finance institution has capital stock owned by 57 member countries. Headquartered in Manila, the Philippines, it promotes the economic and social progress of its developing-country members in the Asian and Pacific region. Its members are: Afghanistan, Australia, Bangladesh, Bhutan, Cambodia, China, Cook Islands, Fiji, Hong Kong, India, Indonesia, Japan, Kazakhstan, Kiribati, South Korea, Kyrgyz Republic, Laos, Malaysia, Maldives, Marshall Islands, Federated States of Micronesia, Mongolia, Myanmar, Nauru, Nepal, New Zealand, Pakistan, Papua New Guinea, Philippines, Samoa, Singapore, Solomon Islands, Sri Lanka, Taiwan, Tajikistan, Thailand, Tonga, Tuvalu, Uzbekistan, Vanuatu, and Vietnam. There are also 16 non-regional members Austria, Belgium, Canada, Denmark, Finland, France, Germany, Italy, Netherlands, Norway, Spain, Sweden, Switzerland, Turkey, United Kingdom, and United States.

Association of Caribbean States (ACS) It was first proposed by the West Indian Commission in its 1992 Report to the CARICOM Heads of Government as a means of advancing economic integration and functional co-operation. On July 24, 1994, the Convention Establishing the ACS was signed in Cartagena de Indias, Colombia. The member states of the ACS are Antigua and Barbuda, the Bahamas, Barbados, Belize, Colombia, Costa Rica, Cuba, Dominica, the Dominican Republic, El Salvador, Grenada, Guatemala, Guyana, Haiti, Honduras, Jamaica, Mexico, Nicaragua, Panama, St. Kitts and Nevis, St. Lucia, St. Vincent and the Grenadines, Suriname, Trinidad and Tobago, and Venezuela. ACS headquarters are in Trinidad and Tobago.

Association of Southeast Asian Nations (ASEAN) Established on August 8, 1967, in Bangkok, Thailand, with the signing of the Bangkok Declaration, it had five original member countries: Indonesia, Malaysia, Philippines, Singapore, and Thailand. Brunei joined the Association on January 8, 1984, Vietnam on July 28, 1995, Laos and Myanmar on July 23, 1997, and Cambodia on April 30, 1999. The Bangkok Declaration united the ASEAN member countries in an effort to promote economic cooperation and the welfare of the people in the region. The Bangkok Declaration set out guidelines for ASEAN's activities and defined the aims of the organization.

asylum In international law, the protection granted by a state to the citizen of another state (usually a political refugee). The person seeking asylum has no legal right to demand it, while the sheltering state, which has the legal right to grant asylum, is under no obligation to give it. Asylum is thus a right of the state, not of the individual.

atrocities Acts of unusual cruelty. Many contemporary conflicts are marked by atrocities perpetrated on large groups of defenseless persons.

autarchy Political self-rule, complete independence.

authoritarianism A system of government with a concentration of power in a leader or small elite who are not constitutionally responsible to the people—the opposite of constitutional democracy. Rule without law has been justified by conquest, by the need of a people for absolute government, by superior qualities of the ruler, and (in the case of a temporary dictatorship) by emergency conditions.

autonomy Self-governance.

back-channel diplomacy Secret lines of communication between two adversaries, often through an informal intermediary or through a third party.

background guide An informational aid, written by Model U.N. conference organizers, that provides delegates with an overview of a committee and the issues on its agenda.

Bangkok Declaration Signed by Indonesia, Malaysia, Philippines, Singapore, and Thailand in 1967 to form the Association of Southeast Asian Nations (ASEAN), the first regional organization in Asia.

barter system The exchange of goods or services without an intervening medium of exchange or money, either according to established rates of exchange or through bargaining.

Beijing Declaration and Platform for Action Reaffirmed the commitment of governments to eliminate discrimination against women and to remove all obstacles to women's advancement by identifying twelve major areas of concern to be dealt with.

bilateral An agreement or exchange involving two parties only, for example a trade agreement between the U.S. and Japan.

biological warfare The military use of disease-producing agents, such as bacteria and viruses, on humans, animals, or plants.

blockade A procedure whereby a belligerent nation prevents ships carrying vital goods from reaching enemy ports. Occasionally used in peacetime to press for a change in state policies.

border control Full border control requires the capability to deny passage and to act where borders have already been closed.

border monitoring The work of international observers, who observe and report but are not mandated to check the nature of goods crossing the border.

bourgeoisie (French) The group in society that carries on commerce and industry; the middle class; as distinct from landowners, wage earners, farmers.

breach A failure to observe the terms; a break or interruption in friendly relations.

budget A statement of estimated income and expenditure of a given entity, over a given period of time.

buffer zone Also known as an area of separation, a neutral space created by withdrawal of both hostile parties; and as a demilitarized zone, an area in which the parties have agreed not to deploy military forces.

bureaucracy A type of administration characterized by specialization, professionalism, and security of tenure.

capital A city that is the seat of government of a state or nation; money used in business—the wealth or assets of a firm. Capital is one of the three main factors of production, the others being land and labor.

Caribbean Community and Common Market (CARICOM) The agreement for the union was signed by the prime ministers of Barbados, Guyana, Jamaica, and Trinidad and Tobago at Chaguaramas, Trinidad, on July 4, 1973, and entered into force on August 1, 1973. CARICOM's headquarters are in Georgetown, Guyana.

Caribbean Development Bank (CDB) Promoting economic development and cooperation, it provides long-term financing for productive projects in CARICOM member countries and U.K.-dependent territories in the Caribbean. Members include: Anguilla, Antigua and Barbuda, the Bahamas, Barbados, Belize, British Virgin Islands, Canada, Cayman Islands, Dominica, France, Grenada, Guyana, Jamaica, Mexico, Montserrat, St. Kitts and Nevis, St. Lucia, St. Vincent and the Grenadines, Trinidad and Tobago, Turks and Caicos Islands, United Kingdom, and Venezuela. The Bank was established in 1969; headquarters are in St. Michael, Barbados.

casualties The total losses of personnel in an operation of warfare, both injured and killed.

Caucasus The region in Central Asia composed of Armenia, Azerbaijan, and Georgia, nations that were granted independence from the Soviet Union in 1991. Although beset by conflict, this region remains significant to world energy markets as a transit area for oil and natu-

ral gas exports from the Caspian Sea to Europe.

caucus A meeting of legislators of any one party to discuss parliamentary strategy and party policy.

cease-fire line The forward limit of the positions occupied by the troops of opposing sides at the suspension of hostilities between them.

censorship The suppression or prohibition of the expression of thoughts or actions considered to be contrary to the common good.

Central American Common Market (CACM) Created in 1960, it functions along with three other Latin American trading blocs—the Latin American Free Trade Area, the Caribbean Free Trade Association, and the Andean Group—to endorse import-substitution-industrialization through regional integration efforts.

Central Asian Union (CAU) Founded in 1994 as a response to the failure of the 1993 CIS Foreign Trade Agreement; it serves to establish regional economic cooperation and integration among its member nations. It is currently composed of Uzbekistan, Kazakhstan, Kyrgyzstan, and Tajikistan.

chaebol A Korean term referring to the large domestically owned conglomerates that have dominated Korean industries since the 1960s, such as Daewoo.

checks and balances A system of dividing power among the executive, legislative, and judicial branches of a government.

chemical warfare The use of chemical compounds, usually toxic agents, in warfare. Included in this group are chemical defoliants and herbicides that are put to military purposes, such as those used in the Vietnam War.

civil disobedience The refusal to obey the demands or commands of a government or occupying power without resorting to violence or active measures of opposition. Its usual purpose is to force concessions from the government or occupying power. Civil disobedience has been a major tactic and philosophy of nationalist movements in Africa and of labor and anti-war movements in many countries. It is also called passive resistance.

civil society Refers to the interplay of institutions, organizations, and behaviors arising

from relationships between the state, the business world, and the family.

civil war A war between the government of a state and a faction of the same state, or between two factions or parts of a state, neither clearly recognized as the government thereof. A specifically termed civil war was the war between the United States government and the southern states combined in the Confederate States of America from 1861 to 1865. Two chief problems were resolved in the retention of the southern states in the Union and in the abolition of slavery.

civilian A person not a member of any military forces.

Clinton Doctrine Interventionist policy adopted by NATO, based on the principle that nations of the free world would take such measures on behalf of basic human rights in other countries, when they have the opportunity to do so.

coalition Temporary alliance between two or more political units for the purposes of joint action.

coalition government A parliamentary government in which the cabinet is composed of members of more than one party.

coercion Forced compliance through fear and intimidation.

Cold War The open yet restricted rivalry that developed after World War II between the United States and the Soviet Union and their respective allies—a war fought on political, economic, and propaganda fronts, with limited recourse to weapons, largely because of fear of a nuclear holocaust.

collaboration A joint effort by two or more persons for the accomplishment of a specific purpose, such as a literary or scientific endeavor. It can also refer to cooperating with the enemy.

collective defense An alliance among states against external threats.

collective goods Goods and services enjoyed in common.

collective security agreement An agreement by participating nations that they will take joint military action against any nation that attacks any one of them. The North Atlantic Treaty is an example.

commission A body created to perform a particular function, whether administrative, legislative, or judicial.

Commission on Human Rights (CHR) Established by ECOSOC Resolution 5 in 1946, the Commission was directed to prepare recommendations and reports regarding an international bill of rights, international declarations or conventions on civil liberties, the status of women, freedom of information, the protection of minorities, the prevention of discrimination on the basis of race, sex, language, or religion, and any other matters concerning human rights. The Commission, which has 53 elected members, meets annually.

Commission on Narcotic Drugs (CND) Established by ECOSOC in 1946, it assists the Council in supervising the application of international conventions and agreements dealing with drugs.

Commission on the Status of Women (CSW) One of the first bodies established by the U.N. Economic and Social Council, it was set up in 1946. It monitors the situation of women and promotes their rights in all societies around the world. The Commission prepares recommendations and reports for the U.N. on any issue affecting women. In the case of urgent problems, the Commission can press for immediate international action to prevent or alleviate violations of women's rights.

Commission on Sustainable Development (CSD) Established in December 1992, it seeks to ensure effective follow-up of the Rio Earth Summit. It is a functional committee of the Economic and Social Council and has 53 members.

commodity trade The international trade in primary goods (raw or partly refined materials, whose value mainly reflects the costs of finding, gathering, or harvesting them). They are traded for processing or incorporation into final goods. Examples are crude oil and rubber.

Common Market for East and Southern Africa (COMESA) Established in 1994 to replace the Preferential Trade Area (PTA) for Eastern and Southern Africa. Its objective is to create a substantial economic and trading unit able to overcome internal trade tariffs and barriers faced by individual states, and to promote peace and security in the region.

Commonwealth of Independent States (CIS) Established in December 1991, it is an association of 12 republics of the former Soviet Union: Russia, Ukraine, Belarus (formerly Byelorussia), Moldova (formerly Moldavia), Armenia, Azerbaijan, Uzbekistan, Turkmenistan, Tajikistan, Kazakhstan, and Kyrgyzstan (formerly Kirghiziya). Georgia held observer status before joining the CIS in November 1993.

communiqué An official document, usually in the form of an announcement to the public or the press.

communism A doctrine based on revolutionary Marxist socialism and Marxism-Leninism that was the official ideology of the USSR.

Comprehensive Nuclear Test-Ban Treaty (CTBT) Opened for signature on September 10, 1996, it established a global verification regime to be overseen by two organs, a plenary body composed of all the states parties—also known as a plenary commission—and a provisional technical secretariat.

concentration camp An internment center for political prisoners and members of minority groups, usually established by executive decree or military order, citing "reasons of state security" or simply to punish—or worse. The inmates of such camps are often chosen on the basis of their identification with a group rather than as individuals.

conciliation The process of bringing two sides in a dispute to agree to a compromise. The conciliator is a third party not involved in the dispute. The agreement must be voluntary; the process of conciliation does not compel the disputants to accept the proposed solution.

confederation A federal system of government in which sovereign constituent governments create a central government but power remains with constituent governments.

conservatism A political ideology generally characterized by a belief in individualism and minimal government intervention in the economy and society; as well as a belief in the virtue of the status quo and general acceptance of traditional morality.

constituency A body of citizens entitled to elect a representative to a legislative or other public body.

constitution The fundamental rules and principles by which a state is organized.

constitutionalism The belief that governments will defer to the rules and principles enshrined in a constitution and uphold the rule of law.

convention A practice or custom followed by the government although not explicitly written into the constitution or in legislation.

Council of Arab Economic Unity (CAEU) A body fostering economic integration among Arab nations. Its activities include compiling statistics, conducting research, and promoting a customs union. The Council, established in 1964 and headquartered in Amman, Jordan, oversees the Arab Common Market, which is composed of Egypt, Iraq, Jordan, Libya, Mauritania, Syria, and Yemen.

Council of Europe (COE) Established in May 1949, it encourages unity and social and economic growth among members, which include: Austria, Belgium, Cyprus, Denmark, Finland, France, Germany, Greece, Hungary, Iceland, Ireland, Italy, Liechtenstein, Luxembourg, Malta, Netherlands, Norway, Portugal, San Marino, Spain, Sweden, Switzerland, Turkey, and United Kingdom. COE headquarters are in Strasbourg, France.

counteroffensive A large-scale military offensive undertaken by a force previously on the defensive.

coup d'etat A sudden, forceful stroke in politics, especially the violent overthrow or alteration of an existing government.

Dayton Peace Accords An agreement between Bosnia, Herzegovina, Croatia, and the Federal Republic of Yugoslavia in 1995 to respect the sovereignty of each nation and to settle future disputes concerning these countries peacefully.

de facto Latin phrase meaning "by the fact of." For example, if a revolution has just taken place, the new government will be the de facto authority, i.e., the actual, existing authority, regardless of whether it has any legal claim to the position. De facto is the opposite of de jure.

de jure Latin phrase meaning "from the law," "by right." The opposite of de facto.

deadlock A stoppage or standstill resulting from the action of equal and opposed forces.

decontamination The process of rendering any person, object, or area safe by absorbing, destroying, or neutralizing chemical or biological agents or by removing radioactive material.

deficit financing Practice in which a government spends more money than it receives as revenue. The term usually refers to a conscious attempt to stimulate the economy by lowering tax rates or increasing government expenditures.

delegate A person authorized to act for others; a representative. To delegate means to give someone the authority to act as one's agent or representative.

delegation A group of delegates, often representing a larger group.

demilitarize To free from organized military control, to remove any military character.

demilitarized zone (DMZ) The area between the forward line of the parties, into which they have agreed not to deploy military forces and which may be placed under the control of a peacekeeping operation.

democracy A form of government in which the right to make political decisions is exercised directly by the whole body of citizens. In direct democracy, citizens rule directly through procedures of majority rule. In representative democracy, citizens exercise the same right not in person but through representatives chosen by them.

Department of Peacekeeping Operations (DPKO) The main U.N. office for dealing with peacekeeping and peace-building activities.

deportation Expulsion of an alien whose presence in a country is deemed inconsistent with the public welfare. Deportation has often had a broader meaning, including exile, banishment, and the transportation of criminals to penal settlements.

deregulation A government policy designed to remove regulations on market or other activity.

devaluation An official reduction in the exchange value of a currency by lowering its gold equivalency or its value relative to another currency.

devolution The redistribution or delegation of political power away from a centralized body to a lower, often regional, authority.

diplomacy The conduct of relations between nations, as in making agreements.

diplomatic immunity Special rights given to diplomats, including immunity from the laws that operate in the country to which they are assigned.

directive A military communication in which policy is established or a specific action is ordered for the purpose of governing conduct or procedure.

disarmament The reduction or removal of armed forces and armaments.

displaced person Someone rendered homeless as a result of war or disaster. An individual fleeing such conditions who crosses a border is considered a "refugee." Anyone who takes flight but never leaves his/her country is an "internally displaced" person.

doctrine of operations A broad statement of policy that incorporates acceptable techniques, procedures, and methodologies to guide operations and resolve issues likely to be encountered in the field.

domestic Pertaining to matters of national internal interest and control, as opposed to international matters.

draft resolution A document that has been approved by the chairperson for discussion in formal debate; it is written in the form of a U.N. resolution but has not been passed by the committee.

duty free No payment of a duty or a tax is required.

Economic Commission for Africa (ECA) Established in 1958 and based in Addis Ababa, Ethiopia, the ECA comprises 53 African states, which are represented on the Commission by their ministers of finance and planning. ECA's primary purpose is to promote growth and development in all areas of Africa.

Economic Commission for Europe (ECE) Established in Geneva in 1947, ECE brings together 55 nations of North America, Europe, and Central Asia to facilitate their economic cooperation.

Economic Commission for Latin America and the Caribbean (ECLAC) Located in Santiago, Chile, ECLAC works to promote economic and social development among 41 countries of the region.

Economic Community of Central African States (SADC) Established in 1983 to work for a common market by eliminating customs duties and restrictions. Member states include Burundi, Cameroon, Central African Republic, Chad, Congo, D.R. Congo, Equatorial Guinea, Gabon, Rwanda, Sao Tome and Principe, and Angola.

Economic Community of West African States (ECOWAS) Established in May 1975 by the Treaty of Lagos, ECOWAS is an economic association of 16 West African nations aimed at creating a full customs union as well as at encouraging social and cultural fellowship. Members include Benin, Burkina Faso, Cape Verde, Côte d'Ivoire, Gambia, Ghana, Guinea, Guinea-Bissau, Liberia, Mali, Mauritania, Niger, Nigeria, Senegal, Sierra Leone, and Togo. Community headquarters are in Abuja, Nigeria.

Economic Community of West African States Cease-Fire Monitoring Group (ECOMOG) Non-standing military force established by the Economic Community of West African States (ECOWAS) to deal with security, suppress rebellion and encourage negotiations in the aftermath of the collapse of the Republic of Liberia in 1990. ECOMOG was replaced by the United Nations Mission in Sierra Leone (UNAMSIL) in 1999.

economic growth The increase in a nation's production of goods and services, often measured in terms of gross national product (GNP). In 1999, for example, the economic growth rate of the U.S., measured in terms of the GNP, was 5.4%, which is considered a fairly high rate of growth.

Economic and Social Commission for Asia and the Pacific (ESCAP) Established in 1947 as the Economic Commission for Asia and the Far East (ECAFE) ESCAP works to channel the growth momentum of its stronger member states to the rest of the countries in the region. Currently there are 51 member states in ESCAP, whose headquarters are in Bangkok, Thailand.

Economic and Social Commission for Western Asia (ESCWA) Established in 1973 as the Economic Commission for Western Asia, ESCWA received its current designation in 1985. Located in Amman, Jordan, ESCWA works to promote economic and social growth and development in the region. It had 13 members in 2002.

Economic and Social Council (ECOSOC) The U.N. organ designed to discuss international economic and social issues; it has 54 member states, which are elected for three-year terms by the U.N. General Assembly.

economic warfare An extreme degree of economic competition between two or more states. Such tactics as the boycott and the discriminatory tariffs usually mark this degree of competition.

economy The entire system of production, distribution, and consumption of goods and services in a country.

ecotourism Sustainable development plans that involve the provision of conservation measures, the inclusion of meaningful community participation, and the profitability and self-sustainability of such measures.

embargo A government order prohibiting the entry or departure of commercial ships at its ports, especially as a war measure. Also refers to any restriction imposed on commerce by law.

embassy A body of diplomatic representatives, specifically one headed by an ambassador.

envoy A diplomatic agent of any rank. The term is specifically a part of the title of a diplomatic agent of the second rank.

espionage Spying or the use of spies, especially for political or military purposes.

ethnic cleansing The expulsion, imprisonment, or killing of ethnic minorities by a dominant majority group.

ethnocentrism Belief in the inherent superiority of one's own cultural or ethnic group.

Euro Area Consists of 12 European countries (Austria, Belgium, Finland, France, Germany, Greece, Ireland, Italy, Luxembourg, Netherlands, Portugal, and Spain) who use the euro as the common currency.

European Coal and Steel Community (ECSC) Established by the Treaty of Paris in 1952, it is also the first treaty organization of the European Union. Its purpose is to create a unified product market for steel and coal, lift restrictions on imports and exports, and create a cohesive labor market for its member nations.

European Constitutional Convention A meeting aimed to define the future meaning and purpose of the European Union.

European Convention on Human Rights (Convention for the Protection of Human Rights and Fundamental Freedoms) Ensures the protection of basic human rights and liberties, and is the core document of the Council of Europe, which was founded in 1949.

European Free Trade Association (EFTA) A regional organization established in December 1959 by the Stockholm Convention as an alternative to the Common Market, EFTA was designed to provide a free trade area for the industrial products of member countries.

European Union (EU) Headquartered in Brussels, Belgium, this group of 15 member states (Austria, Belgium, Denmark, Finland, France, Germany, Greece, Ireland, Italy, Luxembourg, Netherlands, Portugal, Spain, Sweden, and United Kingdom) aims to promote economic and social progress for a strong European presence in the world, as well as to ensure a free, secure and just European citizenship.

executive A small group of elected officials who direct the policy process and oversee the array of departments and agencies of government.

exile A prolonged living away from one's country or community, usually forced. Can also refer to banishment, sometimes self-imposed.

extort To get (money, other items of value) by violence, threats, or misuse of authority.

extremist One who supports ideas, doctrines, or policies beyond the norm, usually in politics.

facilitator In diplomacy, a neutral person or country that brings warring parties or states to a meeting and helps them exchange views and, possibly, come to a preliminary agreement—a less formal role than that of mediator or broker in a treaty negotiation.

faction An association of individuals organized for the purpose of influencing government toward actions favorable to their interests; known also as an interest group.

famine An acute and general shortage of food.

federalism A system of government in which sovereignty is distributed between a central government and several provincial or state governments.

Food and Agriculture Organization (FAO) Headquartered in Rome, Italy, FAO was founded in 1945 with a mandate to raise levels of nutrition and standards of living, to improve agricultural productivity, and to better the condition of rural populations.

foreign affairs Matters concerning the policy of a country in its relation to other countries.

Former Soviet Union (FSU) A term used to identify the successor nations to the Soviet Union (USSR). This group of 15 countries includes Armenia, Azerbaijan, Belarus, Estonia, Georgia, Kazakhstan, Kyrgyzstan, Latvia, Lithuania, Moldova, Russia, Tajikistan, Turkmenistan, Ukraine, and Uzbekistan.

free trade Trade carried on without governmental regulations, especially international trade conducted without protective tariffs, customs duties, and so on.

free trade area (FTA) The territory covered by a cooperative arrangement among two or more nations, pursuant to the General Agreement on Tariffs and Trade, that removes trade barriers. The arrangement generally includes a customs union with a common external tariff, although there are exceptions.

G-7 The Group of Seven First made up of the seven most industrialized nations—Canada, France, Germany, Italy, Japan, United Kingdom, and United States—the group now includes the Russian Federation and is more often referred to as the G-8.

G-8 This Group of Eight Formed by Argentina, Brazil, Colombia, Mexico, Panama, Peru, Uruguay, and Venezuela, in the 1980s for mutual support during the Latin American debt crisis, the group now has seven members, as Panama's membership was terminated in 1990.

General Agreement on Tariffs and Trade (GATT) This 1947 agreement was incorporated into and superseded by the World Trade Organization in January 1995. During successive "rounds" of international negotiations, the 100-plus members of GATT established the norms and rules of international trade, with the aim of reducing trade barriers. WTO offers a dispute-settlement system for enforcing those rules (see WTO).

General Assembly (GA) The main deliberative body of the United Nations. Each of the 191 member nations is represented and has a vote.

genocide The systematic killing or extermination of a whole people or nation.

gerontocracy A form of government composed of a group of elders, such as that which existed in China during the Deng Xiaoping era.

good offices Procedure for friendly intervention, for the maintenance of peace, by a nation between two powers whose differences might well lead to armed conflict. The intervening nation offers its suggestions as to possible means of settling the differences.

grassroots Originating among or carried on by the common people.

gross national product (GNP) The value of all the goods and services produced by a country in a one-year period. GNP is used as a means of assessing the condition of a nation's economy.

guerrilla A member of a small force of irregular soldiers, usually volunteers, who make surprise raids against supply lines, and so on.

Hanoi Summit The 1998 summit of the Association of Southeast Asian Nations (ASEAN) in which the Hanoi Plan of Action was adopted, articulating the goals of strengthening macroeconomic and financial cooperation, enhancing greater economic integration, promoting technological, social, human resource, and environmental development, as well as enhancing peace, security, and ASEAN awareness in the international community.

head of government The person in effective charge of the executive branch of a government. In a parliamentary system, this refers to the prime minister.

head of state An individual who represents the state but does not exercise political power.

heavily indebted poor countries (HIPCs) Countries facing unsustainable debt burdens that have at the same time established significant track records of economic reform through International Monetary Fund (IMF) and World Bank-supported programs, qualifying for special debt-relief assistance from the IMF and the World Bank.

hegemony The preponderant position of a state within a group of states.

host nation support (HNS) Civilian and military assistance rendered by the host country to U.N. peacekeeping forces deployed within or staging through that country.

ideology A system of beliefs and values that explains society and prescribes the role of government.

immunity Exemption from the application of a rule or jurisdiction.

Implementation Force: Yugoslavia (IFOR) Following the signing of the Bosnian Peace Agreement in Paris on December 14, 1995, NATO was given a mandate by the U.N., on the basis of Security Council Resolution 1031, to implement the military aspects of the Peace Agreement. IFOR is the NATO body that carries out that mandate.

indictment 1a. The action or the legal process of indicting; b. the state of being indicted. 2. a formal written statement framed by a prosecuting authority and found by a jury (as a grand jury) charging a person with an offense. 3. an expression of strong disapproval—"an indictment of contemporary morality".

indigenous Born, growing, or produced naturally in a region or country; native.

infiltration Movement (usually on the ground) through or into an area or territory occupied by either friendly or enemy troops or organizations.

inflation 1. An inflating or being inflated. 2. an increase in the amount of currency in circulation, resulting in a fall in its value and rise in prices; it may be caused by an increase in the volume of paper money issued or of gold mined, or a relative increase in expenditures, as when the supply of goods fails to meet the demand. The opposite is deflation.

influence A form of power based on the ability to persuade others to support a desired objective.

infrastructure The structure that underlies and makes possible all economic activity in a country. Infrastructure includes utilities and communications and transportation facilities. Sometimes the term is extended to include such assets as the level of education among a country's citizens as well as their industrial and administrative experience and skills.

Inter-American Development Bank (IADB) (Spanish Banco Interamericano de Desarrollo, BID) A regional financial institution, it was set up to help accelerate economic and social development in Latin America and the Caribbean. The Bank was established in 1959 and began operations in October 1960; headquarters are in Washington, D.C. The 28 regional members include: Argentina, Bahamas, Barbados, Belize, Bolivia, Brazil, Canada, Chile, Colombia, Costa Rica, Dominican Republic, Ecuador, El Salvador, Guatemala, Guyana, Haiti, Honduras, Jamaica, Mexico, Nicaragua, Panama, Paraguay, Peru, Suriname, Trinidad and Tobago, United States, Uruguay, and Venezuela. The IDB has 16 non-regional members Austria, Belgium, Denmark, Finland, France, Germany, Israel, Italy, Japan, Netherlands, Norway, Portugal, Spain, Sweden, Switzerland, and United Kingdom.

interdependence Dependence on each other or one another; mutual dependence.

INTERFET The multinational force authorized by the United Nations Security Council to restore peace and security in East Timor and to provide support for the United Nations Assistance Mission in East Timor (UNAMET).

intergovernmental organization (IGO) Any body that consists of two or more member states.

International Atomic Energy Agency (IAEA) Established in 1957 and headquartered in Vienna, Austria, the Agency serves as the world's foremost center for nuclear information and cooperation. IAEA is also the chief inspector of the world's nuclear facilities.

International Bank for Reconstruction and Development (IBRD) Established in July 1944 at the U.N. Monetary and Financial Conference in Bretton Woods, New Hampshire, the bank opened for business on June 25, 1946. Its mission was to reduce poverty and improve living standards by promoting sustainable growth and investment in people through loans, technical assistance, and policy guidance.

International Conference on Population and Development Held in Cairo, Egypt in 1994, its participants discussed a variety of issues pertaining to abortion, immigration, reproductive health, female empowerment, urbanization, and healthcare, as outlined in the eventual Programme of Action.

International Court of Justice (ICJ) also known as the World Court, is the main judicial organ of the U.N. for settling legal disputes between member states and giving advisory opinions to the U.N. and its agencies. It comprises 15 judges elected by the General Assembly. The ICJ is headquartered in the Peace Palace in The Hague, Netherlands.

International Criminal Court (ICC) The court's Statute was adopted on July 17, 1998, at the United Nations Conference on the Establishment of an International Criminal Court in Rome. At the request of the United States, the Statute was adopted by a non-recorded vote (120 in favor, 7 against, with 21 abstentions). It was then opened for signature along with the Final Act; 127 delegations signed the Final Act and 10 signed the Statute. In 2002, the 60 signatures required to ratify the Statute was exceeded, and the International Criminal Court will come into being on July 1, 2002.

International Criminal Police Organization (INTERPOL) Established on June 13, 1956, it promotes international cooperation among police authorities in fighting crime.

International Criminal Tribunal for the Former Yugoslavia (ICTY) Established by S/Res/827 on May 25, 1993, the ICTY is mandated to prosecute persons responsible for serious violations of international humanitarian law committed in the territory of the former Yugoslavia since 1991.

International Criminal Tribunal for Rwanda (ICTR) An institution created in 1994 with the authority to punish crimes against humanity committed in the territory of Rwanda and by Rwandans in neighboring states.

International Development Association (IDA) Created in 1960, it makes loans on easy, concessional terms to the poorest of the developing nations.

International Labour Organization (ILO) Set up in 1919, the organization became a specialized agency of the United Nations in 1946. The ILO seeks to promote improved working and living conditions by establishing standards that reduce social injustice in areas such as employment, pay, health, working conditions, and freedom of association among work-

ers. Its headquarters are in Geneva, Switzerland.

international law The rules generally observed and regarded as binding in the relations between and among states.

International Law Commission (ILC) Established by A/Res/174 (II) in 1947 with a membership of 15 persons of recognized competence in international law, it encourages the progressive development of international law and its codification. The membership of the Commission currently stands at 34.

International Maritime Organization (IMO) Called the Inter-Governmental Maritime Consultative Organization (IMCO) at its founding in 1948, it had a name change in 1982. The organization is now a U.N. specialized agency headquartered in London responsible for improving maritime safety and preventing pollution from ships.

International Monetary Fund (IMF) Established at the Bretton Woods Conference in July 1944, it began work in Washington, D.C., in March 1947. It provides financial advice and funding to countries that are experiencing balance of payments difficulties. Such assistance begins with "crisis management"—an initial stopgap loan, with strict rules for spending it (IMF "conditionality")—followed by consultations with government leaders to design new fiscal and monetary policies for the long term. The Fund is supported by its members, who make contributions "according to [their] size and importance to trade," a quota that determines the number of votes allocated to each.

international order The combination of major actors, rules, mechanisms, and understandings to manage the co-existence and interdependence of states.

international regimes The pattern of regular cooperation governed by implicit and explicit expectations between two or more states.

international relations A subject of political study concerned with the interaction of independent states.

interoperability The ability of military systems, units, or forces to provide services to and accept services from other systems, units, or forces and to operate effectively together; especially crucial for communications equipment.

intervention 1. An intervening 2. any interference in the affairs of others; especially, interference of one state in the affairs of another.

joint task force (JTF) A U.S. concept, it denotes the bringing together of Navy, Army, Air Force, and Marine units for a specific mission.

Joint United Nations Program on HIV/AIDS (UNAIDS) The body began work in 1995 as the main advocate for global action on HIV/AIDS under the sponsorship of UNICEF, UNDP, UNFPA, UNESCO, WHO, and the World Bank.

judicial 1. Of judges, law courts, or their functions. 2. allowed, enforced, or set by order of a judge or a law court. 3. administering justice. 4. like or befitting a judge; hence. 5. fair; unbiased; carefully considering the facts, arguments, etc., and reasoning to a decision.

judiciary The branch of government with the power to resolve legal conflicts that arise between citizens, between citizens and government, between levels of government, between corporate entities, or between corporate entities and any of the former.

junta A Spanish word meaning a group of individuals forming a government, especially after a revolution or coup d'etat.

Karachi Agreement Document signed by India and Pakistan in 1949 establishing a ceasefire line as a result of disputes over the status of the State of Jammu and Kashmir.

Kyoto Protocol 1997 treaty resulting from the U.N. Framework Convention on Climate Change, this agreement outlines goals to limit greenhouse gas emissions and honor gas reduction commitments among the signatory nations.

Latin America and Caribbean Region (LAC) The most urbanized region in the developing world, it includes South America, the isthmus of Central America, the islands of the Caribbean Sea, and Mexico. Deep wealth inequalities characterize this region, creating the need for public sector health and education reform.

Latin American Economic System This regional intergovernmental organization's objectives include the promotion of common economic interests with third countries or in international arenas and cooperation among member states in support of economic and social development. The ultimate goal is to bring economic prosperity to the region through price protection of basic commodities and the creation and maintenance of export markets.

League of Arab States (LAS) Established on March 22, 1945, this national and regional organization promotes closer ties between the 22 member countries and aims to coordinate joint economic, cultural, and security policies between them. The members are Algeria, Bahrain, Comoros, Djibouti, Egypt, Iraq, Jordan, Kuwait, Lebanon, Libya, Mauritania, Morocco, Oman, Qatar, Saudi Arabia, Somalia, Sudan, Syria, Tunisia, UAE, Yemen, and Palestine Liberation Organization. The League of Arab States headquarters are in Cairo, Egypt.

Less-Developed Country (LDC) A country characterized by a low standard of living, limited industrial capabilities, and long-term impediments to economic growth.

liaison A linking up or connecting to, so as to coordinate activities, especially of a military nature.

liberate To release from slavery, enemy occupation, and the like.

Lima Consensus An agreement between participating governments, resulting from the Eighth Regional Conference on Women of Latin America and the Caribbean, to ensure that women's rights and emerging issues such as globalization and trade liberalization are observed in any future internationally agreed documents from the U.N. Special Session on Women.

limited government A state restricted in its exercise of power by the constitution and the rule of law.

Line of Control in Kashmir Seven hundred kilometer contentious frontier separating Indian and Pakistani forces in Kashmir, agreed upon by India and Pakistan in the 1949 ceasefire negotiations over disputes of the status of that territory.

liquidation (of peacekeeping mission) Activities executed in the closure of a field mission. Includes the physical withdrawal of equipment, supplies, and personnel and a variety of administrative closure actions.

lobbying An activity of interest groups aimed at influencing governors and the public.

local government Any government that is not state or federal, such as county, city, town, village.

Lusaka Ceasefire Agreement Signed by the Democratic Republic of Congo (DRC), Angola, Namibia, Zimbabwe, Rwanda, Uganda and rebel groups in 1999 to stop war in the Democratic Republic of Congo as a result of dissatisfaction with the DRC's political voice in the international system.

majority government A parliamentary government in which the party in power has over 50% of the seats in the legislature.

Manila Social Forum 1999 gathering of more than 250 policy makers who reviewed the issues of global labor markets, promoting reduction of urban and rural poverty, and building social protection programs.

massacre 1. The act or an instance of killing a number of usually helpless or unresisting human beings under circumstances of atrocity or cruelty 2. a cruel or wanton murder 3. a wholesale slaughter of anmals 4. an act of complete destruction.

Memorandum of Understanding (MOU) A binding agreement between two member states regarding an issue of bilateral concern.

Millennium Partnership for African Recovery Program (MAP) A development initiative aimed to remove African countries from stages of underdevelopment through modernizing efforts to improve investment, information, and communications technology.

Millennium Summit Conference that took place from September 6-8, 2000 at the United Nations Headquarters in New York City, assembling 150 Heads of State and Government in the largest-ever gathering of world leaders. The goal of the Summit was to tackle current and future global challenges, including poverty eradication, reversing the spread of HIV/AIDS, and protecting the environment.

militarization To infuse with military preparedness and assemblage.

military-industrial cooperation Aims to demonstrate the military and technical abilities of a nation's armaments and military equipment in order to attract overseas investors and expand internationally, among other objectives.

minister 1. Diplomatic agent of the second class. The full title is Envoy Extraordinary and Minister Plenipotentiary. 2. Cabinet member, as a minister of foreign affairs or foreign minister.

ministry 1. Collective term for cabinet, particularly in Great Britain. 2. Office or department of a cabinet minister, as the ministry of war.

Minsk Agreement (Belovezh Accords) Document signed by the governments of Belarus, Russia, and the Ukraine on December 9, 1991, which established the creation of the Commonwealth of Independent States.

Minsk Group A diplomatic forum whose goal is to reach a settlement of the Nagorno-Karabakh conflict between Armenia and Azerbaijan.

missing in action (MIA) Lost during military operations and whereabouts unknown.

mixed economy An economy based on both private and public (government-controlled) enterprises.

monarchy Form of rule in which a queen or king, empress or emperor holds absolute or limited power, usually inherited. In the 20th century most European monarchies became constitutional or limited, meaning that political power was vested in elected officials and the monarch's duties were largely ceremonial. Such monarchies often represent a strong symbol of national identity in the people's minds. In some countries of Africa, the Middle East, and Asia monarchs continue to hold absolute power.

Montreal Protocol Originally signed in 1987 and amended in 1990 and 1992, this is an international pact on protecting the stratospheric ozone layer, which specifically calls for eliminating the production and consumption of harmful chlorofluorocarbons by 2000.

most favored nation (MFN) The clause in a treaty by which one party or both grant to the other all privileges granted to any third state. The unconditional form of the clause grants the privileges with no strings attached. In the conditional form, the privileges are granted in return for a quid pro quo similar to that given by a third state.

multilateral 1. Having many sides 2. involving or participated in by more than two nations or parties (as in multilateral agreements).

Multilateral Investment Guarantee Agency (MIGA) Established on April 12, 1988, as part of the World Bank Group, it encourages the flow of foreign direct investment for economic development to its developing member countries. Its primary means of facilitating investment is through the provision of investment guarantees against the risks of currency transfer, expropriation, and war and civil disturbance (political risks).

multinational 1. The condition of state that has in it more than one nationality in terms of cultural background, such as Switzerland, which is a composite of French, German, and Italian elements 2. A corporation that operates in more than one country.

multiparty system A political party system in which there are three or more major contenders for power.

multipolar A system of actions involving several states.

nation Individuals in a specific geographical area who share common customs, history, language, etc. under the rule of one government.

nation-state A state with a single predominant national identity.

national command A command that is organized by, and functions under the authority of, a specific nation and may or may not be placed under a U.N. commander.

national interest Interests specific to a nation-state, including especially survival and maintenance of power.

nationalism Loyalty and devotion to a nation; especially a sense of national consciousness exalting one nation above all others and placing primary emphasis on promotion of its culture and interests as opposed to those of other nations or supranational groups.

nationalize To take over ownership by a national government. By nationalizing the armament industry, for example, a government becomes the owner of the country's munitions plant.

natural resources Resources provided by nature, such as minerals, forests, and water power.

New African Initiative (NAI) See New Partnership for Africa's Development (NEPAD).

New Partnership for Africa's Development (NEPAD) A merger between the Millenium Partnership for African Recovery Program (MAP) and the Omega Plan, in which African leaders pledged to eradicate poverty, promote sustainable development, and assert their respective countries in the world economy and body politic through the call for a new global partnership based on shared responsibility and mutual interest. Formerly known as the New African Initiative (NAI).

no-confidence vote A vote declaring the incapability of an officer to hold his or her position responsibly, usually requiring 2/3 affirmative vote of members present at the valid meeting.

Non-Aligned Movement (NAM) An alliance of Third World states, it aims to promote the political and economic interests of developing countries. The name originated in a declaration of neutrality issued at the Conference of Non-Aligned Countries in Belgrade, Yugoslavia, in September 1961. NAM interests have included ending colonialism/neo-colonialism, supporting the integrity of independent countries, and seeking a new international economic order.

non-governmental organization (NGO) A private-sector not-for-profit organization that contributes to development in developing countries through such activities as cooperative projects, financial aid, material aid, the dispatch of personnel, the acceptance of trainees, and development education. Some NGOs are accredited by the United Nations or its specialized agencies and can represent their interests before ECOSOC.

North American Free Trade Agreement (NAFTA) An agreement that entered into force in January 1994 among Canada, United States, and Mexico. NAFTA's consumer population (in excess of 360 million) is only slightly smaller than the European Union's economic sphere;

NAFTA's combined output of $6 trillion is about percent larger than that of the European Union.

North Atlantic Treaty Organization (NATO) Formed on April 4, 1949, when 12 independent nations signed the North Atlantic Treaty and committed to each other's defense, it grew by four more nations between 1952 and 1982. Total membership includes Belgium, Canada, Denmark, France, Germany, Greece, Iceland, Italy, Luxembourg, Netherlands, Norway, Portugal, Spain, Turkey, United Kingdom, and United States, and newcomers Czech Republic, Hungary, and Poland.

Nuclear Non-proliferation Treaty (NPT) Taking effect in 1970, it was intended to limit the number of states with nuclear weapons to five United States, Soviet Union, Britain, France, and China. In doing so, the NPT attempted to prevent nuclear weapons sales, halt the nuclear weapons development programs of non-nuclear weapons states, and promote nuclear disarmament and the peaceful use of nuclear technologies and materials. More than 140 states have pledged not to acquire nuclear weapons and to accept the safeguards of the International Atomic Energy Agency. The treaty, however, is not of indefinite duration. One of the provisions of the treaty was to convene a conference 25 years after its entry into force to decide whether the treaty would continue indefinitely or be extended for a specified time.

observer mission Unarmed officers to staff observation posts for monitoring cease-fires and armistices.

Omega Plan An initiative to examine the needs of the African continent in terms of bridging the divide between underdeveloped and developed nations, and to implement the best possible policies aimed at elevating the economic status of the underdeveloped nations.

one-party-dominant system A party system in which political alternatives exist but a single political party dominates the political process as a result of the overwhelming support of the electorate.

order A communication—written, oral, or by signal—that conveys instructions from a superior to a subordinate. In a broad sense, the terms order and command are synonymous. An order implies discretion as to the details of execution, however, and a command does not.

Organization of African Unity (OAU) See African Union (AU).

Organization of American States (OAS) (Pan American Union; Spanish Organización de los Estados Americanos, OEA). A regional organization created in Bogota, Colombia, in April 1948 (entered into force in December 1951), it promotes Latin American economic and social development. Members include Antigua and Barbuda, Argentina, Bahamas, Barbados, Belize, Bolivia, Brazil, Canada, Chile, Colombia, Costa Rica, Cuba (participation suspended), Dominica, Dominican Republic, Ecuador, El Salvador, Grenada, Guatemala, Guyana, Haiti, Honduras, Jamaica, Mexico, Nicaragua, Panama, Paraguay, Peru, St. Kitts and Nevis, St. Lucia, St. Vincent and the Grenadines, Suriname, Trinidad and Tobago, United States, Uruguay, and Venezuela. The OAS secretariat is in Washington, D.C.

Organization for Economic Cooperation and Development (OECD) Providing a forum for discussion of common economic and social issues facing the United States, Canada, Western Europe, Japan, Australia, and New Zealand, OECD was founded in September 1960. It succeeded the Organization for European Economic Cooperation (OEEC), which had administered European participation in the Marshall Plan. OECD seeks "to achieve the highest sustainable economic growth and employment and a rising standard of living in member countries while maintaining financial stability and thus contribute to the world economy." Members include Australia, Austria, Belgium, Canada, Denmark, Finland, France, Germany, Greece, Iceland, Ireland, Italy, Luxembourg, Japan, Netherlands, New Zealand, Norway, Portugal, Spain, Sweden, Switzerland, Turkey, United Kingdom, and United States. OECD headquarters are in Paris, France.

Organization of the Islamic Conference (OIC) An association of 57 member and 3 observer Islamic states aiming to achieve Muslim cohesion in social, economic, and political matters.

Organization for Security and Cooperation in Europe (OSCE) The 55 participating states of this regional security organization are from Europe, Central Asia and North America. As a regional arrangement under Chapter VIII of the Charter of the United Nations, the OSCE was established as a primary instrument in its region for early warning, conflict prevention, crisis management, and post-conflict rehabilitation in Europe.

Pacific Islands Forum Annual gathering representing the heads of all the independent and self-governing Pacific Island countries with an objective to provide these member nations an opportunity to discuss their political views and cooperate on matters of political and economic concern.

Palestinian Liberation Organization (PLO) It was established in May 1964, along with the structure of the Palestine National Council (PNC), the PLO Executive Committee, the National Fund, and the Palestine Liberation Army (PLA) as well as a Palestinian national covenant and basic law. Since then the PLO has been an umbrella organization for various Palestinian factions and resistance groups. It became independent when taken over by Fatah, with Yasser Arafat as chairman, in 1969, and then acquired a more central role in mobilizing Palestinians as well as international support; created a number of organizations to provide education and health care and to relieve the conditions of the Palestinian people, and formed a quasi-governmental structure performing tasks in the areas of internal security, military operations, finances, information, foreign relations.

Pan American Health Organization (PAHO) An international public health agency that aims to better the health and living conditions of people in the Americas. It is the Regional Office of the Americas for the World Health Organization and the organization for health of the Inter-American System.

paramilitary Of, relating to, being, or characteristic of a force formed on a military pattern, especially as a potential auxiliary military force.

parliament A legislative assembly of a government, or other political unit, that sets national or organizational policy.

partisan 1a. Firm adherent to a party, faction, cause, or person, especially one exhibiting blind, prejudiced, and unreasoning allegiance 2a. a member of a body of detached light troops making forays and harassing an enemy; b. a member of a guerrilla band operating within enemy lines.

Partnership for Peace A consultative body where NATO cooperates with its former Cold War enemies, and designed to promote understanding and cooperation among the members on issues of mutual interest, such as conflict resolution and military training and preparedness.

patriotism Love for or devotion to one's country.

peacekeeper Person assigned the task of helping to maintain peace where conflict has just ended. Strictly speaking, "peacekeepers" can include civilian staff (whereas "peacekeeping soldiers" does not); in practice however, the term usually refers to the military component of a peacekeeping operation.

peacekeeping Hybrid politico-military activity aimed at conflict control, which involves a United Nations presence in the field (usually including military and civilian personnel), with the consent of the parties, to implement or monitor the implementation of arrangements relating to the control of conflicts (cease-fires, separation of forces, etc.) and their resolution (partial or comprehensive settlements), and/or to protect the delivery of humanitarian relief.

peacekeeping operation (PKO) Noncombat military operations undertaken by outside forces with the consent of all major belligerent parties and designed to monitor and facilitate the implementation of an existing truce agreement in support of diplomatic efforts to reach a political settlement. PKOs covers peacekeeping forces, observer missions, and mixed operations.

peacemaking Diplomatic process of brokering an end to conflict, principally through mediation and negotiation, as foreseen under Chapter VI of the U.N. Charter. Military activities contributing to peacemaking include military-to-military contacts, security assistance, shows of force, and preventive deployments.

peace-restoration New and tentative concept applying to the multidimensional operations that, while originally mandated under Chapter VI, are forced by realities in the field to turn into a Chapter VII operation, as when humanitarian convoys need to be defended by force of arms or an exclusion zone enforced by air strikes.

plenipotentiary A person invested with full authority to act as a representative of a government.

pluralism The open competition of political interests.

Politburo The elite officials of the Central Committee within the Communist Party. These officials oversee the operations of the Committee and make the major decisions which are eventually passed down to the Party Congress for implementation.

political asylum The granting of refuge by a state to an individual who has fled his country because of persecution.

political culture Attitudes, values, beliefs, and orientations that individuals in a society hold regarding their political system.

political economy The study of the involvement by the state in the economy of the nation-state.

political party An organized group that makes nominations and contests elections in the hope of influencing the personnel and policy of government.

politics A process of conflict resolution in which support is mobilized and maintained for collective action.

populist A member of a political party claiming to represent the common people.

preventive deployment Interposition of a military force to deter violence in a zone of potential conflict where tension is rising among parties.

preventive diplomacy Action to prevent disputes from arising between parties, to prevent existing disputes from escalating into conflicts, and to limit the spread of the latter when they occur.

prime minister The leader of the government and head of the cabinet in parliamentary systems. The prime minister is also the leader of his political party.

private sector That part of the economy made up of business enterprises owned by individuals or groups of individuals, in contrast to the public sector. Also refers to consumer expenditure for goods and services. The private sector accounts for about four-fifths of the economy of the United States.

privatization The process of transferring ownership of a business or industry from government control to a private enterprise.

protectionism The practice of protecting domestic manufacturers from foreign competition by the imposition of tariffs and quotas on imported goods.

protocol A document that records the basic agreements reached in negotiations prior to the final form in which the agreement appears. Protocol also refers to the diplomatic manners that apply in ceremonial and formal business between states (seating arrangements at dinners, procedures at conferences, and so on).

quorum The number of members of a legislature, or of any organization, that must be present before official business may be conducted.

racism 1a. A belief that race is the primary determinant of human traits and capacities and that racial differences produce an inherent superiority of a particular race 2. racial prejudice or discrimination.

rapid deployment force (RDF) A short-notice contingency force, the RDF can be formed both unilaterally and with partners, to be deployed in situations in which its military organization, training, and equipment, such as transport and communications, enable it to cope with a totally civil situation. RDF activities range from disaster relief (earthquakes, floods, and the like), to humanitarian relief, to separating warring sides, to actual warfare.

rapid reaction force (RRF) Name of various specific formations one set up by NATO, another created to support UNPROFOR, another proposed under UNSAS; the generic term used for this type of formation is "rapid deployment force".

referendum 1a. The principle or practice of submitting to popular vote a measure passed on or proposed by a legislative body or by popular initiative b. a vote on a measure so submitted 2. a diplomatic agent's note asking for government instructions.

regionalize To divide into regions or administrative districts; arrange regionally.

reparations Payments demanded of the losers in a war by the victors as compensation for damage suffered, usually to civilians and property. Heavy reparations were exacted by Britain, France, and the U.S. from Germany after World War I.

repatriate To restore or return to the country of origin, allegiance, or citizenship, as with prisoners of war.

resolution a document passed by a committee that expresses the opinions and decisions of the U.N.

reunification To rejoin a group, party, state, or organization that had previously splintered.

rules of engagement (ROE) Directives issued by DPKO that specify how units in PKO's are to act with hostile parties and the population.

SAARC Preferential Trading Agreement (SAPTA) The agreement signed by the South Asian Association for Regional Cooperation (SAARC) in 1993 in order to gradually reduce and eliminate tariff barriers through bilateral and multilateral initiatives.

sanction A coercive economic or military measure, usually adopted by several nations in concert, for forcing a nation violating international law to desist or yield to adjudication.

sanctions monitoring Observing the performance of the authorities of a country in executing an embargo against the target state.

sanctuary A nation or area near or contiguous to a combat area that is exempt from attack by the warring parties.

Security Council The organ of the United Nations with responsibility for maintaining peace and security is composed of five permanent members (France, China, Russian Federation, United Kingdom, and United States) and ten rotating members elected to two-year terms by the General Assembly.

Secretariat the U.N. organ responsible for running the day-to-day affairs of the organization. The Secretariat is made up of international civil servants and led by the Secretary-General.

Secretary-General the chief administrative officer of the U.N. and the head of the Secretariat.

socialism A leftist political ideology that emphasizes the principle of equality and usually prescribes a large role for government in society and the economy via taxation, regulation, redistribution, and public ownership.

Socialists Members of a political party supporting socialist ideas.

solidarity Unity (as of a group or class) that produces or is based on a community of interests, objectives, and standards.

South American Common Market (MERCOSUR) (Mercado del Sur) Composed of Argentina, Brazil, Paraguay, and Uruguay and modeled on the European Community's Treaty of Rome, it aims to establish a common external tariff and eliminate barriers to trade in services. Chile has not sought entry into MERCOSUR, but does have an agreement with Argentina that provides for some similar benefits.

South Asian Association for Regional Cooperation (SAARC) Composed of Bangladesh, Bhutan, India, Maldives, Nepal, Pakistan and Sri Lanka in 1985, this organization aims to promote peace, cooperation, and economic and social progress in South Asia.

Southeast Asian Treaty Organization (SEATO) At its origin, was composed of Australia, France, New Zealand, Pakistan, Philippines, Thailand, United Kingdom, and United States. Founded in 1954 and disbanded three years later, its original objective was to provide defense and economic cooperation to the Southeast Asia and South Pacific area.

Southern African Development Community (SADC) Originally established in 1979 to reduce the economic dependence of its member states on South Africa as well as to increase development. Currently, the SADC strives to increase production, investment, and intraregional trade among its members.

sovereign The highest or supreme political authority.

sovereignty 1a. Supreme power, especially over a body politic b. freedom from external control; autonomy c. controlling influence. 2. One that is sovereign, especially an autonomous state.

Stability and Growth Pact An agreement among Euro Area Members to prevent budgetary slippages and to define a set of rules outlining the need to avoid excessive deficits.

stand-by forces The capabilities made available to the U.N. by states, which may be military formations, civilian police, specialized personnel (civilian and military), services, and/or specialized equipment.

stand-by phase Logistics; first phase in a peacekeeping operation, while a technical survey team is dispatched to the potential mission area, and before or shortly after the Security Council adopts a resolution.

START I A successful Russian-United States treaty that came into force on December 5, 1994 requiring the reduction and limitation of strategic offensive arms to 6,000 accountable warheads on each side as of December 4, 2001.

START II A Russian-United States treaty signed on January 3, 1993, stating that all heavy intercontinental ballistic missiles (ICBMs) and MIRVed ICBMs must be eliminated from each side's deployed forces.

statehood A geographical region classified as a state rather than a territory or dependency.

Structural Adjustment Programs/Policies (SAPs) Economic policies that countries are required to adopt in order to qualify for loans from the World Bank and the International Monetary Fund (IMF) and to help them make payments on current debts owed to commercial banks, governments, and the World Bank.

Sunshine Policy South Korean president Kim Dae Jung's policy of engagement with respect to North Korea.

tariff 1a. A schedule of duties imposed by a government on imported, or in some countries exported, goods b. a duty or rate of duty imposed in such a schedule. 2. A schedule of rates or charges of a business or a public utility.

taxation A compulsory payment levied by a government on its citizens to finance expenditures. It can be levied on income or as a surcharge on prices (sales tax). Income tax is a direct tax (everyone who earns a certain amount has to pay it); a sales tax is an indirect tax (affects only those who buy the taxed goods).

terrorism The systematic use of terror or unpredictable violence against governments, publics, or individuals to attain a political objective. Terrorism has been used by political organizations with both rightist and leftist objectives, by nationalistic and ethnic groups, by revolutionaries, and by armies and security police of governments themselves.

Third World The developing countries of the world, made up mostly of Asian, African, and Latin American countries; also called the South or Developing World.

treaty A formal, binding international agreement that may cover such issues as the regulation of trade, the making of peace, or the forming of military alliances. It forms part of the structure of international law. In the U.S., all treaties proposed by the executive branch and negotiated with a foreign country must be approved by a two-thirds majority in the Senate. The treaty is then ratified by the President.

Treaty of Amsterdam Signed in 1997, this treaty aims to clarify the institutional and political conditions necessary for the European Union to meet foreign, security, social, and commercial policies of the future.

Treaty on Friendship, Cooperation and Mutual Assistance Signed in 1992, this agreement between the governments of Albania, Bulgaria, Hungary, Germany, Romania, Union of Soviet Socialist Republics, and Czechoslovakia aims at fostering peaceful settlements to international disputes, and legalized Russian military presence in Kazakhstan.

Treaty of Maastricht A set of common provisions setting up the European Union, amendments to existing treaties, 16 new articles, 33 declarations, and 17 protocols.

Treaty of Nice Treaty signed in 2001 by European Union member states that is designed to reform European Union institutions to accommodate the influx of new members, and to shape the future direction of the European Union.

truce A suspension of fighting (especially of considerable duration) by agreement of opposing forces.

Trusteeship Council The U.N. body originally given jurisdiction over 11 former colonies. The T.C. agenda shrank as one trust territory after another achieved independence or merged with a neighbor. The last such territory attained its independence in 1994, and the T.C.'s activities were suspended. The roster of permanent members is identical to the Security Council's permanent five.

United Nations Advance Mission in Cambodia (UNAMIC) Established in 1991 to assist the four Cambodian parties preserve their cease-fire agreement before the establishment of the United Nations Transitional Authority in Cambodia (UNTAC) and to employ mine-awareness training of civilian populations.

United Nations Association of the United States of America (UNA-USA) A nonprofit, nonpartisan national organization, it is dedicated to enhancing U.S. participation in the United Nations system and to strengthening that system as it seeks to define and carry out its mission. UNA-USA's action agenda uniquely combines education and public research, substantive policy analysis, and ongoing U.S.-U.N. dialogue. Membership currently exceeds 22,000 individuals who are spread among 175 local chapters in 43 states. UNA-USA is also comprised of several affiliate organizations, such as the Business Council of the United Nations, the Council of Organizations, and the Adopt-a-Minefield Program.

United Nations Centre for Human Settlements (UNCHS) Also known as HABITAT, the center was established in 1977. UNCHS deals with housing and related problems of the urban and rural poor in developing countries.

United Nations Charter The fundamental set of rules according to which the United Nations exists and operates. It was drawn up by the representatives of 50 countries at the United Nations Conference on International Organization, which met at San Francisco from April 25 to June 26, 1945. The delegates deliberated on the basis of proposals worked out by the representatives of China, the Soviet Union, the United Kingdom, and the United States at Dumbarton Oaks, a mansion in Washington, D.C., between August and October 1944. The Charter was signed on June 26, 1945, by the representatives of the 50 countries. Poland, which was not represented at the Conference, signed it later and became one of the original 51 member states. The United Nations officially came into existence on October 24, 1945, when the Charter had been ratified by the five permanent members and by a majority of other signatories. United Nations Day is celebrated on October 24 each year.

United Nations Children's Fund (UNICEF) Founded in 1946 and headquartered in Paris, it is the only U.N. organization devoted exclusively to children and to the protection of children's rights.

United Nations Commission for India and Pakistan (UNCIP) Established by the United Nations Security Council to investigate and mediate the dispute between India and Pakistan over the status of the State of Jammu and Kashmir. UNCIP was terminated in 1949 when India and Pakistan established a ceasefire line to be supervised by the U.N. observers.

United Nations Commission on Narcotic Drugs (UNCND) The central policy-making body within the United Nations system dealing with drug-related matters. It analyses the world drug situation and develops proposals to strengthen the international drug control system to combat the world drug problem.

United Nations Conference on the Environment and Development (UNCED) At this 1992 gathering in Rio de Janeiro, Brazil (the Earth Summit), more than 100 heads of state agreed on a body of principles and actions that integrate the concerns of people, their livelihoods, and the preservation of ecological systems. These principles and actions in the cause of sustainable development are outlined in the publication known as Agenda 21.

United Nations Conference on Trade and Development (UNCTAD) Established in 1964 as a permanent intergovernmental organization, it serves as the principal organ of the General Assembly in the field of trade and development. It is headquartered in Geneva.

United Nations Development Fund for Women (UNIFEM) Created in 1976 and headquartered in New York, it works toward the empowerment of women and gender equity through innovative and experimental activities benefiting women.

United Nations Development Programme (UNDP) Headquartered in New York, it focuses on poverty elimination, environmental regeneration, job creation, and the advancement of women.

United Nations Disaster Relief Organization (UNDRO) Established in 1971 as a clearinghouse for information on relief needs when earthquakes, floods, hurricanes, and other natural disasters strike, it mobilizes and coordinates emergency assistance from around the world.

United Nations Economic Commission for Africa (UNECA) Established in 1958 and composed of 53 Member States, it is one of five regional economic commissions under the United Nations Headquarters and aims to support economic and social development, promote regional integration, and global cooperation for the development of Africa.

United Nations Educational, Scientific and Cultural Organization (UNESCO) Established on November 16, 1945, with headquarters in Paris, it works to contribute to peace and security in the world by promoting collaboration among nations in the areas of education, science, culture, and communication.

United Nations Environment Programme (UNEP) Headquartered in Nairobi, Kenya, provides leadership and encourages partnerships in caring for the environment. The aim is to inspire, inform, and enable nations and people to improve their quality of life without compromising that of future generations.

United Nations Framework Convention on Climate Change To counter global warming, its objective is the stabilization of greenhouse gas concentrations in the atmosphere at a level that would prevent dangerous anthropogenic interference with the climate system, as well as to transfer to developing countries technology and information enabling them to respond to climate change.

United Nations Good Offices Mission in Afghanistan and Pakistan Established in 1988 to ensure the implementation of the Agreements on the Settlement of the Situation Relating to Afghanistan. Its mandate ended in 1990.

United Nations High Commissioner for Human Rights (UNHCHR) was established by the General Assembly on December 20, 1993. The High Commissioner works to prevent and protect against human rights violations.

United Nations High Commissioner for Refugees (UNHCR) The office was created by the General Assembly in 1951 to help the world's refugees. It is headquartered in Geneva and has branches in 122 countries.

United Nations India-Pakistan Observation Mission (UNIPOM) Established in 1965 to monitor the cease-fire along the India-Pakistan border and ended in 1966 with the withdrawal of all India and Pakistan armed personnel.

United Nations Industrial Development Organization (UNIDO) Established by the General Assembly in 1966 and headquartered in Vienna, Austria, this U.N. specialized agency promotes sustainable and environmentally friendly industrial development in developing countries and in countries in transition to market economies.

United Nations Institute for Training and Research (UNITAR) This autonomous body within the U.N., works to enhance the effectiveness of the U.N. through training and research.

United Nations International Drug Control Program (UNDCP) Headquartered in Vienna, it works to combat the global drug problem.

United Nations International Research and Training Institute for the Advancement of Women (INSTRAW) This institution carries out research, training, and information activities to examine, monitor, and enhance the role of women in development.

United Nations Military Observer Group in India and Pakistan (UNMOGIP) Established in 1949 to monitor the ceasefire agreement between India and Pakistan in the State of Jammu and Kashmir and renewed in 1971 to supervise the ceasefire called for by the United Nations Security Council after continued hostilities in that area.

United Nations Mission of Observers in Tajikistan (UNMOT) Established in 1994 to supervise the ceasefire agreement between the Government of Tajikistan and the United Tajik Opposition. UNMOT's mandate was expanded to monitor the implementation of the general peace agreement signed by both parties in 1997. After the mission completed its assigned tasks, its mandate was terminated in May 2000.

United Nations Mission for the Referendum in Western Sahara (MINURSO) Established in 1991 to allow the people of Western Sahara to choose between independence or integration with Morocco.

United Nations Mission in Sierra Leone (UNAMSIL) Established in 1999 to assist in implementing the Lome Peace Agreement, a pledge to end war and institute a unified government in Sierra Leone.

United Nations Mission of Support in East Timor (UNMISET) A successor mission to the United Nations Transitional Authority in East Timor (UNTAET) concentrating on the gradual withdrawal of U.N. involvement from the East Timor territory and continued support of the East Timorese authorities.

United Nations New Agenda for the Development of Africa (U.N.-NADAF) Program designed to structure and implement social and economic development activities of the United Nations system in Africa.

United Nations Observer Mission in Angola (MONUA) Established in 1997 to assist the Angolan parties in developing stability, peace, democracy, and rehabilitation of the nation. It was terminated in 1999 after it became clear that the National Union for the Total Independence of Angola (UNITA) had no intention of complying with the Lusaka Protocol, a ceasefire agreement it had signed with the Angola government in 1994.

United Nations Observer Mission in Georgia (UNOMIG) Established in August 1993 to monitor the compliance of the ceasefire agreement between the Government of Georgia and the Abkhaz authorities in Georgia. As a result of continued fighting in Abkhazia after the signing of the agreement, UNOMIG's mandate was expanded to include 136 observers monitoring the implementation of the 1994 Agreement on a Ceasefire and Separation of Forces.

United Nations Observer Mission in Sierra Leone (UNOMSIL) Established in 1998 to monitor the military, security, and human rights situation in the country by disarming and demobilizing former combatants.

United Nations Observer Mission for Uganda–Rwanda (UNOMUR) Established to monitor the border between Uganda and Rwanda, its role was to verify that no military assistance—lethal weapons, ammunition, or other material of possible military use—was crossing. While the tragic events in Rwanda in April 1994 prevented UNOMUR from fully implementing its mandate, the Observer Mission played a useful role as a confidence-building mechanism in the months following the conclusion of the Arusha Peace Agreement and during UNAMIR's initial efforts to defuse tensions between the Rwandan parties and to facilitate the implementation of that agreement. UNOMUR was officially closed on September 21, 1994.

United Nations Organization Mission in the Democratic Republic of Congo (MONUC) Established by the United Nations Security Council in 1999 to maintain associations between the parties of the Lusaka Ceasefire Agreement and to implement other tasks.

United Nations Population Fund (UNFPA) The largest internationally funded source of population assistance to developing countries began work in 1967.

United Nations Protection Force (UNPROFOR) It was initially established in Croatia as an interim arrangement to create the conditions of peace and security required for the negotiation of an overall settlement of the Yugoslav crisis. On March 31, 1995, the Security Council decided to restructure UNPROFOR, replacing it with three separate but interlinked peacekeeping operations.

United Nations Relief and Works Agency for Palestine Refugees in the Near East (UNRWA) This agency provides education, health, and relief services to Palestine refugees in Jordan, Lebanon, Syria, the West Bank, and Gaza.

United Nations Security Force in West New Guinea (UNSF) Established in 1962 to oversee peace and security in the territory of West New Guinea during its transition period from Netherlands control to Indonesia.

United Nations Special Commission for Iraq (UNSCOM) By its resolution 687 of April 3, 1991, the Security Council established the terms and conditions for a formal cease-fire between Iraq and the coalition of member states cooperating with Kuwait. Section C of this resolution deals with the elimination, under international supervision, of Iraq's weapons of mass destruction and ballistic missiles with a range greater than 150 kilometers, together with related items and production facilities. It also calls for measures to ensure that the acquisition and production of prohibited items are not resumed. The Special Commission was set up to implement the non-nuclear provisions of the resolution and to assist the International Atomic Energy Agency (IAEA) in the nuclear areas.

United Nations Special Initiative on Africa (UNSIA) Designed to articulate United States assistance to Africa, including such goals as partnership building, coordinative efforts, capacity building and synergistic actions.

United Nations Transitional Administration in East Timor (UNTAET) Established in 1999 to administer authority in the territory of East Timor during its transition to independence.

United Nations Transitional Authority in Cambodia (UNTAC) Established in 1992 and incorporating the United Nations Advance Mission in Cambodia (UNAMIC) with a mandate to establish the rule of law and order, free elections, maintenance of human rights, military and civil administration, and resettlement and rehabilitation of Cambodian refugees in Cambodia.

United Nations Verification Mission in the Central African Republic (MINURCA) Established in 1998 to monitor the implementation of the Bangui agreements, ensuring peace and security in the Central African Republic. The mission was terminated in 2000.

Universal Declaration of Human Rights (UDHR) A historic proclamation of the basic rights and freedoms to which all men and women are entitled—the right to life, liberty, and a nationality, to freedom of thought, conscience, and religion; to work; to be educated; to take part in government; and many others. Adopted by the General Assembly on December 10, 1948, a date commemorated every year as Human Rights Day.

war crime A crime, such as genocide or maltreatment of prisoners, committed during or in connection with war.

West African Economic Community (WAEC) (French: Communauté Economique de l'Afrique de l'Ouest, CEAO) Created in 1974, it includes Benin, Burkina Faso, Côte d'Ivoire, Mali, Mauritania, Niger, and Senegal. Togo has observer status. The WAEC/CEAO operates as a free trade area for agricultural products and raw materials and as a preferential trading area for approved industrial products, with a regional cooperation tax (TCR) replacing import duties and encouraging trade among members. The WAEC/CEAO envisions creation of a customs union and coordination of fiscal policies. Community headquarters are in Ouagadougou, Burkina Faso.

Western European Union (WEU) Created in October 1954 (it began operations in May 1955), it promotes mutual defense and progressive political unification of its members. The Union, which serves interests between those furthered by the European Union and the North Atlantic Treaty Organization, has faced the need to change and currently focuses on humanitarian aid, peacekeeping, and crisis management. Members with decision-making power include Belgium, France, Germany, Greece, Italy, Luxembourg, Netherlands, Portugal, Spain, and United Kingdom. In addition there are six associate members, five observers, and seven associate partners. WEU headquarters moved from London, England, to Brussels, Belgium, in December 1992.

Westphalian Doctrine Treaty that ended the Thirty Years' War in Europe in 1648 and provided the model for peace in Europe for nearly two centuries, stating that sovereign states do not get involved in other sovereign states' internal affairs.

white helmets International volunteer rapid-response teams that provide humanitarian relief in the event of natural or man-made emergencies, launched by an initial contribution from Argentina. The term is also used in reference to ECOMOG troops deployed in Liberia by ECOWAS.

working paper A document distributed informally in committee that serves as a vehicle for discussion.

World Bank A multilateral lending agency that directs its efforts towards reducing poverty by promoting sustainable economic growth for nations in assistance.

World Federation of United Nations Associations (WFUNA) Founded in 1946 as a people's movement for the United Nations, it is the only global NGO to support the United Nations, and has been involved in promoting positive relations between people of conflict areas, and as a forum for global dialogues on a wide variety of issues and challenges.

World Food Programme (WFP) The frontline U.N. organization fighting to eradicate world hunger. It is located in Rome, Italy, and began work in 1963.

World Health Organization (WHO) Founded in 1948 and headquartered in Geneva, promotes technical cooperation for health among nations, carries out programs to control and eradicate disease, and strives to improve the quality of human life.

World Intellectual Property Organization (WIPO) (French: Organisation Mondiale de la Proprité Intellectuelle, OMPI) promotes protection of intellectual property around the world through cooperation among states, and administers various "Unions," each founded on a multilateral treaty and dealing with the legal and administrative aspects of intellectual property. Established in 1967, WIPO became a specialized agency of the United Nations in December 1974. The headquarters are in Geneva, Switzerland.

World Meteorological Organization (WMO) established in 1875, was reconstituted and renamed in 1951. The WMO facilitates worldwide cooperation in establishing a network for meteorological, hydrological, and geophysical observations, for exchanging meteorological and related information, and for promoting standardization in meteorological measurements. Headquarters of this U.N. specialilzed agency are in Geneva.

World Tourism Organization (WToO) an intergovernmental technical body associated with the United Nations, that deals with all aspects of tourism. The WTO promotes and develops tourism as a means of contributing to economic development, international understanding, peace, and prosperity; provides a world clearing house for the collection, analysis, and dissemination of technical tourism information; and offers national tourism administrations and organizations a means for multilateral approaches to international discussions and negotiations on tourism policy and practice. Established in November 1974 its headquarters are in Madrid, Spain.

World Trade Organization (WTO) Established on January 1, 1995, it is an international organization of comparable stature to the World Bank and the International Monetary Fund. The WTO facilitates implementation of trade agreements reached in the Uruguay Round by bringing them under one institutional umbrella, requiring full participation of all countries in one new trading system, and providing a permanent forum for discussion of new issues facing the international trading system. The WTO system is available only to countries that (a) are contracting parties to GATT, (b) agree to adhere to all of the Uruguay Round agreements, and (c) submit schedules of market access commitments for industrial goods, agricultural goods, and services.

Zionism An international movement for the establishment of a Jewish national or religious community in Palestine and later for the support of modern Israel.

The Internet provides one of the most heavily used and easily accessible mediums for research and information about the United Nations. Delegates with access to the Internet will soon find that it complements books, such as this Guide, and is invaluable when it comes to obtaining current and historical information for Model U.N. country assignments. The Model U.N. conferences and groups that have their own sites on the World Wide Web invariably have a host of links to other useful websites.

Delegates should remember to check the source of information accessed from the Internet. Always try to use official websites to ensure that the information is accurate. Supplement Internet materials with newspapers, periodicals and books.

The Internet Resources section below is broken down according to what is important to know when preparing for a Model U.N. simulation. As mentioned, every Model U.N. delegate should become familiar with the structure of the U.N. system, the committee in which you will be a participant, your country, your country and region, and the topics you will discuss.

UNITED NATIONS SYSTEM

The United Nations Homepage offers the best primary source of information for Model U.N. delegates. Delegates should become well acquainted with this site. The U.N. Homepage contains U.N. press releases, documents, and numerous links to U.N. organs.

GENERAL

United Nations Home Page
www.un.org
United Nations Links
www.undcp.org/unlinks.html
United Nations News
www.un.org/News/
Official Website Locator for the U.N. System of Organizations
www.unsystem.org

PRINCIPAL ORGANS OF THE UN

General Assembly
www.un.org/ga
Economic and Social Council
www.un.org/esa/coordination/ecosoc
Security Council
www.un.org/docs/scinfo.htm
International Court of Justice
www.icj-cij.org
Secretariat
www.un.org/documents/st.htm
Trusteeship Council
www.un.org/documents/tc.htm

COMMITTEES

United Nations committee websites provide valuable information on committee structure, programs, and resolutions. The following list represents committees commonly simulated in Model United Nations programs and related U.N. bodies. For a complete listing please refer to the United Nations Homepage. As a Model U.N. delegate, you should know the workings of the U.N. system and more important the workings of the committee, commission, or organ on which you will be representing your country.

GENERAL ASSEMBLY COMMITTEES

Plenary
www.un.org/ga/56/plenary/plenary.htm
First Committee: Disarmament and International Security
www.un.org/ga/56/first/first.htm
Second Committee: Economic and Financial
www.un.org/ga/56/second/
Third Committee: Social, Humanitarian and Cultural
www.un.org/ga/56/third/
Fourth Committee: Special Political and Decolonization
www.un.org/ga/56/fourth/
Fifth Committee: Administrative and Budgetary
www.un.org/ga/56/fifth/
Sixth Committee: Legal
www.un.org/law/cod/sixth/index.html

ECONOMIC AND SOCIAL COUNCIL COMMITTEES

Subsidiary Bodies—Functional Commissions
Commission on Human Rights
www.unhchr.ch
Commission on Narcotic Drugs
www.undcp.org
Commission on Population and Development
www.un.org/esa/population
Commission on Science and Technology for Development
www.unctad.org/en/special/ecn16lds4.htm
Commission for Social Development
www.un.org/esa/socdev/
Commission on the Status of Women
www.un.org/womenwatch/
Commission on Sustainable Development
www.un.org/esa/sustdev/

Subsidiary Bodies—Regional Commissions
Economic Commission for Africa
www.uneca.org
Economic Commission for Europe
www.unece.org
Economic Commission for Latin America and the Caribbean
www.eclacpos.org
Economic and Social Commission for Asia and the Pacific
www.unescap.org
Economic and Social Commission for Western Asia
www.escwa.org.lb

United Nations Agencies and Programs

International Law Commission
www.un.org/law/ilc/index.htm
Joint United Nations Programme on HIV/AIDS
www.unaids.org
United Nations Children's Fund
www.unicef.org
United Nations Conference on Disarmament
www.unog.ch/disarm/dconf.htm
U.N. Conference on Trade and Development
www.unctad.org
United Nations Development Programme
www.undp.org
United Nations Development Fund for
Women
www.unifem.org
United Nations Educational, Scientific and
Cultural Organization
www.unesco.org
United Nations Environment Programme
www.unep.org
United Nations High Commissioner for
Human Rights
www.unhchr.ch
United Nations Industrial Development
Programme
www.unido.org
United Nations International Drug Control
Programme
www.undcp.org
United Nations Special Committee on
Peacekeeping Operations
www.un.org/Depts/dpko
World Bank
www.worldbank.org
World Food Programme
www.wfp.org
World Health Organization
www.who.int
Other United Nations Bodies
www.unsystem.org/

COUNTRIES

Embassies, Permanent Missions to the United Nations, and government homepages provide country-specific information. Some nations may not maintain a general government website in English. Delegates should look for ministries of foreign affairs or national parliaments if their nation is not listed. It is helpful if in your country-specific research you find a speech or policy statement by a spokesperson of the country you are representing. Speeches by your country's leaders and/or ambassador may be found on these websites below.

General

Electronic Embassy
www.embassy.org
Permanent Missions to the United Nations
—Geneva
www.unog.ch/genet/permis/misset.htm
Permanent Missions to the United Nations
—New York
www.un.org/overview/missions.htm
Political Resources on the Net
www.politicalresources.net
U.N. Member States
www.un.org/members

Governments

National Government Information
www.un.org/esa/national.htm
Andora
www.andorra.ad/govern/
Angola
www.angola.org
Antigua and Barbuda
www.undp.org/missions/antigua_barbuda/
Argentina
www.presidencia.gov.ar/
Armenia
www.gov.am/en/
Australia
www.nla.gov.au/oz/gov/
Austria
www.austria.gv.at
Azerbaijan
www.president.az/azerbaijan/azerbaijan.htm
Bangladesh
www.bangladeshgov.org
Barbados
www.bgis.gov.bb/
Belarus
www.president.gov.by/index_en.htm
Belgium
www.belgium.fgov.be
Belize
www.belize.gov.bz/
Bolivia
www.ine.gov.bo/
Bosnia and Herzegovina
www.mvp.gov.ba/
Botswana
www.gov.bw/home.html
Brazil
www.mre.gov.br/projeto/mreweb/ingles/
default.htm
Brunei Darussalem
www.mfa.gov.bn/
Bulgaria
www.bulgaria.gourn.bg

Burkina Faso
www.primature.gov.bf/republic/fparlement.htm

Cambodia
www.embassy.org/cambodia/

Canada
www.canada.gc.ca/main_e.html

Cape Verde
www.governo.cv/wwwindex.html

Chile
www.minrel.cl/

China
www.mii.gov.cn/mii/index.html

Costa Rica
www.casapres.go.cr/

Cote D Ivoire
www.guinee.gov.gn/

Croatia
www.vlada.hr/english/contents.html

Cuba
www.cubagob.cu/

Cyprus
www.pio.gov.cy

Czech Republic
www.czech.cz

Denmark
www.um.dk/

Dominica
www.ndcdominica.dm/index.htm

Dominican Republic
www.presidencia.gov.do/

East Timor
www.gov.east-timor.org/

Ecuador
www.mmrree.gov.ec/

Egypt
www.mfa.gov.eg

El Salvador
www.casapres.gob.sv/

Eritrea
www.eriemb.se

Estonia
www.riigikantselei.ee/eng/

Ethiopia
missions.itu.int/~ethiopia/

Federal Republic of Yugoslavia
www.gov.yu

Federated States of Miconesia
www.fsmgov.org

Fiji
fiji.gov.fj

Finland
formin.finland.fi/english/

France
www.premier-ministre.gouv.fr/

Gambia
www.gambia.com

Georgia
www.parliament.ge/

Germany
www.bundesregierung.de

Ghana
www.ghana.gov.gh/sitemap.html

Greece
www.hri.org

Guatemala
www.minex.gob.gt/

Haiti
www.haiti.org/

Honduras
www.sre.hn/

Hungary
www.kancellaria.gov.hu/index_e.html

Iceland
www.stjr.is/interpro/stjr/stjr.nsf/pages/index.html

India
goidirectory.nic.in

Indonesia
www.dfa-deplu.go.id

Iraq
www.uruklink.net/naoi/

Ireland
www.irlgov.ie/

Israel
www.israel.org/mfa/home.asp

Italy
www.esteri.it/

Jamaica
www.cabinet.gov.jm/

Japan
www.mofa.go.jp/

Jordan
www.nic.gov.jo/nis2.html

Kazakhstan
www.president.kz

Korea
www.assembly.go.kr/english/index.html

Kuwait
65.108.14.156/

Latvia
www.am.gov.lv/en/

Lebanon
www.lp.gov.lb/english.html

Lesotho
www.lesotho.gov.ls/

Luxembourg
www.gouvernement.lu/

Madagascar
www.embassy.org/madagascar/

Maldives
www.presidencymaldives.gov.mv/v3/

Malta
www.gov.mt/

Marshall Islands
www.rmiembassyus.org/

Mauritania
www.mauritania.mr/

Mauritius
ncb.intnet.mu/govt/house.htm
Mexico
www.presidencia.gob.mx/
Mongolia
www.pmis.gov.mn
Morocco
www.mincom.gov.ma
Mozambique
www.mozambique.mz/eindex.htm
Myanmar
www3.itu.int/missions/Myanmar/
Namibia
www.opm.gov.na/
Netherlands
www.nl-menu.nl/nlmenu.en/nlmenu.shtml
New Zealand
www.govt.nz/
Nicuragua
www.asamblea.gob.ni/
Norway
http://odin.dep.no/odin/engelsk/index-b-n-a.html
Oman
www.omanet.com
Pakistan
www.pak.gov.pk/
Palestine
www.pna.org
Panama
www.presidencia.gob.pa/portada.htm
Paraguay
www.mre.gov.py/
Peru
www.congreso.gob.pe/index.asp
Philippines
www.dfa.gov.ph/
Portugal
www.min-nestrangeiros.pt/mne/
Qatar
English.mofa.gov.qa
Republic of Mecedonia
www.gov.mk/English/Tela.htm
Romania
www.guv.ro/engleza/index.html
Russian Federation
www.gov.ru
Rwanda
www.rwanda1.com/government/
rwandalaunchie.html
Singapore
www.gov.sg
Slovakia
www.government.gov.sk/english/
Slovenia
www.sigov.si
South Africa
www.gov.za

Spain
www.mae.es/
Sri Lanka
www.priu.gov.lk/
St. Lucia
www.stlucia.gov.lc/
St. Kitts and Nevis
www.stkittsnevis.net
Sudan
www.sudmer.com/
Suriname
www.sr.net/srnet/InfoSurinam/
Swaziland
www.swazi.com/government/
Sweden
www.utrikes.regeringen.se/inenglish/index.htm
Switzerland
www.admin.ch/
Thailand
www.thaigov.go.th/
Trinidad
www.foreign.gov.tt/
Turkey
www.mfa.gov.tr/
Uganda
www.government.go.ug/
Ukraine
www.kmu.gov.ua/index_engl.html
United Arab Emirates
www.uae.gov.ae/
United Kingdom
www.open.gov.uk
United States
www.firstgov.gov/
Uruguay
www.mrree.gub.uy/mrree/cuadro2.htm
Uzbekistan
www.gov.uz
Vanuatu
www.vanuatugovernment.gov.vu/
Venezuela
www.mre.gov.ve/
Vietnam
www.mofa.gov.vn/
Yemen
www.parliament.gov.ye/

MULTILATERAL ORGANIZATIONS

Alliance for Small Island States
www.sidsnet.org/aosis/
Asia-Pacific Economic Cooperation
www.apecsec.org.sg/
Association of Southeast Asian Nations
www.asean.or.id/
Council of Europe
www.coe.fr/index.asp

Economic Community of West African States
www.ecowas.int

European Union
www.europa.eu.int

Food and Agriculture Organization
www.fao.org

G8 Information Centre
www.g7.utoronto.ca

International Atomic Energy Agency
www.iaea.org

International Fund for Agricultural Development
www.ifad.org

International Labour Organization
www.ilo.org

International Monetary Fund
www.imf.org

International Organization for Migration
www.iom.int/

League of Arab States
www.leagueofarabstates.org/

North Atlantic Treaty Organization
hq.nato.int

Organization of African Unity
www.oau-oua.org

Organization of American States
www.oas.org

Organization for Economic Co-operation and
Development
www.oecd.org

Organization for Security and Cooperation
in Europe
www.osce.org

Western European Union
www.weu.int

World Intellectual Property Organization
www.wipo.int

World Trade Organization
www.wto.org

NON-GOVERNMENTAL ORGANIZATIONS (NGOS)

Non-governmental organizations play an integral role in the United Nations system. The following sites provide links to the hundreds of NGO pages on the Internet.

NGO Homepage
www.un.org/esa/coordination/ngo

Committee on NGOs
www.un.org/esa/coordination/ngo/committee.htm

Conference of NGOs in Consultative Status
with the Economic and Social Council of the
United Nations (CONGO)
www.conferenceofngos.org

NGO Global Network
www.ngo.org

NGO Search Engine
www.un.org/esa/coordination/ngo/altavist.htm

U.N. Department of Public Information NGO
Section
www.un.org/dpi/ngosection/index.html

DPI/NGO Directory
www.un.org/MoreInfo/ngolink/ngodir.htm

INTERNATIONAL AFFAIRS

Brookings Institution—Foreign Policy Studies
www.brook.edu/dybdocroot/fp/fp_hp.htm

Carnegie Council on Ethics in International Affairs
www.cceia.org

Council Foreign Affairs
www.foreignaffairs.org

Council on Foreign Relations
www.foreignpolicy2000.org/

Foreign Policy
www.foreignpolicy.com

Foreign Policy in Focus
www.foreignpolicy-infocus.org

International Relations and Security Network
www.isn.ethz.ch

REGIONS

AFRICA

All Africa Global Media
www.allafrica.com

Africa Online
www.africaonline.com

Africa Action
www.africaaction.org

African Studies Internet Resources
www.columbia.edu/cu/lweb/indiv/africa/

Africa Wire
www.africawire.com

THE AMERICAS

Central Intelligence Agency
www.odci.gov

FedWorld
www.fedworld.gov

Latin American Information Network
www.lanic.utexas.edu

Political Database of the Americas
www.georgetown.edu/pdba

Resource Center for the Americas
www.americas.org

United States Department of State
www.state.gov

White House
www.whitehouse.gov

ASIA

Asia News Stand
www.asiadragons.com/news_and_media/
asianews.shtml
Asia Pacific News
www.asiapacificnews.com
Asia Society
www.asiasociety.org
Asia Times Online
www.atimes.com
TIME Asia
www.timeasia.com
News Asia
www.newsasia.com
South Asian Analysis Group
www.saag.org

COMMONWEALTH OF INTERDEPENDENT STATES (CIS)

Democracy and Governance
www.info.usaid.gov/regions/europe_eurasia/
democr02.htm
Russia and NIS Politics
www.departments.bucknell.edu/russian/
politics.html
Statistics of the CIS
www.cisstat.com

EUROPE

Central Europe Online
www.centraleurope.com
European Investment Bank
www.eib.org
The European Union on-line
www.europa.eu.int/
Radio Free Europe/Radio Liberty
www.rferl.org

MIDDLE EAST

Center for Policy Analysis on Palestine
www.palestinecenter.org/framecpac.html
Middle East Insight
www.mideastinsight.org
Middle East Institute
www.mideasti.org
Middle East Research and Information Project
www.merip.org
Middle East Review of International Affairs
www.biu.ac.il/SOC/besa/meria.html
Middle East Times
www.metimes.com
The Washington Institute of Near East Policy
www.washingtoninstitute.org/pubs
Washington Report on Middle East Affairs
www.wrmea.com

TOPICS

Among the various topics addressed by United Nations delegates each year some themes, from children to international law, recur. The following is a brief selection of sites on the general topics. Delegates should also check the websites of committees, international organizations, and NGOs for topical links.

CHILDREN

Childwatch International Research Network
www.childwatch.uio.no
Center for Europe's Children
www.eurochild.gla.ac.uk/default.htm
Convention on the Rights of the Child
www.unicef.org/crc/crc.htm
Database on Research and Information on Children's Rights
child-abuse.com/childhouse/childwatch/cwi/
RI-DB/info.html
UNICEF Resource Centre—Links
www.unicef-icdc.org/siteguide/indexsearch.html

DISARMAMENT

United Nations and Disarmament
www.un.org/Depts/dda
United Nations Institute for Disarmament Research
www.unog.ch/UNIDIR

ENVIRONMENT

Ecolex—Environmental Law Information
www.ecolex.org
EcoNet
www.igc.org/igc/gateway/enindex.html
European Environmental Law Page
www.eel.nl
Geneva Environment Network
www.environmenthouse.ch
UNEPnet
www.unep.org/unep/eia/eis/unepnet/home.htm

UNEP Site Locator
www.unep.org/sitelocator
United Nations System—Wide Earth Watch
earthwatch.unep.net

HUMAN RIGHTS

Amnesty International
www.amnesty.org
Anti-Defamation League
www.adl.org
The National Center for Human Rights Education
www.pdhre.org/chre

Center for the Study of Human Rights
www.columbia.edu/cu/humanrights

Franklin and Eleanor Roosevelt Institute
www.newdeal.FERI.org/FERI

Human Rights Access
www.kurd.org/hrx

Human Rights Internet
www.hri.ca

Human Rights Watch
www.hrw.org/

International Human Rights Law Institute
condor.depaul.edu/~ihrli

International League for Human Rights
www.ilhr.org/

The Israeli Information Center for Human Rights
in the Occupied Territories
www.btselem.org

Lawyers Committee for Human Rights
www.lchr.org

Robert F. Kennedy Memorial Center for
Human Rights
www.rfkmemorial.org

Universal Declaration of Human Rights
www.un.org/Overview/rights.html

50th Anniversary of the Universal Declaration of
Human Rights
www.udhr.org/

University of Minnesota Human Rights Library
www.umn.edu/humanrts

INTELLIGENCE

Awareness of National Security Issues and Response
(ANSIR) Program
www.fbi.gov/hq/nsd/ansir/ansir.htm

Central Intelligence Machinery
www.cabinet-office.gov.uk/cabsec/1998/cim/
cimrep1.htm

Defense Intelligence Agency
www.dia.mil/index.html

Intelligence Online Project
www.icg.org

National Counterintelligence Executive
www.ncix.gov

National Security Agency Official Homepage
www.nsa.gov

Security Intelligence Review Committee
www.sirc-csars.gc.ca

Stratfor
www.stratfor.com

INTERNATIONAL LAW

Center for International Legal Studies
www.cils.org

Global Legal Information Network
lcweb2.loc.gov/glin/glinhome.html

International Criminal Court
www.un.org/law/icc/index.html

International Law Association
www.ila-hq.org

The International Law Page
www.tsunami.nl/cms/default.htm

International Trade Law
www.uncitral.org/en-index.htm

Law of the Sea
www.un.org/Depts/los/index.htm

United Nations Homepage—International Law
www.un.org/law

United Nations Treaty Collection
http://untreaty.un.org

LANDMINES

Adopt-A-Minefield
www.landmines.org

United Nations Mine Action Service
www.mineaction.org

Landmine Free World
vvaf.org/campaign/index.shtml

PEACE AND SECURITY

Bonn International Center for Conversion
bicc.uni-bonn.de

British American Security Information Council
www.basicint.org

Federation of American Scientists
www.fas.org

Foundation for Middle East Peace
www.fmep.org

Institute for the Studies of Conflict, Ideology
and Policy
www.bu.edu/iscip

Institute for Security Studies
www.iss.co.za

Inter-American Development Bank
www.iadb.org/exr/

International Peace Academy
www.ipacademy.org

Monterey Institute
www.miis.edu

National Security Archive
www.gwu.edu/~nsarchiv

National Security Council
www.whitehouse.gov/nsc

Stockholm International Peace Research Institute
www.sipri.se

REFUGEES

Amnesty International-Refugees
web.amnesty.org/ai.nsf/themes/refugees

Refugee Law Center
www.refugeelawcenter.org

The UN Refugee Agency
www.unhcr.ch/cgi-bin/texis/vtx/home

TRADE AND DEVELOPMENT

World Trade Organization
www.wto.org

International Trade Centre
www.intracen.org

UNCTAD—WWW Related Sites
www.unctad.org/en/wwwsites/fwwwsite.htm

WOMEN

R&R Women's Rights Links
www.refuseandresist.org/contact/hotlist.html#rf

Women Watch
www.un.org/womenwatch

**United Nations Division for the Advancement
of Women**
www.un.org/womenwatch/daw

**United Nations International Training Institute
for the Advancement of Women**
www.un-instraw.org

NEWS

ABC News.Com
www.abcnews.go.com

Associated Press
wire.ap.org

British Broadcasting Corporation
news.bbc.co.uk

Cable News Network
www.cnn.com

The Economist
www.economist.com

Financial Times
www.ft.com/news/home/us

Foreign Wire
www.foreignwire.com

Independent Media Center
www.indymedia.org

Le Monde Diplomatique
www.monde-diplomatique.fr/en

MSNBC
www.msnbc.com

The Nation
www.thenation.org

The New York Times
www.nytimes.com

RAND Publications
www.rand.org/PUBS/index.html

Reuters
www.reuters.com/news

Speakout
www.policy.com

Time
www.time.com

Washington Post
www.washingtonpost.com

World Policy Journal
www.worldpolicy.org

World Press
www.worldpress.org

RESEARCH LINKS

GENERAL

CIA World Factbook
www.odci.gov/CIA/publications/factbook

Crisis Web
www.crisisweb.org

Relief Web
www.reliefweb.int

The WWW Virtual Library
www.vlib.org

United Nations Association of the USA
www.unausa.org

STATISTICS

Global Statistics
www.un.org/Depts/unsd/global.htm

WHO Statistical Information System
www.who.int/whosis

UNICEF Statistics on Women and Children
www.unicef.org/statis/index.htm

U.N. Statistics Division
www.un.org/Depts/unsd/

World Bank Group Data & Statistics
www.worldbank.org/data/

IMPORTANT DOCUMENTS OF
THE UNITED NATIONS

This section contains three of the most important documents in U.N. history. The Charter of the United Nations, the Statute of the International Court of Justice, and the Universal Declaration of Human Rights (UHDR).

These documents will serve as valuable reference materials in your preparation. The Charter of the United Nations was signed on June 26, 1945, in San Francisco, at the conclusion of the United Nations Conference on International Organization, and came into force on October 24, 1945. The Statute of the International Court of Justice is an integral part of the Charter.

Amendments to Articles 23, 27, and 61 of the Charter were adopted by the General Assembly on December 17, 1963, and came into force on August 31, 1965. A further amendment to Article 61 was adopted by the General Assembly on December 20, 1971, and came into force on September 24, 1973. An amendment to Article 109, adopted by the General Assembly on 20 December 1965, came into force on June 12, 1968.

The amendment to Article 23 enlarges the membership of the Security Council from 11 to 15. The amended Article 27 provides that decisions of the Security Council on procedural matters shall be made by an affirmative vote of nine members (formerly seven) and on all other matters by an affirmative vote of nine members (formerly seven), including the concurring votes of the five permanent members of the Security Council.

The amendment to Article 61, which entered into force on August 31, 1965, enlarged the membership of the Economic and Social Council from 18 to 27. The subsequent amendment to that Article, which entered into force on 24 September 1973, further increased the membership of the Council from 27 to 54.

The amendment to Article 109, which relates to the first paragraph of the Article, provides that a General Conference of member states for the purpose of reviewing the Charter may be held at a date and place to be fixed by a two-thirds vote of the members of the General Assembly and by a vote of any nine members (formerly seven) of the Security Council. Paragraph 3 of Article 109, which deals with the consideration of a possible review conference during the tenth regular session of the General Assembly, has been retained in its original form in its reference to a "vote, of any seven members of the Security Council," the paragraph having been acted upon in 1955 by the General Assembly, at its tenth regular session, and by the Security Council.

The third historic document included in this section is the Universal Declaration of Human Rights (UHDR). Written by Eleanor Roosevelt, John Humphrey (Canada), and other leaders in 1948, the UHDR remains the United Nations' standard for preservation of human rights around the world.

Charter of the United Nations

We the Peoples of the United Nations determined

to save succeeding generations from the scourge of war, which twice in our lifetime has brought untold sorrow to mankind, and

to reaffirm faith in fundamental human rights, in the dignity and worth of the human person, in the equal rights of men and women and of nations large and small, and

to establish conditions under which justice and respect for the obligations arising from treaties and other sources of international law can be maintained, and

to promote social progress and better standards of life in larger freedom,

And for these ends

to practice tolerance and live together in peace with one another as good neighbours, and

to unite our strength to maintain international peace and security, and

to ensure, by the acceptance of principles and the institution of methods, that armed force shall not be used, save in the common interest, and

to employ international machinery for the promotion of the economic and social advancement of all peoples,

have resolved to combine our efforts to accomplish these aims.

Accordingly, our respective Governments, through representatives assembled in the city of San Francisco, who have exhibited their full powers found to be in good and due form, have agreed to the present Charter of the United Nations and do hereby establish an international organization to be known as the United Nations.

CHAPTER I

PURPOSES AND PRINCIPLES

Article 1

The Purposes of the United Nations are:

1. To maintain international peace and security, and to that end: to take effective collective measures for the prevention and removal of threats to the peace, and for the suppression of acts of aggression or other breaches of the peace, and to bring about by peaceful means, and in conformity with the principles of justice and international law, adjustment or settlement of international disputes or situations which might lead to a breach of the peace;

2. To develop friendly relations among nations based on respect for the principle of equal rights and self-determination of peoples, and to take other appropriate measures to strengthen universal peace;

3. To achieve international co-operation in solving international problems of an economic, social, cultural, or humanitarian character, and in promoting and encouraging respect for human rights and for fundamental freedoms for all without distinction as to race, sex, language, or religion; and

4. To be a centre for harmonizing the actions of nations in the attainment of these common ends.

Article 2

The Organization and its Members, in pursuit of the Purposes stated in Article 1, shall act in accordance with the following Principles.

1. The Organization is based on the principle of the sovereign equality of all its Members.

2. All Members, in order to ensure to all of them the rights and benefits resulting from membership, shall fulfill in good faith the obligations assumed by them in accordance with the present Charter.

3. All Members shall settle their international disputes by peaceful means in such a manner that international peace and security, and justice, are not endangered.

4. All Members shall refrain in their international relations from the threat or use of force against the territorial integrity or political independence of any state, or in any other manner inconsistent with the Purposes of the United Nations.

5. All Members shall give the United Nations every assistance in any action it takes in accordance with the present Charter, and shall refrain from giving assistance to any state against which the United Nations is taking preventive or enforcement action.

6. The Organization shall ensure that states which are not Members of the United Nations act in accordance with these Principles so far as may be necessary for the maintenance of international peace and security.

7. Nothing contained in the present Charter shall authorize the United Nations to intervene in matters which are essentially within the domestic jurisdiction of any state or shall require the Members to submit such matters to settlement under the present Charter; but this principle shall not prejudice the application of enforcement measures under Chapter VII.

CHAPTER II

MEMBERSHIP

Article 3

The original Members of the United Nations shall be the states which, having participated in the United Nations Conference on International Organization at San Francisco, or having previously signed the Declaration by United Nations of 1 January 1942, sign the present Charter and ratify it in accordance with Article 110.

Article 4

1. Membership in the United Nations is open to all other peaceloving states which accept the obligations contained in the present Charter and, in the judgement of the Organization, are able and willing to carry out these obligations.

2. The admission of any such state to membership in the United Nations will be effected by a decision of the General Assembly upon the recommendation of the Security Council.

Article 5

A Member of the United Nations against which preventive or enforcement action has been taken by the Security Council may be suspended from the exercise of the rights and privileges of membership by the General Assembly upon the recommendation of the Security Council. The exercise of these rights and privileges may be restored by the Security Council.

Article 6

A Member of the United Nations which has persistently violated the Principles contained in the present Charter may be expelled from the Organization by the General Assembly upon the recommendation of the Security Council.

CHAPTER III

ORGANS

Article 7

1. There are established as the principal organs of the United Nations: a General Assembly, a Security Council, an Economic and Social Council, a Trusteeship Council, an International Court of Justice, and a Secretariat.
2. Such subsidiary organs as may be found necessary may be established in accordance with the present Charter.

Article 8

The United Nations shall place no restrictions on the eligibility of men and women to participate in any capacity and under conditions of equality in its principal and subsidiary organs.

CHAPTER IV

THE GENERAL ASSEMBLY

COMPOSITION

Article 9

1. The General Assembly shall consist of all the Members of the United Nations.
2. Each Member shall have not more than five representatives in the General Assembly.

FUNCTIONS AND POWERS

Article 10

The General Assembly may discuss any questions or any matters within the scope of the present Charter or relating to the powers and functions of any organs provided for in the present Charter, and, except as provided in Article 12, may make recommendations to the Members of the United Nations or to the Security Council or to both on any such questions or matters.

Article 11

1. The General Assembly may consider the general principles of co-operation in the maintenance of international peace and security, including the principles governing disarmament and the regulation of armaments, and may make recommendations with regard to such principles to the Members or to the Security Council or to both.
2. The General Assembly may discuss any questions relating to the maintenance of international peace and security brought before it by any Member of the United Nations, or by the Security Council, or by a state which is not a Member of the United Nations in accordance with Article 35, paragraph 2, and, except as provided in Article 12, may make recommendations with regard to any such questions to the state or states concerned or to the Security Council or to both. Any such question on which action is necessary shall be referred to the Security Council by the General Assembly either before or after discussion.
3. The General Assembly may call the attention of the Security Council to situations which are likely to endanger international peace and security.
4. The powers of the General Assembly set forth in this Article shall not limit the general scope of Article 10.

Article 12

1. While the Security Council is exercising in respect of any dispute or situation the functions assigned to it in the present Charter, the General Assembly shall not make any recommendations with regard to that dispute or situation unless the Security Council so requests.
2. The Secretary-General, with the consent of the Security Council, shall notify the General Assembly at each session of any matters relative to the maintenance of international peace and security which are being dealt with by the Security Council and shall similarly notify the General Assembly, or the Members of the United Nations if the General Assembly is not in session, immediately the Security Council ceases to deal with such matters.

Article 13

1. The General Assembly shall initiate studies and make recommendations for the purpose of:

　　a. promoting international co-operation in the political field and encouraging the progressive development of international law and its codification;

　　b. promoting international co-operation in the economic, social, cultural, educational, and health fields, and assisting in the realization of human rights and fundamental freedoms for all without distinction as to race, sex, language, or religion.
2. The further responsibilities, functions and powers of the General Assembly with respect to matters mentioned in paragraph 1 (b) above are set forth in Chapters IX and X.

Article 14

Subject to the provisions of Article 12, the General Assembly may recommend measures for the peaceful adjustment of any situation, regardless of origin, which it deems likely to impair the general welfare or friendly relations among nations, including situations resulting from a violation of the provisions of the present Charter setting forth the Purposes and Principles of the United Nations.

Article 15

1. The General Assembly shall receive and consider annual and special reports from the Security Council; these reports shall include an account of the measures that the Security Council has decided upon or taken to maintain international peace and security.
2. The General Assembly shall receive and consider reports from the other organs of the United Nations.

Article 16

The General Assembly shall perform such functions with respect to the international trusteeship system as are assigned to it under Chapters XII and XIII, including the approval of the trusteeship agreements for areas not designated as strategic.

Article 17

1. The General Assembly shall consider and approve the budget of the Organization.
2. The expenses of the Organization shall be borne by the Members as apportioned by the General Assembly.
3. The General Assembly shall consider and approve any financial and budgetary arrangements with specialized agencies referred to in Article 57 and shall examine the administrative budgets of such specialized agencies with a view to making recommendations to the agencies concerned.

VOTING

Article 18

1. Each member of the General Assembly shall have one vote.
2. Decisions of the General Assembly on important questions shall be made by a two-

thirds majority of the members present and voting. These questions shall include: recommendations with respect to the maintenance of international peace and security, the election of the non-permanent members of the Security Council, the election of the members of the Economic and Social Council, the election of members of the Trusteeship Council in accordance with paragraph 1(c) of Article 86, the admission of new Members to the United Nations, the suspension of the rights and privileges of membership, the expulsion of Members, questions relating to the operation of the trusteeship system, and budgetary questions.

3. Decisions of other questions, including the determination of additional categories of questions to be decided by a two-thirds majority, shall be made by a majority of the members present and voting.

Article 19

A Member of the United Nations which is in arrears in the payment of its financial contributions to the Organization shall have no vote in the General Assembly if the amount of its arrears equals or exceeds the amount of the contributions due from it for the preceding two full years. The General Assembly may, nevertheless, permit such a Member to vote if it is satisfied that the failure to pay is due to conditions beyond the control of the Member.

PROCEDURE

Article 20

The General Assembly shall meet in regular annual sessions and in such special sessions as occasion may require. Special sessions shall be convoked by the Secretary-General at the request of the Security Council or of a majority of the Members of the United Nations.

Article 21

The General Assembly shall adopt its own rules of procedure. It shall elect its President for each session.

Article 22

The General Assembly may establish such subsidiary organs as it deems necessary for the performance of its functions.

CHAPTER V

THE SECURITY COUNCIL

COMPOSITION

Article 23

1. The Security Council shall consist of fifteen Members of the United Nations. The Republic of China, France, the Union of Soviet Socialist Republics, the United Kingdom of Great Britain and Northern Ireland, and the United States of America shall be permanent members of the Security Council. The General Assembly shall elect ten other Members of the United Nations to be non-permanent members of the Security Council, due regard being specially paid, in the first instance to the contribution of Members of the United Nations to the maintenance of international peace and security and to the other purposes of the Organization, and also to equitable geographical distribution.

2. The non-permanent members of the Security Council shall be elected for a term of two years. In the first election of the non-permanent members after the increase of the membership of the Security Council from eleven to fifteen, two of the four additional members shall be chosen for a term of one year. A retiring member shall not be eligible for immediate re-election.

3. Each member of the Security Council shall have one representative.

FUNCTIONS AND POWERS

Article 24

1. In order to ensure prompt and effective action by the United Nations, its Members confer on the Security Council primary responsibility for the maintenance of international peace and security, and agree that in carrying out its duties under this responsibility the Security Council acts on their behalf.

2. In discharging these duties the Security Council shall act in accordance with the Purposes and Principles of the United Nations. The specific powers granted to the Security Council for the discharge of these duties are laid down in Chapters VI, VII, VIII, and XII.

3. The Security Council shall submit annual and, when necessary, special reports to the General Assembly for its consideration.

Article 25

The Members of the United Nations agree to accept and carry out the decisions of the Security Council in accordance with the present Charter.

Article 26

In order to promote the establishment and maintenance of international peace and security with the least diversion for armaments of the world's human and economic resources, the Security Council shall be responsible for formulating, with the assistance of the Military Staff Committee referred to in Article 47, plans to be submitted to the Members of the United Nations for the establishment of a system for the regulation of armaments.

VOTING

Article 27

1. Each member of the Security Council shall have one vote.

2. Decisions of the Security Council on procedural matters shall be made by an affirmative vote of nine members.

3. Decisions of the Security Council on all other matters shall be made by an affirmative vote of nine members including the concurring votes of the permanent members; provided that, in decisions under Chapter VI, and under paragraph 3 of Article 52, a party to a dispute shall abstain from voting.

PROCEDURE

Article 28

1. The Security Council shall be so organized as to be able to function continuously. Each member of the Security Council shall for this purpose be represented at all times at the seat of the Organization.

2. The Security Council shall hold periodic meetings at which each of its members may, if it so desires, be represented by a member of the government or by some other specially designated representative.

3. The Security Council may hold meeting at such places other than the seat of the Organization as in its judgment will best facilitate its work.

Article 29

The Security Council may establish such subsidiary organs as it deems necessary for the performance of its functions.

Article 30

The Security Council shall adopt its own rules of procedure, including the method of selecting its President.

Article 31

Any Member of the United Nations which is not a member of the Security Council may participate, without vote, in the discussion of any question brought before the Security Council whenever the latter considers that the interests of that Member are specially affected.

Article 32

Any Member of the United Nations which is not a member of the Security Council or any state which is not a Member of the United Nations, if it is party to a dispute under consideration by the Security Council, shall be invited to participate, without vote, in the discussion relating to the dispute. The Security Council shall lay down such conditions as it deems just for the participation of a state which is not a Member of the United Nations.

CHAPTER VI

PACIFIC SETTLEMENT OF DISPUTES

Article 33

1. The parties to any dispute, the continuance of which is likely to endanger the maintenance of international peace and security, shall, first of all, seek a solution by negotiation, enquiry, mediation, conciliation, arbitration, judicial settlement, resort to regional agencies or arrangements, or other peaceful means of their own choice.
2. The Security Council shall, when it deems necessary, call upon the parties to settle their dispute by such means.

Article 34

The Security Council may investigate any dispute, or any situation which might lead to international friction or give rise to a dispute, in order to determine whether the continuance of the dispute or situation is likely to endanger the maintenance of international peace and security.

Article 35

1. Any Member of the United Nations may bring any dispute, or any situation of the nature referred to in Article 34, to the attention of the Security Council or of the General Assembly.
2. A state which is not a Member of the United Nations may bring to the attention of the Security Council or of the General Assembly any dispute to which it is a party if it accepts in advance, for the purposes of the dispute, the obligations of pacific settlement provided in the present Charter.
3. The proceedings of the General Assembly

in respect of matters brought to its attention under this Article will be subject to the provisions of Articles 11 and 12.

Article 36

1. The Security Council may, at any stage of a dispute of the nature referred to in Article 33 or of a situation of like nature, recommend appropriate procedures or methods of adjustment.
2. The Security Council should take into consideration any procedures for the settlement of the dispute which have already been adopted by the parties.
3. In making recommendations under this Article the Security Council should also take into consideration that legal disputes should as a general rule be referred by the parties to the International Court of Justice in accordance with the provisions of the Statute of the Court.

Article 37

1. Should the parties to a dispute of the nature referred to in Article 33 fail to settle it be the means indicated in that Article, they shall refer it to the Security Council.
2. If the Security Council deems that the continuance of the dispute is in fact likely to endanger the maintenance of international peace and security, it shall decide whether to take action under Article 36 or to recommend such terms of settlement as it may consider appropriate.

Article 38

Without prejudice to the provisions of Articles 33 to 37, the Security Council may, if all the parties to any dispute so request, make recommendations to the parties with a view to a pacific settlement of the dispute.

CHAPTER VII

ACTION WITH RESPECT TO THREATS TO THE PEACE, BREACHES OF THE PEACE, AND ACTS OF AGGRESSION

Article 39

The Security Council shall determine the existence of any threat to the peace, breach of the peace, or act of aggression and shall make recommendations, or decide what measures shall be taken in accordance with Articles 41 and 42, to maintain or restore international peace and security.

Article 40

In order to prevent an aggravation of the situation, the Security Council may, before making the recommendations or deciding upon the measures provided for in Article 39, call upon the parties concerned to comply with such provisional measures as it deems necessary or desirable. Such provisional measures shall be without prejudice to the rights, claims, or position of the parties concerned. The Security Council shall duly take account of failure to comply with such provisional measures.

Article 41

The Security Council may decide what measures not involving the use of armed force are to be employed to give effect to its decisions, and it may call upon the Members of the United Nations to apply such measures. These may include complete or partial interruption of economic relations and of rail, sea, air, postal, telegraphic, radio, and other means of communication, and the severance of diplomatic relations.

Article 42

Should the Security Council consider that measures provided for in Article 41 would be inadequate or have proved to be inadequate, it may take such action by air, sea, or land forces as may be necessary to maintain or restore international peace and security. Such action may include demonstrations, blockade, and other operations by air, sea, or land forces of Members of the United Nations.

Article 43

1. All Members of the United Nations, in order to contribute to the maintenance of international peace and security, undertake to make available to the Security Council, on its call and in accordance with a special agreement or agreements, armed forces, assistance, and facilities, including rights of passage, necessary for the purpose of maintaining international peace and security.
2. Such agreement or agreements shall govern the numbers and types of forces, their degree of readiness and general location, and the nature of the facilities and assistance to be provided.
3. The agreement or agreements shall be negotiated as soon as possible on the initiative of the Security Council. They shall be concluded between the Security Council and Members or between the Security Council and groups of Members and shall be subject

to ratification by the signatory states in accordance with their respective constitutional processes.

Article 44

When the Security Council has decided to use force it shall, before calling upon a Member not represented on it to provide armed forces in fulfilment of the obligations assumed under Article 43, invite that Member, if the Member so desires, to participate in the decisions of the Security Council concerning the employment of contingents of that Member's armed forces.

Article 45

In order to enable the United Nations to take urgent military measures, Members shall hold immediately available national airforce contingents for combined international enforcement action. The strength and degree of readiness of these contingents and plans for their combined action shall be determined, within the limits laid down in the special agreement or agreements referred to in Article 43, by the Security Council with the assistance of the Military Staff Committee.

Article 46

Plans for the application of armed forces shall be made by the Security Council with the assistance of the Military Staff Committee.

Article 47

1. There shall be established a Military Staff Committee to advise and assist the Security Council on all questions relating to the Security Council's military requirements for the maintenance of international peace and security, the employment and command of forces placed at its disposal, the regulation of armaments, and possible disarmament.

2. The Military Staff Committee shall consist of the Chiefs of Staff of the permanent members of the Security Council or their representatives. Any Member of the United Nations not permanently represented on the Committee shall be invited by the Committee to be associated with it when the efficient discharge of the Committee's responsibilities requires the participation of that Member in its work.

3. The Military Staff Committee shall be responsible under the Security Council for the strategic direction of any armed forces placed at the disposal of the Security Council. Questions relating to the command of such forces shall be worked out subsequently.

4. The Military Staff Committee, with the authorization of the Security Council and after consultation with appropriate regional agencies, may establish regional sub-committees.

Article 48

1. The action required to carry out the decisions of the Security Council for the maintenance of international peace and security shall be taken by all the Members of the United Nations or by some of them, as the Security Council may determine.

2. Such decisions shall be carried out by the Members of the United Nations directly and through their action in the appropriate international agencies of which they are members.

Article 49

The Members of the United Nations shall join in affording mutual assistance in carrying out the measures decided upon by the Security Council.

Article 50

If preventive or enforcement measures against any state are taken by the Security Council, any other state, whether a Member of the United Nations or not, which finds itself confronted with special economic problems arising from the carrying out of those measures shall have the right to consult the Security Council with regard to a solution of those problems.

Article 51

Nothing in the present Charter shall impair the inherent right of individual or collective self-defence if an armed attack occurs against a Member of the United Nations, until the Security Council has taken measures necessary to maintain international peace and security. Measures taken by Members in the exercise of this right of self-defence shall be immediately reported to the Security Council and shall not in any way affect the authority and responsibility of the Security Council under the present Charter to take at any time such action as it deems necessary in order to maintain or restore international peace and security.

CHAPTER VIII

REGIONAL ARRANGEMENTS

Article 52

1. Nothing in the present Charter precludes the existence of regional arrangements or

agencies for dealing with such matters relating to the maintenance of international peace and security as are appropriate for regional action, provided that such arrangements or agencies and their activities are consistent with the Purposes and Principles of the United Nations.

2. The Members of the United Nations entering into such arrangements or constituting such agencies shall make every effort to achieve pacific settlement of local disputes through such regional arrangements or by such regional agencies before referring them to the Security Council.

3. The Security Council shall encourage the development of pacific settlement of local disputes through such regional arrangements or by such regional agencies either on the initiative of the states concerned or by reference from the Security Council.

4. This Article in no way impairs the application of Articles 34 and 35.

Article 53

1. The Security Council shall, where appropriate, utilize such regional arrangements or agencies for enforcement action under its authority. But no enforcement action shall be taken under regional arrangements or by regional agencies without the authorization of the Security Council, with the exception of measures against any enemy state, as defined in paragraph 2 of this Article, provided for pursuant to Article 107 or in regional arrangements directed against renewal of aggressive policy on the part of any such state, until such time as the Organization may, on request of the Governments concerned, be charged with the responsibility for preventing further aggression by such a state.

2. The term enemy state as used in paragraph 1 of this Article applies to any state which during the Second World War has been an enemy of any signatory of the present Charter.

Article 54

The Security Council shall at all times be kept fully informed of activities undertaken or in contemplation under regional arrangements or by regional agencies for the maintenance of international peace and se-curity.

CHAPTER IX

INTERNATIONAL ECONOMIC AND SOCIAL CO-OPERATION

Article 55

With a view to the creation of conditions of stability and well-being which are necessary for peaceful and friendly relations among nations based on respect for the principle of equal rights and self-determination of peoples, the United Nations shall promote:

a. higher standards of living, full employment, and conditions of economic and social progress and development;

b. solutions of international economic, social, health, and related problems; and international cultural and educational cooperation; and

c. universal respect for, and observance of, human rights and fundamental freedoms for all without distinction as to race, sex, language, or religion.

Article 56

All Members pledge themselves to take joint and separate action in co-operation with the Organization for the achievement of the purposes set forth in Article 55.

Article 57

1. The various specialized agencies, established by intergovernmental agreement and having wide international responsibilities, as defined in their basic instruments, in economic, social, cultural, educational, health, and related fields, shall be brought into relationship with the United Nations in accordance with the provisions of Article 63.

2. Such agencies thus brought into relationship with the United Nations are hereinafter referred to as specialized agencies.

Article 58

The Organization shall make recommendations for the co-ordination of the policies and activities of the specialized agencies.

Article 59

The Organization shall, where appropriate, initiate negotiations among the states concerned for the creation of any new specialized agencies required for the accomplishment of the purposes set forth in Article 55.

Article 60

Responsibility for the discharge of the functions of the Organization set forth in this Chapter shall be vested in the General Assembly and, under the authority of the General Assembly, in the Economic and Social Council, which shall have for this purpose the powers set forth in Chapter X.

CHAPTER X

THE ECONOMIC AND SOCIAL COUNCIL

COMPOSITION

Article 61

1. The Economic and Social Council shall consist of fifty-four Members of the United Nations elected by the General Assembly.

2. Subject to the provisions of paragraph 3, eighteen members of the Economic and Social Council shall be elected each year for a term of three years. A retiring member shall be eligible for immediate re-election.

3. At the first election after the increase in the membership of the Economic and Social Council from twenty-seven to fifty-four members, in addition to the members elected in place of the nine members whose term of office expires at the end of that year, twenty-seven additional members shall be elected. Of these twenty-seven additional members, the term of office of nine members so elected shall expire at the end of one year, and of nine other members at the end of two years, in accordance with arrangements made by the General Assembly.

4. Each member of the Economic and Social Council shall have one representative.

FUNCTIONS AND POWERS

Article 62

1. The Economic and Social Council may make or initiate studies and reports with respect to international economic, social, cultural, educational, health, and related matters and may make recommendations with respect to any such matters to the General Assembly, to the Members of the United Nations, and to the specialized agencies concerned.

2. It may make recommendations for the purpose of promoting respect for, and observance of, human rights and fundamental freedoms for all.

3. It may prepare draft conventions for submission to the General Assembly, with respect to matters falling within its competence.

4. It may call, in accordance with the rules prescribed by the United Nations, international conferences on matters falling within its competence.

Article 63

1. The Economic and Social Council may enter into agreements with any of the agencies referred to in Article 57, defining the terms on which the agency concerned shall be brought into relationship with the United Nations. Such agreements shall be subject to approval by the General Assembly.

2. It may co-ordinate the activities of the specialized agencies through consultation with and recommendations to such agencies and through recommendations to the General Assembly and to the Members of the United Nations.

Article 64

1. The Economic and Social Council may take appropriate steps to obtain regular reports from the specialized agencies. It may make arrangements with the Members of the United Nations and with the specialized agencies to obtain reports on the steps taken to give effect to its own recommendations and to recommendations on matters falling within its competence made by the General Assembly.

2. It may communicate its observations on these reports to the General Assembly.

Article 65

The Economic and Social Council may furnish information to the Security Council and shall assist the Security Council upon its request.

Article 66

1. The Economic and Social Council shall perform such functions as fall within its competence in connexion with the carrying out of the recommendations of the General Assembly.

2. It may, with the approval of the General Assembly, perform services at the request of Members of the United Nations and at the request of specialized agencies.

3. It shall perform such other functions as are specified elsewhere in the present Charter or as may be assigned to it by the General Assembly.

VOTING

Article 67

1. Each member of the Economic and Social Council shall have one vote.

2. Decisions of the Economic and Social

Council shall be made by a majority of the members present and voting.

PROCEDURE

Article 68

The Economic and Social Council shall set up commissions in the economic and social ?elds and for the promotion of human rights, and such other commissions as may be required for the performance of its functions.

Article 69

The Economic and Social Council shall invite any Member of the United Nations to participate, without vote, in its deliberations on any matter of particular concern to that Member.

Article 70

The Economic and Social Council may make arrangements for representatives of the specialized agencies to participate, without vote, in its deliberations and in those of the commissions established by it, and for its representatives to participate in the deliberations of the specialized agencies.

Article 71

The Economic and Social Council may make suitable arrangements for consultation with non-governmental organizations which are concerned with matters within its competence. Such arrangements may be made with international organizations and, where appropriate, with national organizations after consultation with the Member of the United Nations concerned.

Article 72

1. The Economic and Social Council shall adopt its own rules of procedure, including the method of selecting its President.
2. The Economic and Social Council shall meet as required in accordance with its rules, which shall include provision for the convening of meetings on the request of a majority of its members.

CHAPTER XI

DECLARATION REGARDING NON-SELF-GOVERNING TERRITORITIES

Article 73

Members of the United Nations which have or assume responsibilities for the administration of territories whose peoples have not yet attained a full measure of self-government recognize the principle that the interests of the inhabitants of these territories are paramount, and accept as a sacred trust the obligation to promote to the utmost, within the system of international peace and security established by the present Charter, the well-being of the inhabitants of these territories, and, to this end:

a. to ensure, with due respect for the culture of the peoples concerned, their political, economic, social, and educational advancement, their just treatment, and their protection against abuses;

b. to develop self-government, to take due account of the political aspirations of the peoples, and to assist them in the progressive development of their free political institutions, according to the particular circumstances of each territory and its peoples and their varying stages of advancement;

c. to further international peace and security;

d. to promote constructive measures of development, to encourage research, and to co-operate with one another and, when and where appropriate, with specialized international bodies with a view to the practical achievement of the social, economic, and scientific purposes set forth in this Article; and

e. to transmit regularly to the Secretary-General for information purposes, subject to such limitations as security and constitutional considerations may require, statistical and other information of a technical nature relating to economic, social, and educational conditions in the territories for which they are respectively responsible other than those territories to which Chapters XII and XIII apply.

Article 74

Members of the United Nations also agree that their policy in respect of the territories to which this Chapter applies, no less than in respect of their metropolitan areas, must be based on the general principle of good-neighbourliness, due account being taken of the interests and well-being of the rest of the world, in social, economic, and commercial matters.

CHAPTER XII

INTERNATIONAL TRUSTEESHIP SYSTEM

Article 75

The United Nations shall establish under its authority an international trusteeship system for the administration and supervision of such territories as may be placed thereunder by subsequent individual agreements. These territories are hereinafter referred to as trust territories.

Article 76

The basic objectives of the trusteeship system, in accordance with the Purposes of the United Nations laid down in Article 1 of the present Charter, shall be:

a. to further international peace and security;

b. to promote the political, economic, social, and educational advancement of the inhabitants of the trust territories, and their progressive development towards self-government or independence as may be appropriate to the particular circumstances of each territory and its peoples and the freely expressed wishes of the peoples concerned, and as may be provided by the terms of each trusteeship agreement;

c. to encourage respect for human rights and for fundamental freedoms for all without distinction as to race, sex, language, or religion, and to encourage recognition of the interdependence of the peoples of the world; and

d. to ensure equal treatment in social, economic, and commercial matters for all Members of the United Nations and their nationals, and also equal treatment for the latter in the administration of justice, without prejudice to the attainment of the foregoing objectives and subject to the provisions of Article 80.

Article 77

1. The trusteeship system shall apply to such territories in the following categories as may be placed thereunder by means of trusteeship agreements:

a. territories now held under mandate;

b. territories which may be detached from enemy states as a result of the Second World War; and

c. territories voluntarily placed under the system by states responsible for their administration.

2. It will be a matter for subsequent agreement as to which territories in the foregoing

categories will be brought under the trusteeship system and upon what terms.

Article 78

The trusteeship system shall not apply to territories which have become Members of the United Nations, relationship among which shall be based on respect for the principle of sovereign equality.

Article 79

The terms of trusteeship for each territory to be placed under the trusteeship system, including any alteration or amendment, shall be agreed upon by the states directly concerned, including the mandatory power in the case of territories held under mandate by a Member of the United Nations, and shall be approved as provided for in Articles 83 and 85.

Article 80

1. Except as may be agreed upon in individual trusteeship agreements, made under Articles 77, 79, and 81, placing each territory under the trusteeship system, and until such agreements have been concluded, nothing in this Chapter shall be construed in or of itself to alter in any manner the rights whatsoever of any states or any peoples or the terms of existing international instruments to which Members of the United Nations may respectively be parties.

2. Paragraph 1 of the Article shall not be interpreted as giving grounds for delay or postponement of the negotiation and conclusion of agreements for placing mandated and other territories under the trusteeship system as provided for in Article 77.

Article 81

The trusteeship agreement shall in each case include the terms under which the trust territory will be administered and designate the authority which will exercise the administration of the trust territory. Such authority, hereinafter called the administering authority, may be one or more states or the Organization itself.

Article 82

There may be designated, in any trusteeship agreement, a strategic area or areas which may include part or all of the trust territory to which the agreement applies, without prejudice to any special agreement or agreements made under Article 43.

Article 83

1. All functions of the United Nations relating to strategic areas, including the approval of the terms of the trusteeship agreements and of their alteration or amendment, shall be exercised by the Security Council.

2. The basic objectives set forth in Article 76 shall be applicable to the people of each strategic area.

3. The Security Council shall, subject to the provisions of the trusteeship agreements and without prejudice to security considerations, avail itself of the assistance of the Trusteeship Council to perform those functions of the United Nations under the trusteeship system relating to political, economic, social, and educational matters in the strategic areas.

Article 84

It shall be the duty of the administering authority to ensure that the trust territory shall play its part in the maintenance of international peace and security. To this end the administering authority may make use of volunteer forces, facilities, and assistance from the trust territory in carrying out the obligations towards the Security Council undertaken in this regard by the administering authority, as well as for local defence and the maintenance of law and order within the trust territory.

Article 85

1. The functions of the United Nations with regard to trusteeship agreements for all areas not designated as strategic, including the approval of the terms of the trusteeship agreements and of their alteration or amendment, shall be exercised by the General Assembly.

2. The Trusteeship Council, operating under the authority of the General Assembly, shall assist the General Assembly in carrying out these functions.

CHAPTER XIII

THE TRUSTEESHIP COUNCIL

COMPOSITION

Article 86

1. The Trusteeship Council shall consist of the following Members of the United Nations:

a. those Members administering trust territories;

b. such of the Members mentioned by name

in Article 23 as are not administering trust territories; and

c. as many other Members elected for three-year terms by the General Assembly as may be necessary to ensure that the total number of members of the Trusteeship Council is equally divided between those Members of the United Nations which administer trust territories and those which do not.

2. Each member of the Trusteeship Council shall designate one specially qualified person to represent it therein.

FUNCTIONS AND POWERS

Article 87

The General Assembly and, under its authority, the Trusteeship Council, in carrying out their functions, may:

a. consider reports submitted by the administering authority;

b. accept petitions and examine them in consultation with the administering authority;

c. provide for periodic visits to the respective trust territories at times agreed upon with the administering authority; and

d. take these and other actions in conformity with the terms of the trusteeship agreements.

Article 88

The Trusteeship Council shall formulate a questionnaire on the political, economic, social, and educational advancement of the inhabitants of each trust territory, and the administering authority for each trust territory within the competence of the General Assembly shall make an annual report to the General Assembly upon the basis of such questionnaire.

FUNCTIONS AND POWERS

Article 89

1. Each member of the Trusteeship Council shall have one vote.

2. Decisions of the Trusteeship Council shall be made by a majority of the members present and voting.

PROCEDURE

Article 90

1. The Trusteeship Council shall adopt its own rules of procedure, including the method of selecting its President.

2. The Trusteeship Council shall meet as required in accordance with its rules, which shall include provision for the convening of meetings on the request of a majority of its members.

Article 91

The Trusteeship Council shall, when appropriate, avail itself of the assistance of the Economic and Social Council and of the specialized agencies in regard to matters with which they are respectively concerned.

CHAPTER XIV

INTERNATIONAL COURT OF JUSTICE

Article 92

The International Court of Justice shall be the principal judicial organ of the United Nations. It shall function in accordance with the annexed Statute, which is based upon the Statute of the Permanent Court of International Justice and forms an integral part of the present Charter.

Article 93

1. All Members of the United Nations are ipso facto parties to the Statute of the International Court of Justice.
2. A state which is not a Member of the United Nations may become a party to the Statute of the International Court of Justice on conditions to be determined in each case by the General Assembly upon the recommendation of the Security Council.

. Article 94

1. Each Member of the United Nations undertakes to comply with the decision of the International Court of Justice in any case to which it is a party.
2. If any party to a case fails to perform the obligations incumbent upon it under a judgement rendered by the Court, the other party may have recourse to the Security Council, which may, if it deems necessary, make recommendations or decide upon measures to be taken to give effect to the judgement.

Article 95

Nothing in the present Charter shall prevent Members of the United Nations from entrusting the solution of their differences to other tribunals by virtue of agreements already in existence or which may be concluded in the future.

Article 95

1. The General Assembly or the Security Council may request the International Court of Justice to give an advisory opinion on any legal question.
2. Other organs of the United Nations and specialized agencies, which may at any time be so authorized by the General Assembly, may also request advisory opinions of the Court on legal questions arising within the scope of their activities.

CHAPTER XV

THE SECRETARIAT

Article 97

The Secretariat shall comprise a Secretary-General and such staff as the Organization may require. The Secretary-General shall be appointed by the General Assembly upon the recommendation of the Security Council. He shall be the chief administrative of?cer of the Organization.

Article 98

The Secretary-General shall act in that capacity in all meetings of the General Assembly, of the Security Council, of the Economic and Social Council, and of the Trusteeship Council, and shall perform such other functions as are entrusted to him by these organs. The Secretary-General shall make an annual report to the General Assembly on the work of the Organization.

Article 99

The Secretary-General may bring to the attention of the Security Council any matter which in his opinion may threaten the maintenance of international peace and security.

Article 100

1. In the performance of their duties the Secretary-General and the staff shall not seek or receive instructions from any government or from any other authority external to the Organization. They shall refrain from any action which might reflect on their position as international officials responsible only to the Organization.
2. Each Member of the United Nations undertakes to respect the exclusively international character of the responsibilities of the Secretary-General and the staff and not to seek to influence them in the discharge of their responsibilities.

Article 101

1. The staff shall be appointed by the Secretary-General under regulations established by the General Assembly.
2. Appropriate staffs shall be permanently assigned to the Economic and Social Council, the Trusteeship Council, and, as required, to other organs of the United Nations. These staffs shall form a part of the Secretariat.
3. The paramount consideration in the employment of the staff and in the determination of the conditions of service shall be the necessity of securing the highest standards of efficiency, competence, and integrity. Due regard shall be paid to the importance of recruiting the staff on as wide a geographical basis as possible.

CHAPTER XVI

MISCELLANEOUS PROVISIONS

Article 102

1. Every treaty and every international agreement entered into by any Member of the United Nations after the present Charter comes into force shall as soon as possible be registered with the Secretariat and published by it.
2. No party to any such treaty or international agreement which has not been registered in accordance with the provisions of paragraph 1 of this Article may invoke that treaty or agreement before any organ of the United Nations.

Article 103

In the event of a conflict between the obligations of the Members of the United Nations under the present Charter and their obligations under any other international agreement, their obligations under the present Charter shall prevail.

Article 104

The Organization shall enjoy in the territory of each of its Members such legal capacity as may be necessary for the exercise of its functions and the fulfilment of its purposes.

Article 105

1. The Organization shall enjoy in the territory of each of its Members such privileges and immunities as are necessary for the fulfilment of its purposes.
2. Representatives of the Members of the United Nations and officials of the Organiza-

tion shall enjoy such privileges and immunities as are necessary for the independent exercise of their functions in connexion with the Organization.

3. The General Assembly may make recommendations with a view to determining the details of the application of paragraphs 1 and 2 of this Article or may propose conventions to the Members of the United Nations for this purpose.

CHAPTER XVII

TRANSITIONAL SECURITY ARRANGEMENT

Article 106

Pending the coming into force of such special agreements referred to in Article 43 as in the opinion of the Security Council enable it to begin the exercise of its responsibilities under Article 42, the parties to the Four-Nation Declaration, signed at Moscow, 30 October 1943, and France, shall, in accordance with the provisions of paragraph 5 of that Declaration, consult with other Members of the United Nations with a view to such joint action on behalf of the Organization as may be necessary for the purpose of maintaining international peace and security.

Article 107

Nothing in the present Charter shall invalidate or preclude action, in relation to any state which during the Second World War has been an enemy or any signatory to the present Charter, taken or authorized as a result of that war by the Governments having responsibility for such action.

CHAPTER XVIII

AMENDMENTS

Article 108

Amendments to the present Charter shall come into force for all Members of the Unit-

ed Nations when they have been adopted by a vote of two-thirds of the members of the General Assembly and ratified in accordance with their respective constitutional processes by two-thirds of the Members of the United Nations, including all the permanent members of the Security Council.

Article 109

1. A General Conference of the Members of the United Nations for the purpose of reviewing the present Charter may be held at a date and place to be fixed by a two-thirds vote of the members of the General Assembly and by a vote of any nine members of the Security Council. Each Member of the United Nations shall have one vote in the conference.

2. Any alteration of the present Charter recommended by a two-thirds vote of the conference shall take effect when ratified in accordance with their respective constitutional processes by two-thirds of the Members of the United Nations including all the permanent members of the Security Council.

3. If such a conference has not been held before the tenth annual session of the General Assembly following the coming into force of the present Charter, the proposal to call such a conference shall be placed on the agenda of that session of the General Assembly, and the conference shall be held if so decided by a majority vote of the members of the General Assembly and by a vote of any seven members of the Security Council.

CHAPTER XIX

RATIFICATION AND SIGNATURE

Article 110

1. The present Charter shall be ratified by the signatory states in accordance with their respective constitutional processes.

2. The ratifications shall be deposited with the Government of the United States of

America, which shall notify all the signatory states of each deposit as well as the Secretary-General of the Organization when he has been appointed.

3. The present Charter shall come into force upon the deposit of ratifications by the Republic of China, France, the Union of Soviet Socialist Republics, the United Kingdom of Great Britain and Northern Ireland, and the United States of America, and by a majority of the other signatory states. A protocol of the ratifications deposited shall thereupon be drawn up by the Government of the United States of America which shall communicate copies thereof to all the signatory states.

4. The states signatory to the present Charter which ratify it after it has come into force will become original Members of the United Nations on the date of the deposit of their respective ratifications.

Article 111

The present Charter, of which the Chinese, French, Russian, English, and Spanish texts are equally authentic, shall remain deposited in the archives of the Government of the United States of America. Duly certified copies thereof shall be transmitted by that Government to the Governments of the other signatory states.

In faith whereof the representatives of the Governments of the United Nations have signed the present Charter.

Done at the City of San Francisco the twenty-sixth day of June, one thousand nine hundred and forty five.

Statute of the International Court of Justice

Article 1

The International Court of Justice established by the Charter of the United Nations as the principal judicial organ of the United Nations shall be constituted and shall function in accordance with the provisions of the present Statute.

CHAPTER I

ORGANIZATION OF COURT

Article 2

The Court shall be composed of a body of independent judges, elected regardless of their nationality from among persons of high moral character, who possess the qualifications required in their respective countries for appointment to the highest judicial offices, or are jurisconsults of recognized competence in international law.

Article 3

1. The Court shall consist of fifteen members, no two of whom may be nationals of the same state.

2. A person who for the purposes of membership in the Court could be regarded as a national of more than one state shall be deemed to be a national of the one in which he ordinarily exercises civil and political rights.

Article 4

1. The members of the Court shall be elected by the General Assembly and by the Security Council from a list of persons nominated by the national groups in the Permanent Court of Arbitration, in accordance with the following provisions.

2. In the case of Members of the United Nations not represented in the Permanent Court of Arbitration, candidates shall be nominated by national groups appointed for this purpose by their governments under the same conditions as those prescribed for members of the Permanent Court of Arbitration by Article 44 of the Convention of The Hague of 1907 for the pacific settlement of international disputes.

3. The conditions under which a state which is a party to the present Statute but is not a Member of the United Nations may participate in electing the members of the Court shall, in the absence of a special agreement, be laid down by the General Assembly upon recommendation of the Security Council.

Article 5

1. At least three months before the date of the election, the Secretary-General of the United Nations shall address a written request to the members of the Permanent Court of Arbitration belonging to the states which are parties to the present Statute, and to the members of the national groups appointed under Article 4, paragraph 2, inviting them to undertake, within a given time, by national groups, the nomination of persons in a position to accept the duties of a member of the Court.

2. No group may nominate more than four persons, not more than two of whom shall be of their own nationality. In no case may the number of candidates nominated by a group be more than double the number of seats to be filled.

Article 6

Before making these nominations, each national group is recommended to consult its highest court of justice, its legal faculties and schools of law, and its national academies and national sections of international academies devoted to the study of law.

Article 7

1. The Secretary-General shall prepare a list in alphabetical order of all the persons thus nominated. Save as provided in Article 12, paragraph 2, these shall be the only persons eligible.

2. The Secretary-General shall submit this list to the General Assembly and to the Security Council.

Article 8

The General Assembly and the Security Council shall proceed independently of one another to elect the members of the Court.

Article 9

At every election, the electors shall bear in mind not only that the persons to be elected should individually possess the qualifications required, but also that in the body as a whole the representation of the main forms of civilization and of the principal legal systems of the world should be assured.

Article 10

1. Those candidates who obtain an absolute majority of votes in the General Assembly and in the Security Council shall be considered as elected.

2. Any vote of the Security Council, whether for the election of judges or for the appointment of members of the conference envisaged in Article 12, shall be taken without any distinction between permanent and nonpermanent members of the Security Council.

3. In the event of more than one national of the same state obtaining an absolute majority of the votes both of the General Assembly and of the Security Council, the eldest of these only shall be considered as elected.

Article 11

If, after the first meeting held for the purpose of election, one or more seats remain to be filled, a second and, if necessary, a third meeting shall take place.

Article 12

1. If, after the third meeting, one or more seats still remain unfilled, a joint conference consisting of six members, three appointed by the General Assembly and three by the Security Council, may be formed at any time at the request of either the General Assembly or the Security Council, for the purpose of choosing by the vote of an absolute majority one name for each seat still vacant, to submit to the General Assembly and the Security Council for their respective acceptance.

2. If the joint conference is unanimously agreed upon any person who fulfils the required conditions, he may be included in its list, even though he was not included in the list of nominations referred to in Article 7.

3. If the joint conference is satisfied that it will not be successful in procuring an election, those members of the Court who have already been elected shall, within a period to be fixed by the Security Council, proceed to fill the vacant seats by selection from among those candidates who have obtained votes

either in the General Assembly or in the Security Council.

4. In the event of an equality of votes among the judges, the eldest judge shall have a casting vote.

Article 13

1. The members of the Court shall be elected for nine years and may be re-elected; provided, however, that of the judges elected at the first election, the terms of five judges shall expire at the end of three years and the terms of five more judges shall expire at the end of six years.

2. The judges whose terms are to expire at the end of the above-mentioned initial periods of three and six years shall be chosen by lot to be drawn by the Secretary-General immediately after the first election has been completed.

3. The members of the Court shall continue to discharge their duties until their places have been filled. Though replaced, they shall finish any cases which they may have begun.

4. In the case of the resignation of a member of the Court, the resignation shall be addressed to the President of the Court for transmission to the Secretary-General. This last notification makes the place vacant.

Article 14

Vacancies shall be filled by the same method as that laid down for the first election, subject to the following provision: the Secretary-General shall within one month of the occurrence of the vacancy, proceed to issue the invitations provided for in Article 5, and the date of the election shall be fixed by the Security Council.

Article 15

A member of the Court elected to replace a member whose term of office has not expired shall hold office for the remainder of his predecessor's term.

Article 16

1. No member of the Court may exercise any political or administrative function, or engage in any other occupation of a professional nature.

2. Any doubt on this point shall be settled by the decision of the Court.

Article 17

1. No member of the Court may act as an agent, counsel, or advocate in any case.

2. No member may participate in the decision of any case in which he has previously taken part as agent, counsel, or advocate for one of the parties, or as a member of a national or international court, or of a commission of enquiry, or in any other capacity.

3. Any doubt on this point shall be settled by the decision of the Court.

Article 18

1. No member of the Court can be dismissed unless, in the unanimous opinion of the other members, he has ceased to fulfil the required conditions.

2. Formal notification thereof shall be made to the Secretary-General by the Registrar.

3. This notification makes the place vacant.

Article 19

The members of the Court, when engaged on the business of the Court, shall enjoy diplomatic privileges and immunities.

Article 20

Every member of the Court shall, before taking up his duties, make a solemn declaration in open court that he will exercise his powers impartially and conscientiously.

Article 21

1. The Court shall elect its President and Vice-President for three years; they may be re-elected.

2. The Court shall appoint its Registrar and may provide for the appointment of such other of?cers as may be necessary.

Article 22

1. The seat of the Court shall be established at The Hague. This, however, shall not prevent the Court from sitting and exercising its functions elsewhere whenever the Court considers it desirable.

2. The President and the Registrar shall reside at the seat of the Court.

Article 23

1. The Court shall remain permanently in session, except during the judicial vacations, the dates and duration of which shall be fixed by the Court.

2. Members of the Court are entitled to periodic leave, the dates and duration of which shall be fixed by the Court, having in mind the distance between The Hague and the home of each judge.

3. Members of the Court shall be bound, unless they are on leave or prevented from attending by illness or other serious reasons duly explained to the President, to hold themselves permanently at the disposal of the Court.

Article 24

1. If, for some special reason a member of the Court considers that he should not take part in the decision of a particular case, he shall so inform the President.

2. If the President considers that for some special reason one of the members of the Court should not sit in a particular case, he shall give him notice accordingly.

3. If in any such case the member of the Court and the President disagree, the matter shall be settled by the decision of the Court.

Article 25

1. The full Court shall sit except when it is expressly provided otherwise in the present Statute.

2. Subject to the condition that the number of judges available to constitute the Court is not thereby reduced below eleven, the Rules of the Court may provide for allowing one or more judges, according to circumstances and in rotation, to be dispensed from sitting.

3. A quorum of nine judges shall suffice to constitute the Court.

Article 26

1. The Court may from time to time form one or more chambers, composed of three or more judges as the Court may determine, for dealing with particular categories of cases; for example, labor cases and cases relating to transit and communications.

2. The Court may at any time form a chamber for dealing with a particular case. The number of judges to constitute such a chamber shall be determined by the Court with the approval of the parties.

3. Cases shall be heard and determined by the chambers provided for in this article if the parties so request.

Article 27

A judgement given by any of the chambers provided for in Articles 26 and 29 shall be considered as rendered by the Court.

Article 28

The chambers provided for in Articles 26 and 29 may, with the consent of the parties, sit and exercise their functions elsewhere than at The Hague.

Article 29

With a view to the speedy dispatch of business, the Court shall form annually a chamber composed of five judges which, at the request of the parties, may hear and determine cases by summary procedure. In addition, two judges shall be selected for the purpose of replacing judges who find it impossible to sit.

Article 30

1. The Court shall frame rules for carrying out its functions. In particular, it shall lay down rules of procedure.
2. The Rules of the Court may provide for assessors to sit with the Court or with any of its chambers, without the right to vote.

Article 31

1. Judges of the nationality of each of the parties shall retain their right to sit in the case before the Court.
2. If the Court includes upon the Bench a judge of the nationality of one of the parties, any other party may choose a person to sit as judge. Such person shall be chosen preferably from among those persons who have been nominated as candidates as provided in Articles 4 and 5.
3. If the Court includes upon the Bench no judge of the nationality of the parties, each of these parties may proceed to choose a judge as provided in paragraph 2 of this Article.
4. The provisions of this Article shall apply to the case of Articles 26 and 29. In such cases, the President shall request one or, if necessary, two of the members of the Court forming the chamber to give place to the members of the Court of the nationality of the parties concerned, and, failing such, or if they are unable to be present, to the judges specially chosen by the parties.
5. Should there be several parties in the same interest, they shall, for the purpose of the preceding provisions, be reckoned as one party only. Any doubt upon this point shall be settled by the decision of the Court.
6. Judges chosen as laid down in paragraphs 2, 3, and 4 of this Article shall fulfil the conditions required by Articles 2, 17 (paragraph 2), 20 and 24 of the present Statute. They shall take part in the decision on terms of complete equality with their colleagues.

Article 32

1. Each member of the Court shall receive an annual salary.
2. The President shall receive a special annual allowance.
3. The Vice-President shall receive a special allowance for every day on which he acts as President.
4. The judges chosen under Article 31, other than members of the Court, shall receive compensation for each day on which they exercise their functions.
5. These salaries, allowances, and compensation shall be fixed by the General Assembly. They may not be decreased during the term of office.

6. The salary of the Registrar shall be fixed by the General Assembly on the proposal of the Court.
7. Regulations made by the General Assembly shall fix the conditions under which retirement pensions may be given to members of the Court and to the Registrar, and the conditions under which members of the Court and the Registrar shall have their travelling expenses refunded.
8. The above salaries, allowances, and compensation shall be free of all taxation.

Article 33

The expenses of the Court shall be borne by the United Nations in such a manner as shall be decided by the General Assembly.

CHAPTER II

COMPETENCE OF THE COURT

Article 34

1. Only states may be parties in cases before the Court.
2. The Court, subject to and in conformity with its Rules, may request of public international organizations information relevant to cases before it, and shall receive such information presented by such organizations on their own initiative.
3. Whenever the construction of the constituent instrument of a public international organization or of an international convention adopted thereunder is in question in a case before the Court, the Registrar shall so notify the public international organization concerned and shall communicate to it copies of all the written proceedings.

Article 35

1. The Court shall be open to the states parties to the present Statute.
2. The conditions under which the Court shall be open to other states shall, subject to the special provisions contained in treaties in force, be laid down by the Security Council, but in no case shall such conditions place the parties in a position of inequality before the Court.
3. When a state which is not a Member of the United Nations is a party to a case, the Court shall fix the amount which that party is to contribute towards the expenses of the Court. This provision shall not apply if such a state is bearing a share of the expenses of the Court.

Article 36

1. The jurisdiction of the Court comprises all cases which the parties refer to it and all matters specially provided for in the Charter of the United Nations or in treaties and conventions in force.
2. The states parties to the present Statute may at any time declare that they recognize as compulsory ipso facto and without special agreement, in relation to any other state accepting the same obligation, the jurisdiction of the Court in all legal disputes concerning:
a. the interpretation of a treaty; b. any question of international law; c. the existence of any fact which, if established, would constitute a breach of an international obligation; d. the nature or extent of the reparation to be made for the breach of an international obligation;
3. The declaration referred to above may be made unconditionally or on condition of reciprocity on the part of several or certain states, or for a certain time.
4. Such declarations shall be deposited with the Secretary-General of the United Nations, who shall transmit copies thereof to the parties to the Statute and to the Registrar of the Court.
5. Declarations made under Article 36 of the Statute of the Permanent Court of International Justice and which are still in force shall be deemed, as between the parties to the present Statute, to be acceptances of the compulsory jurisdiction of the International Court of Justice for the period which they still have to run and in accordance with their terms.
6. In the event of a dispute as to whether the Court has jurisdiction, the matter shall be settled by the decision of the Court.

Article 37

Whenever a treaty or convention in force provides for reference of a matter to a tribunal to have been instituted by the League of Nations, or to the Permanent Court of International Justice, the matter shall, as between the parties to the present Statute, be referred to the International Court of Justice.

Article 38

1. The Court, whose function is to decide in accordance with international law such disputes as are submitted to it, shall apply:
a. international conventions, whether general or particular, establishing rules expressly recognized by the contesting states; b. international custom, as evidence of a general practice accepted as law; c. the general prin-

ciples of law recognized by civilized nations;
d. subject to the provisions of Article 59, judicial decisions and the teachings of the most highly qualified publicists of the various nations, as subsidiary means for the determination of rules of law.
2. This provision shall not prejudice the power of the Court to decide a case ex aequo et bono, if the parties agree thereto.

CHAPTER III

PROCEDURE

Article 39

1. The official languages of the Court shall be French and English. If the parties agree that the case shall be conducted in French, the judgment shall be delivered in French. If the parties agree that the case shall be conducted in English, the judgement shall be delivered in English.
2. In the absence of an agreement as to which language shall be employed, each party may, in the pleadings, use the language which it prefers; the decision of the Court shall be given in French and English. In this case the Court shall at the same time determine which of the two texts shall be considered as authoritative.
3. The Court shall, at the request of any party, authorize a language other than French or English to be used by that party.

Article 40

1. Cases are brought before the Court, as the case may be, either by the notification of the special agreement or by a written application addressed to the Registrar. In either case the subject of the dispute and the parties shall be indicated.
2. The Registrar shall forthwith communicate the application to all concerned.
3. He shall also notify the Members of the United Nations through the Secretary-General, and also any other states entitled to appear before the Court.

Article 41

1. The Court shall have the power to indicate, if it considers that circumstances so require, any provisional measures which ought to be taken to preserve the respective rights of either party.
2. Pending the final decision, notice of the measures suggested shall forthwith be given to the parties and to the Security Council.

Article 42

1. The parties shall be represented by agents.
2. They may have the assistance of counsel or advocates before the Court.
3. The agents, counsel, and advocates of parties before the Court shall enjoy the privileges and immunities necessary to the independent exercise of their duties.

Article 43

1. The procedure shall consist of two parts: written and oral.
2. The written proceedings shall consist of the communication to the Court and to the parties of memorials, counter-memorials and, if necessary, replies; also all papers and documents in support.
3. These communications shall be made through the Registrar, in the order and within the time fixed by the Court.
4. A certified copy of every document produced by one party shall be communicated to the other party.
5. The oral proceedings shall consist of the hearing by the Court of witnesses, experts, agents, counsel, and advocates.

Article 44

1. For the service of all notices upon persons other than the agents, counsel, and advocates, the Court shall apply direct to the government of the state upon whose territory the notice has to be served.
2. The same provision shall apply whenever steps are to be taken to procure evidence on the spot.

Article 45

The hearing shall be under the control of the President or, if he is unable to preside, of the Vice-President; if neither is able to preside, the senior judge present shall preside.

Article 46

The hearing in the Court shall be public, unless the Court shall decide otherwise, or unless the parties demand that the public be not admitted.

Article 47

1. Minutes shall be made at each hearing and signed by the Registrar and the President.
2. These minutes alone shall be authentic.

Article 48

The Court shall make orders for the conduct of the case, shall decide the form and time in which each party must conclude its arguments, and make all arrangements connected with the taking of evidence.

Article 49

The Court may, even before the hearing begins, call upon the agents to produce any document or to supply any explanations. Formal note shall be taken of any refusal.

Article 50

The Court may, at any time, entrust any individual, body, bureau, commission, or other organization that it may select, with the task of carrying out an enquiry or giving an expert opinion.

Article 51

During the hearing any relevant questions are to be put to the witnesses and experts under the conditions laid down by the Court in the rules of procedure referred to in Article 30.

Article 52

After the Court has received the proofs and evidence within the time specified for the purpose, it may refuse to accept any further oral or written evidence that one party may desire to present unless the other side consents.

Article 53

1. Whenever one of the parties does not appear before the Court, or fails to defend its case, the other party may call upon the Court to decide in favour of its claim.
2. The Court must, before doing so, satisfy itself, not only that it has jurisdiction in accordance with Articles 36 and 37, but also that the claim is well founded in fact and law.

Article 54

1. When, subject to the control of the Court, the agents, counsel, and advocates have completed their presentation of the case, the President shall declare the hearing closed.
2. The Court shall withdraw to consider the judgement.
3. The deliberations of the Court shall take place in private and remain secret.

Article 55

1. All questions shall be decided by a majority of the judges present.
2. In the event of an equality of votes, the President or the judge who acts in his place shall have a casting vote.

Article 56

1. The judgment shall state the reasons on which it is based.
2. It shall contain the names of the judges who have taken part in the decision.

Article 57

If the judgment does not represent in whole or in part the unanimous opinion of the judges, any judge shall be entitled to deliver a separate opinion.

Article 58

The judgement shall be signed by the President and by the Registrar. It shall be read in open court, due notice having been given to the agents.

Article 59

The decision of the Court has no binding except between the parties and in respect of that particular case.

Article 60

The judgement is final and without appeal. In the event of dispute as to the meaning or scope of the judgement, the Court shall construe it upon request of any party.

Article 61

1. An application for revision of a judgement may be made only when it is based upon the discovery of some fact of such a nature as to be a decisive factor, which fact was, when the judgement was given, unknown to the Court and also to the party claiming revision, always provided that such ignorance was not due to negligence.
2. The proceedings for revision shall be opened by a judgement of the Court expressly recording the existence of the new fact, recognizing that it has such a character as to lay the case open to revision, and declaring the application admissible on this ground.
3. The Court may require previous compliance with the terms of the judgement before it admits proceedings in revision.
4. The application for revision must be made at latest within six months of the discovery of the new fact.
5. No application for revision may be made after the lapse of ten years from the date of the judgement.

Article 62

1. Should a state consider that it has an interest of a legal nature which may be affected by the decision in the case, it may submit a request to the Court to be permitted to intervene.
2. It shall be for the Court to decide upon this request.

Article 63

1. Whenever the construction of a convention to which states other than those concerned in the case are parties is in question, the Registrar shall notify all such states forthwith.
2. Every state so notified has the right to intervene in the proceedings; but if it uses this right, the construction given by the judgement will be equally binding upon it.

Article 64

Unless otherwise decided by the Court, each party shall bear its own costs.

CHAPTER IV

ADVISORY OPINIONS

Article 65

1. The Court may give an advisory opinion on any legal question at the request of whatever body may be authorized by or in accordance with the Charter of the United Nations to make such a request.
2. Questions upon which the advisory opinion of the Court is asked shall be laid before the Court by means of a written request containing an exact statement of the question upon which an opinion is required, and accompanied by all documents likely to throw light upon the question.

Article 66

1. The Registrar shall forthwith give notice of the request for an advisory opinion to all states entitled to appear before the Court.
2. The Registrar shall also, by means of a special and direct communication, notify any state entitled to appear before the Court or international organization considered by the Court, or, should it not be sitting, by the President, as likely to be able to furnish information on the question, that the Court will be prepared to receive, within a time limit to be ?xed by the President, written statements, or to hear, at a public sitting to be held for the purpose, oral statements relating to the question.
3. Should any such state entitled to appear before the Court have failed to receive the special communication referred to in paragraph 2 of the Article, such state may express a desire to submit a written statement or to be heard; and the Court will decide.
4. States and organizations having presented written or oral statements or both shall be permitted to comment on the statements made by other states or organizations in the form, to the extent, and within the time limits which the Court, or, should it not be sitting, the President, shall decide in each particular case. Accordingly, the registrar shall in due time communicate any such written statements to states or organizations having submitted similar statements.

Article 67

The Court shall deliver its advisory opinions in open court, notice having been given to the Secretary-General and to the representatives of Members of the United Nations, of other states and of international organizations immediately concerned.

Article 68

In the exercise of its advisory functions the Court shall further be guided by the provisions of the present Statute which apply in contentious cases to the extent to which it recognizes them to be applicable.

CHAPTER V

AMENDMENT

Article 69

Amendments to the present Statute shall be effected by the same procedure as is provided by the Charter of the United Nations for amendments to that Charter, subject however to any provisions which the General Assembly upon recommendation of the Security Council may adopt concerning the participation of states which are parties to the present Statute but are not Members of the United Nations.

Article 70

The Court shall have the power to propose such amendments to the present Statute as it may deem necessary, through written communications to the Secretary-General, for consideration in conformity with the provisions of Article 69.

Universal Declaration of Human Rights

PREAMBLE

Whereas recognition of the inherent dignity and of the equal and inalienable rights of all members of the human family is the foundation of freedom, justice and peace in the world,

Whereas disregard and contempt for human rights have resulted in barbarous acts which have outraged the conscience of mankind, and the advent of a world in which human beings shall enjoy freedom of speech and belief and freedom from fear and want has been proclaimed as the highest aspiration of the common people,

Whereas it is essential, if man is not to be compelled to have recourse, as a last resort, to rebellion against tyranny and oppression, that human rights should be protected by the rule of law,

Whereas it is essential to promote the development of friendly relations between nations,

Whereas the peoples of the United Nations have in the Charter reaffirmed their faith in fundamental human rights, in the dignity and worth of the human person and in the equal rights of men and women and have determined to promote social progress and better standards of life in larger freedom,

Whereas Member States have pledged themselves to achieve, in cooperation with the United Nations, the promotion of universal respect for and observance of human rights and fundamental freedoms,

Whereas a common understanding of these rights and freedoms is of the greatest importance for the full realization of this pledge,

Now, therefore, The General Assembly proclaims

This Universal Declaration of Human Rights as a common standard of achievement for all peoples and all nations, to the end that every individual and every organ of society, keeping this Declaration constantly in mind, shall strive by teaching and education to promote respect for these rights and freedoms and by progressive measures, national and international, to secure their universal and effective recognition and observance, both among the peoples of Member States them-selves and among the peoples of territories under their jurisdiction.

Article 1

All human beings are born free and equal in dignity and rights. They are endowed with reason and conscience and should act towards one another in a spirit of brotherhood.

Article 2

Everyone is entitled to all the rights and freedoms set forth in this Declaration, without distinction of any kind, such as race, colour, sex, language, religion, political or other opinion, national or social origin, property, birth or other status.

Furthermore, no distinction shall be made on the basis of the political, jurisdictional or international status of the country or territory to which a person belongs, whether it be independent, trust, non-self-governing or under any other limitation of sovereignty.

Article 3

Everyone has the right to life, liberty and security of person.

Article 4

No one shall be held in slavery or servitude; slavery and the slave trade shall be prohibited in all their forms.

Article 5

No one shall be subjected to torture or to cruel, inhuman or degrading treatment or punishment.

Article 6

Everyone has the right to recognition every-where as a person before the law.

Article 7

All are equal before the law and are entitled without any discrimination to equal protection of the law. All are entitled to equal protection against any discrimination in violation of this Declaration and against any incitement to such discrimination.

Article 8

Everyone has the right to an effective remedy by the competent national tribunals for acts violating the fundamental rights granted him by the constitution or by law.

Article 9

No one shall be subjected to arbitrary arrest, detention or exile.

Article 10

Everyone is entitled in full equality to a fair and public hearing by an independent and impartial tribunal, in the determination of his rights and obligations and of any criminal charge against him.

Article 11

(1) Everyone charged with a penal offence has the right to be presumed innocent until proved guilty according to law in a public trial at which he has had all the guarantees necessary for his defence.

(2) No one shall be held guilty of any penal offence on account of any act or omission which did not constitute a penal offence, under national or international law, at the time when it was committed. Nor shall a heavier penalty be imposed than the one that was applicable at the time the penal offence was committed.

Article 12

No one shall be subjected to arbitrary interference with his privacy, family, home or correspondence, nor to attacks upon his honour and reputation. Everyone has the right to the protection of the law against such interference or attacks.

Article 13

(1) Everyone has the right to freedom of movement and residence within the borders of each State.

(2) Everyone has the right to leave any country, including his own, and to return to his country.

Article 14

(1) Everyone has the right to seek and to enjoy in other countries asylum from persecution.

(2) This right may not be invoked in the case of prosecutions genuinely arising from non-political crimes or from acts contrary to the

purposes and principles of the United Nations.

Article 15

(1) Everyone has the right to a nationality.
(2) No one shall be arbitrarily deprived of his nationality nor denied the right to change his nationality.

Article 16

(1) Men and women of full age, without any limitation due to race, nationality or religion, have the right to marry and to found a family. They are entitled to equal rights as to marriage, during marriage and at its dissolution.
(2) Marriage shall be entered into only with the free and full consent of the intending spouses.
(3) The family is the natural and fundamental group unit of society and is entitled to protection by society and the State.

Article 17

(1) Everyone has the right to own property alone as well as in association with others.
(2) No one shall be arbitrarily deprived of his property.

Article 18

Everyone has the right to freedom of thought, conscience and religion; this right includes freedom to change his religion or belief, and freedom, either alone or in community with others and in public or private, to manifest his religion or belief in teaching, practice, worship and observance.

Article 19

Everyone has the right to freedom of opinion and expression; this right includes freedom to hold opinions without interference and to seek, receive and impart information and ideas through any media and regardless of frontiers.

Article 20

(1) Everyone has the right to freedom of peaceful assembly and association.
(2) No one may be compelled to belong to an association.

Article 21

(1) Everyone has the right to take part in the government of his country, directly or through freely chosen representatives.
(2) Everyone has the right to equal access to public service in his country.
(3) The will of the people shall be the basis of the authority of government; this will shall be expressed in periodic and genuine elections which shall be by universal and equal suffrage and shall be held by secret vote or by equivalent free voting procedures.

Article 22

Everyone, as a member of society, has the right to social security and is entitled to realization, through national effort and international co-operation and in accordance with the organization and resources of each State, of the economic, social and cultural rights indispensable for his dignity and the free development of his personality.

Article 23

(1) Everyone has the right to work, to free choice of employment, to just and favourable conditions of work and to protection against unemployment.
(2) Everyone, without any discrimination, has the right to equal pay for equal work.
(3) Everyone who works has the right to just and favourable remuneration ensuring for himself and his family an existence worthy of human dignity, and supplemented, if necessary, by other means of social protection.
(4) Everyone has the right to form and to join trade unions for the protection of his interests.

Article 24

Everyone has the right to rest and leisure, including reasonable limitation of working hours and periodic holidays with pay.

Article 25

(1) Everyone has the right to a standard of living adequate for the health and well-being of himself and of his family, including food, clothing, housing and medical care and necessary social services, and the right to security in the event of unemployment, sickness, disability, widowhood, old age or other lack of livelihood in circumstances beyond his control.
(2) Motherhood and childhood are entitled to special care and assistance. All children, whether born in or out of wedlock, shall enjoy the same social protection.

Article 26

(1) Everyone has the right to education. Education shall be free, at least in the elementary and fundamental stages. Elementary education shall be compulsory. Technical and professional education shall be made generally available and higher education shall be equally accessible to all on the basis of merit.
(2) Education shall be directed to the full development of the human personality and to the strengthening of respect for human rights and fundamental freedoms. It shall promote understanding, tolerance and friendship among all nations, racial or religious groups, and shall further the activities of the United Nations for the maintenance of peace.
(3) Parents have a prior right to choose the kind of education that shall be given to their children.

Article 27

(1) Everyone has the right freely to participate in the cultural life of the community, to enjoy the arts and to share in scientific advancement and its benefits.
(2) Everyone has the right to the protection of the moral and material interests resulting from any scientific, literary or artistic production of which he is the author.

Article 28

Everyone is entitled to a social and international order in which the rights and freedoms set forth in this Declaration can be fully realized.

Article 29

(1) Everyone has duties to the community in which alone the free and full development of his personality is possible.
(2) In the exercise of his rights and freedoms, everyone shall be subject only to such limitations as are determined by law solely for the purpose of securing due recognition and respect for the rights and freedoms of others and of meeting the just requirements of morality, public order and the general welfare in a democratic society.
(3) These rights and freedoms may in no case be exercised contrary to the purposes and principles of the United Nations.

Article 30

Nothing in this Declaration may be interpreted as implying for any State, group or person any right to engage in any activity or to perform any act aimed at the destruction of any of the rights and freedoms set forth herein.

G.A. res. 217A (III), U.N. Doc A/810 at 71 (1948) Adopted on December 10, 1948 by the General Assembly of the United Nations (without dissent)

REGIONS

AFRICA

Adamolekun, Ladipo. ed. *Public Administration in Africa: Main Issues and Selected Country Studies* (Boulder, CO: Westview Press, 1999), 440pp. Addresses the main topics in the discipline, including governance context and reorientation of government, decentralization and intergovernmental relations, public financial management, human resources management, and accountability and transparency.

Frankel, Philip. *Soldiers in a Storm* (Boulder, CO: Westview Press, 2000), 336pp. A study of the role of the military in the creation and development of South Africa's new post-apartheid system. Frankel also examines military disengagement, post-authoritarian political behavior on the part of militaries, and the process of democratic consolidation.

Herbst, Jeffrey. *States and Power in Africa* (Princeton, NJ: Princeton University Press, 2000), 248 pp. An overview of the African state-building process dating from the pre-colonial period through modern times. Herbst presents the fundamental problem of contemporary African leadership, namely how to extend authority over sparsely settled lands. By analyzing the decisions and strategies of African leaders, Herbst also evaluates policy alternatives for dealing with current political challenges.

James, Valentine U. *Environmental and Economic Dilemmas of Developing Countries: Africa in the 21st Century* (Westport, CT: Praeger, 1994), 240pp. An environmental impact assessment of aid assisted projects in Africa, with special regard to the conflicting choice between environmental quality and the issue of development versus human welfare in Africa. Political instability and declining nationalism are also covered. This highly informative book includes case studies that focus on sub-Saharan Africa, especially Nigeria and Ghana.

Nhema, Alfred G. *Democracy in Zimbabwe From Liberation to Liberalization* (Zimbabwe: Univ. of Zimbabwe Publishing, 2002), 214pp. This book examines the dialectics of political liberalization in Zimbabwe, over time, from the settler period to the late nineties. The study takes in theoretical parameters for political and economic concepts and assumptions; and provides a historical overview of settler rule, civil society reactions, and political developments 1945-1979.

THE AMERICAS

Boron, Atilio. *State, Capitalism, and Democracy in Latin America* (Boulder, CO: Lynne Rienner Publishers, Inc., 1995), 251pp. Addresses the main theme of the possibilities and limits of democratic capitalism in Latin America.

Brockett, Charles D. *Land, Peace, and Poverty: Agrarian Transformation and Political Conflict in Central America* (Boulder, CO: Westview Press, 1998), 288pp. Explores the development of the rigid and unequal structures of rural Central American society, the challenge in recent decades to those structures by a restive peasantry, and the role in these conflicts of five governments of the region—Guatemala, Costa Rica, Honduras, El Salvador, and Nicaragua.

Bryan, Anthony T., ed. *The Caribbean: New Dynamics in Trade and Political Economy* (Miami, FL: University of Miami, 1995), 250pp. Caribbean scholars and policy experts analyze the implications for the Caribbean of a world in transition. Effects of external debt and structural adjustment are reviewed. Also highlighted are intra-Caribbean relations and integration projects for the future of hemispheric cooperation.

Farer, Tom, ed. *Beyond Sovereignty: Collectively Defending Democracy in the Americas* (Baltimore, MD: The Johns Hopkins University Press, 1996). 399pp. A mix of country case studies and detailed analyses of crosscutting issues that together review the legal justifications for international action to defend democracy and human rights, analyze the effectiveness of alternative approaches, and assess their significance as precedents for future initiatives.

Garreton, Manuel Antonio M. and Newman, Edward, ed. *Democracy in Latin America: (Re)Constructing Political Society* (New York, NY: United Nations Publications, 2002), 360pp. *Democracy in Latin America* examines democratic transition and consolidation in post-authoritarian and post-civil war Latin America. A range of issues are embraced: dealing with past abuses of human rights by balancing justice and reconciliation; integrating societies into global market economics, with the accompanying social and political impact this has brought; the manner in which external actors—such as the United Nations, international financial institutions, and multinational corporations—have conditioned or facilitated democracy; the role of civil society; the problems of achieving a sense of citizenship in many communities; the perennial indigenous issue; and the pervading gap between the procedure and the substance of democracy.

Glade, William and Rossana Corona, Eds. *Bigger Economies, Smaller Governments* (Boulder, CO: Westview Press Inc., 1996), 395pp. Written after the launch of Latin America's privatization programs, this book answers the questions about what has been achieved for the financial health of government, the efficiency of enterprises and the economies, for capital formation, and for social welfare.

Hausmann, Ricardo and Liliana Rojas-Suarez, eds. *Banking Crises in Latin America* (Washington, D.C: Inter-American Development Bank, 1996), 267pp. Banking crises last longer, affect a larger segment of the industry, and cost the public more in Latin America. In this book, policymakers, academicians, and bankers analyze the main causes of such crises, how governments can manage them more effectively, and how they can be prevented.

Mainwaring, Scott and Timothy R. Scully, eds. *Building Democratic Institutions: Party Systems in Latin America* (Stanford, CA: Stanford University Press, 1995), 474pp.

Highlights the rich variety of parties and party systems in the Latin American region and explores the consequences of the differences. Also questions stereotypes involving the perceptions of the various parties.

Teichman, Judith A. *The Politics of Freeing Markets in Latin America: Chile, Argentina and Mexico* (Chapel Hill, NC: University of North Carolina Press, 2001), 288 pp. Discusses the extent and impact of domestic and international influences on the two-decade long process of market reform in Latin America. Also examines the relationship between democratization and market liberalization in Chile, Argentina and Mexico through the lenses of the World Bank and the International Monetary Fund.

Wiarda, Howard J. and Kline, Harvey F. *Latin American Politics and Development* (Boulder, CO: Westview Press, 2000), 592pp. Organized around Latin America's distinct background and position in world politics and the world economy. Patterns of political development, the dynamics of political behavior, institutions and public policy, and the constant tension between those who favor a political regime in keeping with the authoritarian past, and those who prefer a Latin American version of democracy are also described.

ASIA

Banerjee, Skata. *Warriors in Politics: Hindu Nationalism, Violence, and the Shiv Sena in India* (Boulder, CO: Westview Press, 1999), 204pp. While the theoretical and empirical research of others is an important part of this study, so too are the interviews conducted by the author when she lived in Mumbai during this tumultuous period. Also discussed are the links among masculinity, militarism, and nationalism, which provide an excellent analysis of the factors—economic, political, and ideological—that converge to transform the simmering discontent of the politics of nationalism into violent conflict.

Chandler, David. *A History of Cambodia,* 3rd ed. (Boulder, Co: Westview Press, 2000) 312pp. This clear and concise volume provides a timely overview of Cambodia, a small but increasingly visible Southeast Asian nation. The third edition of this acclaimed text has been completely revised and updated to include all-new material examining the death of Pol Pot and the collapse of the Khmer Rouge.

Cumings, Bruce. *Korea's Place in the Sun—A Modern History* (New York, London: W. W. Norton & Co., 1997), 386pp. This rich narrative focuses upon Korea's fractured and shattered 20th-century history, as well as its travails and triumphs in the modern period.

Ganguly, Sumit. *The Crisis in Kashmir: Portents of War, Hopes of Peace* (New York: Cambridge University Press, 1997), 182pp. Providing a detailed case study of Kashmiri insurgency, the author also makes recommendations for moving toward resolution of the crisis.

Guldin, Gregory E. *What's A Peasant to Do? Village Becoming Town In Southern China* (Boulder, CO: Westview Press, 2000), 304pp. Looks at the growth of town and village enterprises, labor mobility, and the other aspects of rural urbanization to investigate the connection between economic growth and development in contemporary China.

Hrebenar, Ronald J. *Japan's New Party System,* 3rd Ed. (Boulder, CO: Westview Press, 2000), 288pp. Hrebenar explores the political attitudes, election laws, and role of political money in Japan, historically as well as in context of the post-1993 changes.

Ning, Lu. *The Dynamics of Foreign Policy Decision-making in China* (Boulder, CO: Westview Press, 2000), 240pp. Lu Ning, former assistant to a vice-foreign minister of China, draws on archival materials, interviews, and personal experiences to provide unique insights into the formal and informal structures, processes, mechanisms, and dynamics of—and key players in—foreign-policy decision-making in Beijing.

Rashid, Ahmid. *Taliban: Militant Islam, Oil and Fundamentalism in Central Asia* (New Haven, CT: Yale University Press, 2001), 288 pp. A concise history of how the Taliban came to power in Afghanistan before being crushed under the post-9/11 attacks, and how the Taliban fit into the current state of Muslim extremists and religious fundamentalists in the region.

Rosecrance, Richard. *The Rise of the Virtual State: Wealth and Power in the Coming Century* (Boulder, CO: Westview Press, 2000), 288pp. Explains why Japan's kereitsu system, which brought it industrial dominance, is doomed; why Hong Kong and Taiwan will influence China more than vice-versa; and why the European Union will command

the most international prestige even though the U.S. may produce more wealth.

Sodei, Rinjiro. *Were We the Enemy? Transitions: Asia and Asian America* (Boulder, CO: Westview Press, 2000), 208pp. Drawing on primary sources and rich interview data, Sodei has contributed an original scholarly work to the literature on World War II and the Asian-American experience.

Taylor, John G. *East Timor: The Price of Freedom* (London, England: Zed Books, 2000), 272pp. A detailed description of the aftermath of President Suharto's downfall in the wake of the Asian economic crisis, Taylor documents the history of the East Timorese up to the arrival of U.N. peacekeepers and the struggle of the East Timorese to gain their independence from Indonesia.

Ung, Luong. *First They Killed My Father: A Daughter of Cambodia Remembers* (New York,: Harper Perennial, 2001) 238pp. A detailed reference with excellent additional resources for further research. A first-hand account of growing up under the repressive Khmer Rouge regime in Cambodia. Offers explicit insight into the soul and character of Cambodia's history, genocide, and recovery.

Van Kemenade, Willem. *China, Hong Kong, Taiwan, Inc.: The Dynamics of a New Empire* (New York: Albert A. Knopf Publishing, 1997), 423pp. A groundbreaking study from one of Europe's most knowledgeable and experienced special correspondents in Beijing. The first to give an insider's view that examines the internal dynamics of each part of Greater China and the consequences of impending reunification.

EUROPE

Baranovsky, Vladimir. *Russia and Europe: The Emerging Security Agenda* (Oxford: Oxford University Press, 1997) 560pp. The interaction of Russia with Europe as it is emerging in a post-cold war setting.

Bindi, Federiga M. *The Eurogroups, the European Union and the EU Legislative Process* (Oslo, Norway: Norsk Utenrikspolitisk Institutt, 1996), 75pp. A discussion of the concept of Eurogroups within the European Union.

Clark, Howard. *Civil Resistance in Kosovo* (London, England: Pluto Press, 2000), 268pp. An examination of how the nonviolent struggle by Kosovo Albanians upset the

Serbian government's plans for Kosovo. Clark assesses the achievements and limitations of nonviolence in Kosovo to suggest more effective forms of the policy and also presents lessons to consider in future peace efforts.

Laurenti, Jeffrey, ed. *Searching for Moorings: East Central Europe in the International System* (New York: United Nations Association of the United States, 1994), 133pp. After being under the shadow of the Soviet Union for four decades, the former communist states of Central Europe must find their place in the New World Order.

———. *Russia and Eastern and Central Europe: Old Divisions and New Bridges* (Princeton, NJ: Ethnic Relations, 1996) 46pp. A look at the problems of inter-ethnic relations in Central and Eastern Europe and the former USSR.

McCormick, John. *The European Union: Politics and Policies,* 2nd Ed. (Boulder, CO: Westview Press, 1999), 352pp. This second edition has been completely updated and thoroughly revised to take into account recent developments. It incorporates all the changes coming out of the 1997 Treaty of Amsterdam, the launch of the euro in 1999, and the debate over eastern enlargement, and discusses prospects for the EU in the opening years of the 21st century.

Neumann Iver B., Mark Bassin, and Pavel Baev. *Russia and Europe: Conference Proceedings* (Oslo, Norway: Norsk Utenrikspolitisk Institutt, 1996), 61pp. The reconstruction of Russia's geopolitics after the demise of the Soviet Union and the Cold War.

MIDDLE EAST

Boutros-Ghali, Boutros. *Egypt's Road to Jerusalem: A Diplomat's Story of the Struggle for Peace in the Middle East* (New York: Random House, 1997), 365pp. This book describes an earlier chapter of Boutros-Ghali's life, when he was summoned from academia to accompany President Anwar al-Sadat on his historic trip to Jerusalem in 1977. The book does not attempt to digest, justify, or judge Sadat's or the author's actions but is a chronological account drawn from the daily journal that he kept during the four years that he served in Egypt's Foreign Ministry.

Guyatt, Nicholas. *The Absence of Peace: Understanding the Israeli-Palestinian Conflict* (Zed Books, 1998), 144pp. A well-researched, thoughtful book on the Arab-Israeli conflict, focusing on developments since the 1993 Oslo accords.

Held, Colbert C. *Middle East Patterns: Places, People, and Politics* (Boulder, CO: Westview Press, 2000), 688pp. Examines the Middle East from a topical and then a regional, country-by-country perspective. A thoughtful consideration of the physical environment lays the groundwork for emphasis on cultural-political and geopolitical patterns, which are the essence of the study.

Howe, Martin. *Turkey Today: A Nation Divided Over Islam's Revival* (Boulder, CO: Westview Press, 2000), 328pp. This book is a close-up view of some of the many faces of Islam in Turkey.

Lesch, David W. *The Middle East and the United States: A Historical and Political Reassessment,* 2nd Ed. (Boulder, CO: Westview Press, 1999), 496pp. The second edition has been completely revised and updated, examining encounters from the King-Crance Commission following World War I to the current Israeli-Palestinian negotiations and security questions in the Gulf.

Lewis, Bernard. *The Middle East: A Brief History of the Last 2000 Years* (New York: Touchstone Books, Simon and Schuster, 1997), 433pp. From one of the world's foremost authorities on the Middle East, this sweeping, vivid survey, written in a scholarly yet accessible style, is the most comprehensive single-volume treatment of the region's history that has ever been written.

Lewis, Bernard. *What Went Wrong: Western Impact and Middle Eastern Response* (New York: Oxford University Press, 2002), 192. A survey of how Islamic civilization spiraled from worldwide leadership in almost every frontier of human knowledge five or six centuries ago to its current state. Lewis also offers insight into the Arab encounter with the West, contrasting the development of military, economics, and culture in each society.

Makiya, Kanan. *Republic of Fear: The Politics of Modern Iraq* (California: University of California Press) 504pp. Provides the most authoritative and comprehensive account of Iraq's occupation of Kuwait, its expulsion seven months later, and the aftermath of war. Blending compelling narrative history with objective analysis, the writers inquire into the fundamental issues underlying the dispute and probe the strategic calculations of all its participants.

Wengh, Wilhelm and Josef Tittel, Eds. *Documents on the Arab Israel Conflict: The Resolutions of the United Nations Organizations* (Berlin, Berlin Verlag, 1993), 3 vols. Very detailed accounts of United Nations meetings and resolutions from 1947 to 1993.

COMMONWEALTH OF INDEPENDENT STATES AND EASTERN EUROPE)

Campbell, Greg. *The Road to Kosovo: A Balkan Diary* (Boulder, CO: Westview Press, 2000), 288pp. This first-person, on-the-road travel adventure takes us through one of the most dangerous and hate-filled regions on earth—the former republics of Yugoslavia—and into a land still reeling from months of brutal combat.

East European Constitutional Review (NYU School of Law and Central European University, Budapest) <http://www.law.nyu.edu/eecr/>. A publication that gives an understanding of the dilemmas of post socialist legal reform and serves as a vital and lively forum for discussion and debate about pressing issues of the rule of law. Tracks the constitutional development of the region through quarterly offerings of academic articles, roundtables, and symposia by regional and foreign scholars.

Garnett, Sherman W., and Robert Legfold, eds. *Belarus at the Crossroad* (Washington, D.C.: Carnegie Endowment for International Peace, 2000), 199pp. The editors of this book assemble essays written by specialists from Belarus, Russia, Poland, Ukraine, Lithuania, and the United States to focus on Belarus's place in the evolving European security environment.

Kesselman Mark and Krieger Joel, ed. *European Politics in Transition 4th Ed.*(Boston, MA: Houghton Mifflin Company, 2001). Insights into the factors that have affected the economic, political, and social development in Central and Eastern Europe's socialist states since the fall of the Berlin Wall. A comparative study of the politics of Russia, Bulgaria, Hungary and Poland, and an analysis of the success or failure concerning these states in reaching their declared ideological and policy goals.

Kolsto, Pal, Antane, Aina, Holm-Hansen, Jorn, Malkova, Irina, Melberg, Hans O., and

Tsilvich, Boris. *Nation Building and Ethnic Integration in Post-Soviet societies: An investigation of Latvia and Kazakhstan* (Boulder, CO: Westview Press, 1999), 360pp. This book gives an in-depth analysis of ethnopolitics in Latvia and Kazakhstan and explores the reasons why they have been spared the kind of communal violence that erupted in so many other Soviet successor states.

Kolsto, Pal. *Political Construction Sites: Nation Building in Russia and the Post-Soviet States* (Boulder, CO: Westview Press, 2000), 320pp. This book examines the preconditions for Soviet endeavors, the goals the state leaders are aiming at, and the means they employ to reach them.

Ramet, Sabrina P. and Balkan Babel. *The Disintegration of Yugoslavia from the Death of Tito to the War for Kosovo,* 3rd Ed. (Boulder, CO: Westview Press, 1999), 288pp. This book traces the steady deterioration of Yugoslavia's political and social fabric in the years since 1980, arguing that whatever the complications entailed in the national question, the final crisis was triggered by economic deterioration, shaped by the federal system itself, and pushed forward toward war by Serbian politicians bent on power—either within a centralized Yugoslavia or within an "ethnically cleansed" Greater Serbia.

ARMS CONTROL

DISARMAMENT

Arnett, Eric, ed. *Nuclear Weapons After the Comprehensive Test Ban: Implications for Modernization and Proliferation* (New York: Oxford University Press, 1996), 141pp. A study that suggests that the Comprehensive Test Ban has not only continuing and even renewed relevance in the post-Cold War era but is also perhaps more salient in its own right than its critics acknowledge.

Lebow, Richard. *We All Lost the Cold War* (Princeton, NJ: Princeton University Press, 1994), 542pp. From the Princeton studies series in international history and politics, this controversial book is a very thorough account of the events of the Cold War—the actors, the specific conflicts, and the aftermath.

Menon, Bhaskar. *Disarmament: A Basic Guide.* (New York: United Nations, 2001), 61pp. Informative booklet on disarmament

issues which also provides an appendix of intergovernmental organizations (IGOs) to aid further research.

United Nations. *Status of Multilateral Arms Regulation and Disarmament Agreements* (New York: United Nations). Annual publication that includes location and date of entering into force, depository body, and texts of disarmament agreements.

United Nations. *Challenges to Multilateral Disarmament in the Post Cold War and Post Gulf-War Period* (New York: United Nations, 1991), 334pp. The U.N. Department for Disarmament Affairs compilation of topical papers on world disarmament

NUCLEAR WEAPONS

Beckman, Peter R., Paul W. Crumlish., Michael N. Dobkowski, and Stèven P. Lee. *The Nuclear Predicament: Nuclear Weapons in the Twenty-First Century, 3rd Ed.* (Upper Saddle River, New Jersey: Prentice Hall Inc., 2000), 340pp. Thoroughly revised to reflect the changes that the end of the cold war has brought to nuclear issues and to examine our new nuclear future, this interdisciplinary text shows how nuclear weapons have changed the world—militarily, politically, socially, and ethically. Seeking to shake readers out of their nuclear complacency, it examines the evolving nuclear predicament (that nuclear weapons can be massively destructive, yet we are moving into a period when nuclear weapons are more likely to be used) and considers particular strategies to cope with and shape the nuclear future.

Epstein, William. "Nuclear Powers Take a Hard Line," *The Bulletin of the Atomic Scientists* (Chicago: Educational Foundation for Nuclear Science, 1997), pp. 13-15. Discusses the idea of nuclear disarmament and the lack of momentum available for action toward this goal. The author expresses pessimism for future progress of the disarmament movement.

Hopkins, John C. and Weixing Hu, eds. *Strategic Views from the Second Tier: the Nuclear Weapons Policies of France, Britain, and China* (Rutgers, NJ: Rutgers University, Transaction Publishers, 1995), 268pp. Examination of the nuclear weapons policies of France, Britain, and China in the post-Cold War era, focusing on the role of nuclear forces in the new strategic environment and implications for the future.

Karl, David J. *International Security: Proliferation, Pessimism, and Emerging Nuclear Powers* (Boston: MIT Press, 1997), pp. 87-119. Stresses the danger to the U.S. of foreign powers being in control of nuclear weapons and expresses pessimism at the lack of solutions to this problem.

Leeuwen, Marianne, Ed. *The Future of the International Nuclear Non-proliferation Regime* (Norwell, MA: Kluwer Academic Publishers, 1995), 315pp. Focuses on two different parts of the issue of nuclear non-proliferation: pressing cases of proliferation in their regional context and the existing and potential global aids and instruments that can be used in place of nuclear weapons.

Matheson, Michael J. "The Opinions of the International Court of Justice on the Threat of Nuclear Weapons," American Journal of International Law (Washington D.C.: American Society of International Law, 1997) pp. 417-35. Reviews the International Court of Justice's opinions on nuclear weapons for 1996. It indicates that the court does not advise any change in U.S. or NATO policy but is likely to influence the application of the law to the use of force in more conventional circumstances.

McNeill, John H. "The International Court of Justice's Advisory Opinion in the Nuclear Weapons Cases: a First Appraisal," *International Review of the Red Cross* (International Committee of the Red Cross, 1997), pp. 103-17. A review of the opinions handed down by the International Court of Justice. Addresses two questions asked of the International Court of Justice by the World Health Organization and the General Assembly.

Mingst, Karen A. and Karns, Margaret P. *The United Nations in the Post-Cold War Era* (Boulder, CO: Westview Press, 1999), 288pp. Provides an overview of the U.N.'s evolving role in world politics. Discusses such dilemmas as tensions between sovereignty and its erosion, between demands for global governance and the weakness of U.N. institutions, and between the need for leadership and the diffusion of power.

Ollapally, Deepa and Rajagopal, S., eds. *Nuclear Cooperation: Challenges and Prospects* (Bangalore, India: National Institute of Advanced Studies, 1997), 111pp. Approaches the question of nuclear cooperation in a novel fashion by bringing international and security affairs analysts together with specialists in nuclear technology, monitoring and verification, and nuclear power. Considers both technical and political angles of nuclear cooperation.

Rhinelander, John B. and Adam M. Scheinman, Eds. *At the Nuclear Crossroads: Choices about Nuclear Weapons and Extension of the Non-proliferation Treaty* (Lanham, MD: University Press of America, Inc., 1995), 88pp. The book reflects the fundamental interaction between the choices the United States makes on its nuclear weapons policy, on one hand, and its broader nuclear non-proliferation goals on the other.

Schute, Nancy Turtle, ed. *Dismantlement and Destruction of Chemical, Nuclear, and Conventional Weapons.* (Dordrecht, The Netherlands; Norwell, MA: Kluwer Academic Publishers, 1996). A comprehensive look at nuclear weapons and their effects. Reviews topics from dismantling to storage to environmental consequences.

Turner, Stansfield. *Caging the Genies: A Workable Solution For Nuclear, Chemical and Biological Weapons* (Boulder, CO: Westview Press, 1999), 208pp. Admiral Turner details how a plan for weapons reduction could be carried out for biological and chemical weapons and what tactical and strategic differences exist between de-escalation of nuclear and non-nuclear weapons.

INTERNATIONAL ECONOMICS

DEVELOPMENT

Caporaso, James A. *Challenges and Dilemmas of the European Union* (Boulder, CO: Westview Press, 2000) 176pp. An introduction to the EU as well as a discussion of prevalent dilemmas.

Fischer, Thomas C. *The United States, the European Union, and the "Globalization" of World Trade: Allies or Adversaries?* (Westport, CT: Quorum Books, 2000), 360pp. Fischer presents a comprehensive overview of global trade at the start of a new century, from a national, regional, and international viewpoint. The United States, the European Union, Japan, and China are closely examined.

Iatridis, Demetrius S. *Social Justice and the Welfare State in Central and Eastern Europe: The Impact of Privatization* (Westport, CT:

Praeger, 2000), 272pp. With the collapse of the Eastern Bloc, Central and Eastern European states have had to confront fundamental changes in economic, social, and governmental structures. The essays in this collection address significant issues dealing with the frameworks of social justice and equality, policies for families and women, implications for the welfare state, and the impact on health care.

Lister, Margorie. *New Perspectives on European Development Cooperation* (Boulder, CO: Westview Press, 1999), 184pp. This volume assesses Europe's progress in promoting human rights and democracy through mainstreaming gender issues, creating a coherent immigration policy, and cooperating with non-governmental organizations in the southern hemisphere.

Mueller, John, Ed. *Peace, Prosperity, and Politics* (Boulder, CO: Westview Press, 2000), 304pp. As we enter a new century, world affairs have been transformed. A group of political scientists, economists, and historians offer distinct perspectives and proffer different speculations about the new era and the consequences of the emerging relationship between politics and economics.

Srinivasan, T.N. *Developing Countries and the Multilateral Trading System: From GATT To the Uruguay Round and the Future* (Boulder, CO: Westview Press, 1999) 160pp. Assesses the interaction between developing countries and the multilateral trading system from the end of World War II to the present and places the achievements and failures of the Uruguay Round (UR) in that context.

United Nations. *World Development Report* (New York: United Nations) Each edition of this annual publication focuses on a key development issue and includes the "World Development Indicators," more than 30 statistical tables giving economic and social profiles of 128 countries and dozens of charts, tables, and maps.

United Nations Center on Transnational Corporations. *Transnational Banks and the External Indebtedness of Developing Countries* (New York: United Nations, 1992), 48p. This U.N. report is a concise analysis of the relationship between debtors and creditors since the debt crisis of 1982.

BANKING

Gup, Benton E. *International Banking Crises: Large-Scale Failures, Massive Government Interventions* (Westport, CT: Quorum, 1999), 304pp. In July 1997, Thailand devalued its currency. This event sparked financial crises that spread with speed throughout Southeast Asia to Russia. Even the U.S. and South America were affected. Gup and his panel conclude that government actions were at the root of these crises. Banks were pawns in the hands of governments and banks helped fuel the booms that ultimately burst.

Khambata, Dara. *The Practice of Multinational Banking: Macro-Policy Issues and Key International Concepts,* 2nd Ed. (Westport, CT: Quorum, 1996), 320pp. This book presents the growth and development of international banking and the role of large multinational banks in financial markets. International institutions such as the Export-Import Bank, the World Bank, the International Monetary Fund, and the Bank for International Settlements, are all described and their role in international finance and banking is explained.

TRADE

Grayson, George C. *The North American Free Trade Agreement: Regional Community and the New World Order* (Lanham, MD: University Press of America, Inc., 1995), 245pp. Issues surrounding NAFTA's involvement in the world community, particularly involving the United States and Mexico.

Moon, Bruce. *Dilemmas of International Trade* (Boulder, CO: Westview Press, 2000), 250pp. Three central dilemmas are examined: the unequal distribution of income and wealth created by international trade, the tradeoff among competing values that trade requires, and the difficult interrelationship between economic and foreign policy goals within and among trading nations.

Sampson, Gary. P. *The Role of the World Trade Organization in Global Governance* (New York: United Nations University Press, 2001), 298pp. This collection of papers examines how policymakers can address the recent criticism of the World Trade Organization while ensuring the continued trade growth in the global economy.

ENVIRONMENT

ENERGY RESOURCES

International Energy Agency. *Energy in Developing Countries: A Sectoral Analysis* (Paris, OECD, 1994), 130pp. Technical analysis of energy consumption in developing countries.

World Bank. *Energy Efficiency and Conservation in the Developing World: The World Bank's Role* (Washington D.C.: World Bank, 1993), 102pp. One in series of World Bank policy papers, which deals with energy consumption, conservation, and policies in developing nations.

United Nations University. *Earth Negotiations: Analyzing Thirty Years of Environmental Diplomacy* (New York: United Nations, 2002), 312 pp. Examines lessons learned through years of multilateral environmental negotiation.

POPULATION ISSUES

Ginsburg, Faye D. and Rayna Rapp. *Conceiving the New World Order: The Global Politics of Reproduction* (Berkeley, CA.: University of California Press, 1995), 450pp. Addresses the political aspects of government policies on birth control, international population growth, and new social/cultural issues.

Harkavy, Oscar. *Curbing Population Growth: An Insider's Perspective on the Population Movement* (New York: Plenum Press, 1995), 274pp. From the Plenum Series on demographic methods and population analysis, which examines the issues of global birth control, population growth, and food supply policies.

Ramphal, Shridath and Steven W. Sinding, *Population Growth and Environmental Issues* (Westport, CT: Praeger, 1999), 216pp. Scholars, political leaders, and experts in international development issues offer their responses to the need for up-to-date information about the linkage between population growth and three significant environmental issues: global warming, land use, and natural resource management.

Siddiqi, Javed. *World Health and World Politics: The World Health Organization and the United Nations System* (London: Hurst and Company, 1995), 272pp. Thorough analysis of the World Health Organization and United Nations effort to foster international cooperation for the purpose of improving public health, as well as an analysis of the political aspects of food and population issues.

RESOURCE MANAGEMENT

Halvorssen, Anita. *Equality Among Unequals in International Environmental Law: Differential Treatment for Developing Countries* (Boulder, CO: Westview Press, 2000), 216pp. Without the participation of developing countries, universal efforts to deal with global environmental problems cannot be achieved. This study concentrates on showing what has been done on the international plane to promote the participation of developing countries and suggests some of the things that remain to be done.

Lombard, Emmett N. *International Management of the Environment: Pollution Control in North America* (Westport, CT: Praeger, 1999), 216pp. Lombard analyzes the complementary relationship between trade and environment in the merging North American environmental management system comprising Canada, the U.S., and Mexico. He views the development of closer trade relations among the three NAFTA members as having an overall and long-term beneficial impact on the environment, particularly air quality, in North America.

SUSTAINABLE DEVELOPMENT

Desta, Asayehgn. *Environmentally Sustainable Economic Development* (Westport, CT: Praeger, 1999), 265pp. Can sustainable economic development be achieved without strong environmental protections? Bringing together theoretical issues in development economics and a wide range of empirical evidence, this book examines this question and explores ways that environmental sustainability has been—and might be—incorporated into existing theories of economic development.

Hemmati, Minu, Felix Dodds, Jasmin Enayati, and Jan McHarry. *Multi-Stakeholder Processes for Governance and Sustainability—Beyond Deadlock and Conflict* (London: Earthscan, 2002). Examines the current trend of turning to multi-stakeholder processes in resolving social, economic, and environmental debates, with the goal of reaching a fair and equitable state.

Porter, Gareth, Brown, Janet, and Chasek, Pamela. *Global Environmental Politics* (Boulder, CO: Westview Press, 2000), 300pp. Provides a good introduction to global environmental politics, the actors and the issues involved and the socioeconomic factors that have an impact on both the actors and the issues.

Sitarz, Daniel, ed. *Agenda 21: The Earth Summit Strategy to Save Our Planet* (Boulder, CO: Earth Press, 1993), 321pp. The main text of this abridged version is based on the final official United Nations document, "Agenda 21" and the "United Nations Guide to Agenda 21." The text covers environmental aspects of (sustainable) economic development, international cooperation in environmental policy, and the responsible management of natural resources.

SOCIAL AND HUMANITARIAN ISSUES

REFUGEES

Haines, David W. *Case Studies in Diversity: Refugees in America in the 1990s* (Westport, CT: Praeger, 1997), 320pp. This text introduces students to the main groups of refugees in America. Divided into political, sociological, anthropological, and historical approaches, the book discusses the peoples themselves as well as their impact on American society. Case studies include: Cubans, Vietnamese, Soviet Jews, Iranians, and Afghans.

Richmond, Anthony H. *Global Apartheid: Refugees, Racism, and the New World Order* (Toronto; New York: Oxford U. Press, 1994), 327pp. Richmond describes both the social aspects and government policy regarding refugee emigration and immigration, as well as ethnic relations.

Teitelbaum, Michael S. and Myron Weiner, Eds. *Threatened Peoples, Threatened Borders: World Migration and United States Policy* (New York: W.W. Norton, 1995), 336pp. Based on ideas of the American Assembly at Columbia University, this essential book examines the explosion in refugee population and policies enacted to ward off further refugee crises.

United Nations High Commissioner for Refugees. *The State of the World's Refugees: Fifty Years of Humanitarian Action* (New York: United Nations, 2000), 253 pp. Examines the world's efforts in providing relief to refugees over the latter half of the twentieth century. Complete with statistics, maps, graphs, and tables.

HUMAN RIGHTS

Amnesty International. *Amnesty International Report* (London: Amnesty International). Annual overview of human rights violations and country-by-country description of Amnesty's human rights concerns.

Bales, Kevin. *Disposable People: New Slavery in the Global Economy* (Berkeley, CA: University of California Press, 2000), 298pp. Surveys the disturbing extent of slavery in the modern world in a passionate yet scholarly collection of five case studies.

Donnelly, Jack. *International Human Rights* (Boulder, CO: Westview Press, 1997), 240pp. Traces the rise of human rights issues after World War II, through the Universal Declaration of Human Rights, the dark days of the Cold War, the resurgence of interest during the Carter presidency and the Reagan administration's resistance, up to the current post-Cold War era.

Fitzpatrick, Peter, ed. *Nationalism, Racism, and the Rule of Law* (Brookfield: Dartmouth, 1995), 223pp. Based on papers presented at the Annual Gathering of the Critical Legal Conference held at New College, Oxford, in December 1993.

Flood, Patrick J. *The Effectiveness of U.N. Human Rights Institutions* (Westport, CT: Praeger, 1998), 184pp. Since the 1970s, the international community of states has demonstrated increasing willingness to invest U.N. institutions with politico-ethical authority to act on its behalf in addressing human rights abuses. Through trial and error, some of these institutions have had a degree of success in securing better practical observance of international human rights standards. Flood examines the reasons why some structural approaches have had more impact than others.

Gibney, Mark and Frankowski, Stanislaw. *Judicial Protection of Human Rights: Myth or Reality?* (Wesport, CT: Praeger, 1999), 216pp. The key question asked in this volume is to what extent courts have merely tolerated egregious practices or perhaps even lent them a cover of legitimacy—or conversely, the degree to which courts have purposely attempted to bring about some change in stemming governmental abuses.

Ignatieff, Michael. *Human Rights as Politics and Idolatry* (Princeton, NJ: Princeton University Press, 2001), 208 pp. A collection of essays, by Princeton University professor Ignatieff, as well as four other human rights scholars, that analyzes the human rights movement, from its beginnings in the 18th century to the present.

Langley, Winston E. *Encyclopedia of Human Rights Issues Since 1945* (Westport, CT: Greenwood Press, 1999), 424pp. This comprehensive encyclopedia on human rights issues from 1945 to 1998 contains more than 400 entries on incidents and violations, instruments and initiatives, countries and human rights activists.

Meyer, William H. *Human Rights and International Political Economy in Third World Nations: Multinational Corporations, Foreign Aid, and Repression* (Westport, CT: Praeger, 1998), 264pp. What impact do international economic inputs have on human rights in Third World nations? Meyer explores the effects of direct investment by U.S. multinational corporations, economic and military aid, and MNC manufacturing plants.

Natural Resources Defense Council. *Defending the Earth: Abuses of Human Rights and the Environment* (New York: Human Rights Watch, 1992) 106pp. A study on the infringement of the human rights of citizens who participate in environmental protection organizations and groups.

United Nations Division of Human Rights. *Bulletin of Human Rights* (New York: United Nations). A quarterly review in English, Spanish, French and Russian providing vital articles and statistics on current human rights concerns.

WOMEN

Abadian Sousan. "Women's Autonomy and Its Impact on Fertility," *World Development,* v. 24 (Oxford, England: Elsevier Science Inc., 1996), pp. 793-809. This paper seeks to assess empirically the impact of female autonomy on fertility.

Martin, Mart. *The Almanac of Women and Minorities in World Politics* (Boulder, CO: Westview Press, 2000), 504pp. Provides political biographical details on the achievements of women and minorities in the executive, legislative, and judicial branches of every nation (and most dependent territories) in the world.

Pietila, Hilkka. *Making Women Matter: The Role of the United Nations* (Atlantic Highlands, N.J.: Zed Books, 1994). This updated and expanded version contains information on the United Nations' role in female development and women's rights.

Rehof, Lars. *A Guide to the United Nations Convention on the Elimination of all Forms of Discrimination Against Women* (Boston: Kluwer Academic Publishers, 1993), 388pp. From the International Studies in Human Rights series, v. 29. Examines laws that prevent sex discrimination against women.

Shukri, Shirin J.A. *Unequal Partners in Development* (Avebury Ashgate Publishing Limited, UK, 1996), 191pp. Elaboration on the problem of gender inequality, in the process of development, in a rural village in Jordan.

Soiri, Iina. *Radical Motherhood* (Motala, Sweden: Motala Grafiska, 1996), 109pp. The participation of the Northern Namibian Ovambo Women in the Namibian independence struggle and their situation after Namibian independence.

Walter, Lynn, ed. *Women's Rights: A Global View* (Westport, CT: Greenwood Press, 2000) Each case study asks how national, cultural, class, racial, and religious differences have influenced women's rights. Case studies include: Bolivia, China, India, Iran, Israel, Japan, Nigeria, Ojibway, and Zimbabwe.

Winslow, Anne, ed. *Women, Politics, and the United Nations* (Westport, CT: Greenwood Press, 1995), 213pp. Essays on several female-oriented conferences and on the politics of women and development.

INTERNATIONAL LAW

LAW OF THE SEA

Davis, Elizabeth vanwie. *China and the Law of the Sea Convention: Follow the Sea* (Lewiston, N.Y.: Edwin Mellen Press, 1995), 118pp. The subject of this piece is maritime law in the pacific area, based on the United Nations Convention on the Law of the Sea (1982).

Sanger, Clyde. *Ordering the Oceans: The Making of the Law at Sea* (Toronto: U. of Toronto Press, 1987), 225pp. A historical and technical perspective on international laws with respect to sovereign rights on bodies of water that suggest some propositions that may lead toward reaching agreement in complex bargaining.

Singh, Gurdys. *U.N. Convention on the Law of the Sea* (Delhi, India: Academic Publications, 1985) 271pp. A discussion of the conflict-resolution mechanisms available to the international community as dictated by general international law; also an analysis and evaluation of the dispute settlement mechanisms of the Law of the Sea Convention.

Wang, James C.F. *Handbook on Ocean Politics and Law* (New York: Greenwood Press, 1992), 568pp. Very thorough account of maritime law, its history, and marine resources conservation.

INTERNATIONAL COURT OF JUSTICE

Bodie, Thomas J. *Politics and the Emergence of an Activist International Court of Justice* (Westport, CT: Greenwood Press, 1995), 128pp. This book addresses this political/legal dichotomy through doctrinal study and case law. The considerations of previous scholars, as well as state practice and the opinions of various international courts, are included.

INTERNATIONAL CRIMINAL COURT

Schabas, William. *Introduction to the International Criminal Court* (New York: Cambridge University Press, 2001) 416 pp. This book provides an extensive history of the Court and includes the ICC's major documents, such as the Rome Statute, in its appendix.

TERRORISM

Claridge, David. *Terrorism and Political Violence: State Terrorism? Applying a Definitional Model* (London: Frank Cass, 1996), pp. 47-63. Examines the difference between an act of violence and actual state terrorism and the obstacles presented when forming an indictment of terrorism against a state. It also studies the use of terrorism by states and how they compare to previous patterns in history.

Cole, Leonard A. *The Eleventh Plague: The Politics of Biological and Chemical Warfare* (New York: W.H. Freeman & Co. 1997), 300pp. Deals with the terrifying and compelling subjects of biological and chemical warfare and their use in the hands of terrorists. What recent political and technological developments suggest for the future as

well as how to fight this increasingly ominous deadly plague.

Cooley, James. *Unholy Wars: Afghanistan, America, and International Terrorism* (London; Sterling, Va.: Pluto Press, 2000), 144pp. Describes the development of U.S. foreign policy and CIA covert activity in the 1980s that facilitated the training and arming of almost a quarter of a million Islamic mercenaries drawn from around the world.

Damask, Nicholas A. and Abraham H. Miller. *Terrorism and Political Violence: The Dual Myths of "Narco-Terrorism": How Myths Drive Policy* (London: Frank Cass, 1996), pp. 114-131. Describes the myth of narco-terrorism that has emerged. Defines narco-terrorism and presents examples that have led to the development of this idea.

Laurenti, Jeffrey. *Combating Terrorism: Does the U.N. Matter and How* (New York: UNA-USA, 2002), 41pp. This policy report explains the role the United Nations has assumed in the fight against terrorism, both in the past and in the current global crisis, paying special attention to antiterrorism conventions and historic Security Council resolutions requiring global cooperation in the fight against terrorism.

Parenti, Michael *The Terrorism Trap* (San Francisco: City Lights Publishers, 2002), 120pp. An analysis of the economic, religious, and political agendas behind the September 11 attacks/retaliation, with an emphasis on the history of Afghanistan and globalization's impact on terrorism.

Schmid, Alex P. *Transnational Organized Crime: The Links Between Transnational Organized Crime and Terrorist Crimes* (London: Frank Cass, 1996), pp. 40-52. Explores the nature, structure, dynamics, and danger of transnational organized crime and the differences between political, sociological, and economic interpretations of it. Also, briefly explains how it differs from the common definition of terrorist crimes.

Singh, K.R. "International Terrorism as an Instrument of State Policy," *International Studies* (New Delhi: Sage Publications India Put Ltd., 1995), pp. 119-137. Discusses the future of terrorism as a tactic of governments. Brings up the issues of deterrence and self-defense when related with terrorism. Cites examples of governments using terrorists as a means of gaining control. Means of ending terrorism are also discussed.

Volkan, Vamik D. *International Journal of Group Rights: The Psychodynamics of Ethnic Terrorism* (The Netherlands: Kluwer Academic Publishers, 1995), pp. 145-159. Defines both "terrorism" and "ethnicity" and the psychological motivation behind ethnic terrorism. It clarifies some of the personal reasons for this type of terrorism and some of the goals of the victimizer.

Zinn, Howard. *Terrorism and War* (New York: Seven Stories Press, 2002), 144pp. Explores the loss of civil liberties during war, the history of U.S. militarism, and U.S. resistance in wars from World War I to the war in Afghanistan.

GENERAL INTEREST

UNITED NATIONS

Ayton-Shenker, Diana. ed. *A Global Agenda: Issues Before the General Assembly of the U.N.* (New York: United Nations Association of the USA). This annual publication presents the issues faced by each year's session of the General Assembly with pertinent background and history.

Bailey, Sydney Dawson. *The United Nations: A Concise Political Guide* (Lanham, MD: Barnes & Noble Books, 1995), 176pp. The book poses the question: Does the U.N. have a future? Bailey provides a quick resource guide for information on the United Nations' purpose, structure, groups and blocs, peace and security aims, disarmament goals, and human rights.

Glassner, Martin I. *The United Nations at Work* (Westport, CT: Praeger, 1998), 376pp. The purpose of this collection is to examine something generally ignored, even in the professional literature: what the United Nations actually does. The volume consists of original, authoritative, critical analyses of a sampling of key U.N. activities.

Mingst, Karen A. *The United Nations in the post-Cold War Era,* 2nd Ed. (Boulder, CO: Westview Press, 1999), 208pp. Part of a series that examines new dilemmas in world politics. This installment deals with the possible future challenges facing the United Nations.

Ratner, Steven R. *The New United Nations Peacekeeping: Building Peace in Lands of Conflict After the Cold War* (New York: St. Martin's Press: Council on Foreign Relations, 1995), 322pp. Analysis of the rapidly changing role of U.N. peacekeeping missions.

Rikhye, Indar Jit and Kjell Skjelsbaek, eds. *The United Nations and Peacekeeping: Results, Limitations and Prospects, The Lessons of Forty Years of Experience* (London: Macmillan, 1990), 200pp. A compilation of essays by professionals with first-hand experience in peacekeeping; briefly evaluates the historical experiences of peacekeeping and critically analyzes its present potentials and problems. Covers all aspects of peacekeeping, including its management, finance, support, limitations, future, and impartiality.

United Nations. *The Blue Helmets: A Review of United Nations Peacekeeping* (New York: United Nations Department of Public Information, 1996), 350pp. The history of both peacekeeping operations and observer missions, chapter six and one half of the U.N. Charter, are presented here in great detail. The volume contains extensive data concerning each deployment of troops and maps.

United Nations. *A Diplomat's Handbook of International Law and Practice* (New York: United Nations), 606pp. Current developments and practices of states, including judicial decisions in a variety of fields of topical interest. Also includes current issues of interest in diplomatic relations.

Sewall, Gilbert, ed. *Textbooks and the United Nations: The International System and What American Students Learn About It* (New York: UNA-USA, 2002). A groundbreaking study commissioned by UNA-USA and conducted by the American Textbook Council, this report found that most secondary level textbooks in the U.S. are inadequate for teaching students about the United Nations. By analyzing 17 of the nation's most widely used textbooks, the author found that information on the U.N. is almost non-existent, and where present, was often unclear and superficial. Pointing out the critical need for students to understand the global community in which they live, this study provides a call for action for expanded coverage of the U.N. in American classrooms.

Weiss, Thomas G., Forsythe, David P., and Coate, Roger A. *The United Nations and Changing World Politics* (Boulder, CO: Westview Press, 2000), 370pp. Through this book, students of all levels can learn what the U.N. is, how it operates, and what its relationships are with external actors and institutions.

WORLD POLITICS

Kegley, Charles W. and Eugene R. Witkopf. *World Politics: From War to Peace* (New York: Wadsworth Publishing, 2000), 688pp. A through introduction to the principles and trends of world politics.

Foreign Policy (Washington, D.C.: Carnegie Endowment for International Peace). A valuable quarterly publication of important issues of foreign policy.

Stack, John F, Jr. and Hebron, Lui. *The Ethnic Entanglement: Conflict and Intervention in World Politics* (Westport, CT: Praeger, 1999), 192pp. Provides scholars of international relations with a compelling approach to the study of ethnicity.

Weinberger, Casper and Peter Schweizer, with foreword by Lady Margaret Thatcher. *The Next War* (Washington D.C.: Regnery Publishing, 1996), 430pp. This book is composed of hypothetical war scenarios that are sobering yet compellingly readable. It dramatizes the outbreak, progress, and outcome of major wars most likely to occur over the next dozen years. It does not purport to tell the future but aims to lay bare the dangers that America and the world may soon face due to what the authors see as declining U.S. military readiness in the face of escalating world instability.

DIPLOMACY

Kissinger, Henry. *Diplomacy* (New York: Simon & Schuster, 1994) Former U.S. Secretary of State Kissinger surveys the history of diplomacy, while also providing personal accounts of his experiences with prominent world leaders.

Lippman, Thomas W. *Madeleine Albright and the New American Diplomacy* (Boulder, CO: Westview Press, 2000), 368pp. Compiled over a two-and-a-half-year period, account follows Albright's campaign to reshape American diplomacy for the new century.

Soman, Appu K. *Double-Edged Sword: Nuclear Diplomacy in Unequal Conflicts— The United States and China, 1950-1958* (Westport, CT: Praeger, 2000), 272pp. Highlighting the central role of nuclear diplomacy in these crises, this book draws conclusions on the efficacy of such diplomacy, the impact of these crises on the development of policies of massive retaliation and limited war, the consequences of Dulles's

brinkmanship, and the revival of nuclear diplomacy by the Clinton administration in conflicts with non-nuclear adversaries.

CONFLICT RESOLUTION AND PEACEKEEPING

Annan, Kofi. *Prevention of Armed Conflict, Report of the Secretary-General.* (New York: United Nations, 2002,), 106pp. In this report, the Secretary-General conducts a review of actions the U.N. has taken to prevent conflict, monitoring progress that has been achieved in developing the conflict prevention capacity. Annan also make recommendations on how the U.N.'s efforts can be expanded, particularly with the cooperation of member states.

Fahey, Joseph and Richard A. Armstrong. *Peace Reader: Essential Readings on War, Justice, Non-Violence and World Order* (New York: Paulist Press, 1987), 477pp. An excellent collection of classic essays on the subjects of military conflict, human rights, and the maintenance of order and peace.

Laurenti, Jeffrey. *The Preparedness Gap: Making Peace Operations Work in the 21st Century* (New York: UNA-USA, 2000), 48pp. This report on peacekeeping reform addresses concerns in the United States about the relevance of peace operations to American foreign policy as well as the U.S. stake in strengthening of United Nations capabilities.

Langholtz, Harvey J. *The Psychology of Peacekeeping* (Westport, CT: Praeger, 1998), 280pp. Langholtz examines how psychology and other social sciences can offer both theoretical explanations and practical applications in the resolution and amelioration of potentially violent international conflicts.

Paenson, Isaac. *Manual of the Terminology of the Law of Armed Conflicts of International Humanitarian Organizations* (London: Martinus Nijhoff, 1989), 844pp. Each term is defined in the context of a chapter explaining a principle of armed conflicts. The volume is published in English, French, Spanish, and Russian.

Sanders, Isaac. *Developing a Modern International Law on the Rights of Indigenous Peoples.* (Vancouver: University of British Columbia Press, 1994), 52 pp. A background on international rights and laws of indigenous peoples and a plan to secure them. Includes a draft declaration on the rights of indigenous peoples.

PUBLICATIONS BY THE U.N. AND UNA-USA

For a complete list of U.N. publications in print, write to:

U.N. Publications
Sales Section
Room DC2-0853
New York, N.Y. 10017

Web site: www.un.org/Pubs/

U.N. Publications
Sales Section
Palais des Nations
1211 Geneva
Switzerland

For a complete list of UNA-USA publications, call or write to:

Publications Department
UNA-USA
801 Second Avenue
New York, N.Y. 10017-4706

212 907-1300
Fax 212 682-9185
1-866-335-4001

E-mail: unahq@unausa.org
Web site: www.unausa.org